WATERGATE:

An Annotated Bibliography of
Sources in English,
1972-1982

by
MYRON J. SMITH, JR.

The Scarecrow Press, Inc.
Metuchen, N.J., & London
1983

Library of Congress Cataloging in Publication Data

Smith, Myron J.
   Watergate : an annotated bibliography of sources in English, 1972-1982.

   Bibliography: p.
   Includes index.
   1. Watergate Affair, 1972-   --Bibliography.
I. Title.
Z1245.S64 1983 [E860]   016.3641'32'0973   83-4408
ISBN 0-8108-1623-7

Copyright © 1983 by Myron J. Smith, Jr.
Manufactured in the United States of America

for Dennie

"I would say that, as far as the country is concerned ... the Watergate syndrome has probably run its course, and that is to the good."

    --Richard M. Nixon interview with Diane Sawyer, "CBS Morning News," June 7, 1982

CONTENTS

Introduction	vii
Chronology, May 28, 1972-July 3, 1975	1
Watergate Personalities	13
The Impeachment Investigation of Richard Nixon	25
REFERENCE WORKS	37
BIBLIOGRAPHY	47
Records, Video- and Audio-Tape Recordings	311
Appendix: Magazines and Journals Containing at Least One Article Relative to This Bibliography	315
Subject Index	319

INTRODUCTION

Ten years ago on June 17, 1972, security guard Frank Wills was making his rounds in the dark corridors of DC's Watergate office/apartment complex when he discovered a piece of tape on a door latch. Suspicious, he called the police--thereby beginning a 784-day melodrama which revealed the worst political scandal in American history and ended, by resignation, the second term of the 37th President of the United States, Richard Milhous Nixon.

Narrowly, this scandal, usually just called "Watergate," refers to a botched break-in at the Watergate-housed Democratic National Committee headquarters by members of a White House-created Special Investigations Unit known as "the plumbers." Initially discounted by presidential Press Secretary Ron Ziegler as "a third-rate burglary," the arrest of the five men behind the door on which Wills had noticed the tape, and the subsequent effort to hide, evade, and "cover-up" administration involvement by the President and certain associates became a great political crisis, with Constitutional overtones, not previously experienced in this nation.

More broadly, Watergate, "like 'Teapot Dome,' means everything associated with a scandal that became a national trauma."[1] When press, Justice Department, and Congres-

---

1. William Safire, Safire's Political Dictionary (New York: Random House, 1978), p. 779.

sional investigators were finished and trials and pleadings were concluded, Watergate meant not only the break-in at the office building and its cover-up, but a host of associated crimes and questionable actions dating back to the administration's beginnings. A list of wrongdoings would include, among other things, the following items: non-court-approved wiretapping; the illegal back-dating of gift deeds; 1972 campaign political espionage and "Dirty Tricks" directed by men of the Committee to Re-elect the President (CREEP); the solicitation and acceptance of illegal 1972 campaign contributions from many sources, some as diverse as Howard Hughes, Robert Vesco, ITT, and the Milk lobby--often in return for political favors; the "plumbers'" break-in of the office of D. Ellsberg's psychiatrist, L. Fielding; illegal impoundment of Congressionally approved funds; the secret bombing of Cambodia; and the failure, through such tactics as executive privilege and edited tape transcripts, to co-operate fully in the Watergate investigation. The list is long, the personnel involved were many, and the vocabulary was--and is--rich with unusual terms like "stonewalling," "expletives deleted," "bugs," "black bag jobs," "cover-up," etc.

The drama which had transfixed Americans and befuddled foreigners ended in mid-summer 1974. Faced with certain impeachment and removal from office, President Nixon resigned his office at noon on August 9. Within four months, he had been pardoned by his successor, Gerald Ford, and several of his former top associates had been convicted in the last major court action, the Watergate Cover-up Trial. By October 1975 when the office of the Special Prosecutor was closed, over 30 Nixon administration officials, presidential campaign officials, and financial contributors had pleaded or were found guilty of breaking the law. Of these, 25 were jailed. Others not indicted or acquitted emerged with questionable reputations, including Alexander Haig and John Connally.

Today, after a decade, some technical Watergate questions remain unanswered, and the subject of research by future historians of the scandal. Among these are Why was Watergate really broken into?; Who actually authorized the Ellsberg-Fielding break-in?; Who erased the tapes creating the $18\frac{1}{2}$-minute gap?; Why did not the President simply destroy the tapes?; and Who was the Woodward/Bernstein anonymous source "Deep Throat"? Until these questions are answered, interest in this affair will continue.

Following Watergate, reform became the order of the day for several years. Congress, which had long played a subservient role to an "imperial presidency," became more active and sought to legislate changes designed to guard against other excesses. The most notable example of Congressional work in this respect was the House and Senate investigations of the intelligence community. The role of the press, beatified during the scandal, was enhanced until today some are calling it the "imperial media." A "post-Watergate morality" was visited upon all levels of government from town hall to Congress and seeped into the corridors of big business. In some respects, this new morality did drastically alter ethical standards and expectations and may have contributed to President Carter's election in 1976; in some cases, excesses occurred, such as the FBI ploy ABSCAM, leading to further wonderment. Today the "Watergate syndrome," as some would call it, seems to have slowed with the passing of time, but one salient point above all others remains intact: when the chips are down, no one in this country, not even a president, is above the law.

Objectives

For a variety of reasons including the hunt for answers to the questions noted above, Watergate continues to fascinate many Americans. Over the past decade thousands of books, articles, documents, and other publications have flooded from printing presses in an effort to meet--or in some cases create--the demand for information on the scandal. Although the cascade has slowed with only a brief flurry for the tenth anniversary, research and reading on the topic can be expected to continue for years to come.

In preparation for this work, I found only a few bibliographies devoted to Watergate, mostly within the pages of periodicals or at the conclusion of the occasional book or thesis. These contain, at best, only a few hundred citations, often unannotated, and are now outdated. Perhaps the reason for this is that the scandal is no longer front page news and until now was not considered a suitable subject for full bibliographic enterprise.

This bibliography is intended to serve as a working guide to English-language sources concerning the Watergate and associated scandals written during the years 1972-June 1982. While aimed primarily at scholars and students, it should also prove useful to librarians, general readers, and journalists. It may also be interesting to those specialized students known as "Watergate buffs."

This guide is not definitive, but it attempts comprehensiveness in that virtually all factors concerning Watergate are covered. As a reference tool, it will permit users to quickly determine what material is available and help them establish a basis for further research. In general, items are cited which the user might reasonably expect to find in large university, public, or government libraries. In practice, students should be able to find at least many of the more recent book titles in even small- or medium-sized college, public, or high school library collections. Should you be unable to turn up a given reference locally, keep in mind that many if not all items cited are available through interlibrary loan, details of which service can be obtained at your nearest library.

The criteria for selection has been similar to that employed in my many other titles for Scarecrow Press. The following types of published material are represented below: books and monographs, scholarly papers, periodical and journal articles, government documents, doctoral dissertations and masters theses, and some satire. Excluded materials include fiction, obvious children's works, newspaper articles (unless reprinted in other works), poetry, and book reviews.

Arrangement

The bibliographic parts of this volume are organized into two alphabetically-sequential sections, Reference Works and Bibliography. This offers the obvious benefit of non-repetition of citations and the grouping of all works by a given author under his/her name. Each citation receives at least a brief annotation and is numbered for control through the Subject Index.

Other Features

The chronology of Watergate events, from May 28, 1972-July 3, 1975, follows this preface; corrections or additions may be sent to the publisher for use in the next edition.

The people mixed up in Watergate were many; and

naturally the more prominent ones reappear continuously in citations and annotations. To assist users to understand better who these individuals are, brief biographies appear in a section called Watergate Personalities.

The investigation of Watergate by the House Judiciary Committee resulted in articles of impeachment being drawn up against President Nixon. The story of that investigation is nowhere more succinctly told than in a little-known new Judiciary Committee history of itself. The appropriate parts of that history are here reproduced.

Records, video- and audio-tape recordings of events surrounding Watergate were made at that time, and several scholarly proceedings concerning the scandal were taped for wider distribution. Those uncovered have been arranged alphabetically in a brief section which follows the main body of the bibliography.

To assist users who might wish to check further in the periodical literature, a complete list of the journals consulted is added as Appendix A.

Acknowledgments

For their advice, assistance, or encouragement in the formulation, research, and completion of this endeavor, the following persons and libraries are gratefully acknowledged. Their involvement does not necessarily constitute an endorsement of this guide.

West Virginia University Library; Kanawha, Harrison, and Lewis County (WV) Public Libraries; Salem College (WV) Benedum Library.

Gary S. McAllister, Jesse L. Kelley, John Wood, Margaret Allen, and Sam J. Ervin, Jr. all provided encouragement and help.

Dennie, my wife, provided professional stimulation and criticism which only another librarian can; without her prodding and aid, this project would still be wallowing in file boxes.

Myron J. Smith, Jr.
June 1982

CHRONOLOGY, MAY 28, 1972-JULY 3, 1975*

Date:	Event:
May 28, 1972	Democratic National Committee Headquarters at Watergate is broken into, electronic surveillance equipment installed.
June 17, 1972	Five men are arrested at Democratic National Committee Headquarters while attempting to repair electronic equipment.
June 28, 1972	G. Gordon Liddy, counsel to Finance Committee to Re-elect the President (FCRP), is fired when he fails to co-operate with FBI agents investigating the Watergate break-in.
July 1, 1972	John Mitchell resigns as Committee to Re-elect the President (CRP) Chairman.
July 14, 1972	Hugh Sloan resigns as FCRP Treasurer.
July 31 to August 10, 1972	Press reports suggest that money for Watergate break-in came from CRP funds given by Liddy to one of the arrested men.
August 16, 1972	CRP Chairman Clark MacGregor acknowledges that Liddy spent CRP funds for security program.
August 30, 1972	The President announces that Dean has conducted and completed an investigation into the Watergate affair. Claims that no one in the White House or employed by the administration was involved.
September 15, 1972	Bernard Barker, Virgilio Gonzalez, E. Howard Hunt, G. Gordon Liddy, Eugenio Martinez, James W. McCord, Jr., and Frank Sturgis are indicted for their parts in the June 17, 1972, break-in at Democratic National Headquarters.
September 17 to October 25, 1972	Press reports suggest that CRP maintained a secret cash fund controlled by Mitchell, Stans, Magruder, Kalmbach and Haldeman,

*Adapted from U.S. Dept. of Justice, Watergate Special Prosecution Force. Report (Washington, D.C.: U.S. Government Printing Office, 1975) pp. 253-264.

Watergate

Date:	Event:
	which was used to finance the Watergate break-in and other sensitive political projects.
October 26, 1972	MacGregor acknowledges existence of special cash fund, but denies it was used for sabotage against Democrats.
January 8, 1973	Watergate break-in trial begins.
January 11, 1973	Hunt pleads guilty to charges in break-in indictment.
January 15, 1973	Barker, Sturgis, Martinez, and Gonzalez plead guilty to charges in break-in indictment.
January 15 to January 22, 1973	Press reports suggest that Watergate defendants were being paid by unnamed sources --possibly CRP--and that they were promised money and clemency to plead guilty.
January 30, 1973	Liddy and McCord are convicted on all counts of break-in indictment.
February 7, 1973	Senate unanimously passes S. 60, a resolution creating the Select Committee on Presidential Campaign Activities.
March 19, 1973	McCord writes to Judge Sirica alleging that perjury was committed at trial and that defendants were pressured to remain silent.
March 23, 1973	Judge Sirica issues provisional sentences for Watergate break-in defendants, except McCord; makes McCord's letter public.
April 5, 1973	L. Patrick Gray's nomination to become Director of the FBI is withdrawn.
	Judge W. Matt Byrne reports a personal meeting with Ehrlichman, where Ehrlichman suggested a possible future assignment for Byrne.
April 17, 1973	The President announces White House staff will appear before the Senate Select Committee, and that there have been major new developments in the Watergate investigation, that real progress has been made toward finding the truth.
April 19, 1973	Attorney General Richard Kleindienst removes himself from Watergate case. Henry Petersen assumes responsibility for conduct of Watergate investigation.
April 23, 1973	White House issues a statement denying that the President had any prior knowledge of Watergate affair.
April 27, 1973	Gray resigns as acting director of the FBI. Washington Post reports Gray destroyed doc-

Date:	Event:
	uments in Howard Hunt's files after a discussion with Ehrlichman and Dean.
	Judge Byrne reads memo at Ellsberg/Russo trial describing Hunt and Liddy break-in of Dr. Fielding's office.
	Hugh Sloan is accused of submitting false documents to the General Accounting Office. GAO cites CRP and Maurice Stans for four campaign expenditure violations.
April 30, 1973	Haldeman, Ehrlichman, Dean, and Kleindienst resign. The President nominates Elliot Richardson to become new Attorney General.
May 4, 1973	George A. Hearing is indicted on two counts of fabricating and distributing illegal campaign literature (18 USC 612). Pleaded guilty May 11; sentenced to a one-year prison term on June 15.
May 7, 1973	A spokesman for the President denies that there were any offers of clemency to anyone connected with the Watergate affair.
	Richardson announces that he will appoint a special prosecutor.
May 9, 1973	Egil Krogh resigns; claims full responsibility for the Fielding break-in.
May 9 to May 22, 1973	Richardson confirmation hearings are held before the Senate Judiciary Committee.
May 10, 1973	Mitchell, Stans, Robert Vesco and Harry Sears are indicted for attempting to impede a SEC investigation of Vesco.
May 11, 1973	Judge Byrne dismisses all criminal charges against Ellsberg and Russo in Pentagon Papers case.
May 17, 1973	Senate Select Committee begins public hearings.
May 21, 1973	Richardson announces nomination of Archibald Cox as Special Prosecutor.
May 23, 1973	Richardson is confirmed by Senate to become new Attorney General.
May 25, 1973	Richardson is sworn in as Attorney General. Cox is sworn in as Special Prosecutor.
June 12, 1973	Court orders use immunity for Dean and Magruder.
June 25, 1973	Dean tells Senate Select Committee that the President knew of the cover-up as early as September 1972.
June 27, 1973	Dean submits "enemies list" memorandum of August 16, 1971, to Senate Select Committee.

Watergate

Date:	Event:
	Fred LaRue pleads guilty to an information charging one-count violation of 18 USC 371, conspiracy to obstruct justice.
June 30, 1973	Earl Silbert, Seymour Glanzer and Donald Campbell, Assistant U.S. Attorneys for the District of Columbia, withdraw from the Watergate investigation.
July 7, 1973	The President informs the Senate Select Committee that he will not personally appear before the Committee and that he will not grant the Committee access to presidential files.
July 16, 1973	Herbert Kalmbach, in testimony before the Senate Select Committee, claims that John Ehrlichman approved cash payments to the burglars who broke into Watergate.
	Alexander Butterfield informs the Senate Select Committee of the presidential taping system.
July 20, 1973	Liddy refuses to take an oath as a witness before the House Armed Services Subcommittee during a Watergate-related investigation.
July 23, 1973	Senate Select Committee issues subpoenas for White House tapes and documents.
	Special Prosecutor Cox issues grand jury subpoena for tapes and documents needed for investigation into the Watergate cover-up.
July 24, 1973	Ehrlichman tells the Senate Select Committee that break-in at Fielding's office was legal, and that it was undertaken for national security purposes.
July 25, 1973	The President informs Judge Sirica of his decision to refuse to comply with the Special Prosecutor's subpoena.
July 31, 1973	The Washington Post reports that the President did not sign the deed giving his papers to the National Archives, that the deed was not delivered until April 1 of 1970 (nine months after the effective date of the 1969 law prohibiting tax deductions for such gifts) and that the deed was never accepted by the Archives as a formal written document.
August 9, 1973	Senate Select Committee files suit against the President for failure to comply with their subpoena.
August 13, 1973	Grand Jury II is empanelled to investigate campaign contributions, political espionage, "plumbers" and ITT.

Chronology

Date:	Event:
August 16, 1973	Magruder pleads guilty to a one count violation of 18 USC 371, conspiracy to unlawfully intercept wire and oral communications, to obstruct justice and to defraud the United States.
August 29, 1973	Judge Sirica enforces grand jury subpoena to the President for nine presidential conversations.
September 11, 1973	Oral arguments are heard before the U.S. Court of Appeals concerning refusal of the President to comply with the Special Prosecutor's subpoena.
October 1, 1973	Donald Segretti pleads guilty to three counts of violating 18 USC 612, distributing illegal campaign literature.
October 11, 1973	Krogh is indicted on two counts of violating 18 USC 1623, making a false declaration before a grand jury.
October 12, 1973	U.S. Court of Appeals orders the President to produce subpoenaed tapes.
October 19, 1973	The President offers the Stennis tapes compromise. Orders Special Prosecutor Cox to seek no further litigation. Dean pleads guilty to an information charging a one-count violation of 18 USC 371, conspiracy to obstruct justice.
October 20, 1973	Special Prosecutor Cox holds a press conference where he explains his refusal to comply with the President's order. The President orders that the Special Prosecutor be fired. Richardson resigns in protest and Ruckelshaus is fired. Acting Attorney General Bork fires Special Prosecutor Cox. Special Prosecution Force is transferred to the Department of Justice, Criminal Division.
October 23, 1973	The President informs Judge Sirica that he will comply with grand jury subpoena.
October 31, 1973	J. Fred Buzhardt, Special Counsel to the President, informs the Court that two of the subpoenaed tapes do not exist.
November 1, 1973	Acting Attorney General Bork announces the selection of Leon Jaworski to succeed Archibald Cox as Special Prosecutor.
November 2, 1973	Watergate Special Prosecution Force is re-established by an order of the Acting Attorney General.
November 5, 1973	Leon Jaworski is sworn in as the new Special Prosecutor. Segretti is sentenced to serve six months in prison.
November 7, 1973	Senate passes S.R. 194, affirming the au-

Date:	Event:
	thority of the Select Committee to subpoena and sue the President.
November 9, 1973	Final Watergate break-in sentences are handed down.
November 21, 1973	Buzhardt informs Judge Sirica of an $18\frac{1}{2}$-minute gap on the tape of a June 20, 1972, conversation between the President and Haldeman.
	Judge Sirica appoints a panel of scientific experts to examine tapes of presidential conversations handed over in compliance with the July 23rd grand jury subpoena.
November 29, 1973	Dwight Chapin is indicted on four counts of violating 18 USC 1623, making false declarations before a grand jury.
November 30, 1973	Krogh pleads guilty to an information charging one-count violation of 18 USC 241, conspiracy to violate civil rights.
	Judge Sirica holds hearings, in camera, concerning executive privilege claims on three of the subpoenaed tapes.
December 6, 1973	Brief for the U.S. in conviction appeal of G. Gordon Liddy is filed (DNC break-in).
January 7, 1974	Grand Jury III is empanelled to investigate matters similar to those investigations carried out by Grand Jury II.
January 21, 1974	Herbert Porter is charged with a one-count violation of 18 USC 1001, making false statements to agents of the FBI.
January 24, 1974	Krogh is sentenced to a prison term of two to six years, all but six months suspended. October 11 indictment is dismissed.
January 28, 1974	Porter pleads guilty to January 21 information.
February 6, 1974	House of Representatives authorizes House Judiciary Committee to investigate if grounds exist to impeach the President.
February 25, 1974	Herbert W. Kalmbach pleads guilty to a one-count violation of the Federal Corrupt Practices Act, and one count of promising Federal employment as a reward for political activity. He is sentenced to serve 6-18 months and fined $10,000 for the first count, six months for the second. Sentences are to run concurrently.
March 1, 1974	Watergate cover-up indictment: Colson, Ehrlichman, Haldeman, Mardian, Mitchell, Parkinson, and Strachan are charged with offenses stemming from events following the break-in at the Democratic National Headquarters on June 17, 1972.

Chronology

Date:	Event:
March 4, 1974	Briefs for the U.S. in conviction appeals of McCord and Hunt are filed.
March 6, 1974	Hearing is held before Judge Sirica on transfer of grand jury materials to the House Judiciary Committee.
March 7, 1974	Fielding break-in indictment: Barker, Colson, De Diego, Ehrlichman, Liddy, Martinez are charged with offenses stemming from the September 3-4, 1971, break-in at the Los Angeles office of Dr. Fielding.
March 15, 1974	Special Prosecutor Jaworski issues subpoena for specified documents for use in grand jury.
March 18, 1974	Judge Sirica announces decision to permit transfer of grand jury material to the House Judiciary Committee.
March 20, 1974	Haldeman and Strachan file petition for writ of mandamus with U.S. Court of Appeals concerning transfer of grand jury material.
March 21, 1974	U.S. Court of Appeals hears Haldeman and Strachan petition. Denied later in the day.
March 26, 1974	Grand jury materials are transferred to the House Judiciary Committee.
March 29, 1974	President complies with the Special Prosecutor's March 15 subpoena.
April 1, 1974	Brief for the U.S. in conviction appeals of Barker, Martinez, Sturgis, and Gonzalez is filed.
April 3, 1974	Howard E. Reinecke indicted on three counts of perjury.
April 5, 1974	Chapin found guilty on two of three counts.
April 16, 1974	Special Prosecutor issues a trial subpoena for 64 White House taped conversations.
April 28, 1974	Mitchell and Stans are acquitted on all charges in Vesco trial.
April 30, 1974	President submits transcripts of recorded conversations to House Judiciary Committee.
May 3, 1974	Panel of experts appointed by Judge Sirica issues a report on their examination of White House tapes.
May 15, 1974	Chapin is sentenced to serve 10 to 30 months.
May 16, 1974	Kleindienst pleads guilty to a violation of 2 USC 192, refusal to answer pertinent questions before a Senate Committee. Later sentenced to serve 30 days, and fined $100. Sentence is suspended.
May 20, 1974	Judge Sirica enforces Special Prosecutor's trial subpoena of April 16.
May 21, 1974	Magruder is sentenced to a prison term of ten months to four years.

Watergate

Date:	Event:
May 22, 1974	De Diego indictment is dismissed in Fielding break-in case.
May 31, 1974	Supreme Court grants writs of certiorari on enforcement of tapes subpoena. Chief Judge George Hart grants an extension to Grand Jury I. Expiration date set at December 4, 1974.
June 3, 1974	Charles Colson pleads guilty to an information charging one count of obstruction of justice. Previous indictments are dismissed.
June 7, 1974	Court of Appeals denies petition for writ of mandamus to recuse Judge Sirica.
June 14, 1974	Court of Appeals hears oral arguments in the appeals of Liddy, Barker, Martinez, Sturgis, McCord, Hunt, and Gonzalez.
June 21, 1974	Colson is sentenced to serve one to three years in prison and is fined $5,000.
June 26, 1974	Fielding break-in trial begins.
June 27-28, 1974	James St. Clair appears before the House Judiciary Committee to present a defense for the President.
July 8, 1974	Supreme Court hears oral arguments in U.S. v. Nixon.
July 12, 1974	Jury returns guilty verdict against Ehrlichman, Martinez, Liddy and Barker in Fielding break-in trial.
July 23, 1974	David Parr pleads guilty to a one-count charge of conspiracy to make an illegal campaign contribution. He is later sentenced to four months in prison and fined $10,000.
July 24, 1974	Supreme Court unanimously upholds Special Prosecutor's tapes subpoena for Watergate trial.
July 25, 1974	Supreme Court denies petition for writ of certiorari to review ruling concerning recusal of Judge Sirica.
July 27, 1974	Jury finds Reinecke guilty on one count of perjury. House Judiciary Committee adopts Article I of impeachment resolution charging the President with obstruction of justice.
July 29, 1974	John Connally is indicted on two counts of accepting an illegal payment, one count of conspiracy to commit perjury and obstruct justice, and two counts of making a false declaration before a grand jury. Jake Jacobsen is indicted on one count of making an illegal payment to a public official.

Date:	Event:
	House Judiciary Committee adopts Article II of impeachment resolution charging the President with misuse of powers, violating his oath of office.
July 30, 1974	House Judiciary Committee adopts Article III of impeachment resolution charging the President with failure to comply with House subpoenas.
July 31, 1974	Sentences are handed down in Fielding break-in case.
	Harold S. Nelson pleads guilty to charges of conspiracy to make an illegal payment to a Government official, and to make illegal campaign contributions.
August 1, 1974	Associated Milk Producers, Inc., pleads guilty to one count of violating 18 USC 371, and five counts of violating 18 USC 610; fined $35,000 (campaign contributions).
August 2, 1974	Dean is sentenced to serve a prison term of one to four years.
August 7, 1974	Jacobsen pleads guilty to July 29 indictment.
August 9, 1974	Richard Nixon resigns from office.
August 12, 1974	Norman Sherman pleads guilty in a dairy contributions matter to non-willful violation of 18 USC 610, sections 2 and 610.
	John Valentine pleads guilty in a dairy contributions matter to non-willful violation of 18 USC 610, sections 2 and 610.
August 14, 1974	U.S. Court of Appeals denies Haldeman petition for writ of mandamus concerning validity of grand jury.
August 15, 1974	Members of the Special Prosecution Force meet with White House Counsel to discuss status of Nixon materials.
August 22, 1974	U.S. Court of Appeals suggests a three- to four-week continuance for <u>Mitchell et al.</u> trial.
September 2, 1974	Supreme Court denies Ehrlichman's application for stay of trial.
September 8, 1974	President Ford pardons Richard Nixon.
	President Ford announces the agreement between Sampson and Nixon giving Nixon ownership and control over access to Nixon Administration papers.
September 9, 1974	Brief for the U.S. in the conviction appeal of Dwight Chapin is filed.
September 20, 1974	U.S. Court of Appeals denies Strachan's petition for a writ of mandamus.
	U.S. Court of Appeals denies Mitchell and

Watergate

Date:	Event:
	Ehrlichman petitions for writs of prohibition and/or madamus seeking indefinite postponement of the trial.
September 28, 1974	Senate Select Committee completes its work.
September 30, 1974	Strachan's case is severed from <u>Mitchell et al.</u> trial.
October 1, 1974	Watergate cover-up trial begins.
October 12, 1974	Leon Jaworski announces his resignation as Special Prosecutor, effective October 25.
October 17, 1974	Richard Nixon asks the Court to enforce September 7 Nixon-Sampson agreement.
October 26, 1974	Henry S. Ruth, Jr., is sworn in as the third Special Prosecutor.
November 8, 1974	Edward L. Morgan pleads guilty to one count of conspiracy to impair, impede, defeat and obstruct the proper and lawful governmental functions of the IRS. He is sentenced, on December 19, to serve two years in prison, all but four months suspended.
November 9, 1974	Special Prosecutor Ruth, Mr. Buchen, counsel to the President, Mr. Sampson of General Services, and Mr. Knight, of the Secret Service, sign an agreement that permits the Special Prosecutor to gain access to Nixon Administration tapes and documents pertaining to his investigations.
November 11, 1974	Supreme Court denies Haldeman petition for writ of certiorari to review denial of mandamus relating to grand jury extension.
December 6, 1974	Liddy files petition for writ of certiorari in break-in conviction.
December 10, 1974	Tim Babcock pleads guilty to a charge of a one-count violation of making a contribution in the name of another person. Later sentenced to four months in prison.
December 11, 1974	Harry S. Dent, Jr., pleads guilty to a one-count charge of violating the Federal Corrupt Practices Act. He is sentenced to one month unsupervised probation.
December 12, 1974	Court of Appeals affirms the convictions of Liddy and McCord in Watergate break-in.
December 19, 1974	President Ford signs S. 4016 into law--the Presidential Recordings and Materials Preservation Act.
December 23, 1974	Jack Chestnut is indicted on one count of willful violation of 18 USC 610, aiding and abetting an illegal campaign contribution.
December 29, 1974	Watergate cover-up case goes to the jury.

Date:	Event:
January 1, 1975	Jury convicts all but Parkinson in cover-up trial.
January 8, 1975	Dean, Magruder and Kalmbach are released from prison; sentences are reduced to time served.
January 13, 1975	U.S. files memorandum in opposition to Liddy's petition for certiorari.
January 27, 1975	Liddy petition for certiorari is denied.
February 7, 1975	Court of Appeals hears oral arguments in Chapin appeal.
February 10, 1975	McCord files petition for writ of certiorari in break-in conviction.
February 12, 1975	Grand Jury II expires.
February 19, 1975	Frank DeMarco and Ralph Newman are indicted for conspiracy to defraud the U.S. and the IRS in connection with the donation of the pre-presidential papers of Richard Nixon.
February 21, 1975	Sentences handed down in cover-up trial.
February 25, 1975	Court of Appeals affirms convictions of Barker, Martinez, Sturgis, Gonzales and Hunt in Watergate break-in.
March 4, 1975	Brief for the U.S. to reinstate De Diego indictment is filed.
March 10, 1975	At the request of the Special Prosecutor, charges against Strachan are dropped.
March 12, 1975	Maurice Stans pleads guilty to three counts, violation of the reporting sections of the Federal Election Campaign Act of 1971, 2 USC, Section 434 (a) and (b), 441; and two counts violation of 18 USC 610, accepting an illegal campaign contribution.
March 14, 1975	LaRue is sentenced to serve six months in prison.
March 19, 1975	DeMarco and Newman file a motion to have their case transferred.
March 31, 1975	Brief for the U.S. in the conviction appeal of Howard Reinecke is filed.
April 2, 1975	Trial of John Connally begins.
April 16, 1975	Court of Appeals reinstates De Diego indictment.
April 17, 1975	Connally is acquitted on two counts.
April 18, 1975	Court dismisses remaining three counts against Connally on motion of the Special Prosecutor.
April 21, 1975	McCord petition for writ of certiorari is denied.
April 23, 1975	Morgan is released from prison.
May 2, 1975	Brief for the U.S. in the conviction appeal of Ehrlichman, Barker, Martinez, and Liddy is filed (Fielding break-in).

Watergate

Date:	Event:
May 5, 1975	Babcock files appeal of sentence on his guilty plea.
May 6, 1975	U.S. files petition for a writ of mandamus in DeMarco-Newman case.
May 14, 1975	Stans is fined $5,000.
May 19, 1975	Judge Gesell dismisses charges against De Diego at the request of the Special Prosecutor.
May 29, 1975	McCord is released from prison.
June 6, 1975	Court of Appeals hears oral arguments in Reinecke appeal.
June 18, 1975	Court of Appeals hears oral arguments in Ehrlichman appeal (Fielding break-in).
June 23-24, 1975	Richard M. Nixon gives sworn testimony in matters under investigation by the Special Prosecutor.
July 3, 1975	Grand Jury III expires.

WATERGATE PERSONALITIES

Introduction: The following section is designed to assist users of the bibliography by identifying some of the main personalities involved in the Watergate and related Nixon administration scandals. These personalities include direct participants, investigators, prosecutors, reporters, and prominent onlookers. Names are arranged alphabetically, and titles and ages, where provided, are those of 1972.

AGNEW, Spiro T.--Vice-President; resigned 1973 and paid a $10,000 fine for Federal income tax evasion; an international business consultant, Agnew, 53 in 1972, currently resides in Palm Springs, Calif.

ALEXANDER, Donald C.--IRS Commissioner, 1973-1977; presently a member of the NYC and Washington law firm of Morgan, Lewis & Bockius.

ANDERSON, Jack--Syndicated columnist.

BAKER, Howard H., Jr.--U.S. senator from Tennessee; vice-chairman of the Senate Select Committee on Presidential Campaign Activities; presently Majority Leader of the U.S. Senate.

BALDWIN, Alfred C., 3rd.--White House "plumber."

BARKER, Bernard L.--53, former CIA agent and White House "plumber"; arrested in the Watergate break-in; after prison sentence, became a Miami, Florida, building inspector; he retired in January, 1982.

BEARD, Dita--Author of controversial memo concerning fixing of ITT anti-trust suit.

BEN-VENISTE, Richard--29, Assistant Special Prosecutor; later founding partner of a Washington, D.C. law firm and attorney for Philadelphia ABSCAM defendant Howard Criden.

BERNSTEIN, CARL--28, Washington Post reporter, teamed with Bob Woodward (q.v.), whose early reports broke the scandal open; later, with Woodward, wrote the Watergate books All the President's Men and The Final Days and became ABC Washington bureau chief and subsequently head of ABC's investigative team.

BORK, Robert H.--U.S. Solicitor General, 1973-1977; following service as a law school professor, the man who carried out Nixon's order to fire Archibald Cox was appointed a Federal Appeals Court judge in 1981.

BUCHANAN, Patrick J.--White House aide and speech writer; consultant to President Ford, 1974; syndicated New York Times columnist, 1975-1978; presently a columnist for the Chicago Tribune-New York News syndicate.

BURGER, Warren E.--Chief Justice of the United States Supreme Court.

BUTTERFIELD, Alexander P.--46, White House aide who revealed existence of Nixon's secret tapes; FAA administrator, 1973-1975; presently chief financial officer of Global Networks, Inc. and the GMA Corporation.

BUZHARDT, J. Fred--Former Dept. of Defense general counsel appointed Special Counsel to President Nixon for Watergate matters and later succeeded by James D. St. Clair (q.v.).

CAULFIELD, John--43, former New York City policeman and Ehrlichman aide who attempted to keep James McCord (q.v.) from revealing White House connection to Watergate burglary; he presently works for industrialist Robert Abplanalp in Yonkers, New York.

CHAPIN, Dwight L.--31, Presidential Appointments Secretary who served eight months in prison for lying about his orchestration of the "dirty tricks" squad; currently president and publisher of Success magazine.

COLBY, William E.--Executive Director, CIA, 1972-1973; Deputy Director for Operations, 1973, and CIA Director, 1973-1976; presently a member of the Washington law firm of Reid and Priest.

COLSON, Charles W. ("Chuck")--40, White House Special Counsel, often considered worst of Nixon's political advisors; pleaded guilty to obstruction of justice and served seven months in prison. Becoming a "born again" Christian during the Watergate crisis, he founded the cell-block ministry "Prison Fellowship" with the profits from his autobiography Born Again.

CONNALLY, John B.--Secretary of the Treasury; indicted in the Milk Fund scandal in July 1974, but acquitted in April 1975; candidate for the Republican presidential nomination in 1976 and 1980.

COX, Archibald--60, Watergate Special Prosecutor whose demand for access to all relevant presidential tapes resulted in his controversial dismissal on October 20, 1973; Harvard law school professor who continues to teach beyond the mandatory retirement age, he is also national chairman of Common Cause.

CUSHMAN, Gen. Robert E., Jr.--Deputy Director of CIA, 1972-1973; since retired.

DASH, Samuel--47, Chief Counsel to Senate Select Committee on Presidential Campaign Activities; currently gives public lectures and teaches at Georgetown University Law School.

DEAN, John W., 3rd.--33, White House Counsel, fired by the president, who became the central figure in unraveling the Watergate coverup he had helped to create; after serving 4 months in prison, he paid off legal bills with successful autobiography Blind Ambition; he presently resides in Los Angeles with his wife, Maureen, and owns Popular Media.

DE DIEGO, Felipe--Associate of Bernard Barker; indicted in March

1974 for his role in Fielding break-in; all charges dismissed, May 1975.

DOAR, John M.--Former Assistant to the Attorney General who became Special Counsel to the House Judiciary Committee during its impeachment inquiry; later a partner in the New York City law firm of Donovan, Leisure, Newton & Irvine.

EHRLICHMAN, John D.--47, Domestic Affairs Advisor to the President who helped create the Watergate cover-up and was forced to resign in April 1973; convicted and sentenced for both the Fielding and Watergate conspiracies, he served 18 months; divorced and disbarred, he has since written two political novels and his memoirs, has remarried, and resides in Santa Fe, New Mexico.

ERVIN, Sam J., Jr.--75, North Carolina senator and chairman of the Senate Select Committee on Presidential Campaign Activities; acknowledged Constitutional expert and self-styled country lawyer, has retired to his hometown of Morganton to practice law, give public lectures, and write his memoirs.

FELT, W. Mark--59, Deputy Director of FBI; occasionally mentioned in connection with "Deep Throat," the anonymous Woodward/Bernstein source.

FIELDING, Fred F.--Aide to John Dean; not implicated in Watergate scandal; remains in government service as White House General Counsel.

FIELDING, Dr. Lewis--Daniel Ellsberg's psychiatrist whose office was covertly entered by White House "plumbers."

FORD, Gerald R.--Former House Minority Leader confirmed as Spiro T. Agnew's (q.v.) successor as Vice-President; became President of the United States upon Richard Nixon's resignation; defeated in 1976 campaign; retired.

GARMENT, Leonard--Successor to John Dean as White House counsel; involved with Nixon's Watergate defense.

Watergate Personalities

GARRISON, Samuel, 3rd.--Deputy Minority Counsel, House Judiciary Committee.

GENEEN, Harold S.--President, Chief Executive Officer, and Board Chairman of ITT, 1959-1979; Chairman Emeritus, 1980--.

GESELL, Gerhard A.--U.S. District Court for the District of Columbia judge, 1968--.

GOLDWATER, Barry--Senior senator from the State of Arizona.

GONZALES, Virgilio R.--46, associate of Bernard Barker and master locksmith arrested in Watergate break-in; after prison, returned to Miami to run a general store with his wife.

GRAY, L. Patrick, 3rd.--55, Acting Director of FBI duped by White House aides and left, during his confirmation hearings, to "twist slowly, slowly in the wind" before his nomination was withdrawn; charged in 1978 with authorizing illegal FBI break-ins (charges later dropped), he is currently suing the Justice Department. He resides in Mystic, Conn. and practices law.

HAIG, Gen. Alexander M.--47, succeeded Haldeman as White House chief of staff and essentially ran the Oval Office during Nixon's last weeks; later, N.A.T.O. Supreme Commander and then Secretary of State, 1981-1982.

HALDEMAN, Harry R. ("Bob")--45, White House chief of staff until April 1973; convicted in Watergate cover-up and served 18 months in prison; devoted to Nixon during the life of the administration, his 1978 memoirs claim the former president was involved in Watergate from the start; currently vice-president of the Los Angeles-based Murdock Development Co.

HELMS, Richard M.--Director, CIA, 1971-1973; later ambassador to Iran.

HUGHES, Howard R.--Billionaire industrialist; died 1976.

HUNT, E. Howard, Jr.--53, former CIA agent and White House "plumber" who helped plan the Watergate break-in and served 33 months in prison for the event; released in February 1977, he has cleared his legal debts largely by writing spy novels. Remarried after the death of his first wife in a 1972 plane crash, he won a 1981 libel suit against the Liberty Lobby, which had accused him of involvement in the John Kennedy assassination.

JAWORSKI, Leon--66, Watergate Special Prosecutor, succeeding Archibald Cox (q.v.), who won the Supreme Court case (United States v. Nixon) leading to the prosecution's acquisition of the Nixon tapes; after writing his memoirs, he placed a third of the royalties into a scholarship fund for Baylor Law School students; later served as an advisor to his Houston law firm and as a member of the National Foreign Intelligence Board. Died December 1982.

JENNER, Albert E.--Chief Minority Counsel to the House Judiciary Committee during its impeachment inquiry and proceedings; currently the senior partner in the Chicago law firm of Jenner and Block.

KALMBACH, Herbert L.--50, GOP fund raiser and President Nixon's personal lawyer who collected hush money for the Watergate "burglars"; after serving 6 months for breaking campaign contribution laws, he regained the right to practice law in 1977. He is presently a partner in the Santa Ana, Calif. real estate firm of Hillsdale Associates.

KELLEY, Clarence M.--Former Kansas City lawman confirmed as FBI Director following Ruckelshaus (q.v.); served until 1977.

KISSINGER, Henry A.--National Security Advisor, 1968-1973 and Secretary of State, 1973-1977; presently on the faculty at Georgetown University; lectures and has written two large volumes of memoirs.

KLEINDIENST, Richard G.--48, succeeded John Mitchell (q.v.) as Attorney General and served until April 1973; received a 30-day suspended sentence for perjury in connection with his testimony to the Senate Judiciary Committee inquiry into the ITT scandal; acquitted in 1981 of 12 counts of perjury allegedly committed while representing a swindler; disbarred by Arizona Supreme Court in 1982.

KROGH, Egil, Jr.--32, assistant to John Ehrlichman (q.v.) and member of White House "plumbers"; served 4 months on charges stemming from Fielding break-in; later taught government at Golden Gate University before regaining right to practice law in 1980. He is presently an attorney in Seattle, Washington.

LARUE, Frederick C.--44, oilman aide to CREEP Director John Mitchell who handled hush money given to Watergate "burglars"; after serving 5 1/2 months for his participation in the cover-up, he was released and currently runs a Mississippi oil and gas exploration company with his brother.

LIDDY, G. Gordon--41, former FBI agent and county prosecutor turned chief "plumber," who conceived the political surveillance and break-ins and who privately took the blame for the bungled Watergate burglary; refusing to cooperate with the prosecution, he served the longest of any Watergate figure--52 months in prison; his memoirs, Will, were a best seller and in addition to becoming a popular lecture-circuit figure, he is also advisor to an Illinois private-eye firm, Gemstone Security, Ltd.

McCORD, James W., Jr.--47, former CIA agent and CREEP director of security, was caught in the Watergate break-in; an electronics expert, his letter to Judge John Sirica (q.v.) began the unraveling of the cover-up. Presently a fuel-oil executive in Fort Collins, Colo.

MacGREGOR, Clark--Successor to John Mitchell (q.v.) as CREEP director; not indicted for any Watergate activity.

MAGRUDER, Jeb Stuart--37, former Haldeman (q.v.) aide and deputy director of CREEP who helped set up the "plumbers" and participated in the cover-up; after testifying before Ervin panel, he served seven months in prison, where he, like Colson, became a "born again" Christian. Completed master's degree in

Theology from Princeton Theological Seminary and in May 1982 became pastor of the First Presbyterian Church, Burlingame, Calif.

MARDIAN, Robert C.--48, former Assistant Attorney General and counsel to CREEP, who was found guilty of participating in the Watergate cover-up, a conviction overruled upon appeal; currently president of a real estate development firm and vice-president of his family's Phoenix construction firm.

MARTINEZ, Eugenio--50, associate of Bernard Barker (q.v.) arrested in Watergate break-in; after prison, returned to Miami where he is currently head of the leasing department of a local automobile dealer.

MITCHELL, John N.--58, former Attorney General and director of CREEP; found guilty in Watergate cover-up and served 19 months; barred from law practice, he helped form the international business consulting firm Global Research; remains the only major Watergate figure not to have published his recollections.

MITCHELL, Martha--Estranged wife of former Attorney General and CREEP Director John Mitchell, who is known for her pithy interviews and comments to the press concerning the Nixon White House. Died 1976.

NEAL, James F.--42, assistant Watergate Special Prosecutor and chief prosecutor in the cover-up trial; currently practices law in Nashville.

NIXON, Richard M.--59, 37th President of the United States, who resigned on August 9, 1974 in the face of almost certain impeachment; pardoned by Gerald Ford (q.v.) his successor on September 8, 1974; presently resides in Saddle River, N.J.; he writes, travels, and gives occasional interviews.

O'BRIEN, Lawrence F.--Long-time Kennedy associate and Democratic Party chairman, 1970-1972; since 1975, Commissioner of the National Basketball Association.

PARKINSON, Kenneth W.--CREEP attorney; indicted by Watergate grand jury in March 1974 and acquitted on January 1, 1975.

PETERSEN, Henry F.--51, Head, Criminal Division, Justice Department and pre-Cox Watergate investigator who was, in fact, used by Nixon to keep tabs on the affair; presently a partner in the Washington, D.C. law firm of Hundley & Cacheris.

PORTER, Herbert L.--CREEP scheduling director; charged in January 1974 with making false statements to the FBI, sentenced in April and released on May 17, 1974.

RATHER, Dan--CBS News White House correspondent, 1966-1974; presently anchor of the CBS Evening News with Dan Rather.

REBOZO, Charles G. ("BeBe")--Florida banker and Nixon confidant; held no government post.

RICHARDSON, Elliot L.--Former HEW and Defense Secretary confirmed as Attorney General succeeding Kleindienst (q.v.); retired in October 1973 rather than carry out presidential order to dismiss Archibald Cox (q.v.); served in minor government posts in Ford and Carter administrations and presently practices law in Washington, D.C.

RODINO, Peter W.--63, New Jersey congressman, currently, as in 1974, chairman of the House Judiciary Committee.

RUCKELSHAUS, William D.--Former EPA Administrator who served as interim FBI Director succeeding Gray (q.v.) and also retired rather than become involved in the Cox dismissal; presently senior vice-president of Weyerhauser Corp., Tacoma, Washington.

RUTH, Henry S., Jr.--Succeeded Jaworski (q.v.) as the third and final Watergate Special Prosecutor.

SAFIRE, William--Presidential assistant and speechwriter, 1969-1973; New York Times columnist, 1973 to present.

ST. CLAIR, James D.--52, succeeded Buzhardt (q.v.) as White House special counsel who unsuccessfully defended Nixon's tape case before the Supreme Court and did not learn the truth of the President's involvement until the June 23, 1972 tapes were released; currently senior partner in the Boston law firm of Hale & Dorr, and teaches part-time at Harvard Law School.

SAXBE, William--Former Ohio senator confirmed as Attorney General succeeding Richardson (q.v.); ambassador to India, 1975-1977; presently a partner in the Columbus law firm of Chester, Saxbe, Hoffman & Wilcox.

SCHORR, Daniel--CBS News Washington correspondent, 1966-1976, who won three Emmy awards for his Watergate coverage; dismissed in 1976 after leaking Pike Report on intelligence activities; presently senior Washington correspondent for CNN.

SEGRETTI, Donald H.--30, former Treasury Dept. lawyer and political saboteur who tried to undermine the primary campaigns of leading Democratic candidates in 1972; served 4 1/2 months for distributing false campaign material and was disbarred in California for two years; after working in the art-gallery business, returned to the practice of law in Newport Beach.

SILBERT, Earl J.--Principal Assistant Attorney General, 1972-1973, who headed the original Watergate prosecution team; U.S. Attorney for the District of Columbia, 1974-1979; currently a partner in the Washington law firm of Schwalb, Donnenfeld, Bray & Silbert.

SIRICA, John J.--68, Chief Judge of the District Court for the District of Columbia, who pressed for further investigations of the Watergate break-in and cover-up; survived massive heart attack in 1976 (thanks in part to mouth-to-mouth resuscitation); he retired from full-time bench duty in 1977, but still handles select cases. Nicknamed "Maximum John" for his tough sentences.

SLOAN, Hugh W., Jr.--31, Haldeman (q.v.) aide and CREEP treasurer, who resigned when ordered to commit perjury and cooperated with prosecution; presently president of Budd Canada, an Ontario components manufacturer.

STANS, Maurice--64, former Secretary of Commerce and CREEP finance director and chief political fund raiser; fined $5,000 on five counts of violating campaign financing laws; runs Pasadena, Calif., consulting firm; nominated in 1981 to head the Overseas Private Investment Corporation.

STRACHAN, Gordon--White House aide who was indicted in Watergate cover-up but against whom all charges were dropped on March 10, 1975.

STURGIS, Frank A.--47, associate of Bernard Barker (q.v.) arrested in Watergate break-in; after prison, returned to Miami where he sold videotapes until plotting 1981 attempt for Cuban exiles to invade Guantanamo naval base and establish a "free" Cuban government.

THOMPSON, Fred D.--Chief Minority Counsel, Senate Select Committee on Presidential Campaign Activities.

ULASEWICZ, Anthony ("Tony U")--former New York City policeman who acted as "bagman" in the payment of Watergate hush money; sentenced to probation in 1976 for income tax evasion; currently a poultry raiser in Day, New York.

VESCO, Robert L.--Indicted financier; presently a fugitive reportedly living somewhere in the West Indies.

WALTERS, Vernon A.--Deputy Director, CIA; presently retired.

WILLS, Frank--24, security guard at Watergate who called the police and who arrested the 5-man "plumbers" team. He is presently unemployed and living in Washington, D.C.

WOODS, Rose Mary--54, Nixon's long-time personal secretary accused of covering up in her description of a mysterious $18\frac{1}{2}$-minute tape gap; after Nixon resigned, she lived at San Clemente and assisted in the preparation of his post-Watergate memoirs; retired in 1976 on government pension and currently resides in the Watergate complex.

WOODWARD, Robert U. ("Bob")--29, Washington Post reporter teamed with Carl Bernstein (q.v.) whose early reports broke the scandal open; later, with Bernstein, wrote the Watergate books <u>All the President's Men</u> and <u>The Final Days</u>. He was later the <u>Post</u>'s metropolitan editor, and is currently its managing editor for national investigations.

WRIGHT, Charles A.--44, special White House consultant for Supreme Court tapes case; returned to University of Texas-Austin where he continues to teach constitutional law.

ZIEGLER, Ronald--33, White House press secretary and presidential assistant who provided the press with "non-answers" during the scandal. He is currently president of the National Association of Truck Stop Operators.

THE IMPEACHMENT INVESTIGATION OF RICHARD NIXON*

While the details of President Richard M. Nixon's departure from public life may in time slip from memory, the Judiciary Committee's inquiry preceding Mr. Nixon's resignation will leave a lasting impact on the administrations of future Chief Executives.

During the first session of the 93d Congress more than 40 resolutions were introduced in the House of Representatives calling for either the impeachment or an investigation into the possible impeachment of President Richard M. Nixon.[1] Although the October 20, 1973, presidential firing of Special Watergate Prosecutor Archibald Cox precipitated a majority of the resolutions, the specific charges listed against the President confirmed the fact that the dismissal of Mr. Cox was merely the culminating episode in a series of confrontations between the White House and Congress.

Aside from those relating to the firing of Mr. Cox and obstruction of the Watergate investigation, other charges accused President Nixon of:

(1) Violating the First Amendment in the establishment of the "plumbers" unit.
(2) Aiding and abetting the "plumbers."
(3) Concealing the felonies committed by the "plumbers."
(4) Authorizing Government agencies to violate the constitutional rights of citizens (the so-called "Houston Plan"), knowing the conduct he was authorizing was illegal.
(5) Obstructing the proper administration of justice in the Ellsberg case.
(6) Negligently failing to supervise the collection, and permitting illegal use, of campaign funds in his 1972 campaign.

---

*Reprinted from U.S. Congress, House, Committee on the Judiciary. History of the Committee on the Judiciary of the House of Representatives: House Committee Report. Serial no. 15. 97th Cong., 2nd sess. Washington, D.C.: U.S. Government Printing Office, 1982. pp. 28-36, 178.

1. The first Nixon impeachment resolution offered in the 93rd Congress was introduced by Representative Robert F. Drinan (D-Mass.) on July 31, 1973.

(7) Illegally impounding $40 million in funds appropriated by Congress for various domestic programs.

(8) Dismantling the Office of Economic Opportunity despite legislation extending its authority until June 30, 1974.

(9) Usurping the warmaking and appropriation powers of Congress by authorizing the secret bombing of neutral Cambodia and falsification of military reports, and by concealing the bombing from Congress and the American people.

Following the introduction of a series of nine resolutions relating to the impeachment of the President on October 23, 1973, the House Judiciary Committee was formally granted jurisdiction over the inquiry into the charges. By the beginning of the following week, Judiciary Committee Chairman Peter W. Rodino, Jr., had been given the power to issue subpenas relative to the impeachment investigation. On November 15, 1973, the House passed House Resolution 702 by a vote of 367-51 providing $1 million for the Judiciary Committee staff investigation into whether proper grounds existed for the impeachment of the President. Organization of a special impeachment inquiry staff began in earnest shortly thereafter.

On February 6, 1974, the House passed House Resolution 803 by a vote of 410-4 authorizing and directing the Judiciary Committee "to investigate fully and completely whether sufficient grounds exist for the House of Representatives to exercise its constitutional power to impeach Richard M. Nixon, President of the United States of America." The resolution also granted subpena power to the committee, and specifically authorized use of the funds made available under House Resolution 702 to carry out the investigation.

On March 3, 1974, the President's attorney, James D. St. Clair, disclosed before Judge John J. Sirica of the U.S. District Court for the District of Columbia, and principal jurist in the Watergate trials, that President Nixon had decided to provide the Judiciary Committee with all the tapes and documents submitted to the Watergate grand jury. But the event overshadowing all else during the month of March had occurred 2 days earlier: seven former White House aides or officials of President Nixon's Reelection Committee were indicted by the Watergate grand jury for Watergate-related activities. Of special significance to the Judiciary Committee was a secret report and a briefcase of evidence gathered by the grand jury allegedly pertaining to President Nixon's possible obstruction of justice in the case. It was the intent of the jury that the report and briefcase be turned over to the impeachment inquiry staff. Three weeks later on March 26, after district and appellate court decisions, the committee finally received the material.

Meanwhile, the newspapers of the country were flooded with articles addressing the question of exactly what was an impeachable offense. Near the end of February, the constitutional arguments relative to what the Framers of the Constitution meant by the phrase "other high crimes and misdemeanors" in the impeachment clause of article II, section 4, became, at least momentarily, the most important consideration in the inquiry. From the beginning, one of the principal objectives of the impeachment inquiry had been to define the constitutional grounds for impeachment. On March 20, 1974, the Judiciary Committee staff released a study entitled the "Constitutional Grounds for Impeachment," which concluded that a President could be impeached and removed from the office for offenses against the public interest which are not necessarily crimes in the legal sense. A White House staff report released less than a week later argued that only criminal offenses that are found in the Constitution or in the laws of the United States and that are of a serious and public or governmental nature are grounds for impeaching the President. A third staff report on impeachment prepared by the Department of Justice at approximately the same time as the White House and Judiciary reports concluded that there were persuasive arguments for the narrow view that a criminal action is required as well as the broad view that certain noncriminal "political" offenses may justify impeachment. President Nixon had early joined in the discussion on February 25, when he stated, during the course of his first press conference in 4 months, that the Constitution was "very precise" in specifying that impeachment should depend upon proof of criminal conduct.

On April 3, the Joint Committee on Internal Revenue Taxation reported its findings that President Nixon owed $476,431, including interest, on back taxes for 1969 through 1972.

On April 11, the Judiciary Committee, exercising the power granted to it by House Resolution 803, issued a subpena to President Nixon. Demanded by the subpena were tapes and other records of 42 Presidential conversations, which the committee had sought to obtain from the White House for nearly two months. Five days after the issuance of the subpena, Watergate Special Prosecutor Leon Jaworski asked for a subpena ordering President Nixon to produce tape recordings, dictabelts, and memos involving 64 White House conversations. Ultimately this request would, on appeal, reach the Supreme Court.

Less than two weeks later, the Judiciary Committee impeachment inquiry staff, in a status report released on April 24, detailed its work since the release of a similar report on March 1 and identified the areas under investigation at that time. Also noted within the report were 12 allegations which the staff felt did not warrant further investigation. Among the items which should be dismissed according to the staff report were the bombing of Cambodia, the dismantling of the Office of Economic Opportunity, and the impoundment of appropriated funds. Allegations considered by the impeachment inquiry staff but not detailed in the report included:

(1) Domestic surveillance activities by or at the direction of the White House.
(2) Intelligence activities conducted by or at the direction of the White House anticipating the Presidential election of 1972.

(3) The Watergate break-in and related activities, including alleged reports by persons in the White House and others to "cover up" such activities, and other related matters.

Allegations continuing to occupy the attention of the impeachment inquiry staff and discussed at some length in the report were:

(4) Improprieties in connection with the personal finances of the President.
(5) Efforts by the White House to use agencies of the executive branch for political purposes, and alleged White House involvement with election campaign contributions.
(6) Illegal campaign contributions received from labor unions.
(7) Illegal campaign contributions received from foreign nationals in exchange for promises of favorable treatment by Government agencies.

President Nixon, in a conciliatory response on April 4, stated that he would pay the back taxes. On the evening of April 29, in a precedent-setting speech to the Nation, the President announced that he would turn over to the House impeachment investigators--and make public--edited transcripts of White House conversations that "will tell it all" and prove him innocent in the Watergate affair. The President further explained that verification of the transcripts could be made by Chairman Rodino and the ranking minority member of the committee, Representative Edward Hutchinson, by their personally listening to the tapes at the White House. If additional questions should still exist, the President would be willing to submit to written interrogatories.

A few hours prior to the President's televised address, the House approved House Resolution 1027 providing an appropriation of $733,759.31 for continuation of the Judiciary Committee's impeachment inquiry. Two days later, the Judiciary Committee by a narrow vote decided to inform the President by letter that the edited transcripts did not satisfy the demands of the subpena issued to him on April 11.

On May 7, presidential counsel St. Clair confirmed earlier reports that President Nixon would not comply with further requests for taped White House conversations by either the Special Watergate Prosecutor or the House Judiciary Committee. He told reporters that "the only basis for further requests would be a desire by some to erode the Presidency and the President is not going to stand for it." Less than 48 hours later, the Judiciary Committee opened its hearings to determine whether the President of the United States should be impeached.

For the next 3 months, the committee, meeting in executive session, heard from members of the inquiry staff, presidential counsel St. Clair, who earlier had been granted permission to participate in this phase of the investigation, and a number of witnesses. As events developed amidst these proceedings, the committee on three separate occasions sought unsuccessfully to subpena additional White House tapes.

On July 19, 1974, both of the committee's senior counsel argued that by virtue of the evidence presented during the hearings a recommendation for a Senate impeachment trial was warranted.

On the evening of Wednesday, July 24, for the first time in history, formal deliberations of a Congressional committee considering arguments for and against impeachment of an American President were broadcast over the Nation's television and radio networks. Earlier in the day, the Supreme Court by a unanimous vote of 8 to 0 (Associate Justice William H. Rehnquist having disqualified himself from participation in the case) upheld the decision of U.S. District Court Judge John J. Sirica that 64 Watergate tapes requested by Watergate Special Prosecutor Jaworski for use in the September trial of the Watergate defendants had to be released by the White House.

Three days later, on July 27, the Judiciary Committee by a vote of 27 to 11 approved an article of impeachment which specified that President Nixon had personally engaged in a "course of conduct" which "prevented, obstructed and impeded the administration of justice" in the investigation of the Watergate break-in. After a Sunday recess, the committee on Monday, July 29, discussed and then voted 28 to 10 to recommend a second impeachment article in which Mr. Nixon was charged with "repeatedly" engaging in conduct "violating the constitutional rights of citizens, impairing the due and proper administration of justice and the conduct of lawful inquiries, or contravening the laws governing agencies of the executive branch and the purposes of the agencies." A third article approved the following day charged that the President had "failed without lawful cause or excuse" to honor subpenas issued by the committee.

The text of the resolution and the articles of impeachment adopted by the Committee on the Judiciary stated:

Resolution

Impeaching Richard M. Nixon, President of the United States, of high crimes and misdemeanors.

Resolved, That Richard M. Nixon, President of the United States, is impeached for high crimes and misdemeanors and that the following articles of impeachment be exhibited to the Senate:

Articles of impeachment exhibited by the House of Representatives of the United States of America in the name of itself and of all of the people of the United States of America, against Richard M. Nixon, President of the United States of America, in maintenance and support of its impeachment against him for high crimes and misdemeanors.

Article I

In his conduct of the office of President of the United States, Richard M. Nixon, in violation of his constitutional oath faithfully to execute the office of President of the United States and, to the best of his ability, preserve, protect, and defend the Constitution of the United States, and in violation of his constitutional duty to take care that the laws be faithfully executed, has prevented, obstructed, and impeded the administration of justice, in that:

On June 17, 1972, and prior thereto, agents of the Committee for the Re-election of the President committed unlawful entry of the headquarters of the Democratic National Committee in Washington, District of Columbia, for the purpose of securing political intelligence. Subsequent thereto, Richard M. Nixon, using the powers of his high office, engaged personally and through his subordinates and agents, in a course of conduct or plan designed to delay, impede, and obstruct the investigation of such unlawful entry; to cover up, conceal and protect those responsible; and to conceal the existence and scope of other unlawful covert activities.

The means used to implement this course of conduct or plan included one or more of the following:

(1) making or causing to be made false or misleading statements to lawfully authorized investigative officers and employees of the United States;

(2) withholding relevant and material evidence or information from lawfully authorized investigative officers and employees of the United States;

(3) approving, condoning, acquiescing in, and counseling witnesses with respect to the giving of false or misleading statements to lawfully authorized investigative officers and employees of the United States and false or misleading testimony in duly instituted judicial and congressional proceedings;

(4) interfering or endeavoring to interfere with the conduct of investigations by the Department of Justice of the United States, the Federal Bureau of Investigation, the Office of Watergate Special Prosecution Force, and Congressional Committees;

(5) approving, condoning, and acquiescing in, the surreptitious payment of substantial sums of money for the purpose of obtaining the silence or influencing the testimony of witnesses, potential witnesses or individuals who participated in such unlawful entry and other illegal activities;

(6) endeavoring to misuse the Central Intelligence Agency, an agency of the United States;

(7) disseminating information received from officers of the Department of Justice of the United States to subjects of investigations conducted by lawfully authorized investigative officers and employees of the United States, for the purpose of aiding and assisting such subjects in their attempts to avoid criminal liability;

(8) making false or misleading public statements for the purpose of deceiving the people of the United States into believing that a thorough and complete investigation had been conducted with respect to allegations of misconduct on the part of personnel of the executive branch of the United States and personnel of the Committee for the Re-election of the President, and that there was no involvement of such personnel in such misconduct; or

(9) endeavoring to cause prospective defendants, and individuals duly tried and convicted, to expect favored treatment and consideration in return for their silence or false testimony, or rewarding individuals for their silence or false testimony.

In all of this, Richard M. Nixon has acted in a manner contrary to his trust as President and subversive of constitutional government, to the great prejudice of the cause of law and justice and to the manifest injury of the people of the United States.

Wherefore Richard M. Nixon, by such conduct, warrants impeachment and trial, and removal from office.

Article II

Using the powers of the office of President of the United States, Richard M. Nixon, in violation of his constitutional oath faithfully to execute the office of President of the United States and, to the best of his ability, preserve, protect, and defend the Constitution of the United States, and in disregard of his constitutional duty to take care that the laws be faithfully executed, has repeatedly engaged in conduct violating the constitutional rights of citizens, impairing the due and proper administration of justice and the conduct of lawful inquiries, or contravening the laws governing agencies of the executive branch and the purposes of these agencies.

This conduct has included one or more of the following:

(1) He has, acting personally and through his subordinates and agents, endeavored to obtain from the Internal Revenue Service, in violation of the constitutional rights of citizens, confidential information contained in income tax returns for purposes not authorized by law, and to cause, in violation of the constitutional rights of citizens, income tax audits

or other income tax investigations to be initiated or conducted in a discriminatory manner.

(2) He misused the Federal Bureau of Investigation, the Secret Service, and other executive personnel, in violation or disregard of the constitutional rights of citizens, by directing or authorizing such agencies or personnel to conduct or continue electronic surveillance or other investigations for purposes unrelated to national security, the enforcement of laws, or any other lawful function of his office; he did direct, authorize, or permit the use of information obtained thereby for purposes unrelated to national security, the enforcement of laws, or any other lawful function of his office; and he did direct the concealment of certain records made by the Federal Bureau of Investigation of electronic surveillance.

(3) He has, acting personally and through his subordinates and agents, in violation or disregard of the constitutional rights of citizens, authorized and permitted to be maintained a secret investigative unit within the office of the President, financed in part with money derived from campaign contributions, which unlawfully utilized the resources of the Central Intelligence Agency, engaged in covert and unlawful activities, and attempted to prejudice the constitutional right of an accused to a fair trial.

(4) He has failed to take care that the laws were faithfully executed by failing to act when he knew or had reason to know that his close subordinate endeavored to impede and frustrate lawful inquiries by duly constituted executive, judicial, and legislative entities concerning the unlawful entry into the headquarters of the Democratic National Committee, and the cover-up thereof, and concerning other unlawful activities, including those relating to the confirmation of Richard Kleindienst as Attorney General of the United States, the electronic surveillance of private citizens, the break-in into the offices of Dr. Lewis Fielding, and the campaign financing practices of the Committee to Re-elect the President.

(5) In disregard of the rule of law, he knowingly misused the executive power by interfering with agencies of the executive branch, including the Federal Bureau of Investigation, the Criminal Division, and the Office of Watergate Special Prosecution Force, of the Department of Justice, and the Central Intelligence Agency, in violation of his duty to take care that the laws be faithfully executed.

In all of this, Richard M. Nixon has acted in a manner contrary to his trust as President and subversive of constitutional government, to the great prejudice of the cause of law and justice and to the manifest injury of the people of the United States.

Wherefore Richard M. Nixon, by such conduct, warrants impeachment and trial, and removal from office.

Article III

In his conduct of the office of President of the United States, Richard M. Nixon, contrary to his oath faithfully to execute the office of President of the United States and, to the best of his ability, preserve, protect, and defend the Constitution of the United States, and in violation of his constitutional duty to take care that the laws be faithfully executed, has failed without lawful cause or excuse to produce papers and things as directed by duly authorized subpenas issued by the Committee on the Judiciary of the House of Representatives on April 11, 1974, May 15, 1974, May 30, 1974, and June 24, 1974, and willfully disobeyed such subpenas. The subpenaed papers and things were deemed necessary by the Committee in order to resolve by direct evidence fundamental, factual questions relating to Presidential direction, knowledge, or approval of actions demonstrated by other evidence to be substantial grounds for impeachment of the President. In refusing to produce these papers and things, Richard M. Nixon, substituting his judgment as to what materials were necessary for the inquiry, interposed the powers of the Presidency against the lawful subpenas of the House of Representatives, thereby assuming to himself functions and judgments necessary to the exercise of the sole power of impeachment vested by the Constitution in the House of Representatives.

In all of this, Richard M. Nixon has acted in a manner contrary to his trust as President and subversive of constitutional government, to the great prejudice of the cause of law and justice, and to the manifest injury of the people of the United States.

Wherefore Richard M. Nixon, by such conduct, warrants impeachment and trial, and removal from office.

Having completed the hearing phase of its impeachment inquiry before a TV audience estimated unofficially at 70 million viewers, the committee began the task of drafting a report supporting the articles which would be presented to the full membership of the House within approximately two and a half weeks.

As the leadership of the House began preparations for a floor debate on the articles of impeachment, events during the first 9 days of August ended the Nixon Presidency. The month began with pronouncements from the White House that the President would continue his "political struggle." On August 5, however, Nixon's remaining support in Congress began to crumble following his disclosure that 6 days after the Watergate burglary he had ordered a halt to the investigation of the break-in for political as well as national security reasons and he had kept this information from his lawyers and supporters on the Judiciary Committee. In the face of resignation demands by his strongest supporters, President Nixon the following morning told his cabinet that he did not intend to resign and believed that the constitutional process should be allowed to run its course.

By August 7, the principal topic of discussion in Washington was when, not if, the President would resign. That afternoon, the President met with Senate Minority Leader Hugh Scott, Senator Barry Goldwater, and House Minority Leader John J. Rhodes to discuss his precarious position. Apparently the President's decision to resign was solidified later that evening.

In a televised speech from the oval office, Mr. Nixon, at 9 o'clock the following evening, announced that he intended to resign as President of the United States because "it is evident to me that I no longer have a strong enough political base in the Congress to justify [the] effort [to stay in office]." He made no mention of impeachment, but the significance of the Judiciary Committee investigation was self-evident.

President Nixon formally resigned in a letter to the Secretary of State some 14 hours later, shortly after 11:30 a.m. on August 9, 1974. Gerald Rudolph Ford automatically became the Nation's 38th President at that time. Minutes later President Ford was formally sworn in by Chief Justice of the Supreme Court Warren E. Burger. President Ford observed to those gathered for his inauguration that "our long national nightmare is over. Our Constitution works. Our great Republic is a government of laws and not of men."

By choosing to resign rather than face almost sure impeachment by the House and possible conviction in the Senate, Mr. Nixon brought to an end the Congressional proceedings surrounding Watergate. Eleven days after President Ford assumed the Presidency, the House of Representatives formally concluded the impeachment inquiry of Richard M. Nixon by overwhelmingly accepting the Judiciary Committee's report recommending impeachment by a vote of 412 to 3.

A calm settled over the White House and the Nation for the first month of the Ford administration. On the morning of Sunday, September 8, however, President Ford announced that he was granting a full and unconditional pardon to former President Nixon for any Federal crimes he may have committed while in office. A tremendous outpouring of public and Congressional criticism ensued and some Congressmen even suggested that formal impeachment proceedings against Mr. Nixon should be reopened. Judiciary Committee Chairman Rodino, however, declared the next day that "impeachment is dead" and said he had no intention of renewing the inquiry.

Members of the House Judiciary Committee, 93rd Congress, January 3, 1973 to December 20, 1974: Peter W. Rodino, Jr., New Jersey, chairman; Harold D. Donohue, Massachusetts; Jack Brooks, Texas; Robert W. Kastenmeier, Wisconsin; Don Edwards,

California; William L. Hungate, Missouri; John Conyers, Jr., Michigan; Joshua Eilberg, Pennsylvania; Jerome R. Waldie, California; Walter Flowers, Alabama; James R. Mann, South Carolina; Paul S. Sarbanes, Maryland; John F. Seiberling, Ohio; George E. Danielson, California; Robert F. Drinan, Massachusetts; Charles B. Rangel, New York; Barbara Jordan, Texas; Ray Thornton, Arkansas; Elizabeth Holtzman, New York; Wayne Owens, Utah; Edward Mezvinsky, Iowa; Edward Hutchinson, Michigan; Robert McClory, Illinois; Henry P. Smith, III, New York; Charles W. Sandman, Jr., New Jersey; Tom Railsback, Illinois; Charles E. Wiggins, California; David W. Dennis, Indiana; Hamilton Fish, Jr., New York; Lawrence Coughlin, Pennsylvania;[2] Wiley Mayne, Iowa; Lawrence J. Hogan, Maryland; William J. Keating, Ohio;[3] M. Caldwell Butler, Virginia; William S. Cohen, Maine; Trent Lott, Mississippi; Harold V. Froehlich, Wisconsin; Carlos J. Moorhead, California; Joseph J. Maraziti, New Jersey;[4] Delbert L. Latta, Ohio;[5] Paul N. McCloskey, Jr., California.

---

2. Resigned from Committee, March 7, 1973.
3. Resigned from Congress, noon, Jan. 3, 1974.
4. Elected to Committee, May 29, 1973.
5. Elected to Committee, Feb. 13, 1974; resigned from Committee, Nov. 21, 1974.

REFERENCE WORKS

Introduction: The purpose of setting this section off from the main body of the bibliography below is to provide the user with a variety of sources for additional research into the complexities of the Watergate scandal. Current and retrospective English-language sources relative to this topic can be located in Part A, "Bibliographies," and Part B, "Abstracts and Indexes." Although almost every Watergate book has some sort of chronology, a few are listed in the annuals cited in Part C. Terminology useful in interpreting language or concepts, "Watergate words" if you will, can be found in the political dictionaries listed in Part C. Users should also be certain to check the footnotes and bibliographies (where provided) in the books, scholarly journal articles, dissertations, and documents borrowed as the result of viewing titles in the main body of this work.

PART A: Bibliographies

1. American Historical Association. Writings on American History. Millwood, N.Y.: Kraus Reprint, 1973--. Writings were begun in the years after World War I and until 1961 were published by the GPO. Kraus issued a multi-volume set covering the years from 1962-1972 with annual volumes thereafter. For students of Watergate, it is those annual volumes after 1973 that are of value and which will continue to be of assistance as long as they are issued.

2. Anderson, David A. and Brandon C. Janes, eds. Privacy and Public Disclosures Under the Freedom of Information Act. Tarleton Law Library Legal Bibliography Series, no. 11. Austin, Tx.: Tarleton Law Library, University of Texas, 1976. 173p. A useful guide to the pre-1976 literature on the FOA; valuable for those who would know how the FOA fared under Nixon.

3. Bellush, J. and A. Walling. "Watergate: A Preliminary Bibliography." National Civic Review, LXIII (February 1974), 110-114. Very preliminary; examines the likes of Chester Lewis, et al., Watergate: The Full Inside Story (q.v.) and the New York Times paperback The Watergate Hearings: Break-in and Cover-up (q.v.). Not unlike Newsweek's "Breaking for the Gate" noted below.

Watergate   38

4. Bibliographic Index. New York: H. W. Wilson Co., 1973--.
    v. 27--. A valuable source to bibliographies relative to our
    topic, both alone and as parts of other works.

5. "Breaking for the Gate." Newsweek, LXXXII (October 1, 1973),
    103-104. A brief look at the start of the Watergate book
    flood; compare with Bellush above.

6. Bremer, Howard F., ed. Richard M. Nixon, 1913--: Chro-
    nology, Documents, Bibliographic Aids. Dobbs Ferry, N.Y.:
    Oceana, 1975. 250p. RMN's chronology, selected presiden-
    tial documents, and bibliography; covers the man's entire
    political career with good attention to Watergate, but is now,
    sadly, outdated.

7. The Cumulative Book Index. New York: H. W. Wilson Co.,
    1972--. Valuable for publishing information on new Water-
    gate book titles as they appear. Quarterly, annual cumula-
    tion, no annotations.

8. Darr, Richard K. and Oyeleka Abiba, eds. Watergate Bibliog-
    raphy. River Falls, Wisc.: River City Research, 1974.
    64p. The first pamphlet-length Watergate guide, now out-
    dated.

9. Davison, Kenneth E., ed. The American Presidency: A Guide
    to Information Sources. Detroit, Mich.: Gale Research,
    1982. 200p. Covers the entire field of the presidency with
    some attention to the scandal, but not much.

10. Dick, Barrett. "A Researcher's Guide to the Watergate Affair."
    Law Library Journal, LXXI (February-August 1978), 77-82,
    266-269, 420-424. Perhaps the most useful to that date of
    all of the bibliographic guides presented in journals. Part
    I provides historic background and unannotated listing of ma-
    terials in legal periodicals; Part II covers books; Part III
    covers the articles in National Journal Reports and CQ
    Weekly Reports, again non-annotated. About the only ser-
    ious drawback for the non-legal student is the use of the
    abbreviated legal bibliography format in article citation.

11. Forthcoming Books. New York: R. R. Bowker, Co., 1973--.
    v. 8--. This tool, with its companion Subject Guide to
    Forthcoming Books, will give the user advance information
    on new Watergate-related titles.

12. Greenstein, Fred I., Larry Berman, and Alvin S. Felzenberg.
    Evolution of the Modern Presidency: A Bibliographic Sur-
    vey. Washington, D.C.: American Enterprise Institute for
    Public Policy Research, 1977. Unpaged. A vital tool for
    those who would examine the literature of the modern pres-
    idency and the Watergate affair. In addition to the scandal

itself, sections are devoted to the process of impeachment, succession to the office, executive privilege, etc. Eighty-five mostly-well-annotated citations are provided on the topic of Watergate and Nixon's resignation.

13. Harrell, Karen F. The Role of Television in U.S. Politics and Government: A Bibliography, 1961-1981. Public Administration Series Bibliography P-814. Monticello, Ill.: Vance Bibliographies, 1981. 12p. A slim and inexpensive starting place for those interested in a number of citations on this aspect of the Watergate affair.

14. Johnson, Gretchen and Janice Koyama, comps. A Guide to Library Materials on the Watergate Affair, Nixon to Ford: A Crisis Resolved. Long Beach, Calif.: Library, Social Science Department, California State University, 1974. 8p. A useful in-house publication, given the limitation of its date.

15. Kingsley, T. C. The Federal Impeachment Process: A Bibliographic Guide. Ithaca, N.Y.: Cornell University Libraries, 1974. 29p. Similar in some respects to the Johnson work cited immediately above; covers the literature of the process as a whole and not just as it related to the Nixon case.

16. McPherson, Harry. "Why Read Any More About Nixon?: A Review Article." Washington Magazine, XI (July 1976), 179-184. Looks at the 1973-1976 flood of Watergate items, especially books, analyzes titles, and suggests reasons for the question in the title.

17. Paperbound Books in Print. New York: R. R. Bowker Co., 1973--. v. 18--. Provides listings for paperbacks, including originals and reprints, dealing with Watergate.

18. Rosenberg, Kenyon and Judith K. Watergate: An Annotated Bibliography. Littleton, Co.: Libraries Unlimited, 1975. 141p. Books, newspaper and periodical articles, and government reports are covered in a chronological, month-by-month non-indexed listing from June 1972-August 1974; each of the 975 entries is annotated, this being especially useful for articles from such news magazines as Time and Newsweek. The only book-length bibliography on Watergate previous to this one, the Rosenbergs' work might more profitably have been held up in press until information on the pardon and papers squabble could be included.

19. Sale, Kirkpatrick. "Laying the Dust: Review Article." New York Review of Books, XXII (December 11, 1975), 5-9. An examination of the Watergate titles to that date, with analysis and comparison.

20. Smith, Myron J., Jr. Intelligence, Propaganda, and Psychological Warfare, Covert Operations, 1945-1980. Vol. II of The Secret Wars: A Guide to Sources in English. Santa Barbara, Calif.: ABC/Clio, 1981. 389p. Watergate entries appear on pages 259-263.

21. _____. TV News: Reporters, Programming, and Events, 1949-1982. Jefferson, N.C.: McFarland, forthcoming. Provides complete coverage of the role of network television news in covering the Watergate affair.

22. Smith, S. C. Bibliography-Executive Privilege. New Haven, Conn.: Yale University Library, 1973. 41p. Somewhat similar to the Kingsley title above on impeachment in that this library guide covers the literature of the process as a whole and not just as it related to the Nixon case.

23. Subject Guide to Books in Print. New York: R. R. Bowker, 1973--. v. 16--. This list (actually an index to the Books in Print main volumes) provides an annual comprehensive list of titles available for purchase in the English language, mostly from U.S. sources. Users should check various headings, e.g., Watergate; Nixon, Richard M.; etc.

24. United States. Library of Congress. Library of Congress Catalog, Books-Subjects: A Cumulative List of Works Represented by Library of Congress Printed Cards. Washington, D.C.: U.S. Government Printing Office, 1972--. v. 22--. Users should look under Watergate and Nixon, Richard M.; lists not only books but pamphlets and government documents.

25. Verticle File Index. New York: H. W. Wilson Co., 1972--. v. 41--. Useful for locating pamphlets and government documents related to the Watergate affair.

26. Von Hoffman, Nicholas. "Unasked Questions: A Review Article." New York Review of Books, XXIII (June 10, 1976), 3-8. An analysis of Watergate books, especially memoirs, to mid-1976.

PART B: Abstracts and Indexes

27. Access: The Supplementary Index to Periodicals. Syracuse, N.Y.: Gaylord Publications, 1975--. v. 1--. Provides citations to magazines not usually found in any of the H. W. Wilson Co. indexes; Watergate-related articles can be found under both names and subjects, e.g., Nixon, Richard M.; Haldeman, H. R.; Investigations, Government.

28. America: History and Life--A Guide to Periodical Literature. Santa Barbara, Calif.: ABC/Clio Press, 1972--. v. 8--.

Provides coverage of literature on contemporary events such as Watergate, ITT, etc.; much more sophisticatedly divided now than earlier, with not only abstracts but well-arranged bibliographic entries by subject. Appears much more frequently (quarterly) than Writings on American History.

29. Barrer, Lester A. and Myra E., eds. Documented Index to the Richard Milhous Nixon Impeachment Proceedings; Including the Watergate and Related Investigations, Hearings, and Prosecutions. 2 vols. New York: Today Publications and News Service, 1975-1976. Not an index to ongoing information sources, but to the documents developed during the 1972-1974 Watergate crisis; should be employed in conjunction with the documents presented throughout the main body of the bibliography.

30. Bernan Associates. Checklist of Congressional Hearings and Reports. Washington, D.C., 1972--. v. 14--. Useful for checking hearings and reports that might have something to do with the Nixon crisis, e.g., the 1981 confirmation hearings of Alexander Haig.

31. Biography Index. New York: H. W. Wilson Co., 1972--. v. 25--. A noted reference tool which provides listings to books, articles, and other materials about a variety of personnel in many walks of life; for our purposes, this is an important source for ongoing information about members of the Watergate cast of characters.

32. Botlorff, Robert M., ed. Popular Periodical Index. New York, 1973--. v. 1--. Although some of the magazines covered are different (its chief strength), the purpose of this tool is the same as Access--to index materials not covered in the Wilson indexes.

33. Business Periodicals Index. New York: H. W. Wilson Co., 1972--. v. 14--. Extremely useful for citations to Watergate-related articles from business and interest group publications as well as some popular magazines.

34. CBS News Index: Key to the Television News Broadcasts. Sanford, N.C.: Microfilming Corp. of America, 1975--. v. 1--. Provides access to the content and location of the topics covered in the CBS News Television Broadcasts microform series, which now consists of a basic 1963-1974 set with annual supplements.

35. California News Index. Claremont, Calif.: Center for California Public Affairs, 1972--. v. 2--. Indexes the Los Angeles Times, San Diego Union, Sacramento Bee, and San Francisco Chronicle.

36. The Christian Science Monitor Index. Corvallis, Ore.: Helen M. Cropsey, 1972--. v. 12--. Indexes the noted daily.

Watergate

37. Congressional Information Service. <u>CIS/Annual--Part I, Abstracts of Congressional Publications and Legislative Histories; Part II, Index to Congressional Publications and Public Laws</u>. Washington, D.C., 1972--. Monthly, with annual cumulations; dissects all of the 1972-1975 hearings of various Congressional committees on the Watergate affair, and some such as the Senate Foreign Relations Committee hearings on the Haig nomination, which did not touch on Watergate until much later.

38. <u>Current Contents: Social and Behavioral Sciences</u>. Philadelphia, Pa.: Institute for Scientific Information, 1972--. v. 4--. Reproduces journal contents pages, including those from journals containing articles relating to this topic.

39. <u>Dissertation Abstracts International: "A" Schedule</u>. Ann Arbor, Mich.: University Microfilms, 1973--. v. 4--. A continuation of <u>Dissertation Abstract</u>'s original coverage of the humanities and social sciences; users should examine not only history and political science, but journalism and mass media.

40. <u>Editorials on File</u>. New York: Facts on File, Inc., 1972--. v. 3--. Gives users a handy reference to press editorials about the various facets of the Watergate affair from ITT to impeachment and from the "plumbers" to the pardon.

41. Educational Resources Information Center. <u>Resources in Education</u>. Washington, D.C.: U.S. Government Printing Office, 1973--. v. 8--. An index to those papers and reports reprinted on microfiche as ERIC documents; look in the index under Nixon, Watergate, and Presidents.

42. Garrison, Lloyd W., ed. <u>ABC PoliSci: Advance Bibliography of Contents, Political Science and Government</u>. Santa Barbara, Calif.: ABC/Clio, 1972--. v. 4--. Reproduces contents pages of politically-oriented journals, including those which have articles relating to our topic.

43. Garza, Hedda, comp. <u>The Watergate Hearings: Index to the Senate Select Committee Reports</u>. Washington, D.C.: Scholarly Resources, Inc., 1981. 625p. A guide to who said what when during the Ervin hearings.

44. <u>Humanities Index</u>. New York: H.W. Wilson Co., 1975--. v. 1--. Broken off from the old <u>Social Sciences and Humanities Index</u>, the last few volumes of which need to be employed in conjunction with Watergate; users can find articles of value by checking the headings Nixon, Richard M. and Watergate.

45. <u>Index to Legal Periodicals</u>. New York: H.W. Wilson Co., 1972--. v. 65--. Especially useful for citations to articles dealing with executive privilege and impeachment.

46. Johnson, Catherine, ed. TV Guide 25 Year Index, 1953-1977. New York: Triangle Publications, 1979. 506p. A guide to articles appearing in the popular weekly magazine; much on the relationship of television to Watergate.

47. Journalism Abstracts. Los Angeles, Calif.: Association for Education in Journalism, 1962--. v. 1--. Now published by the University of Minnesota, this tool is a guide to PhD and MA/MS papers with subject/author listings; especially useful in the years after 1972 for Watergate and the concept of investigative reporting à la Woodward and Bernstein.

48. Masters Abstracts. Ann Arbor, Mich.: University Microfilms, 1973--. v. 11--. A continuing guide to MA/MS-level study in all areas; examine the headings for history, political science, journalism, and mass communications.

49. National Observer Index. Flint, Mich.: Newspaper Indexing Center, 1972--. v. 3--. Indexes that particular newspaper.

50. New York Times Index. New York: New York Times Company, 1972--. A massive index which includes all NYT stories relating to our topic.

51. Newspaper Index. Wooster, Ohio: Bell & Howell, 1972--. v. 1--. Indexes the Chicago Tribune, Washington Post, Los Angeles Times, and New Orleans Times-Picayune, the middle two being especially noted for their Watergate coverage.

52. Public Affairs Information Service Annual Cumulated Bulletin (PAIS). New York: Public Affairs Information Service, 1972--. v. 57--. Guide to scholarly public affairs journals, some information from newspapers like the Wall Street Journal, and government documents in addition to books and pamphlets.

53. Readers' Guide to Periodical Literature. New York: H. W. Wilson Co., 1972--. Begun in 1900, this is the most famous and basic of periodical indexes, a first step for those who would seek information on the Watergate scandal.

54. Social Sciences and Humanities Index. New York: H. W. Wilson Co., 1972-1974. Discontinued and broken up in 1974, this famous guide lists articles on Watergate in journals a bit too specialized for inclusion in the Readers' Guide to Periodical Literature.

55. Social Sciences Index. New York: H. W. Wilson Co., 1975--. v. 1--. Broken up from the previous citation, this tool provides Watergate article coverage in journals of a social science bent; companion to Humanities Index (q.v.).

56. Sociological Abstracts. New York, 1973--. v. 20--. A useful guide to periodical articles and unpublished papers; users

employing this tool will occasionally uncover items related to Nixon, Watergate, and the sociological/psychological impact of both.

57. Topicator. Littleton, Co.: Thompson Bureau, 1972--. v. 7--. A monthly classified guide to the advertising/broadcasting/media trade press, cumulated quarterly and annually; includes many citations to the role of the media in the Watergate affair.

58. United States. Department of Commerce. Bibliographic Index to Current U.S. Joint Publications Research Service Translations. New York: C.C.M. Information Corp., 1972--. v. 10--. Useful in providing access to foreign press and periodical articles relating to some aspects of Watergate.

59. _____. Superintendent of Documents. Monthly Catalog of U.S. Government Publications. Washington, D.C.: U.S. Government Printing Office, 1972--. v. 77--. Useful for seeking out Congressional hearings related to Watergate, both in 1972-1974 and thereafter.

60. Vanderbilt University Television News Archives. Television News Index and Abstracts: A Guide to the Videotape Collection of the Network Evening News Programs in the Vanderbilt Television News Archive. Nashville, Tenn.: Joint University Libraries, 1974--. v. 1--. A monthly guide to the various evening news reports carried by the major networks.

61. The Wall Street Journal Index. New York: Dow Jones, 1972--. v. 14--. A guide to this noted financial newspaper; Watergate coverage of WSJ articles is much more complete here than in PAIS (q.v.).

PART C: Annuals and Dictionaries

62. Brownson, Charles B., ed. Congressional Staff Directory. Mt. Vernon, Va.: CSD, 1972--. v. 13--. This annual contains biographies of committee staff members; the 1972-1974 volumes are therefore quite useful for knowing who was who with the House Impeachment and Senate Ervin committees.

63. Congressional Quarterly, Inc. Congressional Quarterly Almanac. Washington, D.C., 1972-1975. v. 27-30. This annual is devoted exclusively to Congressional actions; we have noted only the Watergate years, when the White House scandal was paramount.

64. Facts on File Yearbook: The Indexed Record of World Events. New York: Facts on File, Inc., 1972-1975. v. 31-34.

Based on the weekly loose-leaf service, FonF easily keeps the user abreast of developments during the crisis; a number of chronologies and other studies were "bled" out of this annual.

65. Information Please Almanac. New York: Viking Press, 1972-1976. v. 26-30. Each issue contains a useful chronology with both the 1973 and 1974 volumes including "roundups" on Watergate.

66. Plano, Jack C. and Milton Greenberg. The American Political Dictionary. 5th ed. New York: Holt, 1979. 488p. A useful compendium of political terms, but not as entertaining, Watergate-wise, as Safire, below.

67. Safire, William. "Watergate Words." In: his Safire's Political Dictionary. New York: Random House, 1979. pp. 779-780. Safire provides definitions for a host of words from "cover-up" to "executive privilege" to "plumbers" and beyond.

68. United States. National Archives and Records Service. Weekly Compilation of Presidential Documents. Washington, D.C.: U.S. Government Printing Office, 1972--. v. 7--. Definitely a weekly and not an annual; however, this remains the best source for presidential statements on Watergate during the 1972-1974 years; partially analyzed in the main body of the bibliography.

69. "Watergate Voices." Life, II (December 1979), 20+. A series of quotations relating to the scandal.

70. Who's Who in America. Chicago: Marquis Publications, 1972--. v. 24--. A valuable tool for keeping track of Watergate-related individuals.

71. World Almanac and Book of Facts. Garden City, N.Y.: Doubleday, 1972--. v. 104--. Each issue contains a useful chronology with both the 1973 and 1974 volumes including summaries on Watergate; compare Information Please Almanac above.

BIBLIOGRAPHY

Introduction: The citations in this, the main body of the book, are arranged alphabetically by author (individual or corporate) or, where none exists, by title. Each entry receives a number, which will provide the key to the subject index.

72. "ABC Casts a Dragnet to Prove the White House Was Out to Get the Networks." Broadcasting, LXXXVI (January 14, 1974), 13-14.

73. Aberback, Joel D. and Bert A. Rockman. "Clashing Beliefs Within the Executive Branch: The Nixon Administration." American Political Science Review, LXX (June 1976), 456-468. Survey of Federal administrators which shows sharp policy differences between political appointees and civil servants.

74. "About Those Missing Tapes: White House Experts' Story: Exactly What Is Known About the System Set Up by the White House for Recording--'Bugging'--Conversations? How Could That Elaborate System Fail to Record Two Vital Talks Concerning the Watergate Affair? In Sworn Court Testimony, the Men Who Operated the Recorders Tell What They Know About the Mystery of the Missing Tapes." U.S. News and World Report, LXXV (November 12, 1973), 102-106. Excerpts from the transcript of proceedings in the U.S. District Court for the District of Columbia, Judge John J. Sirica presiding, October 31, 1973.

75. Abrahamsen, David. Nixon vs. Nixon: An Emotional Tragedy. New York: Farrar, Straus, 1977. 267p. In an effort to present "the emotional development of Richard Nixon," the author, a psychiatrist, studied the former president's writings and public statements and much of the writing about him, including the transcripts of the House Impeachment and Senate Ervin panels. The result is a psychohistory in which Nixon is portrayed as warring against himself--"exerting fanatical control over his latent hostilities and aggresive impulses which were nurtured, in part, by Nixon's being brought up in a family characterized by unceasing anger and misery." Nixon's self-destructive instinct reached its cosmic conclusion in the Watergate crisis. Of the var-

ious books which placed the man on the couch, this is by far the most reasoned and non-polemic.

76. "The Abuse of Executive Privilege: Reprinted from the Baltimore Sun, March 14, 1973." Congressional Record, CXIX (March 15, 1973), 8325. An editorial.

77. "Abusing the Presidency: Reprinted from the Peoria [Illinois] Journal-Star, March 20, 1974." Congressional Record, CXX (March 26, 1974), 8343. An editorial suggesting that Congress was wrongly in pursuit of Nixon.

78. "Acting Roles in a Fellini Script." Time, CIII (May 20, 1974), 24-25. Concerns who said what in the presidential transcripts.

79. Adam, Corinna. "The Ghost of Richard Nixon." New Statesman and Nation, LXXXVIII (November 8, 1974), 639-640. The post-resignation struggle over who owned the tapes.

80. Adler, Renata. "Reflections on Political Scandal." New York Review of Books, XXIV (December 8, 1977), 20-33. A general consideration with much attention paid to Watergate.

81. _____. "Searching for the Real Nixon Scandal: A Last Inference." Atlantic, CCXXXVIII (December 1976), 76-84, 87-88, 90-95. Suggests that the real scandal lay in the manner in which the Congress, special prosecutor, and courts handled various aspects of the impeachment process prior to Nixon's resignation.

82. "Adversary Relationships." Newsweek, LXXXIII (April 1, 1974), 66-67. The clash between Nixon and various newsmen, especially Dan Rather.

83. "The Advocates." Newsweek, LXXXIII (January 21, 1974), 29-30. Those charged with the President's defense.

84. AFL-CIO. "The Case for the Impeachment of Richard M. Nixon--Now." Congressional Record, CXIX (December 12, 1973), 41209-41212, 41216-41218, 41222-41223. Suggests that the President had committed so many "crimes" that he should be immediately impeached; a polemic.

85. _____. Watergate: An Unfinished Story of Money and Politics Up Through December 1973. Publication no. 150. Washington, D.C., 1974. 164p. Organized labor's history of the Watergate, based on newspaper accounts and the Ervin committee hearings.

86. "After Surrendering Tapes, New Pressures on Nixon." U.S. News and World Report, LXXV (November 5, 1973), 19-21.

Reviews the events immediately following the Saturday Night Massacre, when Special Prosecutor Cox was fired.

87. Agnew, Spiro T. "Address [on Watergate] by the Vice President of the United States." Congressional Record, CXIX (June 12, 1973), 19130-19132. Suggests Ervin panel hearings would obstruct inquiry of the Justice Department; compare reference 89, which is more easily available to the average student.

88. _____. Go Quietly--or Else. New York: William Morrow, 1980. 288p. The former Vice-President's memoirs of his final crisis. Agnew was not directly involved in the Watergate affair, although dirty money would create for him a scandal forcing him from office. His recollections contain some comments on Nixon, his aides, and the Watergate affair.

89. _____. "Senate Hearings Can Hardly Fail to Muddy the Waters of Justice: Excerpts from an Address, June 11, 1973." U.S. News and World Report, LXXIV (June 25, 1973), 26. Taken from the speech reprinted in the Congressional Record as cited above.

90. Aiken, George T. Aiken: Senate Diary, January 1972-January 1975. Brattleboro, Vt.: Stephen Greene, 1976. 370p. A week-by-week journal of a senior U.S. senator which contains observations and reflections on specific events, especially executive-legislative relations during Watergate.

91. "Albatross." Newsweek, LXXIX (June 26, 1972), 69. The relationship of ITT to the White House.

92. Albert, Lee A. and Larry G. Simon. "Enforcing Subpoenas Against the President: The Question of Mr. Jaworski's Authority." Columbia Law Review, LXXIV (May 1974), 545-560. A critique on Nixon's attack on Jaworski's authority to subpoena the president.

93. Album, Michael T. "Government Control of Richard Nixon's Presidential Material." Yale Law Journal, LXXXVII (July 1978), 1601-1635. Reviews the arguments, pro and con, concerning the government's handling of Nixon's papers, especially the famous Oval Office tapes.

94. Alexander, Shana. "Crazy Gang." Newsweek, LXXXI (May 14, 1973), 46. Suggests that the only reason why the people involved in the cover-up would act in such a manner was a certain insanity brought on by excessive power.

95. _____. "Big Graffiti: The White House Transcripts." Newsweek, LXXXIII (May 27, 1974), 35. The transcripts

96. _____. "The Need Not to Know." Newsweek, LXXXII (August 6, 1973), 31. Questions the Nixon administration's operations on a "need-to-know" basis which discouraged insiders from probing any deeper than necessary on Watergate matters.

97. "Alexander M. Haig." In: Eleanora W. Schoenebaum, ed. Political Profiles: The Nixon/Ford Years. New York: Facts on File, 1979. pp. 257-261. Formerly Henry Kissinger's deputy, Haig was brought over to the White House as chief of staff to replace the resigned Bob Haldeman.

98. "Alexander P. Butterfield." People, III (May 19, 1975), 44-46. An assistant to Haldeman, Butterfield revealed the Oval Office tape system during testimony before the Ervin committee.

99. "All the President's Men--And Two of Journalism's Finest." Senior Scholastic, CVII (January 13, 1976), 13-14. Profiles of Washington Post reporters Bob Woodward and Carl Bernstein.

100. "All the President's Men: Criminal Charges Against Them." Newsweek, LXXXIV (August 19, 1974), 50-51. Examines the range of charges against Nixon's people in the Watergate cover-up trial.

101. Allman, T. D. "Nixon Family Soap Opera." New Statesman and Nation, LXXXVIII (August 16, 1974), 208-210. The impact of resignation on the Nixon family.

102. Alpern, David M., et al. "At Last, Nixon Under Oath." Newsweek, LXXXVI (July 7, 1975), 12-13. A discussion of the former President's June 23-24, 1975 sworn testimony in matters under investigation by the Special Prosecutor.

103. _____. "Jaworski Remembers." Newsweek, LXXXVIII (September 6, 1976), 17. Reflections by the ex-Special Prosecutor on various aspects of the Watergate case and his views on Nixon's criminal involvement.

104. _____. "The Legacy of Watergate." Newsweek, XCIX (June 14, 1982), 36-40. A ten-year anniversary remembrance and look at reforms brought about as a direct result of the excesses of the scandal.

105. _____. "Nixon Speaks." Newsweek, LXXXIX (May 9, 1977), 25+. Excerpts from the former president's television interviews with David Frost.

106. _____ and Richard M. Smith. "All About Impeachment." Newsweek, LXXXIII (March 25, 1974), 28-35. A review of the process and a look at the work of the House Judiciary Committee and its staff on the matter with relation to Nixon.

107. Alsop, Joseph. "Mr. Nixon's Roller Coaster--On the Upswing?: Reprinted from the Washington Post, June 10, 1974." Congressional Record, CXX (June 11, 1974), 18827-18828. Written just before the release of the "smoking gun" transcript, this piece suggests that the president could weather an impeachment.

108. _____. "The Tapes--Challenging the Experts: Reprinted from the Washington Post, February 20, 1974." Congressional Record, CXX (February 21, 1974), 3902. A look at the various theories concerning the 18-minute gap.

109. Alsop, Stewart. "The Case for Nixon." Newsweek, LXXXI (May 28, 1973), 116. Suggests that the president's aides and not the chief executive planned and executed the Watergate break-in.

110. _____. "Crazy-Brave and the Phony-Tough." Newsweek, LXXXII (September 10, 1973), 94. The mentality of G. Gordon Liddy.

111. _____. "War, Not Politics: Tactics of the Committee for the Reelection of the President." Newsweek, LXXXI (May 14, 1973), 132. Compares CREEP's dirty tricks and covert activities to wartime occurrences; abridged in Reader's Digest, CIII (August 1973), 55-56 under the title "Watergate Was War, Not Politics."

112. American Bar Association. Symposium on Campaign Financing Regulation, April 25-27, 1975, Tiburon, California. Chicago, 1975. 148p. Examines the various reform ideas in light of the wrongs of the 1972 Nixon re-election campaign.

113. _____. Special Committee to Study Federal Law Enforcement Agencies. Removing Political Influence from Federal Law Enforcement Agencies. Chicago, 1975. Unpaged. Examines various reform ideas in light of the Watergate role of the FBI and, to a lesser extent, the IRS and CIA.

114. American Civil Liberties Union. "A Report to the Special Prosecutor on Certain Aspects of the Watergate Affair, June 18, 1973, by Charles Morgan, Jr., Director." In: U.S. Congress, Senate, Committee on the Judiciary. Nomination of Earl J. Silbert to Be United States Attorney: Hearings. 93rd Cong., 2nd sess. Washington, D.C.: U.S. Government Printing Office, 1974. pp. 5-55. The role of the ACLU in reviewing the initial stages of the

case and its conduct in opposing the work of Earl Silbert, the original Justice Department prosecutor. Silbert's response is found on pp. 56-82.

115. _____. Why President Nixon Should Be Impeached. Washington, D.C.: Public Affairs Press, 1973. 56p. Takes the position that Richard Nixon, in his own statements, admitted the commission of high crimes and misdemeanors by authorizing the wiretaps and plumbers; a low-key polemic which contains a summary of the impeachment procedure and instructions on how citizens could lobby for the president's impeachment.

116. "American Political Institutions After Watergate--A Discussion." Political Science Quarterly, LXXXIX (Winter 1974-1975), 713-749. A review of the strengths and weaknesses of the American system as revealed by the Watergate crisis; takes the position that few were permanently damaged.

117. American University. Department of Communications. "The Press Covers Government: The Nixon Years from 1969 to Watergate." Congressional Record, CXIX (June 13, 1973), S11058-S11071. Taken from the daily issue of the CR, this report was done for the National Press Club with conclusions and recommendations of the Professional Relations Committee of that organization.

118. Americans for Democratic Action. "Watergate Chronology: A Compendium of Scandal and Revelations." Congressional Record, CXX (May 6, 1974), 13307-13310. A review, in chronology form, of the unfolding of various allegations and events during the Watergate crisis after June 1972.

119. Americans for the Presidency. "The Vendetta--Two Wasted Years." Congressional Record, CXX (July 30, 1974), 25683-25684. An examination of the manner in which the "Nixon haters" attempted to hound the president out of office.

120. "Anatomy of a Committee--Impeachment Inquiry Begins: Profiles of the 37 Judiciary Committee Members." CQ Weekly Reports, XXXII (January 26, 1974), 127-130, 157-161. Brief biographies of those members of Congress who would come to decide if articles of impeachment were warranted.

121. "And Much More Yet to Come: The Up-coming Testimony of Nixon Staffers." Time, CII (July 23, 1973), 23-24+. Reviews expected testimony to Ervin Committee of Herbert Kalmbach, John Ehrlichman, H. R. Haldeman, and Gordon Strachan.

122. "And Now, a Right to Burgle?" Time, CII (August 6, 1973), 12-13. Ehrlichman's view on why the Ellsberg burglary was necessary.

123. "And the Mess Goes On." Newsweek, LXXXI (May 21, 1973), 16-21. Revelations concerning Mitchell and Stans in the Vesco case, the mistrial of the Ellsberg case, and continuing statements by Dean and Gray are seen to be undermining Nixon's latest attempt to bolster his administration by speech and staff changes.

124. "And Watergate Simmers On." Newsweek, LXXXII (October 1, 1973), 31-32. Previews Hunt's Ervin Committee testimony and goes over Cox-White House proposals for tape access.

125. "And Where Is the Palace Guard?" Time, CVI (August 11, 1975), 16-17. Reviews the post-Watergate fate of certain Nixon aides.

126. Anderson, Jack. "Contradictions Cited in ITT Case: Reprinted from the Washington Post, March 3, 1972." In: Book V, Part II of U.S. Congress, House, Committee on the Judiciary. Statement of Information: Hearings. 93rd Cong., 2nd sess. Washington, D.C.: U.S. Government Printing Office, 1974. p. 636. The noted columnist released to the public the Dita Beard memo which implicated Mitchell, Kleindienst and others in a plot to settle an antitrust suit against the International Telephone and Telegraph Corp. favorably in exchange for a company pledge to underwrite funding to hold the 1972 Republican National Convention in San Diego.

127. _____. "How 'Gemstone' Broke Magruder: Reprinted from the Washington Post, April 23, 1973." In: U.S. Congress, Senate, Committee on the Judiciary. Nomination of Earl J. Silbert to Be United States Attorney: Hearings. 93rd Cong., 2nd sess. Washington, D.C.: U.S. Government Printing Office, 1974. pp. 161-162. Anderson tells how Liddy's secretary, Sally Harmony, typed a secret memo, codenamed "Gemstone," which when revealed before the Watergate grand jury forced Magruder to begin talking.

128. _____. "Jaworski Wanted to Indict Nixon: Reprinted from the Washington Post, September 12, 1974." Congressional Record, CXX (September 12, 1974), 30964-30965. Suggests the Special Prosecutor believed Nixon was so guilty that he should be made to appear so in the eyes of the law.

129. _____. "Kleindienst Accused in ITT Case: Reprinted from the Washington Post, March 1, 1972." In: Book V, Part II of U.S. Congress, House, Committee on the Judiciary. Statement of Information: Hearings. 93rd Cong., 2nd sess. Washington, D.C.: U.S. Government Printing Office, 1974. p. 635. The Beard memo embroiled the Attorney General, suggesting he had lied about not being involved in the ITT case negotiations.

Watergate   54

130. _____. "Memo Shows Mitchell 'Fix' in ITT Case; ITT, in Return, Pledged $400,000 to GOP; ITT Puts Supporting Evidence in Shredder: Reprinted from the Washington Post, February 29, 1972." In: U.S. Congress, Senate, Committee on the Judiciary. Richard G. Kleindienst--Resumed: Hearings. 92nd Cong., 2nd sess. Washington, D.C.: U.S. Government Printing Office, 1972. pp. 461-462. The memo referred to was that of Dita Beard.

131. _____. "Mitchell, ITT Try to Lie Way Out of Scandal; California Colleagues Say Mitchell Knew All; ITT's Statement Contradicts Evidence on Hand: Reprinted from the Washington Post, March 3, 1972." In: U.S. Congress, Senate, Committee on the Judiciary. Richard G. Kleindienst--Resumed: Hearings. 92nd Cong., 2nd sess. Washington, D.C.: U.S. Government Printing Office, 1972. pp. 464-465.

132. _____. "Secret [Beard] Memo Bares Mitchell-ITT Move: Reprinted from the Washington Post, February 29, 1972." In: Book V, Part II of U.S. Congress, House, Committee on the Judiciary. Statement of Information: Hearings. 93rd Cong., 2nd sess. Washington, D.C.: U.S. Government Printing Office, 1974. p. 634. Claims Mitchell as Attorney General negotiated with Beard on the GPO convention site and the ITT case settlement.

133. _____. "The Watergate Cast: Rebuilding Lives in the Wake of a Fallen Presidency." Parade Magazine (January 7, 1979), 8-10. A review of the 1979 locations and status of those, from Nixon downward, involved in the scandal.

134. _____. "Watergate Jury Called 'Exceptional': Reprinted from the Washington Post, June 13, 1974." Congressional Record, CXX (June 13, 1974), 19255-19256. On the behavior of the jury in the Fielding break-in trial.

135. _____ and George Clifford. The Anderson Papers. New York: Random House, 1973. 275p. An expansion on how Anderson obtained evidence and investigated four of his most successful exposés, including the Dita Beard-ITT case.

136. Anderson, Patrick. "Rushing Toward a Footnote in History." New York Times Magazine (July 8, 1973), 8-9+. A profile of former White House counsel John Dean.

137. Andrews, John K., Jr. "Ex-Nixon Aide--'On Joining the Rebellion': Reprinted from the New York Times, February 2, 1974." Congressional Record, CXX (February 4, 1974), 2040-2041. 1972 campaign-Watergate recollections of a Nixon speechwriter.

138. "Angry Judges." Nation, CCXVI (February 12, 1973), 196-197. Judge Sirica and Judge Byrne.

139. "Animals in the Forest: CIA Tapes." Time, CIII (February 11, 1974), 26. CIA tapes of conversations with the White House "plumbers."

140. "Another Week of Strain." Time, CII (December 17, 1973), 17-18. Reports tape erasure testimony of Haig, Rose Mary Woods, and Lawrence Higby and new developments in the Howard Hughes contribution controversy.

141. Apple, Raymond W., Jr. "Dean is Debunked--Ziegler Disputes His Testimony on Trying to Find Scapegoat: Reprinted from the New York Times, April 20, 1973." In: Book IV, Part III of U.S. Congress, House, Committee on the Judiciary. Statement of Information: Hearings. 93rd Cong., 2nd sess. Washington, D.C.: U.S. Government Printing Office, 1974. p. 1495. The controversy over whether or not top White House aides were maneuvering Dean "to take the fall" over the Watergate cover-up.

142. _____. "Haldeman the Fierce, Haldeman the Faithful, Haldeman the Fallen." New York Times Magazine (May 6, 1973), 38-39+. A look at the rise and fall of the chief of staff of the Nixon White House.

143. _____. "A Subpoena Seeks More Nixon Files: Reprinted from the New York Times, March 22, 1974." In: Book IX, Part II of U.S. Congress, House, Committee on the Judiciary. Statement of Information: Hearings. 93rd Cong., 2nd sess. Washington, D.C.: U.S. Government Printing Office, 1974. p. 970. On Jaworski's March 15 subpoena of specified documents for use by the Watergate grand jury.

144. _____. "Ziegler Assails Jaworski Staff: Reprinted from the New York Times, November 30, 1973." Congressional Record, CXIX (November 30, 1973), 38995-38996. The problems of leaks and procedures by the staff members of the Watergate Special Prosecution Force (WSPF).

145. Archer, Jules. Superspys: The Secret Side of Government. New York: Delacorte Press, 1977. 252p. A flood of "exposés," some more accurate than others, appeared during the post-Watergate mania over the role of intelligence agencies in the American democracy; Archer's work, like many of these, provides some commentary on the wrongdoings of the CIA, FBI, and the White House "plumbers" during the Watergate era.

146. _____. Watergate: America in Crisis. New York: T.Y. Crowell, 1975. 306p. The first major attempt at a com-

prehensive account, this is a straightforward, first person, chronological recapitulation from the break-in to Nixon's pardon. The final chapter concludes that Nixon's insatiable power drive and sense of opportunism foreshadowed Watergate events and that the unfolding of the affair demonstrated how successful he had become in subverting the system of checks and balances.

147. "Archibald Cox." In: Eleanora W. Schoenebaum, ed. Political Profiles: The Nixon/Ford Years. New York: Facts on File, Inc., 1979. pp. 151-153. A capsule biography and role analysis of the first Watergate Special Prosecutor.

148. "Are the Articles [of Impeachment] Sound?" Newsweek, LXXXIV (August 12, 1974), 28-29. A brief examination of the articles in light of the law and history of the impeachment process.

149. Arendt, Hannah. "Home to Roost." In: Sam B. Warner, ed. The American Experience: Perspectives on 200 Years. Boston: Houghton Mifflin, 1976. pp. 61-79. A review of the history of dirty tricks and political espionage in the American system and how they culminated in Watergate.

150. "Arguments on the Eve of a Verdict." Time, CIV (December 30, 1974), 11-13. A look at the closing briefs in the Watergate cover-up trial.

151. Arlen, Michael J. "Prosecutor." New Yorker, LIII (November 28, 1977), 166-173. CBS reporter Dan Rather.

152. _____. "Time, Memory, and News: Televising and Analyzing President Ford's Pardon of Richard Nixon." New Yorker, L (September 30, 1974), 115-118. A review of the sentiments expressed by various network commentators concerning the pardon.

153. "The Arnholt Smith Affair." Newsweek, LXXXII (August 20, 1973), 57. Concerns an illegal $200,000 campaign contribution by a Nixon friend, a California industrialist.

154. "An Arrogant Act of Men Above the Law: The Conspiracy Trial of John Ehrlichman." Time, CIV (July 8, 1974), 16-17. A review of Ehrlichman's role in the Watergate affair, especially the cover-up.

155. Arterton, F. Christopher. "The Impact of Watergate on Children's Attitudes Toward Political Authority." Political Science Quarterly, LXXXIX (June 1974), 269-288. Reprinted in Political Science Quarterly, editors of American Political Institutions in the 1970's: A Political Science Quarterly Reader (New York: Columbia University Press, 1976), pp. 29-48. An examination of children's political attitudes in

December 1973 which showed that that age group expressed "wholly negative" attitudes and "have come to view the President as a figure to be strenuously rejected."

156. _____. "Watergate and Children's Attitudes Toward Political Authority Revisited." Political Science Quarterly, XC (Fall 1975), 477-496. Children's views of the President became much more favorable once Ford became chief executive.

157. "As If We've Turned Some Kind of Corner." Newsweek, LXXXII (December 17, 1973), 24-28. Even with Ford coming in as Veep, Nixon's power continues to erode; more holes appear in the gap story of Rose Mary Woods.

158. "As the Drama--And Agony--Unfolded." Newsweek, LXXXIV (August 5, 1974), 27-28+. What would happen with regards to the tape case United States v. Richard M. Nixon, President heard before the Supreme Court.

159. "As Time Marched On, CBS News Reported the Cadence." Broadcasting, XCIII (September 19, 1977), 110-115. Mentions CBS coverage of Watergate.

160. Ashby, Neal. "A Connecticut Yankee in King Richard's Court: Why Republican Senator Lowell P. Weicker, Jr. Defended the Faith by Defying the King." Lithopinion, IX (Summer 1974), 56-61. An analysis of Weicker's role in the Ervin Committee hearings.

161. Ashman, Charles R. Connally: The Adventures of Big Bad John. New York: William Morrow, 1974. 305p. A review of the Texas politician's career, including his role as Nixon's Treasury Secretary and supposed involvement in the Milk Fund sub-scandal, of which he was later acquitted when brought to trial.

162. Association of the Bar of the City of New York. Committee on Civil Rights. "Executive Privilege: Analysis and Recommendations for Congressional Legislation." Record of the Association of the Bar of the City of New York, XXIX (February 1974), 177-208. A look at the roots of executive privilege, its application by the Nixon administration, including Watergate, and recommendations for reform.

163. _____. "The Law of Impeachment." Record of the Association of the Bar of the City of New York, XXIX (February 1974), 154-176. How the process has grown up in England and America with minor speculation as to how it would fare if employed against President Nixon.

164. Atkins, Ollie. The White House Years: Triumph and Tragedy. Chicago: Playboy Press, 1977. 244p. Atkins was Presi-

dent Nixon's official photographer; his memoirs record the process of White House photography before and during Watergate with some commentary and recollections about guests and staffers, especially Ron Ziegler, with whom he had some difficulties.

165. "Attorney General and White House Staff: Texts of Letters of Resignations from Attorney General Richard Kleindienst and Assistants to the President H. R. Haldeman and John D. Ehrlichman, April 30, 1973." Weekly Compilation of Presidential Documents, IX (May 7, 1973), 431-438. Full texts; no elaboration.

166. "Autumn in the Shade of Watergate." Time, CII (September 24, 1973), 22-23. A review of where the scandal was re: Congressional hearings, White House steadfastness, tapes, etc.

167. "An Awfully Rough Game: Nixon's Displeasure Over Continued Watergate Investigations by the Washington Post." Newsweek, LXXXIII (May 27, 1974), 29. Excerpts from a Nixon tape transcript wherein he threatens to have the FCC block renewal of the newspaper's Florida TV station.

168. "B-B-Bebe and That $200,000." Newsweek, LXXXIV (December 16, 1974), 29+. An examination of an illegal campaign contribution by Nixon's close personal friend, Bebe Rebozo.

169. "Back on the Counterattack." Newsweek, LXXXIII (January 14, 1974), 18-19. A review of these events: James St. Clair in as Nixon's lawyer, the latest on the tape-gap controversy, the release of Bernard Barker and Howard Hunt from jail, and the President's refusal to honor a subpoena for 600 tapes by the Ervin committee.

170. "Bag Job at Dr. Fielding's: Ellsberg Break-in Indictments." Newsweek, LXXXIII (March 18, 1974), 31-39. An in-depth review of events leading to the break-in with emphasis on the activities of the White House "plumbers."

171. Bailey, Thomas A. Presidential Saints and Sinners. New York: Free Press, 1981. 304p. Every president is considered in the light of examples which, the author contends, show his character and ethics; the appraisals are comparative and Nixon is deemed the greatest "sinner."

172. Baker, G. L. "A Man Named [C. Arnholt] Smith and the President." Progressive, XXXVIII (February 1974), 27-30. More on the influence and alleged illegal contributions of Nixon's friend, a California industrialist.

173. Baker, Howard H., Jr. "The Effect of Watergate--'Far More Political Than Legal': An Interview." U.S. News and

World Report, LXXV (August 20, 1973), 50-52. Baker, a Republican member of the Senate Watergate Committee, here presents his views on the aims of the committee, the tapes issue, and lessons emerging both from the hearings and the scandal.

174. _____. "'Some Foolish Mistakes': Howard H. Baker, Jr.'s Report on the Relationship Between the CIA and the Watergate Break-in." Time, CIV (July 15, 1974), 19. Baker reports on the CIA's role, especially its more questionable activities and assistance to the "plumbers."

175. Baker, J. F. "Publisher's Weekly Interviews Dan Rather." Publisher's Weekly, CCXI (May 9, 1977), 8-9. Includes some thoughts on this reporter's Watergate role.

176. Baker, Russell. "Mr. Rodino Goes for a Ride: Reprinted from the New York Times, March 30, 1974." Congressional Record, CXX (July 22, 1974), 24498. A satirical look at the manner by which the House Judiciary Committee chairman, Peter Rodino of New Jersey, supposedly conferred with various factions while running the impeachment inquiry.

177. Bakshian, Aram, Jr. "The Ghosts of Forbidden City." Washingtonian, XII (October 1976), 132-133, 174, 176-179. An update on the fate of the Watergate "cast."

178. Baldwin, Alfred C., 3rd, as told to Jack Nelson. "An Insider's Account of the Watergate Bugging: Reprinted from the Los Angeles Times, October 5, 1972." Congressional Record, CXIX (October 5, 1972), 34032-34035. One of the more important newspaper scoops of the "caper." Baldwin, an ex-FBI agent, sat in for McCord monitoring the wiretaps in the Watergate building and from the Howard Johnson's across the street watched the police pick up his colleagues.

179. Balfour, Nancy. "The U.S. Presidency in Danger." World Today, XXIX (December 1973), 505-513. A British view of the impact of Watergate on the American presidency.

180. Ball, Howard. No Pledge of Privacy: The Watergate Tapes Litigation. Port Washington, N.Y.: Kennikat Press, 1977. 144p. A rather straightforward account from Judge Sirica's initial decision ordering release of the Watergate tapes through the U.S. Supreme Court decision in U.S. vs. Nixon; little attention to analyzing such legal issues as executive privilege.

181. "The Band That Lost the Beat." Time, CV (January 6, 1975), 48-49. A report on the outcome of the Watergate cover-up trial.

182. Bandy, Lee. "State Congressmen Not Ready to Impeach: Reprinted from the Nashville Banner, May 22, 1974." Congressional Record, CXX (May 30, 1974), 17112-17113. A survey of the Tennessee Congressional delegation after publication of the transcripts but before the Supreme Court ruling in U.S. vs. Nixon.

183. No entry.

184. Barber, James D. "The Nixon Brush with Tyranny." Political Science Quarterly, XCII (Winter 1977-1978), 581-605. A review of the administrative operations of the Nixon administration, as well as the illegal manner in which the President attempted to cover up Watergate.

185. _____. "President Nixon and Richard Nixon: A Character Trap." Psychology Today, VIII (October 1974), 113-114+. Barber recapitulates his argument concerning Nixon's outcome (see next entry) and links his thesis to the demise of the Nixon White House; an interesting psychological study designed for the lay reader.

186. _____. Presidential Character: Predicting Performance in the White House. Englewood Cliffs, N.J.: Prentice-Hall, 1972. 479p. One of the most fascinating and controversial books on the American presidency; a second edition was published by the same firm in 1977. Leaders from Taft to Nixon are classified in terms of being active-passive in fulfilling their duties while at the same time channeling positive-negative feelings into politics. Includes a detailed and controversial negative evaluation of Nixon as being an active-negative member of that group (which also included Lyndon B. Johnson) of hard-driving individuals whose frenetic activity seeks to allay underlying insecurities. In this book, written before Nixon's 1972 re-election, it is predicted that after that re-election, the president would suffer a "character-based" tragedy.

187. _____. "Man, Mood, and the Presidency." In: Rex G. Tugwell and Thomas E. Cronin, eds. The Presidency Reappraised. New York: Praeger, 1974. pp. 205-214. On the differences between presidential communications and the public's expectations of leadership from the Oval Office; some comments on the Watergate case.

188. _____. "The Question of Presidential Character." Saturday Review of Literature, LV (September 1972), 62-66. Suggests character of next president the key 1972 campaign issue in an examination of the pasts of Nixon and McGovern for keys to how well each might perform in office.

189. _____. "Strategies for Understanding Politicians." American Journal of Political Science, XVIII (Spring 1974), 443-

467. Provides the fullest methodological exposition of Barber's procedures for classifying presidential character and style.

190. _____. "Tone-Deaf in the Oval Office." Saturday Review World, I (January 12, 1974), 10-14. Examines Nixon's problems in light of his secluded style of operation.

191. Barker, Bernard and Eugenio R. Martinez. "Mission Impossible: The Watergate Burglars--Excerpts from Interviews." Harper's, CCXLIX (October 1974), 50-58. Two of the Watergate "plumbers" recollect their training, mission, and activities until apprehended, as well as their difficulties in obtaining White House support for their trial defense and their time in jail.

191a. Barnes, Dick and H. L. Schwartz, 3rd. "Mexico 'Bugging Money' Rushed from Texas: Reprinted from an Associated Press Dispatch, September 13, 1972." Congressional Record, CXX (August 7, 1974), 27272-27273. A report on how $200,000 in Nixon 1972 campaign contributions was sent down to Mexico and later employed to finance dubious campaign activities, i.e., "dirty tricks."

192. Barone, Michael, Grant Uzifusa, and Douglas Matthews. The Almanac of American Politics: The Senators, the Representatives--Their Records, States, and Districts, 1974. Boston: Gambit, 1974. 1240p. Includes brief data on those involved in the Congressional aspects of Watergate.

193. Barrett, Marvin, ed. AID-Columbia University Survey of Broadcast Journalism: Moments of Truth. New York: T. Y. Crowell, 1975. 274p. Pays special attention to Nixon's relationship with the media during Watergate.

194. Barron, Jerome. "Impeachment on TV--Publicity Would Become All Pervasive: Reprinted from the Washington Post, April 29, 1974." Congressional Record, CXX (May 9, 1974), 13873-13874. Concern that Nixon could not obtain a "fair trial" if the projected Senate proceedings were televised.

195. Bartlett, Charles. "The Ax That Fell on Cox: Reprinted from the Washington Star-News, October 24, 1973." Congressional Record, CXIX (October 24, 1973), 34956-34957. A review of the process whereby Special Prosecutor Archibald Cox was dismissed.

196. Barton, Ansley B. "United States vs. Nixon and the Freedom of Information Act: New Impetus for Agency Disclosure?" Emory Law Journal, XXIV (Spring 1975), 405-424. Assesses the effect of the Supreme Court decision on prospects for obtaining controversial information from various government agencies.

197. Barzman, Sol. "Richard Nixon." In: his Madmen and Geniuses. New York: Follett, 1974. pp. 253-260. A brief review of Nixon's presidency with emphasis on Watergate.

198. Bates, J. Leonard. "Watergate and Teapot Dome." South Atlantic Quarterly, LXXIII (Spring 1974), 145-159. Compares the Nixon crisis with the scandal which rocked the administration of Warren Harding; reprinted in Congressional Record, CXX (June 27, 1974), 21487-21490.

199. Bates, William. "Vagueness in the Constitution: The Impeachment Power." Stanford Law Journal, XXV (June 1973), 908-926. Suggests that the power of the Congress to impeach and try a modern sitting president is not overly specific.

200. "The Battle for Nixon's Tapes." Time, CII (July 30, 1973), 7-15. Recaps the President's reasons for refusing to surrender.

201. "The Battle for Those Tapes Begins." Time, CII (August 13, 1973), 8-9. A review of the White House brief on why the tapes should not be turned over, an examination of pro and con ideas on the subject as well as public opinion on the topic.

202. "The Battle Over Presidential Power." Time, CII (August 6, 1973), 8-21. Nixon's refusal to honor subpoenas is creating a Constitutional crisis.

203. Bayh, Birch. "The Prosecutor: Reprinted from the New York Times, November 14, 1973." Congressional Record, CXIX (November 15, 1973), 37414. The Indiana Democratic Senator's views on the confirmation of the second Watergate Special Prosecutor, Leon Jaworski.

204. Beard, Dita. "Interview with Mike Wallace: Transcript from '60 Minutes,' April 2, 1972." In: U.S. Congress, Senate, Committee on the Judiciary. Richard G. Kleindienst--Resumed: Hearings. 92nd Cong., 2nd sess. Washington, D.C.: U.S. Government Printing Office, 1972. pp. 1641-1644. Details on her ITT memo.

205. "Bebe on the Spot: Howard Hughes' Secret $100,000 Donation." Newsweek, LXXXIII (April 22, 1974), 28-30+. On the role of Nixon friend Charles G. Rebozo in returning a $100,000 cash political contribution he had received from agents of billionaire recluse Howard R. Hughes.

206. Becker, Lee B. "Two Tests of Media Gratifications: Watergate and the 1974 Election." Journalism Quarterly, LIII (Spring 1976), 28-33, 87. Examines the role of the print

and electronic press in covering both events and the effect of coverage of the former on the outcome of the latter.

207. Becker, Theodore L. "Watergate: On Campaigns and Government Anarchy." Society, X (July 1973), 12-13. A satiric discussion of Nixon campaign tactics and how they had "come home to roost."

208. Becker, Theodore M. and Peter R. Meyers. "Empathy and Bravado: Interviewing Reluctant Bureaucrats." Public Opinion Quarterly, XXXVIII (Winter 1974-1975), 605-613. Not only a "how-to-do" primer, but an assessment of the role of discreet interviewing in ferreting out information; contains a few Watergate examples.

209. Beer, Sam H. "Government and Politics: An Imbalance." Center Magazine, VII (March-April 1974), 10-22. An analysis of how the politics of Watergate interfered with the smooth functioning of the Federal government.

210. "Behind the Eight-Ball: The Watergate Tapes Decision by the Supreme Court." New Republic, CLXXI (August 16, 1974), 8-9. A review of the ramifications on Nixon of the high court's decision forcing him to turn over certain Oval Office tapes.

211. "Behind the Nixon Pardon." Nation, CCXXVIII (April 7, 1979), 353, 363-365. New thoughts on the reasons President Ford elected to spare former president Nixon.

212. Behrens, John C. The Typewriter Guerrillas: Closeups of 20 Investigative Reporters. Chicago: Nelson-Hall, 1977. 254p. Reviews the careers of a number of important figures in the coverage of Watergate; those noted, with pages, include: Carl Bernstein, pp. 25-39; Sy Hersh, pp. 127-136; Clark Mollenhoff, pp. 155-168; Jack Nelson, pp. 169-180; and Jim Polk, pp. 201-208.

213. "Benefactors: The Republican Campaign." Time, C (November 13, 1972), 19-20. A review of the contributions given by big-name "fat cats" to the campaign coffers of the 1972 Republican campaign.

214. Bennetts, L. "Archibald Cox: Symbol of Integrity." Biographical News, I (May 1974), 510-511. A brief biography with emphasis on Cox's service as first Watergate Special Prosecutor.

215. _____. "He'd Rather Get the News." Biographical News, I (April 1974), 449-450. A quick examination of the career of CBS News correspondent Dan Rather.

216. _____. "Jeb Stuart Magruder." Biographical News, II

(July 1975), 823-824. Surveys the career of former Haldeman aide and Deputy White House Communications Director who became Deputy Campaign Director of CREEP.

217. Benoit, W. L. "Richard M. Nixon's Rhetorical Strategies in His Public Statements on Watergate." Southern Speech Communications Journal, XLVII (Winter 1982), 192-211. A study of how the former president sought to maximize sympathy and good public opinion while minimizing adverse political fallout regarding his Watergate actions.

218. Ben-Veniste, Richard and George Frampton, Jr. Stonewall: The Real Story of the Watergate Prosecution. New York: Simon and Schuster, 1977. 410p. A self-congratulatory account by two WSPF assistants of efforts to gain data for use in the trial of Nixon's assistants and campaign officials with emphasis on United States vs. Mitchell, et al. One of the first accounts to provide insights into the approaches and styles of Cox and Jaworski, especially the sharp conflicts between the latter and members of the WSPF staff.

219. Berger, Margaret A. "How the Privilege for Governmental Information Met Its Watergate." Case Western Reserve Law Review, XXV (Summer 1975), 747-795. A review of the concept of executive privilege, its practice during the Nixon administration, and its semi-demise with the outcome of United States vs. Nixon.

220. Berger, Raoul. "Congressional Subpoenas to Executive Officials." Columbia Law Review, XXV (June 1975), 865-896. Examines the withholding of information by the President and agencies of the executive and the impact of subpoenas on the delivery of that information before Watergate and after.

221. _____. Executive Privilege: A Constitutional Myth. Cambridge, Mass.: Harvard University Press, 1974. 430p. After examining British and American legal precedents, the author argues that there is no basis for a presidential claim to withhold information from Congress.

222. _____. "The Grand Inquest of the Nation." Harper's, CCXLVII (October 1973), 12-13, 18, 20-23. Suggests that Nixon's claim to precedent for executive privilege is without foundation and that his withholding of information from Congress is a perversion of the doctrine of separation of powers; reprinted in Congressional Record, CXIX (October 2, 1973), 32624-32627.

223. _____. "Impeachment: An Instrument of Regeneration--How It Works and Why It Must Be Used Now." Harper's, CCXLVIII (January 1974), 14, 16, 18-19, 22. Explains how the process works to renew political life and why its

use would resolve the question of whether Nixon were fit to remain as chief executive; reprinted in Congressional Record, CXIX (December 12, 1973), 41227-41229.

224. _____. Impeachment: The Constitutional Problems. Cambridge, Mass.: Harvard, 1973. 345p. Written before Watergate and with no references later than 1971, this work, which considers English and early American history, concludes that impeachment is a remedy of last resort. A second paperback edition with a few Watergate comments was published by the New York firm of Bantam Books in a 400-page 1974 edition. Berger's book became something of a Watergate impeachment crisis bible and was widely quoted by those interested in the process with regards to its possible use on Richard Nixon.

225. _____. "The Incarnation of Executive Privilege." UCLA Law Review, XXII (October 1974), 4-29. Examines the roots of the concept and its use--and misuse--during the Watergate era.

226. _____. "Mr. Nixon's Refusal of Subpoenas--'A Confrontation with the Nation': Reprinted from the New York Times, July 8, 1974." Congressional Record, CXX (July 11, 1974), 23061-23062. Concerns the constitutional crisis created by the President's refusal to honor the tape subpoenas and possible outcomes should he continue to elect to defy them.

227. _____. "President, Congress, and the Courts." Yale Law Journal, LXXXIII (May 1974), 1111-1155. An historical-legal case which discusses the Jefferson/Marshall argument regarding subpoenaing the President, questioning whether a president can be indicted without impeachment or whether impeachment can occur only on indictable grounds, and presents the anti-impeachment arguments of presidential lawyer St. Clair. Reprinted in Congressional Record, CXX (May 8, 1974), 13806-13817.

228. _____. "The Prosecutor: Reprinted from the New York Times, November 7, 1973." Congressional Record, CXIX (November 7, 1973), 36301-36302. Examines the legal ramifications of the Cox firing and suggests the further need for a Special Prosecutor on the Watergate case.

229. Bergman, Larry and M. Roback. "Nixon's Lucky City: C. Arnholt Smith and the San Diego Connection." Ramparts, XII (October 1973), 32-35+. Reviews the charges of impropriety regarding the California industrialist and the plan to settle the ITT case in exchange for money to fund holding the 1972 Republican convention in San Diego.

230. Berkeley, E. C. "Bernard L. Barker: Portrait of a Watergate Burglar." Computers and Automation, XXI (Novem-

ber 1972), 26-28. Looks at the background and motives of one of the men caught in Democratic headquarters in the Watergate complex.

231. Berman, Daniel I. "Impeachment--Did Nixon Do His Duty?: Reprinted from the Salt Lake Tribune, May 31, 1974." Congressional Record, CXX (June 25, 1974), 20928-20929. Suggests that if the President were performing his office satisfactorily he had nothing to fear from the impeachment process.

232. "Bernard L. Barker." In: Eleanora W. Schoenebaum, ed. Political Profiles: The Nixon/Ford Years. New York: Facts on File, Inc., 1979. pp. 34-35. Another profile of one of the Watergate burglars.

233. Bernstein, Barton J. "The Road to Watergate and Beyond: The Growth and Abuse of Executive Authority Since 1940." Law and Contemporary Problems, XL (Spring 1976), 58-86. A lengthy exposé of pre-Watergate presidential power abuses such as bugging, dirty tricks, etc., with some comments on how they reached their zenith under Nixon.

234. Bernstein, Carl. "Watergate: Tracking It Down." Quill, LXI (June 1973), 45-48. A brief review of the investigative techniques employed by the author and Bob Woodward in pursuing the details of the Watergate story.

235. _____ and Bob Woodward. All the President's Men. New York: Simon and Schuster, 1974. 349p. Released in the late spring of 1974 even before Nixon's resignation, this account is by the two Washington Post reporters whose investigative journalism first revealed the Watergate story for more than the simple police-beat burglary. Presented in a choppy, some would say pedestrian writing style, the chronological story of the two youngsters dogged pursuit from first suspicions through "a trail of false leads, lies, secrecy, and high-level pressure" to the final point where the tale's pieces fell together in a Pulitzer-prize winning whole makes this one of the two or three most famous Watergate books. One of the most devastating detective stories of modern American history, which reads like a mystery thriller, Woodward and Bernstein's account of their successes and blunders, their competition, presidential aides, and the inner workings of the newspaper world of the Washington Post stands as an important source of contemporary history, especially for those users of this guide who did not follow the day-to-day newspaper or television accounts of the 1972-1974 period. Many photos. With the exception of John and Mo Dean's books (q.v.), this is the only Watergate account to be made into a motion picture: in 1976, Warner Brothers released a film version of All the President's Men with Robert Redford and Dustin Hoffman portraying the two Post reporters.

236. _____. "FBI Finds Nixon Aides Sabotaged Democrats: Reprinted from the Washington Post, October 10, 1972." In: Book VII, Part IV of U.S. Congress, House, Committee on the Judiciary. Statement of Information: Hearings. 93rd Cong., 2nd sess. Washington, D.C.: U.S. Government Printing Office, 1974. pp. 1658-1659. Part of the long string of Woodward-Bernstein exposés on the Watergate investigation, this one tying White House personnel into the case.

237. _____. "Gray Hearing Calls Nixon Aide: Reprinted from the Washington Post, March 14, 1973." In: Book III, Part II of U.S. Congress, House, Committee on the Judiciary. Statement of Information: Hearings. 93rd Cong., 2nd sess. Washington, D.C.: U.S. Government Printing Office, 1974. pp. 800-801. How L. Patrick Gray, 3rd asked John Dean to appear to answer questions concerning the fate of certain Watergate evidence during the former's Senate confirmation hearings.

238. _____. "Hearing [on Gray] Shunned by Dean--Aide to Nixon Instead Offers Written Reply: Reprinted from the Washington Post, March 15, 1973." In: U.S. Congress, House, Committee on the Judiciary. Statement of Information: Hearings. 93rd Cong., 2nd sess. Washington, D.C.: U.S. Government Printing Office, 1974. pp. 895-896. Follow-up to the previous citation.

239. _____. "Watergate Data Destruction Charged: Reprinted from the Washington Post, September 20, 1972." In: U.S. Congress, Senate, Committee on the Judiciary. Nomination of Earl J. Silbert to Be United States Attorney: Hearings. 93rd Cong., 2nd sess. Washington, D.C.: U.S. Government Printing Office, 1974. pp. 137-139. Woodward and Bernstein tell how Mitchell ordered Mardian and Fred La Rue to destroy certain CREEP financial records.

240. Besen, Stanley M. and Bridger M. Mitchell. Watergate and Television: An Economic Analysis. RAND Report R-1712-MF. Santa Monica, Calif.: RAND Corp., 1975. 40p. A study of viewer behavior in connection with the 1973 Ervin Committee hearings which showed that PBS and cable broadcasting would expand, not diminish, the total viewing audience; reprinted in Communication Research, III (July 1976), 243-260.

241. Bethell, Tom. "The Myth of the Adversary Press." Harper's, CCLIV (January 1977), 33-40. The press does not automatically set out to clash with any president, even Nixon, but when wrongdoing is uncovered, the public has a right to know about it.

242. Bickel, Alexander M. "How Might Mr. Nixon Defend Himself?" New Republic, CLXX (June 1, 1974), 11-13. Sug-

gests the President admit wrongdoing and ask for public forgiveness.

243. _____. "The Tapes, Cox, and Nixon." New Republic, CLXIX (September 29, 1973), 13-14. Contends the tapes case should be dismissed and that, since Cox was a direct subordinate of the Justice Department, Nixon himself could fire the Special Prosecutor at any time.

244. _____. "Watergate and the Legal Order: Civil Disobedience and the Attack on Morality." Commentary, LVII (January 1974), 19-25. Suggests that the Watergate case was an inevitable follow-up to the legal and social morass growing out of Vietnam.

245. _____, Chairman. Watergate, Politics, and the Legal Process: An AEI Round Table Held on 13 and 14 March 1974 at the AEI, Washington, D. C. Washington, D. C.: American Enterprise Institute for Public Policy Research, 1974. 80p. A discussion among various participants, with special attention to the problems of illegal 1972 campaign contributions to CREEP and the use of some of the cash to pay hush money.

246. Biemiller, Andrew J. "Congress' Time for Decision." American Federationist, LXXXI (February 1974), 10-13. The impeachment inquiry and need for its resolution.

247. "Big John [Connally] Indicted." Time, CIV (August 12, 1972), 21. For his alleged role in the Milk Fund scam.

248. "Big Numbers: The Questionable Political Contributions of Robert L. Vesco." Nation, CCXVI (March 19, 1973), 355. How Maurice Stans took a secret $200,000 cash contribution from a man charged with fraud by the Securities and Exchange Commission (SEC).

249. "Bipartisan End to Patience." Time, CIII (April 22, 1974), 14-16. Republicans join Democrats in calling for Nixon's impeachment.

250. Black, Charles L. Impeachment: A Handbook. New Haven, Conn.: Yale University Press, 1974. 80p. Outlines the Constitutional process leading to a president's removal and discusses issues springing from such an action, relating many to the specifics of the Nixon case, e.g., a definition of "high crimes" and a look at executive privilege.

251. Blackmun, Harry A. "Thoughts on Watergate: Excerpts from a Speech of United States Supreme Court Justice Harry A. Blackmun at the American Bar Association Breakfast, August 5, 1973." In: Buel W. Patch, ed. Historic Documents of 1973. Washington, D. C.: Congressional Quar-

terly, Inc., 1974. pp. 723-728. Deplores the ethics of those government officials whose behavior led to the crisis and suggests the "very glue of our governmental structure seems about to become unstuck."

252. Blackstock, Paul W. "The Intelligence Community Under the Nixon Administration." Armed Forces and Society, I (February 1975), 231-250. Includes reviews of the illegal activities of the IRS, FBI, and CIA before and during the Watergate affair.

253. Blake, H. M. "Beyond the ITT Case." Harper's, CCXLIV (June 1972), 74-78. Suggests a pattern of illegal activities performed by members of the Nixon administration; ironically, the article was published during the same month as the Watergate break-in.

254. Blake, R. A. "The President's Jury of 200 Million." America, CXXX (May 25, 1974), 412-414. An analysis of public opinion on the final stages of the Watergate struggle between Nixon and the Congress.

255. Blanchard, Robert O. Congress and the News Media. New York: Hastings House, 1974. 506p. In Part III, "Conflict and Co-operation," there is a lengthy discussion of the free press vs. fair trial issues surrounding the Watergate hearings (House and Senate) with articles by Jerome Barron, Judge Sirica, Spiro Agnew, and Woodward/Bernstein.

256. Blankenburg, William B. "Nixon vs. the Networks: Madison Ave. and Wall Street." Journal of Broadcasting, XXI (Spring 1977), 163-176. Examines the manner in which the president attempted to control broadcast news via exerting influence on licensing and other economic "soft points" of the media industry.

257. Block, Herbert. Herblock Special Report. New York: W. W. Norton, 1974. 256p. A presentation of 450 of the famed cartoonist's anti-Nixon caricatures.

258. Blumenthal, Fred. "What Happened to the Cop Who Arrested the Watergate Five?: Reprinted from Parade Magazine, June 15, 1974." Congressional Record, CXX (June 18, 1974), 19722-19723. The only biographical piece on Sgt. Paul Leeper of the District of Columbia Police Department.

259. Boeth, Robert and V. E. Smith. "The Helms File." Newsweek, XC (October 10, 1977), 31-32. A review of the CIA career of Helms, with some attention to his role in the Watergate cover-up.

260. Bonafede, Dom. "Administration Tries Public Relations to Reestablish Image and Promote Its Efforts." National Journal, V (June 1973), 908-912. The administration counterattack during the Ervin hearings.

261. _____. "Alexander Butterfield." Washington Magazine, XI (November 1975), 17. Fate of the man who revealed the Oval Office tapes.

262. _____. "Anti-Impeachment Plans Focus on Law, Politics, and Media." National Journal, VI (May 11, 1974), 685-691. St. Clair's plans to exploit all three to the best advantage in an effort to head off impeachment and trial.

263. _____. "CRP Continues Uncertain Existence As It Grapples with Watergate Controversy." National Journal, V (May 26, 1973), 764-765. The post-1972 election campaign fate of the Committee to Reelect the President.

264. _____. "Charles W. Colson, the President's 'Liaison with the Outside World.'" National Journal, II (1973), 1689-1694. Examines the responsibilities and background of the President's Special Counsel in a period before the public discovered his role in Watergate.

265. _____. "A Conversation with Ron Ziegler." Washington Journalism Review, I (April-May 1978), 46-49. Wide-ranging over a variety of subjects, Nixon's former press secretary spends much time analyzing press relations during Watergate.

266. _____. "Dual Capacity [of Press Secretary and Presidential Assistant] Brings Power to Ronald Ziegler." National Journal, VI (1974), 324-327. A profile of this combative aide who had his hands full dealing with the packs of investigative and straight reporters seeking details on Watergate.

267. _____. "Executive Office in Transitional Stage, According to the President's Senior Aides [Alexander Haig and Bryce N. Harlow]." National Journal, V (April 25, 1973), 1239-1244. Includes an outline of White House efforts to restore the prestige and popularity of the Nixon presidency.

268. _____. "Haldeman, Ehrlichman Departures to Bring Major Changes in Administration." National Journal, V (1973), 633-636. Speculations on the changes noted in the title of the previous citation.

269. _____. "Haldeman's 'Lessons of Watergate.'" National Journal, VIII (1976), 904. Views of Nixon's former chief of staff on the scandal's effects.

270. _____. "Inner Circle Convinced Transcripts Will Benefit

Nixon." National Journal, VI (1974), 754. Suggests that the move will, despite the deletions, show the President's honesty.

271. _____. "Judiciary Impeachment Vote Is Expected." National Journal, VI (1974), 861. Speculation on the action of the House Judiciary Committee.

272. _____. "Nixon and Ford: Study in Contrasts." National Journal, VI (1974), 1210. A comparison of presidential styles.

273. _____. "Nixon Believes [Impeachment Panel] Tactics Are Wrong." National Journal, VI (1974), 978. Concern over procedures and leaks to the press.

274. _____. "Nixon-Ford Breach Becomes More Obvious." National Journal, VI (1974), 829. As Nixon's impeachment probability increases, his VEEP places distance between himself and the fall of the current presidency.

275. _____. "Nixon Legal Defense Increases Office Costs, Staff." National Journal, VI (June 1974), 976-977. The expenses of Watergate as borne by the taxpayers.

276. _____. "Sixty Per Cent of Ford's Top Staff Was Appointed by Nixon." National Journal, VI (1974), 1537-1541. Remarks on the holdovers from the fallen presidency.

277. _____. "Watergate Disrupts Staff: Changes in Personnel Operations Expected." National Journal, V (1973), 620-621. The effects on the White House staff of the removal and resignations of Dean, Ehrlichman, and Haldeman.

278. _____. "White House Fund Raisers Enjoy Edge in GOP Scramble for Campaign Dollars." National Journal, IV (September 30, 1972), 1517-1523. On CREEP's fundraising activities.

279. _____. "Ziegler's Added Responsibility Includes Keeping the Press Informed." National Journal, V (1973), 866-873. On Ron Ziegler's becoming White House Press Secretary.

280. _____ and Andrew J. Glass. "Haig Revamping [White House] Staff, Shifts in Patronage Policy Likely." National Journal, V (April 6, 1974), 495-511. On Alexander Haig's work as White House Chief of Staff.

281. "Bork: A Professor Caught in the Storm." Time, CII (November 5, 1973), 18. A profile of U.S. Solicitor General Robert H. Bork who carried out Cox's firing on October 20, 1973.

282. "The Bottom Line." Nation, CCXVIII (April 6, 1974), 418-419. Impeachment would be the next to last act of Watergate.

283. Boudin, Leonard B. "The Presidential Pardons of James R. Hoffa and Richard M. Nixon: Have the Limitations on the Pardon Power Been Exceeded?" University of Colorado Law Review, XLVIII (Fall 1976), 1-39. Written in the wake of Ford's pardon of Nixon, this article questions the wisdom of the former President's pardon as well as Nixon's pardon of the imprisoned labor leader, who subsequently disappeared.

284. "Boy Scout Without Honor." Time, CIII (June 3, 1974), 14-15. Profiles Jeb Stuart Magruder.

285. Boyan, A. Stephen, Jr., ed. Constitutional Aspects of Watergate: Documents and Materials. Dobbs Ferry, N.Y.: Oceana Press, 1976. A collection of readings from official Watergate documents and other materials on the crisis' various topics, e.g., impeachment, executive privilege, etc.

286. Boyarsky, Bill. "[California Secretary of State Edmund G.] Brown [Jr.] Sues to Force GOP to Return 'Gift'--U.S. Court Suit Contends International Telephone and Telegraph Subsidiary's $100,000 for Convention Violates Law: Reprinted from the Los Angeles Times." Congressional Record, CXVIII (May 11, 1972), 17092-17093. The involvement of the Sheraton Corp. in the scam to fund a 1972 Republican National Convention in San Diego; Boyarsky's series is perhaps the most complete on the convention scandal.

287. _____. "Donors Assured on Tax Deductions--Justice Department Aids GOP Convention Drive: Reprinted from the Los Angeles Times." Congressional Record, CXVIII (May 11, 1972), 17092. Further efforts to get the Republicans to San Diego.

288. _____. "GOP Convention's 'Blank Check' Told--San Diego Underwriting by [Sheraton] Company Could Soar: Reprinted from the Los Angeles Times." Congressional Record, CXVIII (May 11, 1972), 17091. An initial detailed revelation concerning the underhanded attempt to secure the GOP Convention for San Diego.

289. _____. "International Telephone and Telegraph Woes Cost San Diego's Port $450,000 Rent--Firm Won Concessions Due to Cable Plant, Hotel Construction Difficulties: Reprinted from the Los Angeles Times. Congressional Record, CXVIII (May 11, 1972), 17093. Results of the exposure of the Sheraton gambit.

290. _____. "Top San Diego Hotelman Tells of $24,000 Aid: Reprinted from the Los Angeles Times." Congressional Record, CXVIII (May 11, 1972), 17091-17092. Assistance given to help sponsor the GOP convention.

291. Boyd, James. "Following the Rules with Dita and Dick." Washington Monthly, IV (July 1972), 5-16+. Settlement of the ITT case, the role of lobbyist Dita Beard and various Justice Department officials, including Richard Kleindienst.

292. _____. "The Plumbers' Trial: A Case of Surplusages." Harper's, CCXLIX (October 1974), 65-73. On the overlapping of the various Watergate trials.

293. Boyd, Marjorie. "Is the President a Perjurer?" Washington Monthly, VII (October 1975), 33-38. Questions Ford's role as House Minority Leader during the Watergate investigation and his statements concerning the pardon of Richard Nixon.

294. _____. "The Watergate Story: Why Congress Didn't Investigate Until After the Election." Washington Monthly, V (April 1973), 37-45. Suggests that a combination of politics, lack of sufficient evidence, and lethargy slowed the Congress' involvement.

295. Braden, Tom. "An Atmosphere of Dark Suspicions." Congressional Record, CXX (December 10, 1974), 38888. The lingering debate over Ford's pardon of Nixon.

296. Bradford, Hank and Tom Moore. The National Watergate Test. Los Angeles, Calif.: Price/Stern/Sloan Publishers, 1973. 63p. A paperback containing anecdotes and satire; illustrated.

297. Brams, Stephen J. "Game Theory and the White House Tapes Case." Trial, XIII (May 1977), 49-53. The effort to obtain the tapes becomes a subject for a sophisticated training game for young lawyers and students.

298. Branch, Taylor. "Crimes of Weakness." Harper's, CCXLVIII (October 1974), 40-43. Contends that Watergate represented a weakness of character in Nixon and his aides.

299. _____. "Gagging on 'Deep Throat.'" Esquire, LXXXVI (November 1976), 10+. The continuing effort to learn the identity of Woodward and Bernstein's anonymous source.

300. _____. "Why We Will Impeach Him." Harper's, CCXLVIII (May 1974), 23-24+. Because the scandal could not, for the national good, be allowed to continue.

301. _____, et al., eds. "American Character--Trial and Triumph: A Symposium." Harper's, CCXLIX (October 1974), 39-43+. While the Nixon gang's character was weak, that of the American people and system in resolving the struggle within the bounds of the Constitution proved to be extremely strong.

302. Brant, Irving. Impeachment: Trials and Errors. New York: Alfred A. Knopf, 1973. 202p. Presents a non-traditional view by suggesting that, if impeachment in fact amounts to a bill of attainder, the courts have power to act on cases as opposed to legislatures.

303. Breckenridge, Adam C. The Executive Privilege: Presidential Control Over Information. Omaha: University of Nebraska Press, 1974. 188p. Argues there is little evidence that executive privilege can be definitively defined; suggests, however, that a president's being allowed to withhold at least certain categories of national secrets is essential to the constitutional and political independency of the presidency.

304. Breiner, Richard M. "David Brinkley, Harry Reasoner, Eric Sevareid, and Howard K. Smith: An Examination of Apparent Role Fulfillment of TV Network News Commentators During Crisis Periods in 1973-1975." Unpublished PhD Dissertation, Kent State University, 1980. Has much to say about the role of those men in helping to mold public opinion during the Watergate crisis.

305. Breslin, Jimmy. How the Good Guys Finally Won: Notes from an Impeachment Summer. New York: Viking Press, 1975. One of the more entertaining and unusual Watergate books, with the "good guys" identified as Tip O'Neill, Peter Rodino, and John Doar. Noted police writer Breslin suggests that politics served America during the summer of 1973 as O'Neill, behind the scenes, set the Congressional impeachment bureaucracy into uncheckable motion. Excerpted in Book Digest, II (October 1975), 68-92.

306. Brill, Steven. "The Mean Country." American Lawyer, III (July 1981), 5+. A profile of G. Gordon Liddy.

307. "Broadcasting the Impeachment Debates: Reprinted from the Washington Post, July 19, 1974." Congressional Record, CXX (July 24, 1977), 25053. A report on the effects of the televised hearings.

308. Broder, David S. "The 'Nixon People': Reprinted from the Washington Post, August 14, 1974." Congressional Record, CXX (August 15, 1974), 28524. Makes an important point: not all of Nixon's aides were either bad or involved in Watergate.

309. _____ and Spencer Rich. "Impact [of Watergate]--GOP Lawmakers, Party Chiefs Join Demands for Prompt Cleanup: Reprinted from the Washington Post, April 28, 1973." In: Book IX, Part I of U.S. Congress, House, Committee on the Judiciary. Statement of Information: Hearings. 93rd Cong., 2nd sess. Washington, D.C.: U.S. Government Printing Office, 1974. p. 136. The impact of the scandal had early reached a point where Republican politicos demanded the effects be "contained" as soon as possible.

310. Broderick, Albert. "Citizen's Guide to the Impeachment of the President: Problem Areas." Catholic University Law Review, XXIII (Winter 1973), 205-254. Looks at the question of process and procedures and finds precedent may not always apply in the Nixon case; nevertheless, as impeachment was a political process, citizen input is vital.

311. _____. "The Politics of Impeachment." American Bar Association Journal, LX (May 1974), 554-556+. As the Constitution makes impeachment a political rather than a judicial concern, citizen input to the Congress during and before the process is crucial; reprinted in Congressional Record, CXX (May 15, 1974), 14958-14960.

312. _____. "What Are Impeachable Offenses?" American Bar Association Journal, LX (April 1974), 415-419. An analysis of "high crimes and misdemeanors" which suggests that the offenses are what the impeachment panel say they are.

313. Brower, B. "The Conscience of Leon Jaworski." Esquire, LXXXIII (February 1975), 89-97+. Examines the second Special Prosecutor's beliefs concerning Nixon's guilt in the Watergate cover-up.

314. Brown, Clifford W., Jr. "Ripon Political Analysis: Watergate." Ripon Quarterly, I (Summer 1974), 3-18. This Republican group concludes that Watergate is disastrous for the GOP.

315. Brown, Janellen H. "An Investigation of the Effects of News and Public Affairs Media Consumption on Individuals' Issue Accuracy and Political Discussion." Unpublished PhD Dissertation, University of Oregon, 1978. Contains some mention of the opinions held by persons who followed the Watergate moves and countermoves and those who did not.

316. Brown, Lee. Reluctant Revolution: On Criticizing the Press in America. New York: David McKay, 1974. 242p. Includes a discussion of the press's role in Watergate.

317. Brownfield, Allan C. "Richard Whalen Dissects the Political

Landscape: Reprinted from the Anaheim [California] Bulletin, November 18, 1974." Congressional Record, CXX (November 20, 1974), 37663. Includes some comments on the effects of Watergate on the 1974 Congressional elections.

318. Brumfield, Bob. "Who Needs a Special Prosecutor?: Reprinted from the Cincinnati Enquirer, November 6, 1973." Congressional Record, CXIX (November 6, 1973), 36058. Suggests that the country needs a new prosecutor to get to the bottom of the tapes controversy.

319. Bruno, Herbert. "The Nixon Boosters: Where Are They Now?" Newsweek, LXXXIII (May 27, 1974), 63-64. The whereabouts of Nixon's supporters within Congress and without is a mystery because they have all but disappeared.

320. Buchanan, Bruce. The Presidential Experience: What the Office Does to the Man. Englewood Cliffs, N.J.: Prentice-Hall, 1978. 198p. The author analyzes the performances of post-FDR presidents in an effort to reveal how the trappings of presidential "royalism" distorted their ability to perceive reality, why the structure of the office promoted widespread secrecy and deception, and shows how the well-informed American can predict presidential behavior. In his section on Nixon, for example, Buchanan concludes that "no reasonably objective and informed observer could have missed predicting that the firing of Archibald Cox would destroy Nixon's moral-symbolic hold on the people."

321. Buchanan, Patrick J. Conservative Votes, Liberal Victories: Why the Right Has Failed. New York: Quadrangle Books, 1975. 184p. The noted conservative Nixon speechwriter contends that the media, especially CBS News and the Washington Post, represented "the most formidable obstacle in the path of a conservative counterreformation in the United States." Draws on some examples from his White House service.

322. _____. "Mr. Nixon Is Down and Hypocrisy Is King in the National Capital: Reprinted from the New York Times, June 13, 1974." Congressional Record, CXX (June 13, 1974), 19147-19148. One of Nixon's most conservative speech writers observes how the President's opponents "finally won."

323. Buchen, Philip W. "Pardon and Agreement on Presidential Materials." Weekly Compilation of Presidential Documents, X (September 16, 1974), 1108-1118, 1123-1129. Remarks at a news conference by Ford's presidential counsel.

324. Buckley, James L. "Why Richard Nixon Should Resign the Presidency: Statement, March 19, 1974." National Re-

view, XXVI (April 12, 1974), 413-415. The conservative Senator from New York and brother of National Review chief William F. Buckley, Jr., called for Nixon's quitting in order to avoid a messy impeachment and trial and for the good of the nation.

325. Buckley, William F., Jr. "As It Might Have Gone." National Review, XXV (June 8, 1973), 650. A review of the opening of the Ervin Committee hearings.

326. _____. "Colson, Nixon, and the Courts." National Review, XXVII (April 2, 1974), 884-885. On the beginning of the Fielding break-in trial.

327. _____. "Immunity for Everyone?" National Review, XXV (June 22, 1973), 703. On the practice of granting immunity to witnesses before the Ervin committee.

328. _____. "Impeach the Speech, Not the President." New York Times Magazine (May 20, 1973), 30+. Concerns Nixon's speech announcing the resignation of Haldeman and Ehrlichman and the firing of John Dean.

329. _____. "Is Nixon a Fool?" National Review, XXV (May 25, 1973), 598-599. Comments on his handling of the Watergate affair thus far.

330. _____. "ITT Talk." National Review, XXIV (May 12, 1972), 544-545. A review of the charges and countercharges of Justice Department involvement in an illegal settlement of an ITT antitrust suit.

331. _____. "Nixon and Goldwater." National Review, XXV (August 31, 1973), 962. The Arizona Republican Senator's support was crucial to the President.

332. _____. "Nixon and Resignation." National Review, XXVI (March 1, 1974), 276. Supports the views of James Buckley, cited above.

333. _____. "Presidential Tapes." National Review, XXV (August 17, 1973), 910-911. On their revelation and value to the Watergate investigation.

334. _____. "Reflections on the Resignation." National Review, XXVI (August 30, 1974), 954. Seen as necessary for the good of public order.

335. _____. "Too Much: The Transcripts." National Review, XXVI (June 7, 1974), 664-665. Revulsion over the contents.

336. _____. "What Happened." National Review, XXVII (May

23, 1975), 576. A brief review of the Watergate crisis and its ending.

337. Buchwald, Art. "I Am Not a Crook!" New York: G. P. Putnam, 1974. 250p. A collection of Buckwald pieces (more than 100) which satirize the events connected with the Watergate affair. One of a series of topical collections the author has published over the years.

338. "Bugging Inside the White House: When It Is Suddenly Discovered That Every Word in the President's Office Is Recorded, the Effects Reach Beyond the Watergate Case Itself." U.S. News and World Report, LXXV (July 30, 1973), 16-19. Examines the implications of the Oval Office bugs, quoting foreign and domestic political leaders on the news.

339. "Bugs at the Watergate: Bugging of Democratic National Committee Offices." Time, C (July 3, 1972), 10-11. A quick description of the burglary and the men involved showing a tentative link to CREEP via McCord and to the White House through Colson and Hunt.

340. Bundy, McGeorge. "Vietnam, Watergate, and Presidential Powers." Foreign Affairs, LVIII (Winter 1979), 397-407. Shows how the deepening domestic crisis cut into the power of the Nixon administration to deal with closing down the Vietnam war and restraining Hanoi after the Paris accords.

341. Burby, John F. "[Charles E.] Wiggins Explains His Complex Role in [the Impeachment] Proceedings." National Journal, VI (August 24, 1974), 1262-1266. The role of the California Republican member of the House Judiciary Committee who attempted to protect the President's interests.

342. _____. "Committee Approaches Halfway Point in Allegation List." National Journal, VI (1974), 902. Examines the work of the House Judiciary Committee.

343. _____. "Conclusions Elusive As Initial Phase of [Impeachment] Inquiry Ends." National Journal, VI (June 8, 1974), 857-860. On the search for "high crimes" with which to form impeachable offenses.

344. _____. "Cover-up Is Focus as [Impeachment] Inquiry Nears Final Stage." National Journal, VI (July 20, 1974), 1065-1973. A review of the House Judiciary Committee's examination of the Watergate cover-up.

345. _____. "Impeachment Committee Ponders 'Question of High Privilege.'" National Journal, VI (May 18, 1974), 723-733. A review of the House Judiciary Committee's problems with executive privilege and the White House's refusal to release the actual tapes.

346. _____. "Inquiry Members Maintain Issue Remains in Doubt." National Journal, VI (1974), 930-931. The problems of the House Judiciary Committee in coming up with conclusive indictments.

347. _____. "Nixon Is Notified Transcripts Fail to Satisfy Subpoena." National Journal, VI (1974), 671-672. On the continuing pursuit of the actual tape recordings, as opposed to the President's presentation of edited transcripts.

348. _____. "Nixon Survival Doubtful as New Watergate Tapes Released." National Journal, VI (1974), 1209. On the release of the famed "smoking gun" tapes which showed the President having a role in the cover-up.

349. _____. "President Forces Test of Executive Privilege Concept." National Journal, VI (May 25, 1974), 783-786. On the Supreme Court case United States vs. Nixon.

350. _____. "Profiles of Members Show How Judiciary [Committee] Divides [on Impeachment]." National Journal, VI (July 6, 1974), 989-1004. Examines the backgrounds and affiliations of members to see who would vote for impeachment.

351. _____ and Richard E. Cohen. "Three Articles Voted by Judiciary Committee." National Journal, VI (August 3, 1974), 1141-1154. Contains the texts of the articles and a record of the roll-call votes; see also U.S. News and World Report, LXXVII (August 12, 1974), 72-73.

352. Burke, Richard. "Dean's Laws." Across the Board, XIV (September 1977), 79-81. How the President's counsel operated in support of the cover-up and then switched sides to testify against Nixon.

353. Burkholder, Donald R. "The Caretakers of the Presidential Image." Presidential Studies Quarterly, IV (Summer-Fall 1974), 35-43. A review of President Nixon's media and public opinion specialists; originally published in Michigan Academician, VI (Spring 1974), 445-457.

354. Burlingham, Bo. "Paranoia in Power: [Tom C.] Huston's Domestic Spy Plan." Harper's, CCXLIX (October 1974), 26-37. A review of the short-lived domestic intelligence operation which haunted the Nixon administration during the Watergate hearings.

355. Burnham, David. "Inquiry to Focus on IRS Policies--Independent Federal Agency Plans Review to Pinpoint Service Shortcomings: Reprinted from the New York Times, March 14, 1974." Congressional Record, CXX (July 23, 1974), 24778. Provides information on the Nixon plan to use the IRS against the "White House enemies."

356. Burns, Thomas S. Tales of ITT: An Outsider's Report. Boston: Houghton, Mifflin, 1974. 246p. A former ITT vice-president's wry account is underlaid with a devastating seriousness concerning his ex-employer.

357. Buschel, Bruce, Albert Robbins, and William Vitka. The Watergate File. New York: Flash Books; dist. by Quick Fox, Inc., 1973. 158p. A paperback review of events in the crisis from the break-in through the Ervin Committee hearings; emphasizes the criminal aspects of the case.

358. "But Will the Talk About the Watergate Never End?" Life, LXXII (September 15, 1972), 32-33. Includes the resignations or firings of CREEP employees Mitchell, McCord, Liddy, and Sloan.

359. Cadden, Victoria. "Unmaking of a President: Comments by House Judiciary Committee Wives." McCall's, CII (October 1974), 76+. Recollections of the impeachment inquiry and hearings by spouses of those House members involved; much on the tension felt and the momentousness of the occasion.

360. Califano, Joseph A., Jr. "Richard Nixon--The Resignation Option: An Address to the National Capitol Chapter, American Society for Public Administration, May 17, 1973." Congressional Record, CXIX (May 21, 1973), 16353-16355. An early assessment of the reasons why it would be well if the President considered resignation over the sticky impeachment process.

361. _____. "On the Impeachable Offenses of Richard Nixon: An Address to the District of Columbia Chapter, Federal Bar Association, November 27, 1973." Congressional Record, CXIX (December 5, 1973), 39610-39614. Suggests that Nixon's people had caused enough crimes to be committed that he, as the responsible official, could be made to bear responsibility during an impeachment.

362. _____. A Presidential Nation. New York: W. W. Norton, 1975. 338p. LBJ's chief domestic policy aide and Carter's HEW Secretary herein suggests the need for an active presidency, but one which is kept in check by such strong countervailing institutions as the Congress. Includes examples from the author's past as well as some Watergate observations.

363. "California Poll: Views on Press Coverage of the Watergate Case." Time, CIII (June 17, 1974), 42. Public opinion mostly supported press exposure of the affair.

364. "Campaign Gifts and Political Fortunes: The Milk Co-operatives." Business Week (July 21, 1973), 60-61. Concerns the

breaking of the Milk Fund affair, one of the sub-scandals of Watergate.

365. Campbell, Bruce A. "Racial Differences in the Reaction to Watergate: Some Implications for Political Support." Youth and Society, VII (June 1976), 439-460. Contends that Blacks and other minorities were not unhappy with the outcome of the Watergate case, although many expected Nixon to survive the crisis.

366. Camper, David. "Mr. Law-and-What?" Newsweek, LXXXIII (May 27, 1974), 74-75. On the Watergate trial of former Attorney General and CREEP boss John Mitchell.

367. "Can Mr. Nixon Stay Afloat?" Newsweek, LXXXI (May 14, 1973), 28-31. Examines Nixon staff changes, paraphrases Nixon speech announcing resignations of Haldeman and Ehrlichman, and reviews John Dean's damaging allegations.

368. "Can Public Confidence Be Restored?" Time, CII (August 20, 1973), 9-10. Public opinion of Nixon's job performance low in the wake of the Ervin Committee hearings.

369. Candee, Daniel. "The Moral Psychology of Watergate." Journal of Social Issues, XXXI (Summer 1975), 183-195. Examines the power corruption of the Nixon staffers involved in Watergate and their various philosophies on why they had the right to act in the manner they chose.

370. Cannon, Lou. "Nixon--A Restless and Sleepless Man in the White House: Reprinted from the Washington Post, January 28, 1974." Congressional Record, CXX (January 30, 1974), 1515-1516. Contends the President is a very private individual who seeks much White House solitude to ponder his moves in the deepening Watergate morass.

371. "Canto 476: Rose Mary Woods." National Review, XXV (December 21, 1973), 1394+. Examines the President's secretary's statement on how she caused the famous 18-minute tape gap.

372. Cantone, Victor. "Fourteen Papers Publish Full Nixon Transcript." Editor and Publisher, CVII (May 11, 1974), 7+. How major and not-so-major newspapers published Nixon's edited transcripts of White House taped conversations in full.

373. "Carl Bernstein." In: Eleanora W. Schoenebaum, ed. Political Profiles: The Nixon/Ford Years. New York: Facts on File, Inc., 1979. pp. 47-48. A brief biography of the Washington Post reporter.

374. Carpenter, Elizabeth. "Good News: The Plusses of Water-

gate." Newsweek, LXXXII (October 8, 1973), 24-25. Examines public opinion and suggests that the scandal is causing more people to become interested and involved in politics.

375. Carter, Bill, et al. "Saturday Night Survivors." Newsweek, LXXXVI (October 20, 1975), 14. The second anniversary of Cox's firing brings an assessment of the event and the course of the nation during Watergate.

376. "The Case Against Private Citizen Nixon: Should He Now Stand Trial?" Senior Scholastic, CV (September 26, 1974), 16-18. Pro and con views on the desirability of having the resigned president answer for his role in Watergate; written and released before Ford's pardon became effective.

377. "A Case of Moral Bankruptcy: Reprinted from the New York Post, December 11, 1973." Congressional Record, CXIX (December 11, 1973), 40921-40922. An editorial reviewing and condemning the White House public relations effort called "Operation Candor."

378. "The Case of the Doctored Transcripts." Time, CIV (July 22, 1974), 18-20. Reveals that Nixon's edited transcripts released to the public contained significant differences from the tapes made available just before the President's resignation.

379. "The Case of the Sealed Envelope: Reprinted from the Chicago Tribune, March 2, 1974." Congressional Record, CXX (March 5, 1974), 5400. On the handing down by the Watergate grand jury of indictments against a number of White House officials involved in the cover-up.

380. "The Case of the Watergate Plumbers." U.S. News and World Report, LXXVII (July 15, 1974), 20. Reviews the court verdict in the Fielding break-in case.

381. "Cash in Politics: The Drive for Cleanup Runs into Snags." U.S. News and World Report, LXXV (August 20, 1973), 26-28. Reports on Congressional hearings and apparent inaction on the matter of illegal contributions and the general handling of donation of cash by and for political candidates.

382. "'Catch-22': Illegal Corporate Campaign Contributions." Newsweek, LXXXIII (April 22, 1974), 88+. Many companies found they were illegal if they gave and would not be permitted government business if they did not.

383. Catledge, Turner. "Historic Confrontation Between the Government and the Press." Loyola Law Review, XX (Janu-

ary 1974), 1-10. Explores the relationship between the President and the press, the anti-Nixon feeling among press people, and the press' investigation of Watergate.

384. Caven, Sherri. 20th Century Gothic: America's Nixon. San Francisco, Calif.: Wigan Pier Press, 1979. 330p. One of the more off-beat Watergate titles which suggests a Watergate pattern known as gothic imagery--a vision of life in which good and evil are locked in mortal winner-take-all combat. The manner by which the President came to hold that vision and the effect it had on his career are examined in confusing detail.

385. CBS, Inc. Face the Nation: The Collected Transcripts from the CBS Radio and Television Broadcasts, 1954-1978. 21 vols. Sanford, N.C.: Microfilming Corp. of America, 1979. Microfilm editions for 1972-1974 are important here as many of the figures interviewed had Watergate comments. The same material was published by Scarecrow in hardback beginning in 1975.

386. Chaffee, S. H., ed. "The Watergate Experience." American Politics Quarterly, III (October 1975), 355-472. A review by various writers of the whole Watergate crisis with comments on the effects of the affair for the future of American government.

387. "Chairman [Peter] Rodino at the Center." Time, CII (November 12, 1973), 38. A look at the chairman of the House Judiciary Committee, that group which would conduct the impeachment inquiry.

388. Chancellor, John. "Did the Press Hatchet the President on Watergate?: Excerpts from an Interview." Senior Scholastic, CIII (November 8, 1973), 12-13. Contends that press coverage was, mostly, fair.

389. "Charges Against the White House." U.S. News and World Report, LXXVI (March 11, 1974), 21-24. Recounts grand jury indictments against seven former White House staff members and lists all previous Watergate indictments and sentences.

390. "Charges: Articles of Impeachment." Time, CIV (July 29, 1974), 12+. Text excerpts from the articles voted by the House Judiciary Committee.

391. "Charles W. Colson." In: Eleanora W. Schoenebaum, ed. Political Profiles: The Nixon/Ford Years. New York: Facts on File, Inc., 1979. pp. 137-139. Recounts the White House career of Nixon's special counsel.

392. Charlton, Linda. "[Patrick] Buchanan Scores the Media Anew--

Nixon Aide Addresses Parley in Capitol--Two Others [Richard Harwood and Richard N. Goodwin] Defend News Coverage: Reprinted from the New York Times, July 18, 1974." Congressional Record, CXX (July 22, 1974), 24496-24497. Buchanan's controversial stand on blaming the press for Nixon's difficulties; see also the Buchanan citations cited above.

393. Chesen, Eli S. President Nixon's Psychiatric Profile: A Psychodynamic-Genetic Interpretation. New York: Wyden, 1973. 245p. After analyzing Watergate television coverage and much of the written material on Nixon's life and philosophy, the author sketches the President's personality traits and psychological tendencies; compares Nixon and his associates to a theoretical model labeled "Steve Cleansman" and pays, like most psychologists, special attention to the man's early life, particularly the role of religion in his character development.

394. _____. "What Makes Nixon Tick?--One Psychiatrist's Analysis: Reprinted from the Washington Star-News, November 25, 1973." Congressional Record, CXIX (November 26, 1973), 37944-37946. Presents more briefly the thoughts given in the author's book (q. v.).

395. Cheslik, Francis E. "Presidential Influence on the Media: A Descriptive Study of the Administrations of Lyndon B. Johnson and Richard M. Nixon." Unpublished PhD Dissertation, Wayne State University, 1977. Examines the manner in which both administrations reacted to press coverage, both in person and through various executive departments and commissions.

396. Chester, Lewis, Cal McCrystal, Stephen Arts, and William Shawcross. Watergate: The Full Inside Story. London: Deutsch, and New York: Ballantine Books, 1973. 280p. After toiling 12-hour days for a dozen weeks, members of the London Sunday Times Insight Team present a paperback review of events through the Ervin Committee hearings which also takes some swipes at U.S. press coverage and reviews defensive Nixon administration attacks on reportage. Written for a British audience.

397. Chomsky, Noam. "Watergate and Other Crimes." Ramparts, XII (June 1974), 31-36. Contends the Nixon administration was crime-ridden from Cambodia through ITT to Watergate.

398. "Chronology of Watergate Events, June 17, 1972-March 23, 1973." In: Buel W. Patch, ed. Historic Documents, 1973. Washington, D.C.: Congressional Quarterly, Inc., 1974. pp. 423-425. A brief recapitulation from the break-in to Nixon's meeting with his aides in which he orders all to "stonewall" it.

399. Church, Frank. "The Watergate Fallout." World Studies, I (Spring 1974), 27-55. The about-to-be chairman of the Senate Intelligence Committee writes that Watergate was caused by an extra-constitutional expansion of the president's war/emergency powers.

400. Cirino, Robert. The Power to Persuade: Mass Media and the News. New York: Bantam Books, 1974. 246p. Contends that the media is often biased in its presentation of the news; presents some examples from the Watergate affair.

401. Clancy, Paul R. Just a Country Lawyer: A Biography of Senator Sam Ervin. Bloomington: Indiana University Press, 1974. 310p. Traces the legal and political career of the Democratic North Carolina Senator who headed the Watergate committee often named for him; compare with Ervin's memoirs cited below.

402. Clarey, Everett B. "Each Branch Shall Be Independent: The Burr-Watergate Syndrome." California Bar Journal, LIX (January-February 1974), 17-18, 20, 22-23, 78-81. Examines the similarities between Watergate and the John Marshall-Thomas Jefferson confrontation in the Aaron Burr case.

403. Clark, E. "The Luckless Watergate Four." Newsweek, LXXXII (November 19, 1973), 45-46. On the conviction of the four Cubans caught in the Democratic headquarters in the Watergate.

404. Cleghorn, Reese. "Watergate: 'Just Politics?'" Christian Century, CXXX (May 30, 1973), 620-621. Hopes the public will not dismiss the case as "just politics."

405. Clem, Alan L., et al. The Making of Congressmen: Seven Campaigns of 1974. North Scituate, Mass.: Duxbury Press, 1976. 275p. A detailed examination of the Congressional races in seven different districts; among other factors, considers the effects of Watergate on the various outcomes.

406. Clemons, Walter. "Humanizing Nixon." Newsweek, LXXXV (March 3, 1975), 71-72. A fresh look at the recently-resigned chief executive.

407. Clifford, George. "The 'Plumbers' Plot to 'Get' Jack Anderson." Argosy, CCLXXXI (January 1975), 14+. Argues that the White House dirty tricks squad wanted to eliminate Anderson due to his consistent muckraking; the story was later confirmed by G. Gordon Liddy in his memoirs (q.v.).

408. Cohen, Richard E. "Court Hears Arguments on Extent of Ex-

ecutive Privilege." National Journal, VI (July 13, 1974), 1056-1058. The Supreme Court case, United States vs. Nixon.

409. _____. "Impeachment Committee Marks Time, Awaits Staff Findings." National Journal, VI (1974), 522-524. Reviews the work of the committee and examines how its staff sought evidence and legal precedents.

410. _____. "Impeachment Studies Agree Offenses Need Not Be Indictable." National Journal, VI (1974), 319-323. A consideration of what "high crimes" were by the staff and members of the House Judiciary Committee.

411. _____. "Richardson Moves to Assert His Control Over Watergate-Shaken Justice Department." National Journal, V (July 14, 1973), 1011-1018. On the confirmation of Richard Kleindienst's successor and his pledge to appoint a special prosecutor.

412. _____. "Watergate May Alter Style, but Not Substance of Power." National Journal, VI (1974), 1340-1349. Examines the impact of the scandal on what is known as "presidential power."

413. _____ and Jules Witcover. A Heartbeat Away: The Investigation and Resignation of Vice President Spiro T. Agnew. New York: Viking Press, 1974. 373p. Although this volume details the circumstances of Agnew's resignation over tax evasion, it also sets the Watergate climate and presents the scandal from the viewpoint of the former Maryland governor.

414. Colby, William. "A Changing Agency--And Watergate." In: his Honorable Men: My Life in the CIA. New York: Simon and Schuster, 1978. pp. 289-328. Gives a CIA Director's eye-view of the spy agency's role in Watergate, especially the attempted use of Langley to block the initial FBI investigation.

415. _____. "Kid Gloves: The Watergate Testimony of William E. Colby." New Republic, CLXIX (July 21, 1973), 9-10. Colby's comments before the Ervin Committee are analyzed.

416. Collier, Barney. Hope and Fear in Washington (the Early Seventies): The Story of the Washington Press Corps. New York: Dial Press, 1975. 254p. The role of the press in covering the Nixon administration is fully explored with appropriate space to the media's exposure and continuing pursuit of the Watergate affair.

417. Collins, Nancy. "Twenty Questions for Dan Rather: An Interview." Playboy, XXVI (May 1979), 183+. A few of the

questions relate to the CBS reporter's controversial role in covering Nixon during Watergate.

418. Collins, Patric. "GOP Contributions--More Money Tied to [Bernard] Barker: Reprinted from the Washington Star-News, August 10, 1972." Congressional Record, CXIX (August 11, 1972), 27889-27890. Barker's role in obtaining "laundered" money from Mexico to CREEP.

419. Colson, Charles W. "Before the Fall." Boston, LXVIII (April 1976), 78-82. The former presidential special counsel remembers the inner workings of the Nixon White House and his own role in the Watergate affair.

420. _____. Born Again. New York: Chosen Books; dist. by Revell, 1976. 351p. While claiming innocence of many of the legal charges laid to his door, this feared Nixon political operator reviews and admits at least moral culpability for the numerous "dirty tricks" he performed on behalf of his once-revered presidential leader; the book tells not only of his rise and fall, but of his religious quest and conversion. Excerpted in Book Digest, III (November 1976), 26+.

421. _____. "Colson's Guilty Plea." In: Robert A. Diamond, ed. Historic Documents, 1974. Washington, D.C.: Congressional Quarterly, Inc., 1975. pp. 443-448. The former special counsel's plea in the Fielding break-in trial.

422. _____. "'I Never Questioned Whether It Was Right': Statement at Sentencing." Newsweek, LXXXIV (July 1, 1974), 16-18. Comments regarding the ethics of his role in the break-ins and their cover-up.

423. _____. "Night Out for the President." New Statesman and Nation, XCI (April 30, 1976), 566-568. The activities of the "plumbers" at the Watergate.

424. _____. "Nixon--Fly Now, Pay Later?: Charles Colson's Manifesto." Newsweek, LXXXIV (July 1, 1974), 16-18. Colson's testimony concerning Nixon's urging him to spread false information about Daniel Ellsberg; analyzes how the former Special Counsel's statements impacted on the impeachment proceedings then under way.

425. _____. "Nixon's Night Out." Harper's, CCLII (March 1976), 31-34. Life in the White House and the Watergate cover-up.

426. _____. "Watergate or Something Like It Was Inevitable: An Interview." Christianity Today, XX (March 12, 1976), 4-7. Considers the illegal operations of the Nixon admin-

istration and the corruption of various people from the President downward brought on by great political power.

427. _____. "Watergate Ten Years After: Tapping It for the Truth." Christianity Today, XXVII (June 18, 1982), 36-38. A review of the events and a philosophical quest for betterment brought on by the crisis.

428. "The Colson Connection." Newsweek, LXXXI (June 25, 1973), 24-25. Biographical information and a look at the vague and as yet unprovable involvement of the special counsel.

429. "The Colson Saga: CIA." National Review, XXVI (July 19, 1974), 794+. Colson's role with the CIA and FBI in the cover-up; holds the former Special Counsel's blaming of the CIA as ludicrous.

430. "Colson's Weird Scenario." Time, CIV (July 8, 1974), 16. His blaming the CIA for the Watergate break-in.

431. Commager, Henry Steele. "America's No. 1 Shortage--Leadership: Reprinted from the Boston Globe, November 11, 1973." Congressional Record, CXIX (November 28, 1973), 30515-30516. The distinguished historian's comments are designed to show that Watergate preoccupation was preventing the President from functioning as a leader.

432. _____. "Five Grounds for Impeaching the President: An Address." Congressional Record, CXX (June 28, 1974), 21767-21768. Using precedent, the historian suggests five ways in which Nixon laid himself open to impeachment and removal from office.

433. _____. "'High Crimes': Reprinted from Newsday, May 12, 1974." Congressional Record, CXX (June 20, 1974), 20175-20176. On the House Judiciary Committee's decision to proceed to articles without having any indictable crimes to point to.

434. _____. "Learning from the Tragedy: A Time Essay." Time, CIV (August 19, 1974), 88. On the values of a strong well-balanced Federal system.

435. _____. "The Presidency After Watergate." New York Review of Books, XX (October 18, 1973), 49-53. Argues that the constitutional powers of the presidency are ill-defined and therefore dangerous.

436. _____. "Watergate and the Schools." Today's Education, LXIII (September 1974), 20-24. The effects of the crisis on the teaching of social studies.

437. "Complaint Filed by the Senate Select Committee on Presiden-

tial Campaign Activities [and] Answer Filed by Attorneys for the President in Response to the Committee's Complaint Regarding Subpoena of Recordings and Documents, August 24, 1973." Weekly Compilation of Presidential Documents, IX (September 3, 1973), 1041-1043. Text of the Senate Committee's suit against the President for his failure to comply with its subpoena and text of the White House response.

438. "Confused Alarms of Struggle: The Watergate Tapes Controversy." Time, CII (September 17, 1973), 22-23. Judge Sirica's order demanding the turn-over of the tapes, the White House appeal, and the efforts of Special Prosecutor Cox and the Ervin Committee to get their hands on them.

439. "Congress and the Subpoena Power: Reprinted from the Wall Street Journal, June 18, 1974." Congressional Record, CXX (June 19, 1974), 19984-19985. A review of the legalities and their application in the Watergate case.

440. "Congress--Black Wednesday: Reactions to the Watergate Tape Transcripts." Time, CIII (May 20, 1974), 24-26+. The comments of various members of Congress to the edited and publicly-released White House tape transcripts.

441. "Congress Facing Test: Reprinted from the San Diego Union, March 19, 1974." Congressional Record, CXX (April 3, 1974), 9695. An editorial on the impeachment inquiry.

442. "Congress Must Insist on Own Prosecutor: Reprinted from the Cleveland Plain-Dealer, October 28, 1973." Congressional Record, CXIX (October 30, 1973), 35505. An editorial demanding Congressional control over a new prosecutor to replace the discharged Archibald Cox.

443. "Congress Questions Nixon's Pardon." C.Q. Weekly Report, XXXII (1974), 2593-2594. The hearings on Ford's action and any possible deal.

444. "Congress vs. White House--Most Crucial Test Yet." U.S. News and World Report, LXXVI (April 22, 1974), 25-26. On the continuing demand by the House Judiciary Committee for the White House tapes and Nixon's refusal to honor subpoenas.

445. Congressional Quarterly. "The Power of Impeachment." In: its Guide to the Congress of the United States. 2nd ed. Washington, D.C., 1976. p. 211. Briefly outlines the power and the process.

446. _____. Presidency, 1974. Washington, D.C., 1975. 268p. Reviews events, messages, news conferences, and major statements of Richard Nixon and Gerald Ford.

447. _____. Watergate: Chronology of a Crisis. Washington, D.C., 1975. 1,039p. A very detailed day-by-day examination of the significant events, personalities, court cases, and Congressional inquiries.

448. "Connally's Milkman." Newsweek, LXXXIII (April 29, 1974), 37. More on John Connally and the Milk Fund case.

449. _____. "Connally's Spilt Milk." Time, CII (April 29, 1974), 23. Virtually the same information as in the previous citation.

450. Conner, Cliff. "The Left and Watergate." International Socialist Review (December 1973), 12-17+. Shows Russian and Chinese reaction to the scandal and explains why U.S. socialists sought the impeachment of the President.

451. "Constitutional Issues Raised by the Watergate Tapes." Congressional Record, CXX (December 9, 1974), 38553-38557. On privacy and the recordings as well as the ownership of presidential papers.

452. Conyers, John, Jr. "Views on Impeachment." Freedomways, XIV (Fall 1974), 303-313. The Michigan Democratic member of the House Judiciary Committee voted for the impeachment articles and here explains why he did so.

453. _____. "Why Nixon Should Have Been Impeached." Black Scholar, VI (October 1974), 2-8. Repeats the views of the previous citation.

454. Cook, Fred J. The Crimes of Watergate. New York: Franklin Watts, 1981. 183p. An excellent title for younger readers; chronicles the Watergate scandal from the 1972 break-in to the 1974 pardon of Richard Nixon.

455. Cook, J. Frank. "Papers of Public Officials: An Analysis of the Archivist's Dilemma." In: U.S. Congress, House, Committee on House Administration, Subcommittee on Printing. The Public Documents Act: Hearings. 93rd Cong., 2nd sess. Washington, D.C.: U.S. Government Printing Office, 1974. pp. 61-72. Explains the difficulties of ownership, care, and access to controversial papers with many references to those of Nixon.

456. _____. "Private Papers of Public Officials." American Archivist, XXXVIII (July 1975), 299-324. Same thrust as the previous citation.

457. Cooper, Arthur. "Up Against a Stone Wall." Penthouse, VIII (November 1976), 53. Concerns the cover-up activities of Ehrlichman and Haldeman.

458. Copeland, Miles. "Unmentionable Uses of the CIA." National Review, XXV (September 14, 1973), 990-997. Domestic secret operations, especially Watergate.

459. Copley, Helen K. "Beyond Sadness Lies the Pride: Reprinted from the Springfield [Illinois] State Journal Register, August 9, 1974." Congressional Record, CXX (August 14, 1974), 28300-28301. On Nixon's resignation.

460. Cornwell, Elmer E., Jr. "The President and the Press: Phases in the Relationship." Annals of the American Academy of Political and Social Science, no. 427 (September 1976), 53-64. Contends there is a pattern common to all presidents; much mention of the irregularities in the press-White House relationship during Nixon's stewardship.

461. "Corruption in the Campaign." New Republic, CLXVII (October 28, 1972), 5-7. Ties the moral corruption of Watergate with other campaign-related sub-scandals such as the ITT case.

462. Costello, Mary. "Presidential Impeachment." Editorial Research Reports, II (1973), 925-946. Reviews what was then known about the process and speculates on how it would be employed if push-came-to-shove re: Nixon.

463. Cottin, Jonathan C. "Republicans Stung by Watergate Scandal: Seek to Separate the Party from the White House." National Journal, V (1973), 757-763. A review of Republican shock over the extent of the scandal as revealed by the Ervin Committee hearings.

464. Coughlin, E. K. "Putting Richard Nixon on the Couch." Chronicle of Higher Education, XVII (February 13, 1979), 3-4. On the prediliction for psychoanalyzing Nixon in an effort to find character-defect causes for Watergate.

465. Coulbourn, Keith. "One Friend of the President: Reprinted from the Atlanta Journal-Constitution, January 28, 1975." Congressional Record, CXXI (January 29, 1975), 1817-1818. Profiles George N. DuMas of Savannah, Georgia, who led a write-in campaign on Nixon's behalf during the final stages of the Watergate crisis.

466. "Could the President's Tapes Be Altered?" Time, CII (November 5, 1973), 17. Notes technical ways in which tapes could be altered and the manner in which such alterations could be detected.

467. "Count on the Tapes: Now About 200, and Still Climbing." U.S. News and World Report, LXXVI (May 27, 1974), 19.

Lists the figures on tapes requested and subpoenaed, those turned over, those transcribed, and those unacknowledged.

468. "Counterattack and Counterpoint: The Testimony of H. R. Haldeman, Richard Helms, and L. Patrick Gray." Time, CII (August 13, 1973), 9-10+. Nixon administration officials testify before the Ervin Committee in an effort to defuse the comments and charges of John Dean.

469. "Counterattack: Nixon's Bold Gamble--President's Aim, to Convince People He Has Nothing to Hide on Watergate [and] Blunt the Impeachment Drive; That's Why He Bared His Intimate Talks with Aides, but the Strategy Carries a Big Risk." U.S. News and World Report, LXXVI (May 13, 1974), 13-15. On the strategy behind release of the White House transcripts.

470. "The Court and the Tapes." Newsweek, LXXXIV (July 15, 1974), 21+. Examines the questions to be answered by the Supreme Court in the case, United States vs. Nixon.

471. "Court Gets a 'C': The Watergate Tapes Decision--Opinions of Constitutional Experts." Time, CIV (November 4, 1974), 96. A belated review of the outcome of United States vs. Nixon.

472. "Court Order Requiring Production of Recordings and Documents--Brief of Petitioners Filed by Attorneys for the President Requesting the U.S. Court of Appeals to Vacate Judge Sirica's Order, September 10, 1973." Weekly Compilation of Presidential Documents, IX (September 17, 1973), 1100-1122. Test of the White House appeal.

473. "Court Order Requiring Production of Recordings and Documents--Petition for Writ of Mandamus Filed by Attorneys for the President Requesting That the Court Order Be Vacated, September 6, 1973." Weekly Compilation of Presidential Documents, IX (September 10, 1973), 1061-1963. Text of the petition.

474. "Court Proceedings: Senate Select Committee on Presidential Campaign Activities, Amended Answer and Response to Plaintiff's Memorandum on Remand Filed by Attorneys for the President, January 17, 1974." Weekly Compilation of Presidential Documents, X (January 21, 1974), 43-61. Text of the amended answer.

475. "Court Proceedings: Senate Select Committee on Presidential Campaign Activities--Brief Filed by Attorneys for the President in Opposition to the Committee's Motion for Summary Judgement, September 24, 1973." Weekly Compilation of Presidential Documents, IX (October 1, 1973), 1174-1196. Full text of the brief.

476. Courtney, Jeremiah. "Electronic Eavesdropping, Wiretapping, and Your Right to Privacy." Federal Communications Bar Journal, XXVI (January 1973), 1-60. The conflict between the first two and the latter has received greater attention, the author claims, due to the Watergate affair.

477. "The Court's Hard Questions." Newsweek, LXXXIV (July 22, 1974), 48B+. Recaps the arguments of Jaworski and St. Clair before the Supreme Court in United States vs. Nixon.

478. "Court's Historic Ruling Narrowing President's Power." U.S. News and World Report, LXXVII (August 5, 1974), 16-17. Argues that more than Watergate is involved; that the decision on the bounds of executive privilege in United States v. Nixon demonstrates that a president cannot put himself above the law or courts.

479. "Courts on White House Tapes, October 12, 1973." In: Buel W. Patch, ed. Historic Documents, 1973. Washington, D.C.: Congressional Quarterly, Inc., 1974. pp. 839-858. U.S. District Court order, decisions of Court of Appeals, and two dissenting opinions.

480. "The Coverage: Calm and Massive." Time, CIV (August 19, 1974), 73-74. Press coverage of Nixon's resignation.

481. "Covering Watergate: Success and Backlash." Time, CIV (July 8, 1974), 68-73. A review of the coverage of the scandal by press and television with comments on the good and bad points of the coverage.

482. No entry.

483. "The Cover-up Comes Apart." Newsweek, LXXXIII (May 13, 1974), 39-40+. Reviews the White House cover-up difficulties from March 21, 1973 until John Dean's Ervin Committee testimony.

484. "The Cover-up of the Cover-up." Nation, CCXVII (July 2, 1973), 2-3. Details the complexities of the cover-up and why it had to fall apart; the main goal was a continued and massive disclaimer by all White House officials from Nixon down.

485. "The Cover-up Prosecutor: James F. Neal." Time, CIV (October 21, 1974), 110-111. A profile of the lawyer who presented the government case in the Watergate cover-up trial, following Jaworski's retirement.

486. Cox, Archibald. "Can the System Work?--Commencement Address, Stanford University, June 16, 1974." Congressional Record, CXX (August 7, 1974), 27316-27318. Remarks by the first Watergate prosecutor on the soundness of the American constitutional system re: Watergate.

487. _____. "Cox at Cambridge: An Interview." New Yorker, L (January 20, 1975), 25-28. Views of the first special prosecutor on the Watergate case given during a visit to one of England's great universities.

488. _____. "Cox, Ready to Shovel Some Snow: An Interview." Time, CII (November 5, 1973), 24. Reflections after his firing by Nixon on the "Saturday Night Massacre."

489. _____. "Ends." New York Times Magazine (May 19, 1974), 27-28+. Looks for the causes behind Watergate and proposes reforms.

490. _____. "Even the President Is Subject to the Rule of Law: Arguments from a Brief." U.S. News and World Report, LXXV (August 27, 1973), 83. Excerpts from the special prosecutor's court brief requesting access to the Watergate tapes.

491. _____. "Executive Privilege." University of Pennsylvania Law Review, CXXII (1974), 1383-1438. A comprehensive post-"Saturday Night Massacre" essay which calls for greater judicial power over presidential claims of privilege.

492. _____. "If We Have the Will: An Address, June 12, 1975." Current, CLXXV (September 1975), 3-11. On the return to a system of checks and balances in the American government.

493. _____. "An Interview." Publisher's Weekly, CCIX (March 1, 1976), 8-9. A review of Cox's role in Watergate with emphasis on pursuit of the presidential tapes.

494. _____. "On Formulating an Approach to Impeachment: Reprinted from the New York Times, January 24, 1974." Congressional Record, CXX (January 30, 1974), 1494. The former prosecutor's views on the process' application in the Watergate affair.

495. _____. "Some Reflections on Possible Abuses of Governmental Power." Record of the Bar of the City of New York, XXVIII (December 1973), 811-827. Discusses his pre-October 1973 investigation, suggests ways in which his effectiveness can be measured, and calls for a governmental return to concepts of right and wrong rather than simple political expediency.

496. _____. "Watergate and the Constitution of the United States." University of Toronto Law Journal, XXVI (Spring 1976), 125-139. Argues that the manner in which the crisis was resolved demonstrates that the American constitutional system works. Reprinted from the British Journal of Law and Society, II (1975), 1+.

497. Cox, Arthur M. The Myths of National Security: The Peril of Secret Government. Boston: Beacon Press, 1975. 231p. Written during the height of the Senate intelligence investigations, this work details the wrongdoing of American intelligence services, with some attention paid to their involvement in the Watergate scandal.

498. Cox, Tricia N. "My Father and Watergate." Ladies Home Journal, XLI (April 1974), 136, 164. Recounts the family support for the first special prosecutor and, as only a daughter could, remembers the pressures on Archibald Cox before and during the tapes crisis that led to his firing.

499. "Cox and His Army." New York Times Magazine (January 13, 1974), 32-34+. Looks at Cox's background and personality and how his actions led to terminal White House irritation.

500. "Cox Invited Firing: Reprinted from the Columbia [South Carolina] Record, October 23, 1973." Congressional Record, CXIX (November 7, 1973), 36136. By his constant pursuit of material which Nixon, his employer, had said was covered by executive privilege.

501. "[Cox] Not Free from Blame: Reprinted from Labor Digest, October 29, 1973." Congressional Record, CXIX (October 31, 1973), 35594. Same thrust as the previous citation.

502. "Cox Objectivity Suspect: Reprinted from the Bismarck [North Dakota] Tribune, October 31, 1973." Congressional Record, CXIX (November 5, 1973), 35912. Finds Cox an eastern establishment liberal who could not give Nixon a fair shake.

503. "Crack in Ehrlichman's Stone Wall." Time, CIV (July 22, 1974), 26-27. The former domestic advisor's testimony during the Watergate coverup trial.

504. Cranston, Alan. "Campaign Funds: How to Cure the Corruption." Nation, CCXVII (September 17, 1973), 242-244. After a brief review of known Watergate-related excesses, suggests limits on the amounts non-candidates can contribute to campaigns; the author is a California Democratic U.S. Senator.

505. "CREEP Marches On." Time, CII (July 30, 1973), 6. On the fate of Nixon's reelection organization in the wake of the Ervin hearings.

506. "Creeping Paralysis: Effect on Government Functions." Time, CI (June 18, 1973), 35. The effects on government activities of the constant barrage of Watergate revelations.

507. "Crime in the Suites." Forbes, CXVI (August 15, 1975), 17-20. A review of the ITT-Sheraton-Justice Department plan to hold the 1972 GOP convention in San Diego.

507a. Crockett, H. Dale. Focus on Watergate: An Examination of the Moral Dilemma of Watergate in the Light of Civil Religion. Macon, Ga.: Mercer University Press, 1982. 120p. A brief review of the ethics and character of those involved in the plot directly and of the ethical climate of the United States during the years before and during the crisis.

508. Cromwell, Gardner. "Constitutional Responsibility of Congress to Pursue Impeachment and Trial Remedies in a Proceeding Once Commenced or After a President Resigns: Memorandum." Congressional Record, CXX (September 17, 1974), 31346-31348. Addresses the question of what, if anything, should be done by the Congress in continuing the Nixon impeachment once the President had stepped down.

509. Cronin, Thomas E. The State of the Presidency. Boston: Little, Brown, 1975. 355p. While debunking many post-Watergate claims for presidential reform, this noted scholar of the presidency, in describing the organizational life of the office, goes to great lengths to detail the work of--and warn against the growth of--the White House staff. Contains a number of views on the effects of Watergate based on the author's previous work and interviews with staffers. A second, 417-page, edition was published by the same firm in 1980, a revision which argues less against the White House staff and more for reason in expectations of the office, while continuing to reject the most outlandish calls for reform. More Ford/Carter anecdotes than in the first edition, which is still recommended for students of Watergate.

510. No entry.

511. "Crossfire Cuts Gray." Time, CI (April 2, 1973), 12-13. Comments on Gray's Watergate involvement; predicts his Senate confirmation as FBI Director will be denied.

512. Crouse, Timothy. The Boys on the Bus: Riding with the Campaign Press Corps. New York: Random House, 1973. 383p. "The" 1972 election history in journalism circles; Crouse explains what it was like for print and broadcast reporters to follow the 1972 candidates, and reports on a number of questionable activities which during the Ervin committee hearings came to be known as "dirty tricks."

513. _____. "Gambits of Desperation: The White House Five Defense Lawyers." Rolling Stone (January 16, 1975), 24-29. Looks at the defense and defense lawyers of the

former White House aides during the Watergate coverup trial.

514. "The Crowded Blotter of Watergate Suspects: A Checklist of the Charges." Time, CI (May 14, 1973), 23. Explores the current occupations of and charges against 17 White House staff members.

515. Crowell, Todd. "San Clemente: Nixon's Beach-Town Beachhead." Coast, XVI (September 1975), 24-27. A look at the beach-front presidential property known during the Nixon administration and Watergate as the "Western White House."

516. Cunliffe, Marcus. American Presidents and the Presidency. 2nd ed., rev. New York: McGraw-Hill, 1976. 446p. A pictorial history which focuses on the men and issues which have influenced America's highest political office with some reflection on the extent of presidential power; Nixon and Watergate included.

517. "Curbs and Loose-Talk: Reprinted from the Washington Star-News, July 2, 1974." Congressional Record, CXX (July 9, 1974), 22483. An editorial on the leaks and attempted containment of same coming out of the House Judiciary Committee impeachment inquiry.

518. Curland, Philip. "Watergate and the Constitution: An Address, University of Chicago Alumni Club, Washington, D.C., May 10, 1974." Congressional Record, CXX (June 6, 1974), 18204-18206. Presents comments on how the constitutional system of the U.S. was working in the Watergate case with regard to the involvement of the Congress and the courts.

519. Dabney, Dick. "Amazing Grace: Looking for the Real Chuck Colson." Washingtonian, XIII (April 1978), 110-115. Reviews the White House career of Colson and his Watergate involvement and wonders over his apparent conversion to fundamentalist religion.

520. _____. Good Man: The Life of Sam J. Ervin. Boston: Houghton Mifflin, 1976. 356p. A biography of the North Carolina Democratic Senator who chaired the Select Committee on Presidential Campaign Activities in 1973-1974.

521. "Damaged Nixon: Reprinted from the Times of London, September 16, 1973." Congressional Record, CXIX (September 19, 1973), 30538. A British view of the effects of the Ervin committee hearings on the President's ability to govern and retain the confidence of the American people.

522. "Damaging Deletions from the Tapes." Time, CIII (June 24, 1974), 31-32. Examines differences between the transcripts released by the White House and those held by the House Judiciary Committee.

523. "Dan Rather." In: Current Biography Yearbook 1975. New York: H. W. Wilson Co., 1976. pp. 337-340. A biography of the man who was CBS News White House correspondent during the Watergate mess.

524. _____. In: Eleanora W. Schoenebaum, ed. Political Profiles: The Nixon/Ford Years. New York: Facts on File, Inc., 1979. pp. 507-508. Contains mention of his controversial reporting during Watergate.

525. "Dan Rather: Lightning Rod in White House Hostility." Broadcasting, LXXXV (December 10, 1973), 67. Points out White House dislike for the CBS newsman.

526. Dancey, C. L. "The Pardon and the TV: Reprinted from the Peoria [Illinois] Star-Journal, September 10, 1974." Congressional Record, CXX (September 18, 1974), 31695-31696. Critical of TV news analysis of President Ford's move.

527. _____. "Watergate Reviewed: Reprinted from the Peoria Star-Journal, June 18, 1974." Congressional Record, CXX (June 19, 1974), 19796. Examines the crisis, the idea of Nixon-haters, and suggests possible outcomes.

528. _____. "Why the Impeachment Fire Burns: Reprinted from the Peoria Star-Journal, January 25, 1974." Congressional Record, CXX (February 6, 1974), 2472. Because the people are fearful no justice will otherwise come out of the Watergate case.

529. "Daniel Schorr." In: Eleanora W. Schoenebaum, ed. Political Profiles: The Nixon/Ford Years. New York: Facts on File, Inc., pp. 576-578. Schorr was every bit as aggressive a CBS reporter on the Watergate case as Dan Rather; he later was dismissed for leaking a special report of a House Intelligence panel.

530. Danielson, George E. "Presidential Immunity from Criminal Prosecution." Georgetown Law Journal, LXIII (May 1975), 1065-1069. Reports on whether or not an incumbent president can be tried for crimes in a regular court, as opposed to an impeachment tribunal.

531. Daniloff, Nicholas. "Falling." Nieman Reports, XXVIII (Autumn 1974), 3-8. An examination of the fall of Nixon's presidency and the role of the press in covering it.

532. Dash, Samuel. Chief Counsel: Inside the Ervin Committee-- The Untold Story of Watergate. New York: Random House, 1976. 275p. An account of the author's role as chief counsel in the inner workings of the Senate Select Committee on Presidential Campaign Activities, 1973-1974, with emphasis on the double-dealing and position-jockeying of

the committee's various lawyers. Several new items appear in the story, including details on how Cox tried to quash the committee's investigation, which he saw as rivalling his own; how Rebozo's lawyers outwitted committee counsel, thus avoiding an important subpoena; the role of television in the hearings; and the pro-White House role of committee member Senator Howard Baker. An interesting Ervin memo (appended) recalls a meeting between the North Carolina Democrat and Baker and President Nixon just before the Cox firing. Other tidbits like this make Dash's book interesting reading.

533. Davenport, J. A. "A Bigger Coverup: Political Contributions by Organized Labor." National Review, XXVI (August 2, 1974), 867-868. Rightly points out that the illegal contributions of labor unions to both the GOP and Democratic 1972 presidential campaigns were not covered with the same fierceness as those of large corporations and wealthy individuals.

534. David, Lester. The Lonely Lady of San Clemente: The Story of Pat Nixon. New York: T. Y. Crowell, 1978. 235p. The only book-length biography of the former first lady; includes much information on the effect of the Watergate crisis on the Nixon family.

535. Davis, I. "John and Maureen Dean." Biographical News, II (July 1975), 735-736. Profiles the former White House counsel and his wife, both of whom published memoirs of their Watergate experiences.

536. Davis, Sally. "Picking up the Pieces with John and Mo Dean." Los Angeles, XX (May 1975), 54+. Similar to but more lively than the previous entry, with emphasis on their post-Watergate lives.

537. Dean, John W., 3rd. Blind Ambition: The White House Years. New York: Simon and Schuster, 1976. 415p. In one of the most important and candid Watergate memoirs, the former Counsel to the President recalls his White House service from his 1970 appointment to 1975, when Judge Sirica reduced his prison sentence to time served. Always noted for his photographic memory, Dean pictures, in lively style, the events, conversations, and locales of his service with special attention, naturally, to Watergate and his role in it. Accepting his lawyer's advice ("Don't waste their time telling them what a nice guy you are"), the author paints a less-than-flattering portrait of himself, conceding that calculating ambition was the sole standard he applied in scrambling for White House power and influence and admitting that fear of losing status pushed him into criminal acts. Only when he decided, earlier than most, that the cover-up would not work and

that he could be blamed for it did the author elect to turn against the President and his former colleagues, among whom John Ehrlichman is pictured as a unique villain. Dean recounts his famous March, 1973 meeting with President Nixon, his testimony before the Ervin Committee, and his trial and jail term, all with intriguing dialogue. Much of Dean's tale was confirmed by the White House tapes, and to a certain extent by other memoirs, especially those of William Safire (q.v.).

538. ———. "Dean's Watergate Testimony, June 25-29, 1973: Excerpts." In: Buel W. Patch, ed. Historic Documents, 1973. Washington, D.C.: Congressional Quarterly, Inc., 1974. pp. 659-682. Highlights his most important statements before the Ervin panel.

539. ———. "Hearts and Flowers from John Dean: An Interview." Time, CII (July 9, 1973), 13. Post-Ervin hearing interview revealing Dean's feelings about his testimony and earlier role in the cover-up.

540. ———. "How to Rehearse for Deception: Excerpts from John Dean's Testimony." Time, CII (July 9, 1973), 39. Dean's recollection of a session with Ziegler on how the latter should handle press questions on "dirty tricks," down to role playing between the two.

541. ———. "Interview." Playboy, XXII (January 1975), 65-80. Contains much of the same information released a few months later in Dean's book, Blind Ambition, cited above.

542. ———. "John Dean Points a Finger." Newsweek, LXXXII (May 14, 1973), 32-37. Dean's story from the point when he first heard about the Watergate break-in through his decision to talk.

543. ———. "John Dean Warns—'A Mile to Go': An Interview." Time, CI (June 4, 1973), 30-31. Dean tells why he is testifying before the Ervin committee and gives his reaction to recent White House Watergate statements.

544. ———. "My Decision to Testify Against Richard Nixon." New York, IX (September 13, 1976), 37-47. To avoid blame for a cover-up he knew would not work.

545. ———. "Nixon's Role in Watergate: The Testimony of John Dean." U.S. News and World Report, LXXV (July 9, 1973), 11-13. Reports the substance of Dean's testimony before the Ervin committee; an inset quotes the president's May 22 denials.

546. ———. "Portrait of a Presidency: John Dean's Testimony." Newsweek, LXXXII (July 9, 1973), 12-16+. A report of

Dean's testimony, which is contrasted with White House denials and reports attempts to discredit the former counsel's statements.

547. _____. "The President Was Well Aware of What Had Been Going On: Testimony on the Cover-up." U.S. News and World Report, LXXV (July 9, 1973), 14-15. Recounts Dean's testimony concerning his meetings with Nixon in which he laid out details of the cover-up for the President.

548. _____. "Rituals of the Herd." Rolling Stone (October 7, 1976), 38-58. Reflections on the Watergate-involved members of the White House staff and on how the cover-up fell apart.

549. _____. "A Talk with John Dean: An Interview." Newsweek, LXXXI (May 21, 1973), 28-31. Reveals that he never gave the President the report the chief executive claimed, and reports attempts to paint Dean as the Watergate scapegoat.

550. _____. "'There Was a Cancer Growing': Summary of John Dean's Opening Statement." Newsweek, LXXXII (July 9, 1973), 17-26. Recounts Dean's opening statement and subsequent testimony and the anti-Dean questions prepared by White House lawyer J. Fred Buzhardt.

551. _____. "Watergate: Most Damaging Charges Yet by Dean." C.Q. Weekly Report, XXXI (June 30, 1973), 1710-1720. Another report on what Dean said to the Ervin panel.

552. Dean, Maureen. "How I Lived Through Watergate: The Secret Diary of John Dean's Wife." Redbook, CXLV (October-November 1975), 55-62, 96-97+. "Mo's" recollections of her marriage to Dean and the union's subsequent problems, not the least of which was the public exposure of her husband for his Watergate role.

553. _____. "Mo": A Woman's View of Watergate. New York: Simon and Schuster, 1975. 286p. Critics had little use for this volume concerning the great issues of Watergate which was considered fairly plastic and lacking in depth; nevertheless, the volume does add something to the scandal's literature in its descriptions of the pressure under which the Deans operated, and the comings-and-goings on Air Force One, at Camp David, and at the White House. TV producers combined the basic parts of this volume with Dean's Blind Ambition to produce the noted 1979 drama starring Martin Sheehan.

554. "Dean: A Vote of Confidence." Newsweek, LXXXIII (February 11, 1974), 36+. Concerns further attempts to dis-

credit Dean through the White House release of some tape transcripts.

555. "Dean's Case Against the President." Time, CII (July 9, 1973), 6-13. Covers Dean's five-day testimony before the Ervin panel and reports on the Nixon strategy of blaming Dean and John Mitchell for the break-in and cover-up.

556. "Dean's First Day." New Yorker, XLIX (July 9, 1973), 22-23. Describes the room where the Ervin Committee met, how the panel members looked, and the way in which Dean delivered his opening statement.

557. "Debut of White House Tapes, July 16, 1973." In: Buel W. Patch, ed. Historic Documents, 1973. Washington, D.C.: Congressional Quarterly, Inc., 1974. pp. 697-701. Excerpts from a transcript of an exchange at the Ervin Committee hearings on July 16, 1973 between Fred D. Thompson and Alexander W. Butterfield.

558. "A Decade Later, Watergate's Veterans Are Winners, Losers--And Everything in Between." People, XVII (June 14, 1982), 100-102+. A report on the status of the main characters in the case.

559. "Decline and Fall." Time, CIV (August 19, 1974), 53-55. A review of the final events of the Watergate affair.

560. "'Deep Throat': Narrowing the Field." Time, CVII (May 3, 1976), 17-18. On the continuing search for the identity of Woodward and Bernstein's anonymous administration source.

561. "Deepening Doubts for Top Cop: Senate Confirmation Hearings for L. Patrick Gray." Time, CI (May 19, 1973), 13-14. The acting FBI chief is scored for his handling of Watergate.

562. "Deeper and Deeper: The Walters Memoranda." National Review, XXV (June 22, 1973), 666. LTG Vernon Walters, Deputy CIA chief, and his June 23, 1972 report on CIA involvement with laundered Mexican money.

563. "Defending Nixon." Time, CI (May 28, 1973), 61. Editorials attacking press coverage of Nixon as unfair.

564. "Deferred Analysis: End of CBS's Instant Analysis After Presidential TV Addresses." Time, CI (June 18, 1973), 72. A network effort to avoid charges of bias.

565. DeFrank, T. "Stonewall Nixon at War." Newsweek, LXXXIII (June 3, 1974), 22-25. Examines Nixon's refusal to answer tape subpoenas.

566. "Defining the Charges: Reprinted from the Wall Street Journal, July 24, 1974." Congressional Record, CXX (July 29, 1974), 25618. Seeks clear language in the impeachment charges.

567. "Delay, Divide, Discredit." Nation, CCXIX (July 6, 1974), 3-4. Nixon's last-ditch strategy to avoid impeachment.

568. "Delayed Reaction: No More Commentaries Immediately After Presidential Speeches." Newsweek, LXXXI (June 18, 1973), 74. The CBS action.

569. Demaris, Ovid. The Director: An Oral Biography of J. Edgar Hoover. New York: Harper & Row, 1975. 405p. Hoover died early on in the Watergate affair, but was contacted by Dean for aid in building the initial cover-up.

570. _____. Dirty Business: The Corporate-Political Money-Power Game. New York: Harper's Magazine Press, 1974. 442p. Presents the thesis that the U.S. government is dedicated simply to the protection of property; institutions and individuals involved in this unusual tale include: President Nixon, Bebe Rebozo, Howard Hughes, John Connally, Robert Vesco, and ITT.

571. "Democracy and Presidential Power: Maintaining the Balance." Presidential Studies Quarterly, XI (Spring 1981), 200-298. A review of various contemporary issues with a strong look backwards at Watergate.

572. DeMott, Benjamin. "Gentlemen of Principle, Priests of Presumption." In: Christopher W. E. Bigsby, ed. Approaches to Popular Culture. Bowling Green, Ohio: Bowling Green State University Press, 1976. pp. 264-274. On the high drama of the Ervin Committee hearings.

573. "Denials and Still More Questions." Time, C (October 30, 1972), 18-19. Reviews White House condemnation of press criticism and links Jeb Stuart Magruder to break-in payoffs and the hiring of G. Gordon Liddy.

574. Dershowitz, A. M. "Unchecked Wiretapping: Before Watergate and After." New Republic, CLXXII (May 31, 1975), 13-17. Reviews FBI and "plumbers" bugging during the Nixon administration and contends illegal wiretaps were still functional in spring, 1975.

575. "Desperate Gamble for Survival: Release of Transcripts of Tapes." Newsweek, LXXXIII (May 13, 1974), 16-17+. Why Nixon chose to release the edited White House transcripts.

576. "The Detectives Hunt for Illegal Givers." Business Week

(July 14, 1973), 27-28. Watergate investigators search for illegal corporate donors to the 1972 presidential election campaigns.

577. Diamond, Edwin. "Psychojournalism: Nixon on the Couch." Columbia Journalism Review, VII (March-April 1974), 7-11. Comments on the practice of some journalists of seeking psychological reasons for the President's Watergate actions.

578. ———. "TV and Watergate: What Was, What Might Have Been." In: Michael C. Emery and Ted C. Smythe, eds. Readings in Mass Communications: Concepts and Issues in the Mass Media. 2nd ed. Dubuque, Ia.: William C. Brown, 1974. pp. 393-396. Analyzes the role of television in covering the unfolding Watergate drama, with special attention to the Ervin hearings.

579. ———. "Tape Shock: The Nixon Transcripts." Columbia Journalism Review, XIII (July-August 1974), 5-9. On the negative public relations the White House experienced after the American audience read the transcripts or listened to excerpts on television.

580. ———. The Tin Kazoo: Television, Politics, and the News. Cambridge, Mass.: M.I.T. Press, 1975. 269p. A veteran commentator examines the dynamic medium of television and contends that electronic journalism is neither as influential as many believed or as close to its stories as necessary to reflect accuracy. Examples chosen for coverage include Watergate, especially the Senate Ervin Committee and House Judiciary Committee hearings.

581. Diamond, Robert A., ed. Impeachment and the U.S. Congress. Washington, D.C.: Congressional Quarterly, Inc., 1974. 60p. Looks at the process, precedents, and machinery of impeachment, with emphasis on the spring-summer 1974 crisis.

582. Dickerson, Nancy. Among Those Present: A Reporter's View of 25 Years in Washington. New York: Random House, 1976. 238p. A veteran network television reporter's recollections, with some mention of television's role in the Watergate affair.

583. Dickinson, William R., comp. Watergate: Chronology of a Crisis. 2 vols. Washington, D.C.: Congressional Quarterly, Inc., 1973-1974. Arranged in chronological order with excerpts from or entire reprintings of articles from C.Q. Weekly Reports for the June 1972-summer 1974 issues; includes complete texts of various letters, documents, statements, testimonies, and memos, as well as biographies of participants and suggestions for reform.

584. "Dirty Politics: A Bumper Crop of Complaints in 1972."
C.Q. Weekly Reports, XXX (November 18, 1972), 3046-3047. Many of these reports would be given substance during the Ervin committee hearings.

585. "Did Watergate Break the Ice Between the White House and the Media?" Broadcasting, LXXXIV (May 7, 1973), 21-22. Argues that Nixon, who had warred with the press since assuming office, needed the press and would use it to try to get his posture of innocence across to the public.

586. "The Dimensions of Watergate." National Review, XXVI (August 30, 1974), 966-967. A brief review of the importance of the crisis.

587. "The Disposition of the White House Tapes: Documents." Congressional Record, CXX (September 16, 1974), 31174-31186. Materials on the arrangements made for the storage and dissemination of the Watergate tapes.

588. Dissinger, George. "Representative [Bob] Wilson Bares Details of Convention Gift Offer: Reprinted from the San Diego Evening Tribune, March 3, 1972." In: U.S. Congress, Senate, Committee on the Judiciary. Richard G. Kleindienst--Resumed: Hearings. 92nd Cong., 2nd sess. Washington, D.C.: U.S. Government Printing Office, 1972. p. 899. On ITT chairman Harold S. Geneen's guarantee of $400,000 for a GOP convention in San Diego.

589. Doane, D. P. "How Time Has Treated the Watergate Crew." U.S. News and World Report, XCII (June 14, 1982), 51-55. Current fate and whereabouts of those involved in the case.

590. Doar, John M. and James D. St. Clair. "Nixon: The Case for and Against." U.S. News and World Report, LXXVII (August 5, 1974), 11-15. Pro- and anti-impeachment views of the House Judiciary Committee counsel and the President's chief defense lawyer respectively.

591. Dobrovir, William A., et al. Offenses of Richard Milhous Nixon: A Guide for the People of the United States--Bribery and Other High Crimes and Misdemeanors. New York: Quadrangle Books, for Public Issues Press, 1974. 169p. A review of the Watergate case and its various issues in an effort to show that sufficient crimes have been committed and linked to the President that he should be removed from office; this polemic was first published in 1973 by the Washington, D.C. firm of A. B. Zill and was subtitled "A Lawyer's Guide for the People of the United States of America."

592. "Donald H. Segretti." In: Eleanora W. Schoenebaum, ed. Political Profiles: The Nixon/Ford Years. New York:

Facts on File, Inc., 1979. pp. 586-587. The former Treasury Department lawyer who directed a campaign of political espionage and "dirty tricks" against the Democrats in 1972.

593. Donner, Frank. "Domestic Political Intelligence." In: Howard Frazier, ed. Uncloaking the CIA. New York: Free Press, 1978. pp. 165-173. Contains some mention of the Agency's Watergate involvement.

594. _____. "Electronic Surveillance: The National Security Game." Civil Liberties Review, II (Summer 1975), 15-47. Includes a review of bugging related to Watergate.

595. _____ and Richard I. Lavin. "From the Watergate Perspective: Kangaroo Grand Juries." Nation, CCXVII (November 19, 1973), 519-533. Looks at the use of grand juries to gather inside information.

596. Donovan, Hedley. "Good Uses of the Watergate Affair." Time, CI (May 14, 1973), 24-25. Nixon's "palace guard" is out, free press is a proven fact, and presidential power is being checked.

597. Dorfman, Ron. "Miasmas of Watergate: The Truth Is Bad Enough." Nation, CCXVII (July 30, 1973), 73-75. The paranoia caused by the scandal is causing wild charges of conspiracies and cover-ups, including a deliberate plot to down the plane carrying Mrs. E. Howard Hunt.

598. Dorman, Michael. Dirty Politics: From 1776 to Watergate. New York: Delacorte Press, 1979. 301p. Details examples of dirty politics, including spying, sabotage, and smear campaigns; fully discusses Watergate and various moves for reform in and out of Congress.

599. Dorsen, Norman and John H. F. Strattuck. "Executive Privilege, the Congress, and the Courts." Ohio State Law Journal, XXXV (Spring 1974), 1-40. The authors explain why, in their opinion, Nixon's assertion of discretionary executive privilege on the tapes issue is without basis in law, and discuss what a president's right to confidentiality should be. Reprinted under the title, "Executive Privilege: The President Won't Tell," in U.S. Library of Congress, Congressional Research Service. Resolved That the Powers of the Presidency Should Be Curtailed. Washington, D.C.: U.S. Government Printing Office, 1974. pp. 172-205.

600. Dough, George. "Sam Ervin." In: his Leaders in Profile. New York: Sperr and Douth, 1975. pp. 848-859. A brief profile of the Senate Watergate Committee chairman.

601. Douglass, Bruce. "Watergate and Political Realism." Chris-

tian Century, XCI (October 9, 1974), 929-932. Suggests that the ethics of the Watergate gang got them into trouble before truth and justice rebalanced the situation.

602. Dowling, Tom. "Using the Nuremberg Defense for Watergate: Reprinted from the Washington Star-News, May 28, 1973." Congressional Record, CXIX (June 5, 1973), 18210-18211. On the plea of many that they were simply "following orders."

603. "Down to the Bedrock in the Impeachment Probe." U.S. News and World Report, LXXVI (May 6, 1974), 26-28. On the release and substance of the White House transcripts.

604. Downie, Leonard. The New Muckrakers. Washington, D.C.: New Republic Book Company, 1976. 296p. Examines investigative reporting by newsmen and profiles a number of them who were in one way or another involved in covering Watergate.

605. Doyle, James. Not Above the Law: The Battles of Watergate Prosecutors Cox and Jaworski--A Behind the Scenes Account. New York: William Morrow, 1977. 420p. Recollections of the official spokesman of the WSPF, describing the prosecutor's staff, its relations with Cox and Jaworski, its reactions to the Cox firing, and the work of the Nixon White House to demoralize it and block its task. The disputes within the WSPF unit are outlined, as well as the disputes over indicting Nixon; White House aides Haig and Buzhardt are special villains. The book was well received by most reviewers.

606. _____. "Saturday Night Live: An Insider's Report on the Crucial Events of October 20, 1973, When Nixon Ousted Cox and Provoked the Fateful Massacre." New York Times Magazine (May 15, 1977), 40, 42, 45-46, 48-49. Contains the same information as found in the appropriate section of the previous citation.

607. Drew, Elizabeth. "Reporter in Washington, D.C.: Autumn Notes--1." New Yorker, XLIX (March 11, 1974), 42-101. Daily coverage of Watergate and related events from September 5, 1973 through October 25, 1973; extremely detailed.

608. _____. Washington Journal: The Events of 1973-1974. New York: Random House, 1975. 428p. Without making any judgements, the author chronicles on an almost daily basis the who, what, when, and where of Watergate from September 1973 through Nixon's resignation, providing details on such strategies as "Operation Candor" and the White House transcripts, intervening issues such as the Middle East alert, and the efforts of the House Judiciary

Committee (covered by the last quarter of the book) to come to grips with the impeachment process. Well written and filled with fascinating anecdotes and trivia.

609. _____. "Watergate Diary, May 1973." Atlantic, CCXXXII (August 1973), 60-70. Notes on Watergate happenings during May, including the events surrounding John Dean.

610. Drinan, Robert F. "Resolution of the Impeachment of President Nixon." Computers and Automation, XXII (September 1973), 28-30+. Father Drinan was a Democratic Congressman from Massachusetts who voted for the President's impeachment.

611. "The Drive to Discredit Dean." Time, CIII (February 11, 1974), 12-14. Outlines the latest attempts to discredit Dean's Ervin panel testimony through the release of selected tapes.

612. Drummond, Roscoe. "Point of View--Ervin, Rodino, et al.-- How About It?: Reprinted from the Christian Science Monitor, June 20, 1974." Congressional Record, CXX (June 21, 1974), 20674-20675. Argues that unfair leaks from the various Congressional committees involved with Watergate are hurting Nixon.

613. _____. "Watergate Reform Number One: Reprinted from the Christian Science Monitor, September 28, 1973." Congressional Record, CXIX (October 2, 1973), 32612. On the need for reform in political contribution laws.

614. DuBois, Larry. "Howard Hughes: Political Connections and Business Affairs." Playboy, XXVIII (September 1976), 74-76, 82, 112, 180-190; XXIX (April 1977), 94-96, 98, 106, 154, 193-194, 196-198. Reports on Hughes' contribution to the 1972 Nixon reelection campaign, among other issues.

615. Dunham, Roger and Armand Mauss. "Waves from Watergate." Pacific Sociological Review, XIX (1976), 469-490. Presents, as the subtitle reads, "Evidence Concerning the Impact of the Watergate Scandal Upon Political Legitimacy and Social Control."

616. "Dwight Chapin." In: Eleanora W. Schoenebaum, ed. Political Profiles: The Nixon/Ford Years. New York: Facts on File, Inc., 1979. pp. 120-121. A brief biography of the former Presidential Appointments Secretary who was convicted of perjury.

617. Dygert, James H. The Investigative Journalist: Folk Heroes of a New Era. Englewood Cliffs, N.J.: Prentice-Hall, 1976. 282p. Examines the idea of investigative reporting and profiles many involved with it at the time of Watergate.

618. "Dynamic Duo." Newsweek, LXXX (October 30, 1972), 76-77. An early profile of Washington Post reporters Woodward and Bernstein.

619. "E. Howard Hunt." In: Eleanora W. Schoenebaum, ed. Political Profiles: The Nixon/Ford Years. New York: Facts on File, Inc., 1979. pp. 317-320. A biography of the former CIA agent and White House "plumber" who was early caught up in the web of the Watergate break-in.

620. "E. Howard Hunt, Master Storyteller." Time, CI (June 11, 1973), 20-21. Wonders if Hunt's Ervin panel testimony matches his spy thrillers penned under the name David St. John.

621. Eagly, Alice H. and Shelly Chaiken. "Why Would Anyone Say That?: Causal Attribution of Statements About the Watergate Scandal." Sociometry, XXXIX (September 1976), 236-243. Reviews a number of the untrue statements made by various participants in the Watergate drama and analyzes why they were issued.

622. Edelstein, Alexander S. Media Credibility and the Believability of Watergate. Washington, D.C.: American Newspaper Publishers Association, 1974. Unpaged. Argues that press credibility rose as the result of Watergate reporting; reprinted in Communication Research, I (October 1974), 426-439.

623. "The Edited Transcripts--Opinions of National Leaders (Excerpts): Reprinted from the 'Talk of the Town' column, New Yorker, May 20, 1974." Congressional Record, CXX (May 28, 1974), 16551-16552. Many of those quoted did not believe the transcripts showed Nixon to be as innocent as he claimed.

624. Edmondson, Madeline and Alden D. Cohen. The Women of Watergate. New York: Stein and Day, 1975. 288p. Capsule biographies of the wives, daughters, and political women involved in Watergate, with emphasis on the newsmakers: the Nixon women, Rose Mary Woods, Martha Mitchell, and Maureen Dean.

625. "Effects of the Nixon Pardon." U.S. News and World Report, LXXVII (September 23, 1974), 19-22. While many were opposed to it, many also hoped that it would heal the nation's wounds.

626. Efron, Edith. "Is There Truth in Charges of Anti-Nixon Bias?" TV Guide, XXII (May 11, 1974), A3-A4. A long-time opponent of the bias she saw in network television news, Efron contends that the charge of bias is accurate. Reprinted in Congressional Record, CXX (May 13, 1974), 14185-14186.

627. "Egil Krogh." In: Eleanora W. Schoenebaum, ed. Political Profiles: The Nixon/Ford Years. New York: Facts on File, Inc., 1979. pp. 365-366. A brief biography of a former assistant of John D. Ehrlichman who became tied up with the White House "plumbers."

628. Ehrlichman, John D. "Ehrlichman Hangs Tough." Newsweek, LXXXII (August 6, 1973), 18-26. Summarizes his Ervin Committee testimony, including his national security rationale for the Ellsberg break-in; contrasts his statements with those of other witnesses, especially John Dean.

629. _____. "Ehrlichman on the CIA: 'No Recollection of a Call.'" C.Q. Weekly Report, XXXI (June 2, 1973), 1351-1357. Reports he did not ask CIA to frustrate the FBI check on the Watergate break-in.

630. _____. "Ehrlichman Reviews Haldeman." Time, CXI (March 6, 1978), 26+. Nixon's former domestic aide's views on the published memoirs of his colleague, H. R. "Bob" Haldeman (q.v.).

631. _____. "Ehrlichman's Opening Statement." C.Q. Weekly Report, XXXI (July 28, 1973), 2044-2047. In which he went before the Ervin panel and tried to "stonewall it."

632. _____. "Ehrlichman's Story: 'I Was Had.'" Newsweek, LXXXIV (December 23, 1974), 20+. Testimony on Watergate delivered during the cover-up trial; very different from the Ervin panel comments.

633. _____. "Ehrlichman on the Stand: 'I Was Deceived by Nixon.'" U.S. News and World Report, LXXVII (December 23, 1974), 41. Same data as the previous entry.

634. _____. "The Top Aide Tells How Nixon Sold Him Out." New West, II (May 23, 1977), 76+. Elaborates on his Watergate cover-up trial testimony.

635. _____. "What I Have Learned." Parade Magazine (September 26, 1982), 4-5, 7. "When I heard the Nixon tapes, as my attorneys and I prepared for the cover-up trial, it became crystal clear that Richard Nixon had been involved in the cover-up within a week of the Watergate burglary."

636. _____. Witness to Power: The Nixon Years. New York: Simon and Schuster, 1982. 432p. The latest and one of the largest of the Watergate memoirs in which the one-time domestic affairs counsel recalls his experience in the White House, especially the Watergate scandal; Ehrlichman writes well, but his memoirs often descend into rationalization and vengeful commentary directed at all of his perceived opponents from President Nixon (who sold him out) to John Dean

(the traitor) to the reporter every staffer hated, Dan Rather. Excerpted, with an interesting interview, in Book Digest, IX (May 1982), 14-26.

637. "Ehrlichman--Guilty in Plumbers Case." U.S. News and World Report, LXXVII (July 22, 1974), 17. The verdict in the Ellsberg break-in case.

638. "The Ehrlichman Mentality on View." Time, CII (August 6, 1973), 22-27. Analyzes Ehrlichman's ethics as revealed in his Ervin panel testimony, especially his contentions as to the necessity of the Ellsberg burglary.

639. "Ehrlichman's Defense: A Counterattack." U.S. News and World Report, LXXV (August 6, 1973), 14. Lists his rebuttal of the testimony of previous Ervin Committee witnesses.

640. Eilberg, Robert. "The Investigation by the Committee on the Judiciary of the House of Representatives into the Charges of Impeachable Conduct Against Richard M. Nixon." Temple Law Quarterly, XLVIII (1975), 209+. A review of the impeachment inquiry process conducted in the spring and summer of 1974.

641. Eisenhower, David. "Last Days in a Nixon White House." Good Housekeeping, CLXXXI (September 1975), 89+. The President's son-in-law tells of the pressures on the first family of the Nixon resignation dilemma and decision.

642. _____. "Our Hardest Year: An Interview." McCall's, CII (August 1975), 24+. Provides information similar to that in the previous citation.

643. "Electronic Eavesdropping: Watergate Comes Full Circle." C.Q. Weekly Report, XXXI (1973), 2321-2324. Discusses the widespread allegations about illegal wiretaps such as those unsuccessfully planted in the Watergate.

644. "Elliot E. Richardson." In: Eleanora W. Schoenebaum, ed. Political Profiles: The Nixon/Ford Years. New York: Facts on File, Inc., 1979. pp. 524-528. A biography of the Attorney General who succeeded Richard Kleindienst and quit rather than carry out the President's order to fire Watergate Special Prosecutor Archibald Cox.

645. Elliott, Karen J. "The Pardon of Nixon Was Timely, Legal, Jaworski Believes: Reprinted from the Wall Street Journal, October 16, 1974." In: U.S. Congress, House, Committee on the Judiciary, Subcommittee on Criminal Justice. Pardon of Richard M. Nixon and Related Matters: Hearings. 93rd Cong., 2nd sess. Washington, D.C.: U.S. Government Printing Office, 1974. pp. 147-148. The second special prosecutor's views on Ford's action.

646. "Ellsberg Break-in Indictments: Texts, March 7, 1974." In: Robert A. Diamond, ed. Historic Documents, 1974. Washington, D.C.: Congressional Quarterly, Inc., 1975. pp. 205-214. The prosecution of Ehrlichman, et al., for the "plumbers'" act.

647. Elms, Alan C. Personality in Politics. New York: Harcourt, Brace, Jovanovich, 1976. Provides a broad functional analysis of the evidence concerning the role played by personality characteristics in political behavior; includes numerous references to Nixon.

648. "Embarrassment of Riches: CREEP Funds." Nation, CCXVI (March 26, 1973), 388. Editorial on the amount of cash-- some illegal--collected by the President's 1972 re-election organization.

649. "Encyclopedia of Evidence." Newsweek, LXXXIV (July 22, 1974), 21-25. A capsule history of Watergate distilled from the more than 4,000 pages of the House Judiciary Committee's report.

650. "The End Begins with Bitter Fratricide at Trial." Time, CIV (October 28, 1974), 12-14. On the conflicting and often bitter testimony at the Watergate coverup trial.

651. "End of Watergate Coverup Trial: Excerpts from Documents and Transcripts Introduced at the Watergate Coverup Trial That Ended January 1, 1975 with the Conviction of Four of the Five Defendants on All Charges." In: Robert A. Diamond, ed. Historic Documents, 1974. Washington, D.C.: Congressional Quarterly, 1975. pp. 991-1002. Includes testimony by Haldeman, Ehrlichman, Mitchell, and Stans.

652. "End of the Greatest Uncertainty." Time, CIV (September 16, 1974), 14+. The Ford pardon removed the question of a trial for Nixon in civil court.

653. "Enter Professor Bork: Robert H. Bork, Solicitor General." Time, CII (October 1, 1973), 112+. Biography of the man who in 20 days would carry out the Cox firing.

654. Entman, Robert M. "The Imperial Media." In: Arnold J. Meltsner, ed. Politics and the Oval Office: Towards Presidential Government. San Francisco, Calif.: Institute for Contemporary Studies, 1981. Chpt. 4. Reviews the role of the media in covering the White House; includes the author's thoughts on the press and Watergate.

655. Ephron, N. "Ken Clawson Is No Joke." New York, VI (June 3, 1974), 58-64, 67. Deputy director of communications at the Nixon White House.

656. Epstein, Edward Jay. <u>Agency of Fear: Opiates and Political Power in America.</u> New York: G. P. Putnam, 1977. 352p. Investigative reporter Epstein, whose recent credits include books on television news and the world diamond market, here draws a connection between the White House "plumbers" unit and the administration's effort to ferret out illegal drug dealers.

657. _____. "Did There Come a Time When There Were 43 Different Theories of How Watergate Happened?" <u>Esquire,</u> LXXX (November 1973), 127-132. Lists and assesses the various theories thus far offered on the basis of Watergate, i.e., who masterminded it, target or data sought, how it could happen, the cover-up, etc., and reviews the strengths and weaknesses of each.

658. _____. "How the Press Handled the Watergate Scandal." <u>Editor and Publisher,</u> CVI (October 20, 1973), 5+. Argues that the press did not uncover the affair but simply picked up on investigations already under way.

659. _____. "The Krogh File: The Politics of Law and Interest." <u>Public Interest,</u> XXXIX (Spring 1975), 99-124. Egil Krogh, the "plumbers," and the Ellsberg break-in.

660. Ervin, Sam J., Jr. "Campaign Practices and the Law: Watergate and Beyond." <u>Emory Law Journal,</u> XXIII (1974), 1+. Calls for election reform to halt the campaign ills documented by his panel.

661. _____. "Controlling 'Executive Privilege.'" <u>Loyola Law Review,</u> XX (Spring 1974), 11-31. Documents how this concept was a creation of the executive branch and not the Constitution; illustrated with testimony and statements from earlier Senate inquiries into the practice.

662. _____. "'Executive Privilege': The Need for Congressional Action." <u>Illinois Bar Journal,</u> LXII (1973), 66+. Provides almost the same documentation as in the last citation, together with a call for reform, especially in light of President Nixon's handling of the tapes. Reprinted in <u>Case and Comment,</u> LXXIX (January-February 1974), 39-48.

663. _____. "Hill Country Sayin's of Sam Ervin." <u>Time,</u> CI (April 16, 1973), 13. A brief biography featuring folksy quotes.

664. _____. "A Personal Account by Senator Sam J. Ervin, Jr., of His Meeting with President Richard M. Nixon Regarding the Release of Transcripts of the White House Tapes, October 19, 1973." In: Samuel Dash, <u>Chief Counsel: Inside the Ervin Committee--The Untold Story of Watergate.</u> New

York: Random House, 1976. pp. 267-272. A brief statement of recollection written especially for Dash's book.

665. _____. "The Separation of Powers." Center Magazine, VII (January-February 1974), 8-10. A brief review of the constitutional concept with a note on how it was out of kilter under Nixon and his post-Hoover predecessors.

666. _____. "'To Obtain the Truth'--Why Senator Sam Ervin Presses Ahead: An Interview." U.S. News and World Report, LXXIV (June 18, 1973), 19. Ervin discusses his reasons for holding hearings, despite a request from Archibald Cox that he not do so.

667. _____. The Whole Truth: The Watergate Conspiracy. New York: Random House, 1981. 320p. After reading Nixon's memoirs, the chairman of the Senate Select Committee on Presidential Campaign Activities decided to write this volume to "set the record straight" and correct what he considered to be many errors in the former President's account. It is generally agreed by reviewers that this account is one of the most clearly organized, cleverly written, and informative of all the participant accounts. Loaded with many of the down-home phrases for which he was famous, The Whole Truth answers several remaining questions, especially regarding the Ervin-Baker-Nixon meeting prior to the Cox firing. A fine piece of work by the man many considered the Senate's finest constitutional expert.

668. _____. "Why the Senate Is Investigating Watergate." U.S. News and World Report, LXXIV (May 28, 1973), 106-107. Text of the Senator's opening remarks at the Watergate hearings on May 17, 1973.

669. _____. The Wisdom of Sam Ervin. Edited by Bill Adler. New York: Ballantine Books, 1973. 177p. A paperback devoted to the wit and down-home sayings of the Senate Watergate Committee's chairman.

670. _____ and Howard H. Baker, Jr. "Text of Statements at Opening of the Special Senate Committee's Watergate Hearings, May 17, 1973." In: Buel W. Patch, ed. Historic Documents, 1973. Washington, D.C.: Congressional Quarterly, Inc., 1974. pp. 549-556. Provides reasoning for why the hearings were held.

671. "The Ervin Agenda." New Republic, CLXVIII (April 14, 1973), 7-8. On the formulation of the Senate Special Committee and its upcoming hearings.

672. "The Ervin Committee's Last Hurrah." Time, CIV (July 22, 1974), 27-28+. An examination of the panel's final report with emphasis on the financial relationship of Nixon and Bebe Rebozo.

673. "The Ervin Hearings." New Republic, CLXVIII (June 2, 1973), 7-8. Concerns their process and Watergate details uncovered.

674. "Ervin's Chief Investigator: Sam Dash, Counsel for the Senate Committee." Business Week (May 19, 1973), 46. A brief profile.

675. "An Ethics Student Rationalizes Watergate." Christian Century, XC (July 4, 1973), 723-724. Discusses the Ervin panel testimony of Jeb Magruder.

676. Evans, J. Claude. "Executive Privilege and Judicial Prerogatives." Christian Century, XC (July 4, 1973), 723-724. Examines the privilege conflict between Nixon and Sirica over the Watergate tapes and related materials.

677. Evans, Les. "Watergate and the White House." International Socialist Review (December 1973), 4-11+. Examines Nixon's background and the unrest in America from the Kennedy assassination through Vietnam as a basis for Watergate.

678. _____ and Allen Myers. Watergate and the Myth of American Democracy. New York: Pathfinder Press, 1976. 206p. Evans' contribution is the same as the previous citation; Myers' portion consists of a series of articles first published in Intercontinental Press between September 17 and December 17, 1973, with one new article for the book. These American Trotskyites wonder how the capitalist system could ever let itself get into the expense of Watergate, but conclude that the scandal is "the symptom of a far-advanced disease of the whole government system and a confirmation of the Marxist critique of U.S. capitalism."

679. Evans, Rowland and Robert Novak. "The Impact of Dean's IRS Testimony: Reprinted from the Washington Post, July 24, 1974." Congressional Record, CXX (August 1, 1974), 26441. On Nixon administration efforts to use the IRS against the "White House enemies."

680. _____. "Scandal?--They Like Impeachment Even Less: Reprinted from the Washington Post, January 20, 1974." Congressional Record, CXX (January 21, 1974), 185. Views of the people of Newark, Ohio.

681. _____. "The Secret Destruction of Howard Hunt's Notebooks: Reprinted from the Washington Post, March 27, 1974." Congressional Record, CXX (April 11, 1974), 10789-10790. How Dean "deep-sixed" them into the Potomac River.

682. _____. "With an 'Expected' Pardon: Reprinted from the

Washington Post, September 12, 1974." Congressional Record, CXX (September 12, 1974), 30964. On the idea of a deal between Ford and Nixon.

683. Evans, Thomas E., 3rd. "Executive Privilege and Congress: Perspectives and Recommendations." DePaul Law Review, XXIII (Winter 1974), 692-736. An historical review of the concept with ideas for making it more compatible with the information needs of Congress.

684. Evarts, Dru, and Guido H. Stempel. "Coverage of the 1972 Campaign by TV, News Magazines, and Major Newspapers." Journalism Quarterly, LI (Winter 1974), 645-648. Comments on the amount of Watergate information provided.

685. Everett, Terry. "In Defense of Nixon: Reprinted from the Enterprise [Alabama] Enterprizer, October 31, 1973." Congressional Record, CXIX (November 14, 1973), 37118-37119. Supports the removal of Archibald Cox.

686. "Evidence: Fitting the Pieces Together." Time, CIV (July 22, 1974), 20-25. Summarizes recently-released Judiciary Committee evidence and presents James D. St. Clair's defense of the President.

687. "Examining the Record of That Meeting in March: The Controversial March 21, 1973 Meeting Between Richard M. Nixon, John Dean, and H. R. Haldeman." Time, CIII (March 18, 1974), 10-11. Reviews the differences in the statements of the three men concerning the payment of hush money to the Watergate burglars.

688. "Excerpts from the Tapes." New Republic, CLXX (May 11, 1974), 13-33. A reprinting from the White House edited transcripts.

689. "Excerpts of Papers on Milk Supports, ITT Decision." C.Q. Weekly Report, XXXII (1974), 57-62. From evidence developed by the House Judiciary Committee.

690. "An Excess of Executive Privilege Versus the Truth: Reprinted from the Washington Post, July 16, 1973." Congressional Record, CXIX (July 16, 1973), 24052. An editorial on the continuing White House "stone-wall."

691. "Executive Cover-up: Reprinted from the New York Times, March 14, 1973." Congressional Record, CXIX (March 15, 1973), 8324. An editorial on executive privilege.

692. "Executive Privilege--The President Does Not Have an Absolute Privilege to Withhold Evidence from a Grand Jury." Harvard Law Review, LXXXVII (May 1974), 1557-1568. A review of the privilege concept and Nixon's use of it

vis-à-vis the delivery of material to the Watergate grand jury.

693. "Executive Privilege: What the Argument Is All About." U.S. News and World Report, LXXV (July 30, 1973), 18. Examines the concept of a president's withholding information from Congress for various reasons, with special attention to Nixon's refusal to supply requested Watergate data.

694. "Exit Jaworski." Newsweek, LXXXIV (October 21, 1974), 38. On the return to private practice of the second Watergate Special Prosecutor.

695. "Exit Nixon." Time, CIV (August 19, 1974), 13B-14+. On Nixon's resignation and retirement to San Clemente.

696. "Exposing the Big Cover-up." Newsweek, LXXXI (May 28, 1973), 26-31. Mainly concerns James McCord's letter to Judge Sirica charging that the Watergate break-in was the work of important administration officials.

697. "Facing the Court and Counting the House." Time, CIV (July 15, 1974), 12-13. Nixon's two-front battle with the Supreme Court over the tapes and the House Judiciary Committee on impeachment.

698. "Facing the Music: The Nixon Interviews." New Republic, CLXXVI (June 4, 1977), 2+. Comments on the former president's televised interviews with Englishman David Frost.

699. "Facing up to Resignation or Impeachment." Time, CIII (February 4, 1974), 30-31. Outlines the ideas on both and suggests Nixon may soon have to make a decision.

700. "The Failure of Mr. Ford: Reprinted from the New York Times, September 9, 1974." Congressional Record, CXX (September 11, 1974), 30748-30749. A negative editorial concerning Ford's September 8 pardon of former president Nixon.

701. Fairlie, Henry. "The Lessons of Watergate: On the Possibility of Morality in Politics." Encounter, XLIII (October 1974), 8-27. A long review of the immoralities in politics, especially during the Nixon years, with a call for a return to or at least an improvement in politics worthy of the American system.

702. "The Fairness Problem Re-examined: Has the Press Done a Job on Nixon?" Columbia Law Review, XII (January-February 1974), 50-58. Examines the basis for the long-running press-Nixon feud in the context of the fairness doctrine of the FCC.

703. "Fake: Hearings on the ITT Affair." Newsweek, LXXIX (March 27, 1972), 28+. Wonders if the Dita Beard memo is a hoax.

704. "The Fall of Richard Nixon: World Reaction to a Historic Shock." Atlas (September 1974), 11-19. Excerpts from newspapers around the world.

705. "Fallout from Ford's Rush to Pardon." Time, CIV (September 23, 1974), 11-14+. Asserts that public opinion was against the Nixon pardon.

706. "Fallout from the ITT Affair." Fortune, LXXXV (May 1972), 151-152. Effects of the scandal on business and government.

707. "Fallout of Stardom: Sam Ervin's Special Watergate Panel." Newsweek, LXXXII (July 9, 1973), 18. Increased status for the various members, most of whom were previously little known by the American public.

708. Fallows, James. "Chapter Two of Moral Myopia: The Watergate Committee and Its Staff." Washington Monthly, V (January 1974), 12-20. Argues that some of the tactics of the Ervin panel were no more moral than the alleged illegalities of the White House.

709. "Fateful Trial Closes a Sorry Chapter." Time, CV (January 13, 1975), 9-14. A review and assessment of the recently-finished Watergate cover-up trial.

710. "Fateful Vote." Newsweek, LXXXIV (August 5, 1974), 18-22. The vote of the House Judiciary Committee on articles of impeachment.

711. "The Fateful Vote to Impeach." Time, CIV (August 5, 1974), 10-18. Contains the same information as the previous citation.

712. "FBI Chief L. Patrick Gray." C.Q. Weekly Report, XXXI (1973), 378. A brief biography of Hoover's acting successor.

713. "Feeling of Betrayal: Businessmen's Opinions." Time, CI (June 4, 1973), 78. Reactions to exposure of illegal campaign contributions.

714. Feiffer, Jules. Feiffer on Nixon: The Cartoon Presidency. New York: Random House, 1974. 64p. A slim volume of cartoons and satire by the noted political cartoonist.

715. Feldman, Trude B. "Julie Eisenhower's Fight for Her Father." McCall's, CI (February 1974), 86+. Reviews the

youngest Nixon's daughter's outspoken defense of her father's integrity.

716. _____. "The Quiet Courage of Pat Nixon." McCalls, CII (May 1975), 74-75+. Examines the trials and traumas of the former first lady during Watergate and the subsequent California "exile" of her husband.

717. Felt, W. Mark. The FBI Pyramid: From the Inside. New York: G. P. Putnam, 1978. 351p. Recollections of the former Deputy Director of the FBI, whom some thought might be the anonymous Woodward and Bernstein source called "Deep Throat."

718. Fernandez, Julio. White House Enemies; Or, How We Made the Dean's List. New York: New American Library, 1973. Unpaged. A paperback loaded with Watergate caricatures, cartoons, and satire.

719. Ferrer, Jose M., 3rd. "An Awful Lot of Lawyers Involved." Time, CII (July 9, 1973), 50-51. Examines ethical and other considerations for the legal profession of having so many lawyers involved in Watergate wrongdoings.

720. Fields, Howard. High Crimes and Misdemeanors--"Wherefore Richard M. Nixon Warrants Impeachment": The Dramatic Story of the Rodino Committee. New York: W. W. Norton, 1978. 330p. A reporter's view of the inside workings of the House Judiciary Committee and its staff as it considered the process of impeachment, investigated and chose charges, drew up and voted the articles in mid-summer 1974. Behind-the-scenes maneuvering of key committee members for and against Nixon and the work of John Doar and his staff are fleshed out with details from private conversations, though little attention is paid to a review of those articles which did not win adoption. Much of what is discussed was actually seen by viewers during the televised impeachment hearings, but for those who did not watch them, this book, together with the committee's final report, is a good starting place from which to study the panel's considerations.

721. Finch, Gerald B. "Impeachments and the Dynamics of Public Opinion: A Comment on 'Guilty, Yes--Impeachment, No.'" Political Science Quarterly, LXXXIX (1974), 301-324. A comment on the article by P. J. McGeever cited below. Finch advances a "cross pressures" theory on why people feared the unsettling effects of impeachment more than they did an obviously guilty president.

722. "Finding the Perfect Prober." Time, CI (May 28, 1973), 24. Looks at the legal background of Archibald Cox.

723. "The Firestorm." New York Times Magazine (January 13, 1974), 48+. Reviews the almost universal condemnation of Nixon for the Cox dismissal.

724. "Firing of Watergate Prosecutor: Texts of Numerous Letters and Statements Leading to and Following the Dismissal of Special Watergate Prosecutor Archibald Cox." In: Buel W. Patch, ed. Historic Documents, 1973. Washington, D.C.: Congressional Quarterly, Inc., 1974. 859-881. All review the tapes controversy and opinions on the dismissal.

725. Firmage, E. B. "The Law of Presidential Impeachment." Utah Law Review, XXIV (Winter 1973), 681-704. A study of the constitutional procedure and its precedents; compare with the work of Raoul Berger cited above.

726. Flatto, Edie. "Impeachment of a President: Reflections on Watergate." Contemporary Review, CCXXIII (September 1973), 129-131. A British review of the process in America and a look to its possible employment in the Watergate case.

727. _____. "The Impeachment of Richard M. Nixon." Contemporary Review, CCXXVI (March 1975), 146-148. A follow-up to the previous citation that concentrates on TV coverage of the House Judiciary Committee hearings.

728. Fletcher, Joseph. "Situation Ethics and Watergate." Theology Today, XXXI (January 1975), 343-345. Comments on the lack of morality of those White House aides who let expediency and power dictate their actions rather than right, honor, or good.

729. "Flight from Reality?" Newsweek, LXXXIII (June 17, 1974), 16-19. Reveals Nixon's condemnation by the grand jury as an unindicted co-conspirator and Judge Gesell's citing of the President for stonewalling in the Fielding trial.

730. Florestano, Patricia S. "The Characteristics of White House Staff Appointees from Truman to Nixon." Presidential Studies Quarterly, VII (Fall 1977), 184-191. Some are noted for their ability to act with honor and reason, all for their devotion to their chiefs, including some like Nixon's who would commit illegal acts for him.

731. "Following the Footprints of Rose Mary's Baby: List of Secret Contributors to the President's Re-election Campaign." Newsweek, LXXXII (July 23, 1973), 20. Includes names like Howard Hughes, Bebe Rebozo, etc.

732. "Following the Milk Trail, with an Excerpt from the March 23, 1971 Watergate Tape Transcript." Newsweek, LXXXIV

(July 29, 1974), 32+. Reviews evidence developed on the case by the House Judiciary Committee.

733. Fonzi, Gaeton. "The Man Who Does It All for Women." Gold Coast Pictorial, XIII (January 1977), 50+. Portrays G. Gordon Liddy as a devoted family man.

734. Footlick, J. K. "The Search for T-R-U-T-H." Newsweek, LXXXIV (November 18, 1974), 80-81. Judge Sirica's role in the Watergate coverup trial.

734a. "For the Record: The Report on Impeachment." C.Q. Weekly Report, XXXII (1974), 2352-2358. Excerpts from the final report of the House Judiciary Committee.

735. Ford, Gerald R. "Address to the Congress: The Presidential Address Delivered Before a Joint Session of Congress, August 12, 1974." Weekly Compilation of Presidential Documents, X (August 19, 1974), 1029-1035. In which the new President pledges to end the national nightmare of Watergate.

736. _____. "Ford--'An American Tragedy ... Someone Must Write the End to It.'" U.S. News and World Report, LXXVII (September 23, 1974), 20-21. The President's remarks concerning the pardon of Richard Nixon.

737. _____. "Ford Memoirs--Behind the Nixon Pardon." Nation, CCXXVIII (April 7, 1979), 353+. An analysis of that section of the former President's memoirs which detail how he came to pardon the Watergate President.

738. _____. "Ford Says No Deals Made on Nixon Pardon." C.Q. Weekly Report, XXXII (1974), 2907-2909. Ford's statement on how the decision was made.

739. _____. "Ford's Own Story of the Nixon Pardon--'No Deals--Period': Statement." U.S. News and World Report, LXXVII (October 28, 1974), 20-21+. Same data as in the previous citation.

740. _____. "Ford's Testimony on the Nixon Pardon." In: Robert A. Diamond, ed. Historic Documents, 1974. Washington, D.C.: Congressional Quarterly, Inc., 1975, 887-900. Contains the same data as the last two entries on the President's testimony before the Criminal Justice Subcommittee of the House Judiciary Committee on October 17, 1974.

741. _____. "Nixon--'Has Suffered Enough.'" Time, CIV (September 16, 1974), 12-13. Details on the presidential pardon.

742. _____. "Pardon for Former President Nixon: The President's Remarks Announcing His Decision to Grant the Pardon, September 8, 1974." Weekly Compilation of Presidential Documents, X (September 16, 1974), 1102-1103. Text of the pardon and Ford's brief remarks.

743. _____. "The President Tells More About the Nixon Pardon." U.S. News and World Report, LXXVII (September 30, 1974), 19. Continues to insist no deals were made.

744. _____. "The President's News Conference of August 28, 1974." Weekly Compilation of Presidential Documents, X (September 2, 1974), 1069-1073. He answers questions relative to the pardon.

745. _____. Public Papers of the Presidents of the United States: Gerald R. Ford, Containing the Messages, Speeches, and Statements of the President, August 9, 1974-December 31, 1974. Washington, D.C.: Published for the Office of the Federal Register, U.S. National Archives and Records Service by the U.S. Government Printing Office, 1975. 841p. Contains Ford's official releases from the day he took over from Nixon through the pardon episode to the new year.

746. _____. "Swearing in of the President and the President's Remarks Following His Swearing in As the 38th President of the United States, August 9, 1974." Weekly Compilation of Presidential Documents, X (August 12, 1974), 1023-1025. Ford's brief call for national unity.

747. _____. A Time to Heal: An Autobiography. New York: Harper & Row, 1979. 384p. The former president's memoirs of his political career include a view of his selection as Agnew's successor and his elevation to the Oval Office upon the resignation of Richard Nixon. Considerable space is given to the question of Nixon's pardon and Ford forcefully sets out his reasons for taking the chance which cost him so much in the eyes of his fellow citizens at the polls in November 1976.

748. _____. "Vice-President Ford: 'Why I Will Not Run in '76.'" U.S. News and World Report, LXXV (December 17, 1973), 24-30. An interview in which he also discusses the handling of Watergate.

749. Ford, William D. and Daniel H. Pollitt. "Who Owns the Tapes?" North Carolina Central Law Journal, VI (Spring 1975), 197-203. Considers the legality of presidential papers ownership and the claims by former president Nixon that the tapes were a part of his personal papers as opposed to his public materials.

750. "Forgotten Cubans." Time, CII (September 24, 1973), 26. Considers the fate of the actual Watergate burglars.

751. "The Formal Charges Against President Nixon." U.S. News and World Report, LXXVII (August 12, 1977), 72-73. A review of the articles of impeachment voted by the House Committee on the Judiciary.

752. Foster, Leo. "Impeachment--The Doctrine of Separation of Powers: An Address to the Tallahassee Bar Association." Congressional Record, CXX (March 11, 1974), 6027-6029. Examines the impeachment concept and the role of the Congress in implementing it against an incumbent president.

753. "Four Key Convictions in the Watergate Affair." U.S. News and World Report, LXXVIII (January 13, 1975), 15-17. The jury finds Ehrlichman, Haldeman, Mitchell, and Mardian guilty in the Watergate coverup trial.

754. "Four Nixon Aides Found Guilty in Cover-up." C.Q. Weekly Report, XXXIII (January 4, 1975), 57-59. Same data as in the last entry.

755. "Four Walls Close in on Nixon: The Charles Colson Trial." Time, CIII (June 17, 1974), 13-15. After revealing events of the week, including Nixon's being named an unindicted co-conspirator, Colson's statement upon pleading guilty is printed.

756. Fowlkes, Diane L. "Realpolitik and Play Politics: The Effects of Watergate and Political Gaming on Undergraduate Students' Political Interest and Political Trust." Simulation and Games, VIII (December 1977), 419-438. Suggests the process a useful tool for instructors in political science.

757. Fox, Frank and Stephen Parker. "Why Nixon Did Himself In: A Behavioral Examination of His Need to Fail." New York, VI (September 9, 1974), 26-32. Argues without exactly saying so that the former president was something of a political masochist.

758. Frampton, George T., Jr. "Some Practical and Ethical Problems of Prosecuting Public Officials." Maryland Law Review, XXXVI (Spring 1976), 5-38. Includes references to both the cases of Richard Nixon and Spiro T. Agnew.

759. "Frank A. Sturgis." In: Eleanora W. Schoenebaum, ed. Political Profiles: The Nixon/Ford Years. New York: Facts on File, Inc., 1979. pp. 628-629. One of the Watergate burglars later convicted.

760. Frazier, Catherine S. "The Tragedy of Watergate." Mid-

west Quarterly, XV (October 1973), 8-15. Reviews the case and its influence on what the author sees to have been the greater accomplishments of the Nixon presidency.

761. Freeman, D. N. "Freedom of Speech Within the Nixon Administration." Communication Quarterly, XXIV (Winter 1976), 3-10. Examines its virtual non-existence.

762. Freeman, Richard B., ed. Watergate, the Unmaking of a President: Lexington, January 12-February 9, 1975. Lexington, Ky.: University of Kentucky Art Gallery, 1975. 96p. A catalog of an exhibition held at the UK art gallery, most of which is illustrated.

763. Freund, Paul A. "The Supreme Court, 1973 Term--Foreword: On Presidential Privilege." Harvard Law Review, LXXXVIII (Fall 1974), 13-39. Reviews the Supreme Court involvement in the argument of executive privilege in United States vs. Nixon; reprinted in Congressional Record, CXX (November 26, 1974), 37513-37520.

764. Friedman, Leon, ed. The Justices of the United States Supreme Court, Their Lives and Major Opinions, Vol. V: The Burger Court, 1969-1978. New York: Chelsea House, 1978. 510p. Biographical data as well as the facts related to various Nixon administration cases, especially United States v. Nixon.

765. _____. United States v. Nixon: The President Before the Supreme Court. New York: Chelsea House, 1974. 644p. Includes Judge Sirica's August 1973 opinion on the tapes, the September 1973 Court of Appeals findings, petitions and memos of opposing counsel to the court, both the Special Prosecutor's and President's main briefs in the case, supplemental briefs, the ACLU's amicus curia, transcripts of the oral arguments before the high court, and the unanimous ruling rendered by the Burger court.

766. Friedman, Roger. "Stampede." Nation, CCXVIII (May 4, 1974), 549-550. Concerns the White House transcripts.

767. Friedman, Saul. "[Lucien] Nedzi Spurs Probe of Watergate: Reprinted from the Detroit Free Press, May 24, 1974." Congressional Record, CXX (August 8, 1974), 27576. The role of the CIA in the case is sought by the chairman of the House Armed Services Committee's Subcommittee on Intelligence.

768. Friendly, Fred W. "Impeachment on TV--An Obligation to Communicate Directly: Reprinted from the Washington Post, May 4, 1974." Congressional Record, CXX (May 9, 1974), 13875. On the public's need and right to see the process live.

769. _____. "Paying the High Price of a President in an Isolation Booth." New York, VI (June 11, 1973), 61-64+. The televised Ervin panel hearings as noted by a distinguished figure in broadcasting.

770. Frohmayer, David B. "An Essay on Executive Privilege." In: Weaver Constitutional Law Series, no. 1 (Chicago: American Bar Association, 1974), pp. 1-17. Another review of the concept which argues that the president has no constitutional right to keep data from Congress; reprinted in the daily Congressional Record, CXX (April 30, 1974), S6603-S6607.

771. _____. "The Separation of Powers: An Essay on the Vitality of a Constitutional Idea." Oregon Law Review, LII (Spring 1973), 211-235. A review of the growing constitutional issue over the allocation between the legislative and executive branches of the vast array of Federal power; Section III:B deals with the question of executive privilege in disputes between the two branches.

772. "From the Summit to the Moment of Truth?" Newsweek, LXXXII (July 2, 1973), 12-16. Previews John Dean's possible testimony and administration efforts to discredit it in advance.

773. Frost, David. "How Frost Made Nixon Sweat." Esquire, LXXXIX (March 1, 1978), 82-88+. In which the author reveals the manner in which his questions were researched and posed so as to get the maximum response from the former President during the televised interviews.

774. _____. "I Gave Them a Sword": Behind the Scenes of the Nixon Interviews. New York: William Morrow, 1978. 320p. The first part of the volume is built around the business arrangements necessary for the Englishman to get the former President to agree to the videotaped interviews; the larger part, however, is devoted to the author's recollections of his strategies, questions, and conduct of the interviews. Much of the material is culled from the 28 hours of video-taped interviews and for those who did not watch them, the material presented on Watergate, including Nixon's admission that he had let down the American people, is significant. At this point in time, however, readers would have found verbatim transcripts of material more valuable than the many recapitulations.

775. _____. "Interview." Playboy, XXV (April 1978), 67+. Contains much of the information presented in the previous citation, only in question-and-answer form.

776. Fry, Brian R. "The Nixon Impeachment Vote: A Speculative Analysis." Presidential Studies Quarterly, XI (Summer

1981), 387-394. A review of the House Judiciary Committee proceedings wondering if the articles would have been accepted by the full house or the president convicted by a Senate trial.

777. "Frying Fish with the Folks at Home." Time, CII (August 27, 1973), 16-18. Concerns the constituent reaction to members of the Ervin panel as well as witty sayings of the committee's Chairman.

778. Fuller, Jack. "The Short, Sensational Law Career of Jill Volner." Chicago Tribune Magazine (January 15, 1978), 28-29. A member of the Special Prosecutor's staff.

779. "Furor over Watergate Leaks." U.S. News and World Report, LXXVII (July 1, 1974), 22+. Coming out of the House Judiciary Committee.

780. "Further Notes on Nixon's Downfall." Time, CVII (April 5, 1976), 26-28.

781. "Further Tales from the Transcripts: Excerpts." Time, CIII (May 20, 1974), 29-32. Additional excerpts from the White House transcripts.

782. "The Fuse Burns Ever Closer: Admission of Guilt by Egil Krogh." Time, CII (December 10, 1973), 24. Krogh's conviction in the Fielding break-in and the indictment of Dwight Chapin.

783. "G. Gordon Liddy." In: Current Biography Yearbook 1980. New York: H. W. Wilson, 1981. pp. 225-228.

784. _____. In: Eleanora W. Schoenebaum, ed. Political Profiles: The Nixon/Ford Years. New York: Facts on File, Inc., 1979. pp. 376-377. The last two entries are brief biographies of the Watergate man who refused to talk before any court or committee.

785. Galbraith, John K. "John Dean, Ambition, and the White House." In: his Annals of an Abiding Liberal. Edited by Andrea D. Williams. Boston: Houghton, Mifflin, 1979. pp. 341-345. Dean is seen as a victim and tool in the power-lust of the Nixon administration.

786. "Gallery of the Guilty." Time, CV (January 13, 1975), 10-11. Profiles of those convicted in the Watergate cover-up trial.

787. Galloway, George B. History of the House of Representatives. 2nd ed., rev. by Sidney Wise. New York: T. Y. Crowell, 1976. An institutional history from 1787-1975, with much of the final section devoted to the question of Nixon's impeachment.

788. Gallup, George. "The Gallup Poll--Nixon Failing to Recover Popularity: Reprinted from the Washington Post, October 4, 1973." Congressional Record, CXIX (October 4, 1973), 33096-33097. Public opinion in the wake of the Ervin panel hearings.

789. Gans, Herbert J. Deciding What's News: A Study of the CBS Evening News, NBC Nightly News, Newsweek and Time. New York: Pantheon, 1979. 393p. Reminiscent of Halberstam's study (q.v.), this work provides details on how these various media reported and responded to the crisis of Watergate.

790. Garrett, James B. and Benjamin Wallace. "Cognitive Consistency, Repression-Sensitization, and Level of Moral Judgement: Reactions of College Students to the Watergate Scandal." Journal of Social Psychology, XCVIII (February 1976), 69-76. Reviews the reactions of certain tested underclassmen to the facts and perceptions of Watergate.

791. Gartner, Alan. What Nixon Is Doing to Us. New York: Harper & Row, 1973. 258p. A polemic which reviews the ills of the Nixon administration, both with regard to Watergate and other issues.

792. Gates, Gary P. Air Time: The Inside Story of CBS News. New York: Harper & Row, 1978. 440p. An institutional history with much on the network's Watergate coverage; compare with Halberstam below.

793. Genovese, Michael A. "The Supreme Court As a Check on Presidential Power." Presidential Studies Quarterly, VI (Winter-Spring 1976), 40-44. A brief review with emphasis on United States v. Nixon.

794. Gesell, Gerhard A. "Court Rejection of 'National Security' Defense: Excerpts from U.S. District Court Judge Gerhard A. Gesell's Opinion Rejecting the Rationale of 'National Security' as a Defense in the Case Involving the Break-in at the Office of Daniel Ellsberg's Psychiatrist, May 24, 1974." In: Robert A. Diamond, ed. Historic Documents, 1974. Washington, D.C.: Congressional Quarterly, Inc., 1975. pp. 411-418. A rejection of the Ehrlichman thesis that the "plumbers'" assignment was one undertaken for the national good.

795. Getlein, Frank. "The Entertainers." Commonweal, CIV (March 18, 1977), 164-166. Finds little of value in the Nixon-Frost interviews.

796. "Getting the Watergate Story Out." Newsweek, LXXXIV (September 23, 1974), 39+. Reviews the number of "instant" paperback titles on the topic.

797. "Giving the American Way: Secret List of Nixon Contributors." Time, CII (July 16, 1973), 10. Those who gave legally and illegally to the 1972 campaign.

798. Glass, Andrew J. "Impeachment Maneuvers." New Leader, LVII (February 4, 1974), 3-4. By both the White House and the House Judiciary Committee.

799. _____. "Watergate Diminishes Nixon's Leverage, Forces a Series of Legislative Compromises." National Journal, V (1973), 1049-1056. The effect of the scandal on Nixon's program in Congress.

800. _____. "Watergate Splinters Republicans As Influence of President Nixon Declines." National Journal, V (1973), 1717-1721. A look at the break-down of GOP party loyalty in Congress.

801. _____ and S. L. Harrison. "House Establishes Procedures to Handle Moves to Impeach the President." National Journal, V (October 27, 1973), 1616-1620. Turns the matter over to Rodino's Judiciary Committee.

802. Goldberg, Arthur. "The Question of Impeachment." Hastings Constitutional Law Quarterly, I (1974), 5+. Views on the process by a former Supreme Court justice.

803. Goldman, Peter. "Breach of Faith." Newsweek, LXXXV (May 12, 1975), 53-54. A review of Theodore H. White's (q.v.) thoughts on the Nixon affair.

804. _____. "Haldeman Speaks Out." Newsweek, XCI (February 27, 1978), 29-31. Highlights from the memoirs of the former White House chief-of-staff.

805. _____. "Nixon on His Fall." Newsweek, LXXXIX (June 6, 1977), 28+. As recorded in his interview with David Frost.

806. _____. "The President's Palace Guard." Newsweek, LXXXI (March 19, 1973), 24-28. A look at White House aides Haldeman, Ehrlichman, and Dean.

807. _____. "Richard Nixon's Final Days." Newsweek, LXXXVII (April 5, 1976), 25-26+. A look at the tormented last week of Nixon's presidency.

808. _____. "Was Justice Finally Done?" Newsweek, LXXXV (January 13, 1975), 19-20+. On the outcome of the Watergate cover-up trial.

809. Goldwater, Barry. "Barry Goldwater Speaks His Mind on Richard Nixon: An Interview." U.S. News and World Report, LXXVI (February 11, 1974), 38-42. In which the

Arizona Republican Senator suggests that Nixon might want to resign rather than face certain impeachment.

810. _____. With No Apologies: The Personal and Political Memoirs of a United States Senator. New York: William Morrow, 1979. 320p. Goldwater's recollections include his views on the Watergate crisis and his visit, together with Senator Scott and Congressman Rhodes, to President Nixon in an effort to get him to resign.

811. Goodwin, Richard N. "Presidential Power and the Rule of Law: Reprinted from the Los Angeles Times, March 31, 1974." Congressional Record, CXX (April 2, 1974), 9225-9227. Contends that the former is not above the latter.

812. _____. "A Time for Clipping White House Wings: Reprinted from the Washington Post, March 19, 1974." Congressional Record, CXX (March 20, 1974), 7423-7425. Contains essentially the same sentiments as the last entry.

813. Gordon, Slade. "Reflections on an Inoperative Administration: An Address to the Seattle Rotary Club, March 20, 1974." Congressional Record, CXX (April 1, 1974), 9091-9093. Contends government in Washington has all but broken down; the speaker was Attorney General of Washington State.

814. Gotbaum, Victor. "One Vote Against Mr. Nixon's Resignation." Congressional Record, CXX (April 1, 1974), 9107. Views of a labor leader.

815. Gouran, Denis S. "The Watergate Cover-up: Its Dynamics and Its Implications." Communication Monographs, XLIII (August 1976), 176-186. Looks at the way in which the tangled web was woven.

816. Graham, Katherine. "The Activism of the Press." Nieman Reports, XXVIII (Spring-Summer 1974), 21-25. On the value of investigative reporting by the owner of the Washington Post.

817. Graham, John. "Mr. Jaworski Presses On." New Statesman and Nation, LXXXVII (February 8, 1974), 174-175. A British view of the Special Prosecutor's pursuit of evidence.

818. _____. "The Net Closes on Nixon." New Statesman and Nation, LXXXVII (March 8, 1974), 313-314. A review of new evidence in the case since the first of the year.

819. _____. "Nixon Runs out of Friends." New Statesman and Nation, LXXXVII (April 26, 1974), 567-568. On the loss of presidential support from key senators like Goldwater and Buckley.

820. Granberg, Donald. "An Analysis of the House Judiciary Committee's Recommendation to Impeach Richard Nixon." Political Psychology, II (Fall Winter 1980), 50-65. Examines the psychology of the moment during the incredible amount of behind-the-scenes politicking on the committee.

821. "The Grassroots of Impeachment: Reprinted from the Chula Vista [California] Star-News." Congressional Record, CXX (February 6, 1974), 2456-2457. Public opinion on the case in Chula Vista.

822. Gray, L. Patrick, 3rd. "The FBI Gets a 'New Look': An Interview with the Acting Director." U.S. News and World Report, LXXIII (July 10, 1972), 58-62. The man who would not be confirmed suggests ways in which he would like to see Hoover's organization changed.

823. "Gray Clouds." New Republic, CLVIII (March 24, 1973), 7-8. Confirmation problems of the Acting FBI Director.

824. "Gray Goes." Time, CI (April 16, 1973), 16. The President's withdrawal of Gray's nomination.

825. "Gray on the Griddle." Newsweek, LXXXI (March 12, 1973), 21-22. His troubled confirmation hearings.

826. Grayson, Carl T., Jr. and Susan Lukowski, eds. The Impeachment Congress, 93rd U.S. Congress, 1974. Washington, D.C.: Potomac Books, 1974. 29p. A paperback pamphlet providing information on members and various committees.

827. "The Great Tapes Crisis: The Firing of Archibald Cox." Newsweek, LXXXII (October 29, 1973), 22-30. Recounts events prior to and during the "Saturday Night Massacre" as well as Cox's refusal of a proposed compromise to have Senator John Stennis audit the tapes.

828. Greene, Bob. Running: Nixon-McGovern. Chicago: Regnery, 1973. 267p. One reporter's recollections of the 1972 presidential campaign out "on the hustings"; reports many of the events which during the Ervin Committee hearings would come to be known as campaign "dirty tricks."

829. Greene, Jerry. "Capitol Stuff: Reprinted from the New York Daily News, July 2, 1974." Congressional Record, CXX (July 9, 1974), 22482-22483. Commentary on the alleged anti-Nixon bias of the House Judiciary Committee.

830. Greene, R.S. "The Balance of Power, the Impeachment Powers, and the Supreme Power of Congress." Federal Communications Bar Journal, XXXIV (1975), 42-53. Congress should not refuse to use its power when necessary, as in Nixon's case.

831. Gregor, William J. "The Avoidable Institutional Crisis." Congressional Record, CXX (June 4, 1974), 17597-17598. Supports Nixon's refusal of various Watergate-related subpoenas.

832. Griffith, Thomas. "Must Mr. Nixon's Hard-Core Supporters Be Satisfied?: A Time Essay." Time, CIV (August 12, 1974), 23-25. On providing irrefutable evidence of Nixon wrongdoing.

833. _____. "Proper Grounds for Impeachment." Time, CIII (February 25, 1974), 23-24. Questions many of the grounds then being advanced.

834. _____. "Putting Politics in Its Place at the Justice Department." Esquire, LXXXVIII (October 1973), 160-163+. Calls for an end to the political use of the Justice Department and the FBI.

835. Griffiths, D. "Watergate Pair: Woodward and Bernstein." Editor and Publisher, CVI (April 28, 1973), 12-13. A brief profile of the Washington Post reporters.

836. Gross, Martin L. "Conversation with an Author: John Ehrlichman." Book Digest, III (September 1976), 19+. Following the publication of his first novel, Ehrlichman answers a number of questions, several relating to Watergate.

837. Grossberger, Lewis. "Columbia University Law Students Urge Impeachment, Quietly: Reprinted from the New York Post, October 30, 1973." Congressional Record, CXIX (October 30, 1973), 35519-35520. Students express the hope that an impeachment can be handled without it becoming a national crisis.

838. Grossman, Michael B. and Martha J. Kumar. Portraying the President: The White House and the News Media. Baltimore, Md.: Johns Hopkins University Press, 1981. 358p. Covers all presidents since Hoover; the section on Watergate covers the Nixon-press feud and the negative fashion in which both attempted to use the other.

839. _____. "The Refracting Lens: The President As He Appears Through the Media." In: Harold C. Relyea, ed. The Presidency and Information Policy. New York: Center for the Study of the Presidency, 1981. pp. 102-138. A capsulized version of the previous citation.

840. _____. "The White House and the News Media: The Phases of Their Relationship." Political Science Quarterly, XCIV (Spring 1979), 37-53. All modern presidents have had a honeymoon followed by intense questioning, to which some have responded better than others.

841. Grossman, Ronald. "Watergate on Main Street: Reprinted from the Chicago Tribune, July 25, 1973." Congressional Record, CXIX (July 25, 1973), 26028. Public opinion on the case was mixed, but not yet entirely negative.

842. Guerra, David M. "Network Television News Policy and the Nixon Administration: A Comparison." Unpublished Ph.D. Dissertation, New York University, 1974. Suggests that a feud existed between the two and that the networks often set their policies in reaction to the offensive conducted by Nixon, Agnew, Buchanan, and other White House spokesmen who attempted to point out TV bias.

843. "Guerrilla Warfare at Credibility Gap." Time, CII (July 2, 1973), 12-16. An examination of the possible effect of Dean's testimony.

844. Guido, Kenneth J., Jr. The Right of the House Judiciary Committee to All Presidential Documents It Deems Necessary for Its Impeachment Inquiry. Samuel Pool Weaver Constitutional Law Series, no. 1. Washington, D.C.: Common Cause, 1974. 34p. Rejects out of hand Nixon arguments on executive privilege.

845. Gulley, Bill. Breaking Cover. New York: Simon and Schuster, 1980. 288p. A member of the staff of the White House Military Office, Gulley recalls incidents during his service from Johnson to Carter; extremely critical of H.R. Haldeman and Alexander Haig.

846. Gunther, Gerald. "Judicial Hegemony and Legislative Autonomy: The Nixon Case and the Impeachment Process." UCLA Law Review, XXII (October 1974), 30-39. Contends that the Supreme Court case of United States v. Nixon tended to overshadow the importance of the Congressional impeachment process.

847. Gurney, Edward. "Senator Contends Media Has Turned United States Against Nixon: Reprinted from the Sarasota [Florida] Herald-Tribune, April 18, 1974." Congressional Record, CXX (April 30, 1974), 12327. Gurney, a Florida conservative, supported Nixon.

848. Gysling, Erich. "America's Urge for Self-Destruction: Reprinted from Die Weltwoche, June 19, 1974." Congressional Record, CXX (August 1, 1974), 6283-6285. A Swiss view of the Watergate affair.

849. "H. R. Haldeman." In: Eleanora W. Schoenebaum, ed. Political Profiles: The Nixon/Ford Years. New York: Facts on File, Inc., 1979. pp. 261-267. A brief biography of Nixon's first White House chief of staff.

850. Hager, [unknown]. "The Constitution, the Court, and the Cover-up: Reflections on United States v. Nixon." Oklahoma Law Review, XXIX (1976), 591+. Unavailable for review.

851. Haig, Alexander M., Jr. "Amid Turmoil--A Look Inside the White House: An Interview." U.S. News and World Report, LXXVI (June 3, 1974), 19-20. Despite the difficulties of Watergate, the White House and its staff functions as well as a highly-oiled machine.

852. _____. "Events That Led to 'the Firestorm': Excerpts from News Conference, October 23, 1973." U.S. News and World Report, LXXV (November 5, 1973), 66-69. In which the White House chief of staff outlines the administration's reasons for dismissing Archibald Cox.

853. _____ and Charles Alan Wright. "News Conference on the President's Decision to Comply with Court Order Requiring Production of the Tapes, October 23, 1973." Weekly Compilation of Presidential Documents, IX (October 29, 1973), 1275-1283. Given on the Monday following the "Saturday Night Massacre."

854. Halberstam, David. The Powers That Be. New York: Alfred A. Knopf, 1979. 771p. A massive history of Time, Inc., CBS, the Washington Post, and the Los Angeles Times. Halberstam is especially good at describing the concern, competition, and support of the various media in the grand pursuit of the Watergate story. The names are all here: Woodward and Bernstein, Dan Rather and Daniel Schorr, Hugh Sidey, Sy Hersh of the New York Times, Jack Anderson, the media executives and editors who guided or permitted the story to unfold, and the Nixon White House and "palace guard" working to halt the bad news. A valuable source.

855. _____. "Presidential Video." Esquire, LXXV (June 1976), 94-97+. CBS's treatment of presidents, especially Richard M. Nixon.

856. _____. "The Press and Prejudice: The White House Press Corps Relations with Richard M. Nixon, Lyndon B. Johnson, and John F. Kennedy." Esquire, LXXXI (April 1974), 109-114+. While all modern presidents have had some pressmen and accounts which they disliked, Halberstam lists those since Eisenhower and before Ford in the order in which they had difficulty with the media.

857. _____. "Watergate and the System." New Statesman and Nation, LXXXV (May 25, 1973), 757-759. A look at the U.S. political system for British readers expressing hope

that the Ervin panel hearings will begin to right what many perceived as an unbalance between Congress and the White House.

858. Haldeman, H. R., with Joseph DiMona. The Ends of Power. New York: Times Books, 1977. 326p. General Haig's predecessor as White House chief of staff here presents his Watergate memoirs and one of the most interesting of theses: the Democrats and the CIA knew about the burglary in advance and arranged for it to fail. Although the author admits there was a lot of wrongdoing in the affair, his major concern continues to be that the cover-up fell apart because of weaknesses on the part of his "palace guard" colleagues and the ruthless, unethical work of the press. This is not a repentant tome, but one useful for demonstrating the lack of morals and ethics which pervaded some quarters of the Nixon White House. Reviewers generally wrote the book off as "sour grapes" which laid the blame on others; Haldeman's former aides and allies, after taking the heat in his book, naturally condemned it, with Charles Colson being perhaps the most generous in his April 14, 1978 National Review comments: "I am saddened by Bob's book ... it is, in fact, more significant for what it does not say than for what it does."

859. "Haldeman Variations." Newsweek, LXXXII (August 13, 1973), 19-23. A review of Haldeman's testimony before the Ervin panel.

860. Hallett, David. "A Low-Level Memoir of the Nixon White House." New York Times Magazine (October 20, 1974), 39-42+. Recollections of the "palace guard" by a former member of Colson's staff; useful for atmosphere, but as the author was not one of those deeply caught up in Watergate, not overly significant for students of the case.

861. Halperin, Morton H. "Did Richard Helms Commit Perjury." New Republic, CLXXIV (March 6, 1976), 14-17. A review of Helm's role with the CIA and his testimony before Congress.

862. _____. Top Secret: National Security and the Right to Know. New York: Simon and Schuster, 1977. 158p. A study of the executive practice of labelling matters secret, whether they are or not, and withholding information both from Congress and the American people.

863. Halpern, Paul J., ed. Why Watergate? Pacific Palisades, Calif.: Palisades Publishing Co., 1975. 233p. An anthology containing brief items on the crisis as well as the presidency in general.

864. Hamby, Alonzo and Edward Weldon, eds. Access to the Pa-

pers of Recent Public Figures: The New Harmony Conference. Bloomington, IN: Organization of American Historians, 1977. 107p. For our purposes, the most enlightening pieces concern the plight of historians and political scientists seeking access to the Watergate materials held by the National Archives.

865. Hamill, Pete. "Treason, etc.: Reprinted from the New York Post, June 24, 1974." Congressional Record, CXX (July 1, 1974), 21986. A quick review of the evidence gathered for impeachment by the staff of the House Judiciary Committee.

866. Hamilton, James. The Power to Probe: A Study of Congressional Investigations. New York: Random House, 1976. 333p. The Assistant Chief Counsel to the Ervin Committee documents a list of congressional investigations, citing the rights and responsibilities of individuals and the legislative and executive branches of government; naturally, many examples are drawn from the Ervin panel's Watergate hearings as well as those of the House Judiciary Committee involving impeachment.

867. Hampton, Lewis H. "Temptation of a Sacred Cow." Harper's, CCLVII (August 1973), 43-46+. Fears press triumph in Watergate will lead to renewed pressure for shield laws.

868. "Handing the Ball to Bill Saxbe: The New Attorney General." Time, CII (November 12, 1973), 37+. A profile of the Ohio Republican Senator chosen by Nixon to succeed Elliot Richardson in the wake of the Saturday Night Massacre; highlights Saxbe's reputation as a maverick.

869. Hannah, Norman B. "Nixon + Watergate = Communist Indochina." National Review, XXX (June 23, 1978), 772-775. Argues that the Watergate case so debilitated Nixon's hand that Hanoi had an easy time preparing for the takeover of South Vietnam.

870. Hargrove, Erwin C. The Power of the Modern Presidency. Philadelphia, Pa.: Temple University Press, 1974. 353p. The author identifies the crises of the modern presidency while describing the impact of personality and institutionalized trappings on the office; offers a set of prescriptions for limiting executive power in the wake of Watergate.

871. Harrell, Jackson, B. L. Ware, and Wil A. Linkugel. "The Failure of Apology in American Politics: Nixon on Watergate." Speech Monographs, XLII (November 1975), 245-261. Reviews the former president's "I am not a crook" stance throughout and after the Watergate crisis and suggests that, had he been able to admit his mistakes while in office, he might not have been forced to resign.

872. Harris, I. D. "The Psychologies of Presidents." History of Childhood Quarterly, III (Winter 1976), 337-350. An attempt at "a theoretical framework" for understanding presidents using the idea of two psychological types (adult-civilized and peer-civilized) arising out of early childhood. Influenced by older siblings, Richard Nixon "can be regarded as having been peer-civilized."

873. Harris, Richard. "The President and the Press." New Yorker, XLIX (October 1, 1973), 122-128. Reviews Nixon's long-running feud with the press and the status of the battle in the light of Watergate.

874. _____. "Reflections: The Watergate Prosecutions." New Yorker, L (June 10, 1974), 46-63. Argues that some legal practices such as plea bargaining employed to bring Watergate defendants to justice have, in fact, subverted the American system of justice.

875. Harrison, John M. and Harry H. Stein, eds. Muckraking: Past, Present, and Future. State College, Pa.: Pennsylvania State University Press, 1973. 165p. A review of investigative journalism with some comments near the end on the role of certain journalists in the scandals of ITT and Watergate.

876. Hart, J. B. "People on the Cover: Maureen Dean." Redbook, CXLV (October 1975), 2+. A brief biography of John Dean's wife.

877. Harward, Donald W., ed. Crisis in Confidence: The Impact of Watergate. Boston: Little, Brown, 1974. 200p. The texts of sixteen lectures in the Crisis of Confidence series delivered at the University of Delaware in late 1973-early 1974; personal musings and reflections on the possible end of the affair and its significance are provided by personalities as diverse as socialist Michael Harrington, conservative columnist James J. Kilpatrick, Senators Sam Ervin, Edward W. Brooke, Frank Church, and Edmund S. Muskie, Rep. Philip M. Crane, reporters and columnists Carl Rowan, Shana Alexander, Daniel Schorr, Richard J. Barnet, and Tom Wicker, historian James MacGregor Burns, former Attorney General Ramsey Clark, and theorists Gabriel Kolko and Daniel Ellsberg. All agree in optimistic tones that such evils as incursions on individual rights, freedom of the press, poor public morality, secrecy, and leaks can be overcome, but no concrete proposals are provided.

878. "Has President Nixon Extended the Doctrine of Executive Privilege Too Far?: Pro and Con." C.Q. Weekly Report, XXXI (April 14, 1973), 864-865. An early example of the kind of debate which would culminate in United States v. Nixon in late spring 1974.

879. Hays, Brooks. "The Moral Implications of Watergate: An Address to the Southern Baptist Convention, Washington, D.C., June 26, 1973." Congressional Record, CXIX (July 17, 1973), 24276-24277. Public ethics were not all that they should be.

880. Head, Simon. "The Pardoner's Tale." New Statesman and Nation, LXXXVIII (September 13, 1974), 335-336. A review of Ford's pardon of Richard Nixon.

881. "Heading Closer to Impeachment." Time, CIII (March 4, 1974), 15-16+. The work of the House Judiciary Committee and the many problems facing the president.

882. "Hearings Resume, Shakily." Time, CII (October 8, 1973), 26+. On the resumption of the Ervin Committee investigation.

883. "Hearings Under Cover." Newsweek, LXXXI (June 4, 1973), 26-28. Ervin panel testimony of Ulasewicz, McCord, Barker, and Alfred Baldwin.

884. Hearst, William Randolph, Jr. "A Facing of Facts: Reprinted from the Hearst Newspapers, May 5, 1974." Congressional Record, CXX (May 7, 1974), 13588-13589. A conservative publisher comes to favor Nixon's impeachment.

885. Henkin, Louis. "Executive Privilege: Mr. Nixon Loses, but the Presidency Largely Prevails." UCLA Law Review, XXII (October 1974), 40-46. United States v. Nixon is seen to have been politically important in helping to resolve the Watergate case, but the author finds its constitutional significance "less obvious."

886. "Henry E. Petersen." In: Eleanora W. Schoenebaum, ed. Political Profiles: The Nixon/Ford Years. New York: Facts on File, Inc., 1979. pp. 493-494. A brief biography of the assistant Attorney General who headed the Justice Department's Watergate inquiry.

887. Hentoff, Nat. "The Real Legacy of Richard Nixon." Penthouse, X (March 1979), 106-107. Unavailable for review.

888. _____. "Woodward, Bernstein, and 'All the President's Men': Lingering Questions." Columbia Journalism Review, VIII (July-August 1974), 10-15. Questions the accuracy of some of the Post reporter's methods and statements.

889. Herbers, John. No Thank You, Mr. President. New York: W. W. Norton, 1976. 192p. A very readable account by the New York Times' White House correspondent during the last days of Watergate which assesses the flaws of the office and the press. The author scores the excesses of

White House operations (e.g., expensive weekend trips), the intense cloak of secrecy surrounding every aspect of the Nixon administration, the president's and Ron Ziegler's contempt for the press, which Herbers finds both the creator and victim of the over-aggrandized presidency. Filled with anecdotes, the reporter never lets his audience forget that being a White House correspondent is mostly dull work, even during a crisis.

890. _____. "White House Yields Data Subpoenaed by Jaworski in Political Gift Inquiry: Reprinted from the New York Times, March 30, 1974." In: Book IX, Part II of U.S. Congress, House, Committee on the Judiciary. Statement of Information: Hearings. 93rd Cong., 2nd sess. Washington, D.C.: U.S. Government Printing Office, 1974. pp. 971-972. How the Special Prosecutor obtained needed documents on ITT and other illegal contributions.

891. "A Hero Steps Down." Time, CII (December 31, 1973), 13-14. Senator Ervin finishes his hearings.

892. Herschensohn, Bruce. The Gods of Antenna. New Rochelle, N.Y.: Arlington House, 1976. 155p. Written by a deputy special assistant to President Nixon, this slim volume identifies a variety of methods, with some Watergate examples, whereby network news can be presented to accomplish planned results.

893. Hersh, Seymour M. "[General Robert E.] Cushman Okayed CIA Aid to Hunt: Reprinted from the New York Times, May 9, 1973." Congressional Record, CXIX (May 9, 1973), 15084-15085. The Marine Corps general was deputy CIA director at the time.

894. _____. "Kissinger and Nixon in the White House." Atlantic, CCXLIX (May 1982), 35-53+. Reveals the close alliance between the two men, the former's role in bugging his subordinates, and the illegal war run by the two men in Cambodia.

895. Hershey, M. R. "Watergate and Preadults: Attitudes Toward the President." American Journal of Political Science, XIX (November 1975), 703-726. Examines the effect of the crisis on children's attitudes toward political leadership.

896. Hess, Stephen. "Richard Nixon's White House." Present Tense, III (Autumn 1975), 71-74. Intensely secret and largely run by a huge staff.

897. Hickey, Neil. "Should Impeachment Be Televised?" TV Guide, XXII (June 1, 1974), A3-A6. Discusses the arguments on both sides.

898. Higgins, George V. "In Defense of a Prosecutor: Reprinted from the Boston Sunday Globe, March 24, 1974." In: U.S. Congress, Senate, Committee on the Judiciary. Nomination of Earl J. Silbert to Be United States Attorney: Hearings. 93rd Cong., 2nd sess. Washington, D.C.: U.S. Government Printing Office, 1974. pp. 107-109. On Silbert's original work as the Justice Department prosecutor.

899. _____. The Friends of Richard Nixon. Boston: Little, Brown, 1975. 295p. A study of the affair that attempts to reconstruct events from the perspective of Prosecutor Earl Silbert, principal cover-up specialist John Dean, and Special Prosecutor Henry Ruth. The author, a former U.S. Attorney, has filled his book with seemingly illogical heroes and villains: Henry Peterson is seen as stupid, Richard Kleindienst, an admitted perjurer, is defended, and Sam Dash was inept. The only real heroes are the prosecutors Doar, Jim Neal, and Ruth. The entire case is seen as a criminal conspiracy dealt with by criminal procedures, a narrow prism which does not reflect the roles of larger interests such as public opinion, the press, and national ethics.

900. _____. Atlantic, CCXXXIV (November 1974), 41-52. A more compact version of the previous entry.

901. _____. "The Judge Who Tried Harder." Atlantic, CCXXXIII (April 1974), 83-92+. The Watergate efforts of Judge John J. Sirica.

902. "High Noon at the Hearings." Time, CI (June 25, 1973), 9-14. Recaps the testimony of Jeb Magruder and Maurice Stans and previews the upcoming testimony of John Dean.

903. "The High Price of Just Going Along." Time, CI (May 7, 1973), 18-19. The troubles of Jeb Magruder.

904. "The High Price of Security." Newsweek, LXXXI (May 28, 1973), 33-40. FBI/CIA wiretaps of those suspected of "leaking" administration data.

905. "Highlights of the Nixon Presidency, 1969-1974." C.Q. Weekly Report, XXXII (1974), 2092-2118. Reviews the successes as well as the Watergate failure.

906. Hilts, Philip J. "CBS: The Fiefdom and the Power in Washington." Washington Post Potomac (April 21, 1974), 8+. Examines the leading position of this network's news bureau with some attention to its correspondents, e.g., Rather.

907. "Hindsight Saga." Newsweek, LXXXII (July 30, 1973), 18-20.

Reviews a week of Ervin panel testimony from John Mitchell and Robert Mardian.

908. Hirschfield, Robert S., ed. The Power of the Presidency: Concepts and Controversy. 3rd ed. Hawthorne, N.Y.: Aldine Publishing Company, 1982. 502p. Views the subject from the perspective of the Constitution, the courts, the presidents, and academic experts and contains texts of documents, judicial decisions, and professional analysis of the problem of defining the limits of presidential power. Examples with regards to the Nixon administration include Watergate.

909. Hirshberg, Jack. "The Day the Sundance Kid Brought Washington to Its Knees." Los Angeles, XXI (April 1976), 98-100, 171-176. Concerns John Dean's testimony before the Ervin Committee.

910. "Historic Coverage for Historic Events." Broadcasting, LXXXVII (July 29, 1974), 29-30. Network plans to cover impeachment.

911. "Historic Debate Before the Supreme Court--The Watergate Tapes Case: Excerpts from the Transcript, July 8, 1974." U.S. News and World Report, LXXVII (July 22, 1974), 72-75. United States v. Nixon.

912. "Historic Legal Step: The Charges Against Mitchell and Stans." U.S. News and World Report, LXXIV (May 21, 1973), 26. Charges for their role in obtaining illegal campaign contributions.

913. Hoar, William P. "Presidential Atrocities." American Opinion, XX (September 1977), 11-16, 99, 101, 103, 105, 107-108. Unavailable for review.

914. Hofstetter, Richard C. Bias in the News: Network Television Coverage of the 1972 Election Campaign. Columbus: Ohio State University Press, 1976. 213p. An extraordinary attempt to monitor the more than 4,000 campaign stories broadcast on the network evening news shows between July 10 and November 6, 1972, using advanced techniques of social-scientific analysis in an effort to uncover bias for or against various candidates; makes limited reference to the seeming lack of impact Watergate had on public opinion.

915. Hogan, Lawrence J. "The Impeachment Inquiry of 1974: A Personal View." Georgetown Law Journal, LXIII (1975), 1051+. Thoughts of a Maryland GOP Congressman who voted for the impeachment articles.

916. "Holes in the Story." New Republic, CLXX (May 11, 1974), 5-8. Comments on the White House transcripts.

917. "Holiday Test for the President." Time, CII (December 24, 1973), 9-10. Experts look into the 18-minute tape gap.

918. Holtzman, Elizabeth. "Memorandum Analyzing the Testimony of President Ford Before the Subcommittee on Criminal Justice of the House Judiciary Committee." Congressional Record, CXXII (September 30, 1976), 34286-34287. The Democratic New York Congresswoman did not believe Ford's pardon story.

919. "Honorable Men, All." New Republic, LXVIII (June 23, 1973), 6-7. Comments on Ervin panel handling of Maurice Stans.

920. "Honors and Credits." Nation, CCXVI (January 29, 1973), 132-133. CREEP political sabotage by Brigham Young student Thomas Gregory.

921. Horn, David E. "Who Owns Our History?" Library Journal, C (April 1, 1975), 635-639. Objects to National Archives restrictions on the Nixon tapes.

922. Horowitz, Irving L. "The Europeanization of American Politics: Watergate Retrospective." Commonweal, C (April 5, 1974), 103-106. The role of Congress in the affair came to resemble a parliamentary vote of no confidence; reprinted in Current, CLXII (May 1974), 3-9, under the title "Watergate and American Politics."

923. ———. "What the Tapes Really Reveal." Nation, CCXXIV (June 18, 1977), 751-754. Opinions expressed in Nixon's first interview with David Frost.

924. Horsey, R. Kent. Highlights of the Watergate Tapes. Salt Lake City, UT: Hawkes Publications, 1974. Unpaged. Excerpts from the White House transcripts.

925. "Hot on the Trail of Political Cash." Quill, LXII (June 1974), 26. A profile of reporter Jim Polk.

926. Hougan, Jim. "The McCord File." Harper's, CCLX (January 1980), 37-46+. Examines the career of Watergate burglar James McCord, including his famous letter from jail to Judge Sirica.

927. "House Accepts Impeachment Report 412-3." C.Q. Weekly Report, XXXII (August 24, 1974), 2284-2285. On the full House vote to accept the report for the record despite Nixon's resignation.

928. "House Judiciary Approves Ford." C.Q. Weekly Report, XXXI (1973), 3143. As Ford does not directly figure in the Watergate case and after becoming VEEP largely distanced himself from the White House, few citations to his activities are included here.

929. "House Judiciary Committee Impeachment Inquiry: Brief Submitted to the Committee by the Office of the Special Counsel to the President, Dated July 19, 1974, Released July 20, 1974." Weekly Compilation of Presidential Documents, X (July 29, 1974), 840-993. James D. St. Clair's contention that no solid evidence exists against the President.

930. "House Study Sets Broad Grounds for Impeachment." U.S. News and World Report, LXXVI (March 4, 1974), 25-26. The Judiciary Committee report which said a president's impeachable crimes need not be indictable in a court of law.

931. "How Attorneys Judge the Ervin Hearings." Time, CII (July 30, 1973), 44. The senators have been too soft, says a consensus of those interviewed.

932. "How Credible Was John Dean?" Newsweek, LXXXIII (May 13, 1974), 30-31. Despite White House attempts to discredit it, Dean's testimony, on the basis of the transcripts, emerges as fairly accurate, although omitting certain items which increased his culpability.

933. "How Good a Case?" Newsweek, LXXXIV (July 29, 1974), 16-21. An analysis of the House Judiciary Committee's articles of impeachment.

934. "How Gray Tried to Warn Nixon." Newsweek, LXXXI (May 21, 1973), 18. The Acting FBI chief attempted to warn the president that his aides were interfering with his organization's Watergate investigation by attempting to make the burglary appear to be a CIA operation.

935. "How John Dean Came Center Stage." Time, CII (June 25, 1973), 10-11. Concerns Dean's decision to testify.

936. "How Main Street Views Watergate." Time, CI (May 28, 1973), 13-19. Interviews with people in five communities regarding the scandal.

937. "How the Public Feels About Nixon and Watergate." Time, CII (November 19, 1973), 25-26. Shows the decline in the president's standing.

938. "How the Tape Sleuths Did It: Deciphering the Erasures on the Nixon Tapes." Newsweek, LXXXIII (January 28, 1974), 17. The work of Judge Sirica's panel of technicians on the 18-minute gap.

939. "How the White House Views Chances of Impeachment." U.S. News and World Report, LXXVI (May 20, 1974), 22-23. Believes there is no solid evidence against Nixon and that he would survive a Senate trial.

940. "How the World Looks at Watergate." Newsweek, LXXXI (May 14, 1973), 49-50. Excerpts from the world press; much wonderment as to what "all the fuss is about."

941. Hoyt, Kendall K. and Frances Spatz. Drunk Before Noon: The Behind-the-Scenes Story of the Washington Press Corps. Englewood Cliffs, N.J.: Prentice-Hall, 1979. 418p. A very useful view of correspondents assigned to Washington from all over the country; examines their ability to ferret out information as opposed to accepting government handouts, provides details on many of the personalities, and includes some information on the role of the press in the Watergate crisis.

942. Hubbard, H. "All About Impeachment." Newsweek, LXXXIII (March 25, 1974), 28-30+. A review of the process's technical aspects written for lay readers.

943. Huck, S. L. M. "The Tape Chase: Who Controlled the Nixon Tapes?" American Opinion, XVIII (February 1975), 9-16+. The various efforts to pry the tapes out of the White House before Nixon's resignation and the battle over custody once Ford became president are here succinctly reviewed.

944. Huffman, J. A. "Biblical Lessons from Watergate." Christianity Today, XVIII (March 15, 1974), 8-10+. Contrasts the Ten Commandments with the illegalities of Watergate.

945. "Hugh W. Sloan." In: Eleanora W. Schoenebaum, ed. Political Profiles: The Nixon/Ford Years. New York: Facts on File, Inc., 1979. pp. 605-606. Former treasurer of the Finance Committee of CREEP.

946. Hughes, Emmett J. "Exorcists of the Presidency." Newsweek, LXXXIII (May 27, 1974), 13. A former top aide in the Eisenhower administration, the author adds a few comments on the purposes of the current impeachment proceedings.

947. ———. "A White House Taped." New York Times Magazine (June 9, 1974), 17+. Employs the transcripts to analyze the atmosphere of the administration; notes tape-related blunders committed by the White House.

948. "Hughes Connection: Rebozo Testimony to Committee Investigators." Time, CII (October 22, 1973), 25-26. On Howard Hughes' campaign contribution for Nixon's 1972 campaign.

949. "Hughes Contribution: $100,000 Gift." Newsweek, LXXXII (October 22, 1973), 52. Same information as in the last entry.

950. Hume, Brit. "The Anderson Transcripts." More, IV (July

1974), 5-6. Reports on his former colleague's use of leaked House Judiciary Committee information in syndicated columns during the spring of 1974.

951. _____. "Checking out Dita Beard's Memo." Harper's, CCXLV (June 1972), 38-47. How the author conducted an interview with the former ITT lobbyist and how she confirmed the authenticity of her memo.

952. _____. Inside Story. Garden City, N.Y.: Doubleday, 1974. 305p. Hume, who now works for ABC News, here includes a variety of his cases while a former assistant to Jack Anderson; for our purposes, his involvement with the ITT case is the most important covered.

953. Hunt, E. Howard. "Interview." Penthouse, VI (May 1975), 66+. Hunt discusses his CIA career, his recruitment into the "plumbers," his role in the Watergate affair, and his subsequent imprisonment.

954. _____. "Text of Statement in Court, March 23, 1973." In: Buel W. Patch, ed. Historic Documents, 1973. Washington, D.C.: Congressional Quarterly, Inc., 1974. pp. 417-418. Hunt admits his guilt and asks for leniency.

955. _____. Undercover: Memoirs of an American Secret Agent. New York: Berkley Pub. Corp.; dist. by G. P. Putnam, 1974. 338p. Hunt, from prison, recalls his OSS/CIA career, his work as a White House "plumber," his arrest, sentencing, and imprisonment, with almost half the book devoted to his chores for Chuck Colson and his comeuppance. Strong personal anguish emerges over his treatment from government and prison officials for actions which for much of his career he was well-paid and honored. Excerpted in Book Digest, II (March 1975), 78-103.

956. _____. "Watergate--The View from Jail: An Interview." Time, CII (August 27, 1973), 18-21. Hunt reacts to the amount of newly-uncovered Watergate evidence and as in his book, expresses bitterness over his treatment as compared to the others involved.

957. "Hunt's Memo: Watergate Bombshell." U.S. News and World Report, LXXVII (November 18, 1974), 42. In which he suggests more was involved in Watergate than met the eye.

958. Hurst, J. W. "Watergate: Some Basic Issues." Center Magazine, VII (January 1974), 11-25. Reviews the morality question, the idea of separation of powers, presidential power, etc.

959. Hurt, Harry. "Have Conscience, Will Travel." Texas Monthly, V (November 1977), 126+. A career review of the work of Leon Jaworski.

960. Hurtgen, James R. "The Case for Presidential Preogative." University of Toledo Law Review, VII (Fall 1975), 59-85. Argues that there are legitimate occasions when executive privilege is necessary for the protection of the national good.

961. Hurwitz, Leon. "Watergate and Detente: A Content Analysis of Five Communist Newspapers." Studies in Contemporary Communism, IX (Autumn 1976), 244-256. An analysis of the Watergate coverage of five Red papers in an effort to see whether Nixon's problems were perceived as lessening the danger of nuclear conflict.

962. _____, et al. "International Press Reactions to the Resignation and Pardon of Richard M. Nixon." Contemporary Politics, IX (October 1976), 107-123. Demonstrates that much of the world still found it hard to accept that the crimes of Watergate were considered significant enough to warrant such drastic remedies. Based on a content analysis of four elite newspapers.

963. "'I Am Not a Crook.'" New York Times Magazine (January 13, 1974), 58-60+. An analysis of Nixon's speech containing those words.

964. "'I Knew What I Meant.'" Newsweek, LXXXIII (March 18, 1974), 22-26. Recaps the president's latest news conference in which he tried to respond to the implications of a grand jury's belief that he was involved in the Watergate cover-up; notes the contradictory aspects of his statements.

965. "If Nixon Is Impeached, What Then?" U.S. News and World Report, LXXVI (February 4, 1974), 22-29. An interview with Attorney General Saxbe on the mechanics of the process.

966. "The Imaginary Men: Reprinted from the Wall Street Journal, May 7, 1974." Congressional Record, CXX (May 8, 1974), 13848-13849. Reactions to the comments in the White House transcripts.

967. "The Impact of Watergate on Nixon's Popularity." Gallup Opinion Index, XXXII (May 1973), 1-11. The president's popularity has not yet been greatly damaged.

968. "Impeach Nixon!: Reprinted from the Madison [Wisc.] State Journal, August 2, 1974." Congressional Record, CXX (August 2, 1974), 26607. The call from one Republican newspaper which had previously supported the president.

969. "Impeach Nixon: Three Views in a Historic Debate." U.S. News and World Report, LXXVI (February 25, 1974), 20-22. Views of Nixon's lawyer, the Special Prosecutor, and a member of the House Judiciary Committee.

970. "Impeach or Resign: Voices in a Historic Controversy."
Time, CII (November 19, 1973), 20-21. Similar to the last entry.

971. "Impeachment--A Trial for the Nation: Symposium." Reader's Digest, CV (September 1974), 61-63. Published after the Nixon resignation.

972. "Impeachment and the Dilatory Democrats." Progressive, XXXVIII (February 1974), 5-6. Suggests that the Congress' majority party is moving too slowly on the question of impeachment.

973. "Impeachment and the House." New Republic, CLXIX (November 3, 1973), 5-7. On the need for the House to take up the matter in light of the Saturday Night Massacre.

974. "Impeachment: Big Questions." Newsweek, LXXIV (July 1, 1974), 22-25. Wonders what the outcome of the process might be.

975. "Impeachment: Congress Puts Nixon Under a Microscope." U.S. News and World Report, LXXVI (February 18, 1974), 27-29. Reviews the work of the Special Prosecutor, the Ervin Committee, and the latest steps by the House Judiciary Committee in setting loose its impeachment inquiry.

976. "Impeachment Crisis--A Historic Debate Before the Supreme Court: Excerpts from the Official Transcript." U.S. News and World Report, LXXVII (July 22, 1974), 72-75. United States v. Nixon.

977. "Impeachment Crisis--Key Decisions at Hand." U.S. News and World Report, LXXVII (July 22, 1974), 15-17. What to do next in the wake of the Supreme Court decision noted in the last entry.

978. "Impeachment: Down to the Real Issues." U.S. News and World Report, LXXVII (July 29, 1974), 16-18. On the House Judiciary Committee's decision to go ahead with the preparation of its articles.

979. "Impeachment: Fear of the Unknown." Time, CII (July 23, 1973), 28+. A discussion of the process and a review over concern as to what might happen if it were implemented.

980. "Impeachment Fight--The President Comes out Swinging." U.S. News and World Report, LXXVI (January 21, 1974), 16-17. On the start of "Operation Candor."

981. "Impeachment Focus." National Review, XXVI (July 19, 1974), 793-794. Examines the work of the House Judiciary Committee.

982. "The Impeachment Inquiry." In: Congressional Quarterly Almanac 1974. Washington, D.C.: Congressional Quarterly, Inc., 1975. pp. 867-902. A review of the work of the House Judiciary Committee; taken largely from the pages of C.Q. Weekly Report.

983. "Impeachment Inquiry Staff: Large, Young, and Busy." C.Q. Weekly Report, XXXII (March 2, 1974), 540-543. Looks at the make up of the staff and its 43 personalities.

984. "Impeachment Lobby: Emphasis on Grass Roots Pressure." C.Q. Weekly Report, XXXII (1974), 1368-1380. Looks at the effect of public opinion on the work of the Congressmen on the House Judiciary Committee.

985. "Impeachment: Men on the Spot." Newsweek, LXXXIV (July 15, 1974), 14-18+. Looks at the principles: Rodino, Jaworksi, Nixon, etc.

986. "Impeachment: Moving Toward a Decision." C.Q. Weekly Report, XXXII (1974), 1923-1946. The concluding work of the House impeachment inquiry.

987. "The Impeachment of Richard Nixon." New Republic, CLXX (March 16, 1974), 5-8. Looks at the prospects for such a move.

988. "Impeachment Offenses--Two Views: Excerpts from a Report of the House Judiciary Committee Assessing Grounds for Presidential Impeachment and Excerpts from a Similar Study by President Nixon's Legal Advisors." In: Robert A. Diamond, ed. Historic Documents, 1974. Washington, D.C.: Congressional Quarterly, Inc., 1975. pp. 137-144. The House said grounds existed while St. Clair said they did not.

989. "Impeachment: Phase One." Newsweek, LXXXIII (May 20, 1974), 28+. The House inquiry.

990. "Impeachment Prospects." National Review, XXVI (February 1, 1974), 124+. At that point they did not seem promising.

991. "Impeachment: The Case Unfolds." Newsweek, LXXXIII (May 27, 1974), 26+. On the evidence being accumulated by the House Judiciary Committee.

992. "Impeachment: Three Articles Sent to the House Floor." C.Q. Weekly Report, XXXII (August 3, 1974), 2007-2023. Reviews their content and adoption by the Judiciary Committee.

993. "Impeachment Trial Could Kill Major Bills." C.Q. Weekly Report, XXXII (1974), 1632-1635. On a Congressional suspension of business during a trial.

994. "Impeachment Moving Toward a Decision, with a Chronology of Events, July 18-24, 1974." C.Q. Weekly Reports, XXXII (July 27, 1974), 1923-1941. On the final work of the House Judiciary Committee.

995. "'In a Manner Contrary to His Trust.'" Time, CIV (August 5, 1974), 12-13. The articles of impeachment.

996. "In Character: The President's Sudden About-Face on the Watergate Case." Nation, CCXVI (April 30, 1973), 546-547. In light of various allegations, Nixon indicated he will look into the case more closely and "clean it up."

997. "'In Disregard of the Rule of Law....'" Newsweek, LXXXIV (August 12, 1974), 29. The articles of impeachment.

998. "In His Own Right." Newsweek, LXXXII (December 3, 1973), 34+. Leon Jaworski as the second Special Watergate Prosecutor.

999. "Inconclusive Hunt." New Republic, CLXIX (October 6, 1973), 5-7. On Hunt's testimony to the Ervin Committee.

1000. "Indictments Begin: Los Angeles Hearings." Time, CII (September 17, 1973), 21-22. The Fielding break-in quest.

1001. Ingram, Timothy H. "ITT and Watergate: The Colson Connection." Washington Monthly, V (November 1972), 32-36. Suggests that the special counsel played a part in the proceedings.

1002. Inouye, Daniel. "After Watergate: Some Answers from a Senatorial Questioner." ASNE Bulletin (November-December 1973), 10-12. Views of a member of the Ervin panel.

1003. "Inquest Begins: Getting Closer to Nixon." Time, CI (May 21, 1973), 16-28. A lengthy article on the opening of the Ervin Committee hearings with lists of witnesses, problems of TV coverage, and recapitulation of information known to that time.

1004. "Inside the Nixon White House." Newsweek, LXXXIII (January 21, 1974), 21-24. A look at the pressures on the staff as the Watergate case continues to simmer.

1005. "Inside the Watergate Prisons." Newsweek, LXXXIV (July 15, 1974), 26-29. Looks at the fate of men like Dean and Hunt who were in jail before Nixon's resignation.

1006. "Instant Analysis: CBS and Instant Analysis." New Republic, CLXVIII (June 20, 1973), 8-9. On the temporary (as-it-turned-out) CBS decision to abandon IA after presidential speeches.

1006a. "Instant Replay: The ITT Case." Newsweek, LXXXII (November 12, 1973), 29-30+. On evidence developed during the Ervin hearings.

1007. "Integrity and the Presidency: Reprinted from the Christian Science Monitor, November 30, 1973." Congressional Record, CXIX (December 6, 1973), 40120. Calls for more truth in revelations about Watergate.

1008. "An Interim Judgement on the Judge." Time, CIV (November 11, 1974), 21. An assessment of the role of Judge Sirica.

1009. "An Intimate Glimpse of a Private President." Time, CIII (May 13, 1974), 38-39. Excerpts from the White House transcripts relative to Nixon's personality.

1010. "Investigators Turn Attention to Millions in Secret Campaign Funds." U.S. News and World Report, LXXIV (May 14, 1973), 19. Illegal campaign funds some of which was to be hush money.

1011. Irish, Leon E. "An Independent Prosecutor: Reprinted from the Washington Post, November 9, 1973." Congressional Record, CXIX (December 4, 1973), 39499-39500. Calls for a special prosecutor not employed by the Justice Department as Cox was.

1012. "Is Everybody Doing It?" Time, CI (May 21, 1973), 32-33. Contrary to poll results, only a few White House people are involved.

1013. Isenbergh, Max and Joseph. "Does the Constitution Require High Crimes or Misdemeanors for Impeachment?: A Memo." Congressional Record, CXX (May 14, 1974), 14633-14634. Looks at precedent for the answer, which the memo says is "no."

1014. "It Looks Very Grim." Newsweek, LXXXII (November 5, 1973), 21-29. Analyzes the backlash over the "Saturday Night Massacre."

1015. "It Never Stops, Does It?" Newsweek, LXXXII (July 16, 1973), 21-25. Allegations of wrongdoing coming out of the Ervin hearings.

1016. "It Started with $200,000 in a Worn Briefcase: The Involvement of Robert L. Vesco in the Watergate Case." Time, CI (May 21, 1973), 18-19. The hush money-illegal campaign contribution connection.

1017. "The ITT Affair." Time, XCIX (March 13, 1972), 19-20. A review of the case to date.

1018. "ITT Again: White House Involvement in the Anti-Trust Suit." New Republic, CLXIX (November 10, 1973), 7-8. Nixon's role in the case's settlement.

1019. "ITT: Another Cover-up." Newsweek, LXXXIV (July 29, 1974), 36+. Evidence developed by the House Judiciary Committee in its Watergate inquiry.

1020. "ITT Back on the Doorstep: Alleged $400,000 Contribution." Newsweek, LXXXII (August 13, 1972), 21. A huge illegal contribution for the ITT case settlement.

1021. "ITT Case Background: Classic Pattern of Pressures." C.Q. Weekly Report, XXX (March 11, 1972), 519-524. The controversy stemming from the U.S. Justice Department's 1971 settlement without trial of its anti-trust case against ITT; like many of the other citations here, provides data on events, key individuals, etc.

1022. "ITT Continued." New Republic, CLXVI (April 22, 1972), 8-9. Further revelations in the case.

1023. "The ITT Flap." Newsweek, LXXIX (March 13, 1972), 26+. Another review of the case.

1024. "The ITT Scandal." Commonweal, XCVI (May 12, 1972), 229-230. Wonders how it could happen.

1025. _____. New Republic, CLXVI (May 12, 1972), 5-7. A brief analysis of the significance of the case.

1026. "ITT Tries to Kill an Antitrust Story." Business Week (April 29, 1972), 25-26. On the corporation's efforts to defuse press reaction to the mounting scandal.

1027. No entry.

1028. "ITT's Arrogance." New Republic, CLXVI (April 8, 1972), 25-26. In attempting to quash reports of the scandal.

1029. "ITT's Public Relations Fiasco." Business Week (April 1, 1972), 23-24. Same data as the last citation.

1030. "ITT's Small Contribution: Paid and Deferred Taxes." Time, XCIX (April 17, 1972), 86+. Further details on an underhanded arrangement.

1031. Ives, C. F. "Watergate: Two Parables and a Proposition." Modern Age, XX (Spring 1976), 141-152. Watergate happened, the author contends, because the security law is too unreasonable.

1032. Jackson, Brian. "Kalmbach and the Dairymen: The Contribution to the Richard M. Nixon Campaign by Associated Milk Producers, Inc." New Republic, CLXX (April 6, 1974), 19-21. Story based on House Judiciary Committee evidence.

1033. _____. "Milk Money." New Republic, CLXXI (August 10, 1974), 11-12. Further details on the above citation.

1034. _____. "Milking the White House." New Republic, CLXX (January 26, 1974), 15-18. A review of Milk Fund charges based on evidence developed by the Ervin hearings.

1035. Jackson, Nancy B. "The Politics of Revenge." More, IV (February 1974), 5-8. Nixon administration pressure via the FCC on the renewal of license for two Washington Post-owned TV stations in Florida.

1036. Jackson, Robert L. "ITT Lobbyist Puts Knife to Work--Without the Butler: Reprinted from the Los Angeles Times." Congressional Record, CXVIII (May 11, 1972), 17098-17099. On the work of Dita Beard.

1037. _____. "Nixon Aide Recalls Another International Telephone and Telegraph Talk--Kleindienst Was Told of Complaint, Flanigan Says: Reprinted from the Los Angeles Times." Congressional Record, CXVIII (May 11, 1972), 17118-17119. How the Attorney General was brought into the underhandedness of the case.

1038. _____. "Report Links Foreign Account to Nixon Fund--House Banking [Committee] Study Discloses $30,000 Cleared Through Luxembourg Institution: Reprinted from the Los Angeles Times, October 3, 1972." Congressional Record, CXX (August 7, 1974), 27275. On the laundering of money through foreign banks for use in the 1972 campaign.

1039. _____. "Watergate Questioning Leaves Much Unprobed--Prosecutor Explains Limited Testimony by Saying There Is No Evidence of Wider Plot: Reprinted from the Los Angeles Times, January 28, 1973." In: U.S. Congress, Senate, Committee on the Judiciary. Nomination of Earl J. Silbert to Be United States Attorney: Hearings. 93rd Cong., 2nd sess. Washington, D.C.: U.S. Government Printing Office, 1974. pp. 191-192. Jackson reports on Silbert's original findings.

1040. _____. "White House Aides Planned to Misuse IRS, Jaworski Says: Reprinted from the New York Times, May 29, 1974." Congressional Record, CXX (July 22, 1974), 24500. To harass enemies.

1041. _____ and Robert J. Ostrow. "Nixon Voices 'Total Confidence' in Dean After Telephone Talk: Reprinted from the Los Angeles Times, March 27, 1973." In: Book IV, Part I of U.S. Congress, House, Committee on the Judiciary. Statement of Information: Hearings. 93rd Cong., 2nd sess. Washington, D.C.: U.S. Government Printing Office, 1974. p. 324. The event eventually led to Dean's turning state's evidence.

1042. James, Judson L. and Dorothy B. "Lessons of Watergate: The Nixon Campaigns." Current History, LXVII (July 1974), 31-33, 38. Reviews the "dirty tricks" in Nixon's various efforts at winning public office.

1043. "James W. McCord." In: Eleanora W. Schoenebaum, ed. Political Profiles: The Nixon/Ford Years. New York: Facts on File, Inc., 1979. pp. 397-398. A brief biography of the Watergate burglar.

1044. Jaros, Dean. "The Malevolent Unindicted Co-Conspirator: Watergate and Appalachian Youth." American Politics Quarterly, IV (October 1976), 483-508. Reviews young peoples' views of the former president and the pardon which allowed him to avoid prison.

1045. Jaworski, Leon. "An Active Conspirator: Reaction to the Nixon/Frost Interview." Newsweek, LXXXIX (May 16, 1977), 33. The former Special Prosecutor disagrees with several of Nixon's taped Watergate comments.

1046. _____. "The Case Against the President." Criminal Law Bulletin, XIII (1977), 253+. Sets forth the reasons Jaworski believed Nixon was guilty of the charges made against him in Watergate.

1047. _____. "The Most Lustrous Branch: Watergate and the Judiciary." Fordham Law Review, XLV (May 1977), 1267-1280. The second Watergate Special Prosecutor reviews the work of the D.C. federal courts and the Supreme Court in United States v. Nixon.

1048. _____. "Nothing Is Inviolate: An Interview." Time, CII (November 26, 1973), 21. Thoughts on becoming special prosecutor.

1049. _____. "Out to Get the President: The Special Prosecutor's Answer." U.S. News and World Report, LXXVI (April 15, 1974), 20-21. An interview in which Jaworski claims to only be interested in the truth and in justice.

1050. _____. The Right and the Power: The Prosecution of Watergate. New York: Reader's Digest Press; dist. by T.Y. Crowell, 1976. 305p. Weaves excerpts from legal briefs and other documents into a first-person narrative of the Watergate affair as experienced by the author, placing America's ordeal into a legal, moral, and human perspective. Jaworski, whose appointment after Cox's firing was quite controversial, does not step back from the criticism he suffered and the disputes within his staff as to the prosecution of the case. He also addresses the question of an indictment for an incumbent president, desired by early 1974 not only by his staff but by a grand jury. The tapes case and the Ervin/Rodino hearings also receive mention.

1051. _____. "Text of Jaworski's Letter to Senate [Judiciary] Panel on the White House Refusal to Yield Tapes: Reprinted from the New York Times, February 15, 1974." In: Book IX, Part II of U.S. Congress, House, Committee on the Judiciary. Statement of Information: Hearings. 93rd Cong., 2nd sess. Washington, D.C.: U.S. Government Printing Office, 1974. pp. 939-940. Reaction to the White House refusal.

1052. _____. "Watergate Prosecutor Charts the Next Moves: An Interview." U.S. News and World Report, LXXV (December 10, 1973), 37-38. Jaworski discusses his areas of investigation, independence, staff, and other matters.

1053. "Jaworski: Seeing It Through." Time, CIII (February 18, 1974), 10-11. His efforts to obtain further Watergate evidence.

1054. "Jaworski Wins over Skeptics As Worthy Cox Successor: Reprinted from the Baltimore News-American, November 26, 1973." Congressional Record, CXIX (December 11, 1973), 40911. Suggests that even though he was named by Nixon, the new man had shown independence enough to be accepted as a dedicated seeker of the truth.

1055. "Jeb Magruder, a Pragmatist." Newsweek, LXXXI (June 25, 1973), 23. Examines Magruder's ethics in his Watergate actions.

1056. "Jeb Magruder: Another Former White House Aide Heads for Prison." U.S. News and World Report, LXXVI (June 3, 1974), 26. On his sentencing for his Watergate role.

1057. "Jeb Magruder: Lost Compass." Newsweek, LXXXIII (June 3, 1974), 24. Same information as last entry.

1058. "Jeb Stuart Magruder." In: Eleanora W. Schoenebaum, ed. Political Profiles: The Nixon/Ford Years. New York: Facts on File, Inc., 1979. pp. 414-416. A brief biography.

1059. Jenkins, Peter. "Portrait of a Presidency." New Statesman and Nation, LXXXVII (May 17, 1974), 688-692. Ponders the question "How did Watergate happen?"

1060. "A Job Well Done: Reprinted from the Washington Star-News, July 3, 1974." Congressional Record, CXX (July 31, 1974), 25983. An editorial concerning the end of the Ervin Committee.

1061. "John D. Ehrlichman." In: Eleanora W. Schoenebaum, ed. Political Profiles: The Nixon/Ford Years. New York: Facts on File, Inc., 1979. pp. 182-188. A capsule biography of Nixon's domestic advisor.

1062. "John Dean: The Man with the Scarlet 'W.'" Time, CIV (July 29, 1974), 25-26. Reviews his Ervin committee and various trial testimonies.

1063. "John J. Sirica." In: Eleanora W. Schoenebaum, ed. Political Profiles: The Nixon/Ford Years. New York: Facts on File, Inc., 1979. pp. 602-604. A short biography of the chief judge of the U.S. District Court for the District of Columbia.

1064. "John Mitchell Takes the Stand." Time, CII (July 16, 1973), 9-10. Reviews his Ervin Committee testimony.

1065. "John N. Mitchell." In: Eleanora W. Schoenebaum, ed. Political Profiles: The Nixon/Ford Years. New York: Facts on File, Inc., 1979. pp. 442-445. Looks at the career of the former Attorney General and CREEP boss.

1066. "John W. Dean, III." In: Eleanora W. Schoenebaum, ed. Political Profiles: The Nixon/Ford Years. New York: Facts on File, Inc., 1979. pp. 163-166. A capsule biography of the former presidential counsel.

1067. Johnson, Constance. "Brinkley Wants Solid Proof: Reprinted from the [Columbus, Georgia] Sunday Ledger-Enquirer, August 4, 1974." Congressional Record, CXX (August 9, 1974), 27667. Views of Georgia Congressman Jack Brinkley published one day before Nixon released the transcripts of his June 23, 1972 White House meeting-- the "smoking gun."

1068. Johnson, Gerald W. "Watergate: One End, but Which?" American Scholar, XLII (Autumn 1973), 594-603. Suggests the crisis will either add to national insecurity or jolt it into some sort of readjustment.

1069. Johnson, Haynes. "Congress and the Watergate: Reprinted from the Washington Post, July 8, 1973." Congressional Record, CXIX (July 9, 1973), 22867-22868. A survey of Congressional opinion on the case.

1070. _____. "Judiciary Committee Members Splendidly Rising to History: Reprinted from the Washington Post, July 24, 1974." Congressional Record, CXX (July 29, 1974), 25425. Praises the work of the members of the Rodino panel.

1071. Johnson, Richard T. Managing the White House: An Intimate Study of the Presidency. New York: Harper & Row, 1974. 270p. Surveys the managerial practices employed by presidents from FDR to Nixon; shows how Nixon became the most isolated of chief executives and how his organization of his staffers led to Watergate.

1072. Johnson, Robert H., Jr. "Covering the Nixon Resignation." Montana Journalism Review, no. 18 (1975), 40-45. Recollections of an Associated Press (AP) correspondent.

1073. Jones, Stephen. "Was Richard Nixon Guilty?: The Case for the Defense." Oklahoma Bar Association Journal, XLIX (Winter 1978), 251-268. Reviews the final arguments of James D. St. Clair.

1074. Jordan, Barbara with Shelby Hearon. Barbara Jordan, a Self-Portrait. Garden City, N.Y.: Doubleday, 1979. 269p. Recollections by the Black Texas Congresswoman and member of the House Judiciary Committee whose eloquent oratory during the impeachment hearings is long remembered.

1075. Joseph, Ted. "How White House Correspondents Feel About Background Briefings." Journalism Quarterly, L (Autumn 1973), 509-516, 532. Most felt they gave only part of the story, although useful information sometimes not easily available elsewhere was provided.

1076. "Judge John J. Sirica: Standing Firm for the Primacy of Law." Time, CIII (January 7, 1974), 8-20. Focuses on the judge's actions during the first year of the scandal.

1077. "A Judge Commands the President: Watergate Tapes Decision." Time, CII (September 10, 1973), 14-16. Recaps Sirica's main points in his decision on the tapes.

1078. "Judgement Day." Newsweek, LXXXIV (December 30, 1974), 19-20. On the outcome of the Watergate cover-up trial.

1079. "Judging Nixon: The Impeachment Session." Time, CIII (February 4, 1974), 14-18+. On the convening of the 2nd session of the 93rd Congress.

1080. "Judiciary Leaks: Reprinted from the New York Times, June 20, 1974." Congressional Record, CXX (June 20, 1974),

20111. An editorial deploring the leaks, often used by Jack Anderson.

1081. "Julie: Her Father's Daughter." Newsweek, LXXXIV (October 14, 1974), 39-43. A brief profile which notes her spirited defense of the President during Watergate.

1082. "Jury Points a Finger at Nixon." Newsweek, LXXXIII (March 11, 1974), 17-22. Examines Watergate grand jury indictments against Mitchell, Mardian, Ehrlichman, Haldeman, Strachan, Colson, and Kenneth Parkinson, as well as the President's unindicted co-conspirator status.

1083. "The Jury: Silent Decision-Makers." Time, CIV (December 30, 1974), 10-11. Looks at the reasoning of the Watergate coverup trial's jury.

1084. Kalmbach, Herbert. "Kalmbach's Story." Newsweek, LXXXII (July 16, 1973), 23-25. Ervin panel testimony on fund raising and passing of hush money.

1085. Kampelman, Max M. "The Arrogance of the Press." Washingtonian, X (October 1974), 61-62, 64, 66, 68, 70. Watergate was not uncovered by the press as many believe, but by government investigations.

1086. _____. "Congress, the Media, and the President." In: H. C. Mansfield, ed. Congress Against the President. New York: Praeger, 1975. pp. 85-97. Examines the feud between Nixon and the press and suggests that Nixon's impeachment trials were largely due to a hostile media that did not uncover the scandal.

1087. _____. "The Power of the Press: A Problem for Our Democracy." Policy Review, VI (Fall 1978), 7-39. Contains much of the same data as the previous entry.

1088. Kane, Joseph N. Facts About the Presidents: A Compilation of Biographical and Historical Data. 4th ed. New York: Ace Books, 1976. 698p. Includes a full section on Richard M. Nixon.

1089. Kanfer, Stefan. "Sherlock Holmes: The Case of the Strange Erasures." Time, CIII (January 28, 1974), 28-29. Looks at how the 18-minute gap mystery might have been solved by Holmes.

1090. _____. "Watergate on TV: Show Biz and Anguished Ritual." Time, CII (June 25, 1973), 14-15. The televising of the Ervin Committee hearings.

1091. Karst, Kenneth L. and Harold W. Horowitz. "Presidential Prerogative and Judicial Review." UCLA Law Review,

XXII (October 1974), 47-67. A review of the doctrine of executive privilege.

1092. Katula, R. A. "The Apology of Richard Nixon." Today's Speech, XXIII (Fall 1975), 1-5. Analyzes Nixon's talk to his staff after resigning.

1093. Keeffe, Arthur J. "Explorations in the Wonderland of Impeachment." American Bar Association Journal, LIX (August 1973), 885-88. On various efforts to define the law of impeachment.

1094. _____. "The W. S. P. F.: What Was and Could Have Been." American Bar Association Journal, LXIII (January 1977), 139-142. Reviews the trials and difficulties of the Watergate Special Prosecution Force.

1095. Keerdoja, Eileen. "Watergate Anniversary." Newsweek, LXXXIX (June 20, 1977), 10+. Examines the crisis from the perspective of three-five years.

1096. Kelly, Clarence M. "The FBI's Illegal Activities." In: Robert A. Diamond, ed. Historic Documents, 1976. Washington, D. C.: Congressional Quarterly, Inc., 1977. pp. 321-331. Includes a few references to the FBI in Watergate.

1097. Kelly, Kay. A Funny Thing Happened on the Way to San Clemente. Stamford, Conn.: Special Features Workshop, 1977. 250p. A Watergate satire.

1098. Kenny, Gerald J. "The 'National Security Wiretap': Presidential Prerogative and Judicial Responsibility." Southern California Law Review, XLV (Summer 1972), 888-913. Looks at the president's power to install them and the court's responsibility to make sure they are in fact for the national good.

1099. "Key Questions: Review of Conflicting Testimony." Newsweek, LXXXII (August 27, 1973), 18-20. A look at the various statements made to the Ervin Committee.

1100. "A Key Witness Named Dean." Newsweek, LXXXIII (April 8, 1974), 21-22+. Dean's testimony in the various Watergate trials.

1101. Kilpatrick, Carroll. "The Imperial Front Man." Nation (February 21, 1976), 197-199. Examines the role of presidential press secretaries, including Nixon's Ron Ziegler.

1102. _____. "St. Clair Calls Evidence Inadequate: Reprinted from the Washington Post, July 23, 1974." Congressional

Record, CXX (July 24, 1974), 25042. The brief of the President's chief lawyer.

1103. ———. "Ziegler Cites 'Mistakes' by [W. S. P. F.] Legal Staff: Reprinted from the Washington Post, November 30, 1973." Congressional Record, CXIX (November 30, 1973), 38995. Comments on the work of Jaworski's people.

1104. Kilpatrick, James J. "Ample Precedent Aids Nixon on His Position on Evidence: Reprinted from the Washington Star-News, July 24, 1974." Congressional Record, CXX (July 24, 1974), 25058. Support's Nixon's claims on executive privilege.

1105. ———. "Calming Nixon's Legion: Reprinted from the Washington Star-News, August 5, 1974." Congressional Record, CXX (August 6, 1974), 27068. On making conciliatory gestures towards Nixon's supporters.

1106. ———. "Crushing Verdict on Watergate: Reprinted from the Washington Star-News, December 14, 1973." Congressional Record, CXX (January 22, 1974), 211-212. On the President's decline in public opinion polls.

1107. ———. "The Presidency Goes Nowhere." National Review, XXVI (March 1, 1974), 253-255. On how the Watergate crisis had curtailed Nixon's ability to govern.

1108. ———. "Transcripts Answer a Good Many of Our Questions: Reprinted from the Arizona Republic, May 11, 1974." Congressional Record, CXX (May 14, 1974), 14513-14514. A conservative's view of the White House transcripts.

1109. ———. "The Watergate Caper Is No Longer Just Funny: Reprinted from the Washington Star-News, August 8, 1972." Congressional Record, CXIX (August 11, 1972), 27890. On the illegal use of CREEP funds in the light of Washington Post accounts.

1110. Kinkead, Gwen. "The Verdict." Boston, LXVIII (October 1976), 82+. Reviews the opinion on Archibald Cox's service as Watergate Special Prosecutor from the advantage of three years after his dismissal in the "Saturday Night Massacre."

1111. Kirschten, Dick. "Watergate Survivor [Fred F.] Fielding Guards Against Abuses of White House Power." National Journal, XIV (February 13, 1982), 289-292. On the post-Watergate activities of John Dean's assistant.

1112. Kissinger, Henry. Years of Upheaval. Boston: Little,

Brown, 1982. 1,283p. In the second volume of his memoirs (post-1972 period), the former Secretary of State devotes considerable space to his recollections of the Watergate affair and its impact on U.S. foreign policy; the excerpt on the crisis was also published in Time, CXIX (March 8, 1982), 42-48+.

1113. Klein, Carl L. "Objects of 'Lynch Mob Hysteria': Reprinted from the Oak Lawn [Illinois] Star-Tribune, May 19, 1974." Congressional Record, CXX (May 28, 1974), 16563. On the loud clamor for Nixon's removal.

1114. Klein, Herbert G. "Brief for the President: Reprinted from the New York Times, November 16, 1973." Congressional Record, CXIX (November 19, 1973), 37641. The White House Communications Director's opinions on Nixon's non-involvement in Watergate crimes.

1115. _____. "Klein Offers Middle-Ground Perspective on Nixon Wars with the Press." Broadcasting, XCIX (September 22, 1980), 57-59. Suggests there was fault on both sides.

1116. _____. Making It Perfectly Clear. Garden City, N.Y.: Doubleday, 1980. 464p. The author was Press Secretary or Advisor to Richard Nixon during much of the latter's public career. This volume reviews the former President's running debates and feuds with the press, with much sadness showing on his recounting of the Watergate fiasco. Although unhappy with his treatment at the hands of the "palace guard," Klein nevertheless reproduces many memos exchanged with them in an effort to show that mistakes in the Nixon administration's handling of the media can be avoided by future White House occupants. "For the President of the United States," he asserts, "politics and the media are deeply interrelated and a major part of everyday life. A president who loses the ability to communicate effectively with the American people loses the political strength to govern effectively."

1117. No entry.

1118. _____. "The Press vs. White House Spokesmen." TV Guide, XXIII (August 2, 1975), 2-6. Traces the problem back to James Hagerty under Eisenhower before moving forward in time; ample discussion of his problems and Ziegler's before and during the Watergate case.

1119. Kleindienst, Richard G. "Kleindienst Pleads Guilty: Text of Statement, May 16, 1974." In: Robert A. Diamond, ed. Historic Documents, 1974. Washington, D.C.: Congressional Quarterly, Inc., 1975. pp. 407-410. In return for co-operating with Jaworski's ITT investigation, Kleindienst was charged with a minor offense rather than perjury for lying to the Senate Judiciary Committee during his confirmation hearings.

1120. _____. "Text of Kleindienst Statement on ITT: Reprinted from the New York Times, October 31, 1973." In: Book V, Part II of U.S. Congress, House, Committee on the Judiciary. Statement of Information: Hearings. 93rd Cong., 2nd sess. Washington, D.C.: U.S. Government Printing Office, 1974. p. 853. On his role in the mini-scandal.

1121. "Kleindienst Cops a Plea." Newsweek, LXXXIII (May 27, 1974), 31-32. On the Jaworski-Kleindienst deal which gave the latter a lesser charge in exchange for his cooperation.

1122. "Kleindienst: His Role in ITT Anti-Trust Settlement; Kleindienst--White House Role in ITT Case." C.Q. Weekly Report, XXX (March 4 and 11, 1972), 510-511, 664-667. Background information and the Attorney General designate's testimony before his Senate confirmation hearings, March 2-9, 1972.

1123. Kleindienst-ITT Case: Three Main Issues Emerge." C.Q. Weekly Report, XXX (March 18, 1972), 575-579, 627-630. Testimony of Kleindienst, John Mitchell, and ITT chairman Geneen on the antitrust settlement.

1124. Klobuchar, Jim. "The Whole Truth of Watergate: Reprinted from the Minneapolis Star, April 30, 1974." Congressional Record, CXX (May 2, 1974), 13030. Concerns Nixon's frustrations with the public learning of the facts in the case.

1125. Knappman, Edward W., ed. Government and the Media in Conflict, 1970-1974. New York: Facts on File, Inc., 1974. 204p. An examination of the press-Nixon feud drawn from the pages of the weekly service "Facts on File."

1126. _____. Watergate and the White House: June 1972-September 1974. 3 vols. New York: Facts on File, Inc., 1973-1974. Should be compared with the Congressional Quarterly effort cited above. Offers detailed chronologies, excerpts from documents and testimonies as well as the court trials, plus editorials from hundreds of newspapers around the nation. Much of the material, as in the previous entry, is drawn from the weekly service "Facts on File," and while dry reading makes for a useful and permanent record of the crisis.

1127. Knight, John S. "Impeachment Process Strengthens the Nation: Reprinted from the Akron Beacon-Journal, August

4, 1974." Congressional Record, CXX (August 6, 1974), 27046. Another conservative newspaper publisher comes to favor the House Judiciary Committee approach.

1128. "Know-Nothing Mitchell: Hearings on the ITT Scandal." New Republic, CLXVI (March 25, 1972), 5. Comments on the Attorney General's testimony on the case.

1129. Knowles, James W. "The Economic Consequences of Watergate." Business Economics, IX (May 1974), 25-30. Argues that the scandal is bad for business and looks at the effects of the case on business policies.

1130. Koenig, Louis W. "The Presidency Today." Current History, LXVI (June 1974), 249-253, 272. A review of the institution in the light of Watergate.

1131. Kopkind, Andrew. "The Unwritten Watergate Story." More, IV (November 1974), 5-6+. Looks at the corporation men involved in illegal donations but not exposed by the media.

1132. Kraft, Joseph. "Can Mr. Nixon Still Govern?: Reprinted from the Washington Post, June 4, 1973." Congressional Record, CXIX (June 5, 1973), 18013. Suggests that the scandal has not yet overly affected the president's ability to govern.

1133. _____. "Cox's Tape Case: Reprinted from the Washington Post, July 27, 1973." Congressional Record, CXIX (July 27, 1973), 26398-26399. Reviews the Special Prosecutor's pursuit of the Oval Office Watergate tapes.

1134. _____. "Questioning Haig's Role: Reprinted from the Washington Post, September 17, 1974." Congressional Record, CXX (September 17, 1974), 31394-31395. Questions the White House chief of staff's role in obtaining a presidential pardon for Nixon.

1135. _____. "The Watergate and the White House: Reprinted from the Washington Post, March 27, 1973." Congressional Record, CXIX (March 27, 1973), 9904-9905. Looks at the matter of whether the scandal goes high into White House circles or was really "a third-rate burglary."

1136. _____. "The Watergate Caper: Reprinted from the Washington Post, June 25, 1972." Congressional Record, CXVIII (June 26, 1972), 22487. An early analysis of the significance of the break-in.

1137. _____. "Who's Running the Country?" Atlantic, CCXXXIII (April 1974), 57-60+. With Nixon tied up with Watergate, day-to-day operations are pretty much in the hands of various cabinet secretaries.

1138. Kraus, Sidney and Steven H. Chaffee. "The Ervin Committee Hearings and Communications Research." Communications Research, I (October 1974), 339-348. A review of the audience impact studies coming out of the televising of the Ervin panel hearings.

1139. Kremer, William. "The Devil and Watergate." Detroit, II (October 1979), 10+. Reviews the role of the Deputy Director, later Director, of White House communications Ron Ziegler.

1140. Kressel, Marilyn. "Pigs on Two Feet: George Orwell Through the Prism of Watergate." Intellect, CIII (December 1974), 192-195. How close America came to "Big Brotherism" during the pre-scandal era of the case.

1141. Kriebel, Robert. "Excerpts from a Poll: Reprinted from the Lafayette [Ind.] Journal and Courier, June 10, 1974." Congressional Record, CXX (July 1, 1974), 21979-21980. Reviews continuing support for Nixon in the home town of Purdue University.

1142. Krislov, Steve. "Watergate Fallout: Some Bizarre and Not-So-Bizarre Proposals for Changes in the System." Center Report, VII (April 1974), 10-15. On increasing the power of Congress, changing to a parliamentary system, a single 6-year presidential term, etc.

1143. Kristovic, Stephen M. "United States v. Barker: Misapplication of the Reliance on an Official Interpretation of the Law Defense." California Law Review, LXVI (July 1978), 809-843. After Barker was convicted, his petition to the Supreme Court for a writ of certiorari was denied.

1144. Krogh, Egil. "Krogh Denies Break-in Order from Nixon." U.S. News and World Report, LXXVI (February 4, 1974), 21. Comments before sentencing.

1145. _____. "Sentencing of Egil Krogh: Text of Statement Released Immediately Following His Sentencing." In: Robert A. Diamond, ed. Historic Documents, 1974. Washington, D.C.: Congressional Quarterly, Inc., 1975. pp. 33-40. Same data as in last entry.

1146. Kurland, Philip B. "United States v. Nixon: Who Killed Cock Robin?" UCLA Law Review, XXII (1974), 68-75. A review of the historic Supreme Court case.

1147. _____. "Watergate: A Teaching Challenge." Congressional Record, CXX (February 18, 1974), 3139-3142. Presents ideas on how teachers should tell their students about the crisis and its significance.

1148. _____. Watergate and the Constitution. Chicago: University of Chicago Press, 1978. 261p. Calling for a dispersal of power, Kurland focuses on the history of the Constitution and the issues for it raised by the crisis, which actually predated the affair and were, in his opinion, caused by a "bloated" and "Plebiscitary" presidency, overactive courts, and a submissive Congress. Executive privilege, impeachment, appointment and removal, pardons, congressional inquiry powers, etc., are all considered within the context of Watergate and more importantly, the Constitution. His specific suggestions for change include increasing the accountability of presidential staff and strengthening the power of Congress.

1149. _____. "Watergate and the Cult of the Robe: An Address Before the Illinois State Bar Association Annual Convention, June 17, 1974." Congressional Record, CXX (July 11, 1974), 22795-22797. Examines the role of the courts in settling the legal issues of the Watergate case.

1150. _____. "Watergate, Impeachment, and the Constitution." Mississippi Law Journal, XLV (May 1974), 531+. Covers the entire issue and expresses many of the Constitution-based ideas later published in the author's book, cited above.

1151. _____. "The Watergate Inquiry, 1973." In: Arthur M. Schlesinger, Jr. and Roger Burns, eds. Congress Investigates: A Documented History. New York: Chelsea House, 1975. V, 3923-4064. The last in a chronological history of 29 major Congressional investigations in U.S. history to be covered is that of the Ervin Committee in which the author discusses at length the problems of executive privilege as well as the varied testimony of the Watergate witnesses.

1152. Kutner, Luis. "Executive Privilege: Growth of Power over a Declining Congress." Loyola Law Review, XX (Spring 1974), 33-44. Examines the history of the doctrine culminating in the Watergate-related invocation of it by the Nixon people.

1153. _____. "A Legal Note on the Nixon Pardon: Equal Justice Vis-à-vis Due Process." Akron Law Review, IX (1975), 243+. Weighs the conflicting views that Ford's pardon circumvented the system and that Nixon could not get a fair trial.

1154. _____. "Nixon vs. Cox: Due Process of Executive Privilege." St. John's Law Review, XLVIII (March 1974), 441-460. A review of Cox's pursuit of the tapes and the Nixon administration's attempt to employ executive privilege to frustrate his effort.

1155. Kuttner, Bob. "White House Pressure on IRS Detailed." Congressional Record, CXX (July 18, 1974), 24182-24183. Its attempt to have the tax people monitor "enemies."

1156. "L. Patrick Gray." In: Eleanora W. Schoenebaum, ed. Political Profiles: The Nixon/Ford Years. New York: Facts on File, Inc., 1979. pp. 246-248. A capsule biography of the Acting FBI Director.

1157. Labovitz, John R. Presidential Impeachment. New Haven, Conn.: Yale University Press, 1978. 268p. The author, a member of the Nixon impeachment staff, systematically reviews the history of the process in America with special attention to the decisions arrived at in connection with the House Judiciary Committee inquiry. Very clear and quite thorough.

1158. Laing, Robert B. and Robert L. Stevenson. "Public Opinion Trends in the Last Days of the Nixon Administration." Journalism Quarterly, LIII (Summer 1976), 294-302. Argues that "those who viewed the hearings were more likely to favor impeachment and more likely to base their opinions on information provided about Watergate."

1159. Lake, I. Beverely. "The Separation of Powers: An Address, Raleigh, North Carolina, September 14, 1973." Congressional Record, CXIX (September 20, 1973), 30727-30728. Watergate shows a need for Congress to retake some of the power it had abdicated to the executive branch.

1160. Lammers, William W. "Presidential Press-Conference Schedules: Who Hides, and When?" Political Science Quarterly, XCVI (Summer 1981), 261-278. Examines the modern presidency and press conference and suggests that Nixon, as an isolated leader who did not fully appreciate the need for communications, chose the wrong times to make statements and the wrong statements to make at those times.

1161. "The Land of Milk and Honey: The Question of Contributions to Richard M. Nixon's Campaign by the Associated Milk Producers, Inc." Time, CII (December 3, 1973), 22-23. Wonders if a deal were struck over the Milk gift.

1162. Landon, Alf. "The Stability of Our System Will Not Be Affected: An Interview." U.S. News and World Report, LXXIV (May 21, 1973), 20-23. Views of the 1936 GOP presidential candidate on the scandal.

1163. Lang, Kurt and Gladys E. "Televised Hearings: The Impact out There." Columbia Journalism Review, XII (November-December 1973), 52-57. Reviews the televising of the Ervin Committee hearings and the change in public opinion among those who watched them.

1164. _____. "Polling on Watergate: The Battle for Public Opinion." Public Opinion Quarterly, XLIV (Winter 1980), 530-547. Demonstrates the politics of polling during the crisis and the effort each side made to show that the other side was losing its grasp or was not seriously damaged.

1165. Lapham, Lewis H. "As the Watergate Turns." Harper's, CCXXXII (September 1973), 58. Suggests the televised hearings were not very popular with viewers.

1166. Lardner, George, Jr. "Anatomy of a Scandal: The Milk Fund." Reader's Digest, CV (November 1974), 123-127. Examines the 1972 charges that dairy industry officials had made contributions to CREEP in exchange for an increase in federal milk price supports.

1167. _____. "Behind-the-Scenes at the Cox Investigation." Ramparts, XII (January 1974), 21-26. Summarizes Cox's appointment, political background, investigation and dismissal, and the work of his staff.

1168. _____. "Harassing of O'Brien Cited: Reprinted from the Washington Post, May 29, 1974." Congressional Record, CXX (July 22, 1974), 24499-24500. Reports the Jaworski contention that the IRS was ordered to harass the Democratic Party chairman, Lawrence O'Brien.

1169. _____. "Judge Bars Tape Comment: Reprinted from the Washington Post, April 11, 1974." Congressional Record, CXX (April 11, 1974), 10912-10913. Judge Sirica's order that no comments be issued on the raging tape issue.

1170. _____. "Once Doubtful Executive Privilege Expanded in Scope: Reprinted from the Washington Post, March 25, 1973." Congressional Record, CXIX (March 29, 1973), 10392-10394. Nixon's increased use of the process to deny Watergate witnesses and materials.

1171. _____ and Carroll Kilpatrick. "Magruder Resigns U.S. Job--First Among Watergate Figures to Quit: Reprinted from the Washington Post, April 27, 1973." In: Book IV, Part III of U.S. Congress, House, Committee on the Judiciary. Statement of Information: Hearings. 93rd Cong., 2nd sess. Washington, D.C.: U.S. Government Printing Office, 1974. p. 1626. On Magruder's decision to quit the Commerce Department post he was given after having served in CREEP.

1172. Larson, C. V. "A Content Analysis of Media Reporting of the Watergate Hearings." Communications Research, I (October 1974), 440-448. Examines the printed record of the newspapers and news-magazines to see if it accurately reflected the transcripts of the televised hearings.

1173. Lasch, Christopher. "Paranoid Presidency." Center Magazine, VII (March-April 1974), 23-31. Examines reasons why the Nixon administration should feel that everyone was out to see its ruin.

1174. Lasky, Victor. It Didn't Start with Watergate. New York: Dial Press, 1977. 438p. Lasky, famous for his attacks on JFK and LBJ, has here written a pro-Nixon volume--reviews sometimes called it a diatribe--designed to show that many of the transgressions for which Nixon was condemned were freely committed by earlier administrations who were not called to account for them by the press and people. Useful as a counterbalance to the many anti-Nixon books which appeared during and after the affair, it should, however, be used with care due to its complete partisanship.

1175. "Latest U.S. Views on Watergate." Gallup Opinion Index, XXXII (June 1973), 2-13. Public opinion is sampled in the wake of the early phases of the Ervin hearings; Nixon still holds strong in many quarters.

1176. Latham, Aaron. "How the Washington Post Gave Nixon Hell." New York Times Magazine (May 14, 1973), 49-52+. Concerns the many stories pumped out by Woodward and Bernstein.

1177. _____. "The Reporter the President Hates." New York, VI (January 21, 1974), 34-43. Dan Rather.

1178. _____. "Soldier, Spy--Tinkered Out." Esquire, LXXXIX (April 25, 1978), 18. On the CIA career of Vernon A. Walters.

1179. Lawler, Philip F. "A Great Pair of Eggs." American Spectator, XIV (June 1981), 24-26. Bob Woodward and his anonymous source, "Deep Throat."

1180. Lawton, J.H. "Milhouse Rising." Journal of Psychohistory, VI (Spring 1979), 519-542. Once again Nixon is put on the couch to find out how his early childhood and youthful experiences made him the president of Watergate.

1181. Leamer, Laurence. "The Sam Ervin Show." Harper's, CCXLIV (March 1972), 80-86. A review of the Senator's career written a year before he was placed in charge of the Senate Select Committee on Presidential Campaign Activities.

1182. "Learning to Live with the Crisis." Time, CII (July 16, 1973), 11-12. Impact on the families of Nixon staffers.

1183. "The Legal Legacy of Watergate: Citizen Nixon Enmeshed in Criminal Litigation." Time, CIV (August 26, 1974), 18+. Speculates on Nixon's fate before the law; written before the pardon.

1184. Leggett, Robert L. "Nixon's Case Against Nixon: The President's Own Admissions Provide Enough Evidence to Impeach Him." Progressive, XXXVIII (May 1974), 15-18. Argues that sufficient evidence for impeachment exists even before the House Judiciary Committee completes its inquiry; reprinted in Congressional Record, CXX (May 7, 1974), 13614-13615.

1185. Lentz, William W. "Executive Privilege to Withhold Information from Congress: A Constitutional or Political Doctrine?" University of Missouri--Kansas City Law Review, XLII (Spring 1974), 372-389. Argues the latter.

1186. "Leon Jaworski." Current Biography Yearbook 1974. New York: H. W. Wilson Co., 1975. pp. 186-193. A brief biography of the Texas lawyer.

1187. _____. In: Eleanora W. Schoenebaum, ed. Political Profiles: The Nixon/Ford Years. New York: Facts on File, Inc., 1979. pp. 328-330. A somewhat shorter biography than the last entry.

1188. Leopold, Stephen S. "Inside the Watergate Hearings." Maclean's, LXXXVI (December 1973), 19-21+. A review of the Ervin panel hearings written for a Canadian audience.

1189. LeRoy, D. J. "The Public Television Viewer and the Watergate Hearings." Communications Research, I (October 1974), 406-425. The hearings were carried without interruption on PBS and had a definite effect upon viewers.

1190. "Letting It All Out." Time, CIII (May 13, 1974), 82. Reporting on the Watergate tape transcripts.

1191. Levin, Arthur. "The Man Who Nailed Gordon Liddy." Washington Monthly, VI (December 1974), 38-39+. How Liddy was fired from CREEP for failing to cooperate with the FBI's Watergate investigation.

1192. Levin, Murray. "Investigative Reporting As a Research Method: An Analysis of Bernstein and Woodward's 'All the President's Men.'" American Psychologist, XXXV (July 1980), 626-638. Reviews the psychological make-up of the reporters and the stress they operated under.

1193. Lewin, Nathan. "Firing Cox." New Republic, CLXIX (November 3, 1973), 12-13. Contends the act was a "gross miscalculation" on Nixon's part.

1194. _____. "The Supreme Court and the Watergate Tapes." New Republic, CLXX (June 22, 1974), 13-16. A review of the court's verdict in United States v. Nixon.

1195. _____. "That Bulging Briefcase." New Republic, CLXX (March 16, 1974), 13-16. Looks at the question of presidential immunity from indictment.

1196. _____. "Who Gets the Tapes?" New Republic, CLXIX (October 27, 1973), 14-17. Examines the upholding of Sirica's tape decision, but faults it for lack of clarity on how the tapes are to be screened.

1197. Lewis, Anthony. "The End Begins: Reprinted from the New York Times, October 22, 1973." Congressional Record, CXIX (October 30, 1973), 35513. On the Cox dismissal.

1198. _____. "One Day in October: Reprinted from the New York Times, October 20, 1975." Congressional Record, CXXI (October 21, 1975), 33369. Looks back on the Cox dismissal two years earlier.

1199. _____. "A President's Day in Court." New Republic, CLXXI (July 20, 1974), 10-11. On the Supreme Court's verdict in United States v. Nixon.

1200. _____. "Undermining Faith in the System: Reprinted from the Minneapolis Tribune, September 10, 1974." Congressional Record, CXX (September 11, 1974), 30772-30773. The impact of President Ford's pardon of Richard Nixon.

1201. _____. "Why We Are Shaken: Reprinted from the New York Times, October 29, 1973." Congressional Record, CXIX (October 30, 1973), 35513-35514. Examines the ruthlessness of the "Saturday Night Massacre."

1202. Lewis, Carolyn. "The Battle of Capitol Hill." TV Guide, XXIV (July 27, 1974), 24-26. The televised House Judiciary Committee proceedings.

1203. Lewis, Finlay. "Impeachment--Nixon in Crisis: Reprinted from the Minneapolis Tribune, February 3-9, 1974." Congressional Record, CXX (March 26, 1974), 8304-8310. A detailed look at the atmosphere and politics involved in the House Judiciary Committee inquiry.

1204. _____. "Presidential Papers: An Attempt to Own History." Nation, CCXIX (October 19, 1974), 366-369. On the debate between Nixon and the government over access to and ownership of his presidential papers, especially the Watergate tapes.

1205. _____. "Sending Congress a Message." Nation, CCXVIII

(April 20, 1974), 493-495. On grass roots pressure on Congress for Nixon's impeachment.

1206. _____. "Some Errors and Puzzles in Watergate Coverage." Columbia Journalism Review, XII (November-December 1973), 26-32. Examines press coverage of the case and notes a few examples of mistakes in allegations of statements to various sources.

1207. _____. "The Tapes That Ousted Nixon May Become His Richest Asset: Reprinted from the Minneapolis Tribune, August 25, 1974." Congressional Record, CXX (September 19, 1974), 31820-31821. On the ownership issue of Nixon's presidential materials.

1208. Liddy, G. Gordon. "An Interview." Playboy, XXVII (October 1980), 65+. Discusses some of the ideas noted in his book, e.g., holding hand over live flame, plot to kill Hunt in jail, his elaborate espionage plan for 1972 presented to CREEP.

1209. _____. "Watergate's Sphinx Speaks." Time, CXV (April 21, 1980), 58-60+. Recaps the thoughts in Liddy's book, the next entry below.

1210. _____. Will: The Autobiography of G. Gordon Liddy. New York: St. Martin's Press, 1980. 374p. A fascinating story of personality development which led the author to his role in Watergate and difficulties during his subsequent imprisonment. Here he tells of his FBI career and campaign as a prosecuting attorney who tried to win a conviction against LSD advocate Timothy Leary. In a lucid prose style, he details his work with CREEP and the White House "plumbers," the acts which many have called bravado, his extremely-expensive (even by CREEP standards) plans for political dirty tricks against Democrats in 1972, the bungled Watergate burglary done by incompetents, his refusal to testify before any of the groups investigating the case, his stiff prison sentence, and his activities as a pro-Black anti-guards guerrilla while serving the longest term of any of those convicted for Watergate. His memoirs are unrepentant and he still believes his do-or-die attitude towards the re-election of Richard Nixon was the only correct and honorable direction. Liddy's writing and subsequent appearances on college campuses have proved fascinating to many, but one should look behind them for clues to the character of the man--and the men who used him!

1211. Lieberman, Jethro K. Milestones: 200 Years of American Law. New York: Oxford University Press, 1976. Recounts the facts, meanings, and historical contexts of eighteen cases and events judged to be pivotal in American legal history; the final case is that of Richard M. Nixon and Watergate.

1212. Lieberman, Myron. "Watergate: The Bottom Line." Alternative, VIII (December 1974), 18-20. Comments on the morality involved in the affair.

1213. Lim-chun, Lily Y. U.S. v. Nixon and Executive Privilege. FOI Center Report, no. 345. Columbia, Mo.: School of Journalism, University of Missouri, 1975. 8p. A brief review of the impact of the Supreme Court decision on executive privilege.

1214. Lindsay, John. "Colson: Beat the Devil." Newsweek, LXXXIII (June 17, 1974), 19-20. The Fielding break-in trial and Colson's conversion to religion.

1215. _____. "'Options' and 'Scenarios': The (Expletive Omitted) Cover-up." Nation, CCXVIII (May 18, 1974), 617-621. Transcript excerpts contrast Nixon in private and public.

1216. _____. "We Are All Going to Survive." Newsweek, LXXXIII (June 10, 1974), 21-23. Thoughts on the outcome of the crisis.

1217. Lipset, Seymour M. and Earl Raab. "Appointment with Watergate." Commentary, LVI (September and December 1973), 35-43, 4+. Looks at radical movements in U.S. history and how Nixon's background made him an antiradical leader; demonstrates how the political atmosphere in the White House led to the scandal.

1218. "Listening in on Nixon and His Men." Newsweek, LXXXIII (May 13, 1974), 46-92. Excerpts from the White House transcripts.

1219. Littleton, Thomas B. "Serving up News--With a Twist." Columbia Journalism Review, VIII (July-August 1978), 47-48. Ken Clawson and Nixon's press relations.

1220. Locander, Robert. "The President, the Press, and the Public: Friends and Enemies of Democracy." Presidential Studies Quarterly, VIII (Spring 1978), 140-150. Reviews the relationship between the White House and the press and the effect a feud such as that existing during Nixon's tenure has on the information needs of the U.S. public.

1221. Lofton, John D., Jr. "Tape, Cocktails, TV Journalism, and Legal Ethics." TV Guide, XXII (March 2, 1974), A3-A4. Looks at CBS News correspondent Fred Graham.

1222. "Long Road to Nixon's Last Crisis." Newsweek, LXXXIV

(August 19, 1974), 35-36+. A review of the history of the Watergate crisis.

1223. Loory, Stuart H. "The CIA's Man in the White House." Columbia Journalism Review, XIV (September 1975), 11-14. Alexander Butterfield.

1224. "Loyalty and Leniency." Time, CIII (June 17, 1974), 16. The sentencing of Richard G. Kleindienst.

1225. "The Luckless Watergate Four." Newsweek, LXXXII (November 19, 1973), 45-46. On the resentencing of the Watergate "burglars."

1226. Lukas, J. Anthony. "Hughes Connection: What Were the Watergate Burglars Looking For?" New York Times Magazine (January 4, 1976), 8-9+. Suggests Democrats might have known of Howard Hughes' gift and were seeking evidence.

1227. _____. Nightmare: The Underside of the Nixon Years. New York: Viking Press, 1976. 626p. A chronological account, running from 1969 through the Nixon resignation, by a former New York Times reporter, which details most of the illegalities of Nixon's presidency. It's all here: wiretapping of staffers and reporters, the sale of ambassadorships, illegal fund raising, campaign dirty tricks, the president's California and Florida land deals, the Watergate break-in and cover-up, the Agnew resignation, and the influence of Howard Hughes, Bebe Rebozo, ITT, the Milk Fund, etc. The author eschews explicit analysis and commentary, preferring to let his facts speak for themselves--facts drawn mostly from his previous Watergate writings and the Watergate literature available at the time of his research.

1228. _____. "The Story So Far." New York Times Magazine (July 22, 1973), 1+. The story of the scandal to date; draws heavily on Ervin Committee testimony.

1229. _____. "Watergate Questions for Haig." Nation, CCXXXII (January 3, 1981), 1+. Questions raised at his confirmation hearings as Secretary of State concerning his role as Nixon's last White House chief of staff.

1230. _____. "Watergate: The Story Continued." New York Times Magazine (January 13, 1974), 1+. Sequel to the entry before last.

1231. Lurie, Leonard. Impeachment of Richard Nixon: A Call to Action--Now! New York: Berkley Publishing Co., 1973. 208p. Employing the Watergate hearings and newspaper evidence, Lurie contends that the evidence for impeachment of the President is formidable, pinpointing the legal case and drawing upon history and constitutional theory to put the episode into perspective. The paperback was written before the extensive findings of the Ervin and House Judiciary Committees were completed and suggests that Nixon "set out deliberately, knowingly, in a systematic way to subvert and destroy the very processes through which American democracy must operate!"

1232. Lurie, Ranan R. Nixon-Rated Cartoons. Rev. ed. New York: Quadrangle Books, 1974. 320p. A cartoon-laden satire, revised to include the latest Watergate caricatures.

1233. Lyons, Richard L. "Probers Seek Middle Path on St. Clair: Reprinted from the Washington Post, March 26, 1974." Congressional Record, CXX (March 28, 1974), 8653. The inquiry staff of the House Judiciary Committee and the President's lawyer.

1234. _____ and William Chapman. "IRS Link to Nixon Queried-- Democrats Eye Service's Use to Harass: Reprinted from the Washington Post, June 14, 1974." Congressional Record, CXX (July 23, 1974), 24778. On the use of the IRS against Democratic chairman O'Brien.

1235. _____. "Tape Provides No Nixon Link to Milk Fund: Reprinted from the Washington Post, June 6, 1974." Congressional Record, CXX (June 6, 1974), 18006. On evidence not developed by the House Judiciary Committee inquiry.

1236. McBee, Susana. "Richardson Discloses Papers: Reprinted from the Washington Post, November 28, 1973." In: Book IX--Part II of U.S. Congress, House, Committee on the Judiciary. Statement of Information: Hearings. 93rd Cong., 2nd sess. Washington, D.C.: U.S. Government Printing Office, 1974. pp. 771-772. Data on the "Saturday Night Massacre."

1237. McCarthy, Eugene J. "Watergate: Seeing Through a Glass Darkly." Christianity and Crisis, XXXIV (April 29, 1974), 88-92. Thoughts on the morality of the crisis by a well-known philosopher-politician.

1238. McCarthy, Mary. The Mask of State: Watergate Portraits. New York: Harcourt, Brace, Jovanovich, 1974. 165p. Six of the eight chapters in this noted novelist's slim volume were written in the summer of 1972 as immediate and personal reactions to what she saw and heard of the Senate Select Committee hearings; subsequently they were published in the London Observer. Her word-portraits of the leading actors, e.g., Dean, Mitchell, Haldeman, Ehrlichman, Magruder, McCord, Ervin, etc. are incisive and rather unflattering. This is not an objective work; the author freely admits her fascination with the day's speculations. A final chapter argues that the data on hand in 1974 suggests the President himself as the brains behind the Watergate cover-up.

1239. McCartney, James. "The Washington Post and Watergate: How Two Davids Slew Goliath." Columbia Journalism Review, XII (July-August 1973), 8-22. Concerns the investigative reporting of Woodward and Bernstein.

1240. McCord, James W., Jr. "McCord Memo Text." C.Q. Weekly Report, XXXI (May 12, 1973), 1129-1131. The Watergate "burglar's" letter to Judge Sirica stating that there was more involved in the break-in than met the eye and that higher-ups were involved.

1241. _____. "Watergate and the Intelligence Community." Armed Forces Journal International, X (August 1973), 57-58. An early assessment of the role of the CIA and FBI in the case with comments on the effect of same on the politization of the agencies.

1242. _____. Piece of Tape--The Watergate Story: Fact and Fiction. Rockville, Md.: Washington Media Services, 1974. 329p. McCord's memoirs reveal not only his early career but his involvement with the White House "plumbers" in their illegal entries and practices before the Watergate break-in, during which he was arrested. The author assesses the testimonies given by the "Palace Guard" before various committees and in various statements, as well as the President's position, and assures us that they were all guilty of participation, either directly or through cover-up. An interesting account, not easily available, which should be compared with the memoirs of E. Howard Hunt and G. Gordon Liddy.

1243. _____. "Text of Letter to U.S. District Judge John J. Sirica, Read in Court, March 23, 1973." In: Buel W. Patch, ed. Historic Documents, 1973. Washington, D.C.: Congressional Quarterly, Inc., 1974. pp. 416-417. In which McCord points a finger towards others as having been involved in planning and covering up the Watergate break-in.

1244. McDonough, John R., R. Gordon Hoxie, and Richard Jacobs. "Who Owns Presidential Papers?" Manuscripts, XXVII (Winter 1975), 2-11. Disputes Nixon's contention that his White House papers were, in fact, his own private property.

1245. McGeever, P.J. "'Guilty, Yes, Impeachment, No.': Some Empirical Findings." Political Science Quarterly, LXXXIX

Watergate   174

(June 1974), 289-304. The results of a questionnaire sent to 1,000 citizens in a Midwestern metropolitan area showed that, while many believed Nixon guilty of Watergate irregularities, the majority were afraid of the uncertainties of an impeachment. See the comments of Gerald B. Finch cited above.

1246. MacGill, [unknown]. "The Nixon Pardon: Limits on the Benign Prerogative." Connecticut Law Review, VII (1974), 56+. Unavailable for review.

1247. McGovern, George. "Reflections on Watergate and 1972: Reprinted from Newsday, June 16, 1974." Congressional Record, CXX (June 19, 1974), 19971-19972. The defeated 1972 Democratic presidential candidate considers the impact of CREEP's "dirty tricks" effort against him (and other Democrats), and the morality of an administration which would lead certain of its members to burgle Democratic headquarters and then attempt to cover-up the act when it was bungled.

1248. McGrory, Mary. "Can Nixon Answer?: Reprinted from the New York Post, June 26, 1973." Congressional Record, CXIX (June 26, 1973), 21418-21419. Assesses Dean's Ervin Committee testimony.

1249. _____. "Point of View: Reprinted from the Washington Star-News, July 22, 1974." Congressional Record, CXX (July 23, 1974), 24822. The work and opinion of House Judiciary Committee chairman Rodino.

1250. _____. "Who Said What to Whom?" America, CXXVI (March 25, 1972), 307. On the involvement of administration officials in the ITT scandal.

1251. McKenzie, Richard B. and Bruce Yandel. "The Logic of 'Irrational' Politics: Nixon's Reelection Committee." Public Finance Quarterly, VIII (January 1980), 39-55. Concentrates on the massive effort by the Finance Committee to Reelect the President to obtain funds, often from questionable sources and in an illegal manner.

1252. McKibbin, [unknown]. "On Executive Clemency: The Pardon of Richard M. Nixon." Pepperdine Law Review, II (1975), 353+. Unavailable for review.

1253. McKown, Robin. The Resignation of Nixon: A Discredited President Gives up the Nation's Highest Office. New York: Franklin Watts, 1975. 86p. A slim volume which reviews the Watergate crisis for juvenile readers.

1254. McLaughlin, Daniel F. "Colson Claims Nixon Pardon 'Understanding': Reprinted from the Boston Herald-American,

March 23, 1976." Congressional Record, CXX (September 30, 1976), 34288. The former counsel argues that a deal was struck between Nixon and Ford which would assure the latter's pardon of the former.

1255. McLaughlin, John. "Impeachment and Common Sense: An Address to the National Press Club, July 24, 1974." Congressional Record, CXX (August 1, 1974), 26455-26458. A deputy Special Assistant to the President argues against impeachment stressing the trauma it would cause the nation.

1256. McLaughton, H. K. "Constitutional Law--Executive Privilege: Tilting the Scales in Favor of Secrecy." North Carolina Law Review, LIII (December 1974), 419-430. Contends that the doctrine of executive privilege would lessen the public's information about the workings of its government.

1257. McLendon, Winzola. Martha: The Life of Martha Mitchell. New York: Ballantine Books, 1979. A close journalist friend of John Mitchell's outspoken wife offers a behind-the-scenes look at what motivated Martha, her Watergate experiences, and her life after Nixon's resignation.

1258. McLeod, Jack M., et al. "Decline and Fall at the White House: A Longitudinal Analysis of Communications Effects." Communication Research, IV (January 1977), 3-22. Reviews the impact of the media on Nixon's downfall.

1259. _____. "Watergate and the 1974 Congressional Elections." Public Opinion Quarterly, XLI (Summer 1977), 181-195. Demonstrates the impact of the crisis on voters in the 1974 midterm elections and on members of the House Judiciary Committee (many who supported Nixon during the impeachment inquiry subsequently lost reelection bids).

1260. McMenamin, Michael. "How [John] Connally Beat the Milk Fund Rap." Inquiry, III (February 18, 1980), 11-17. An analysis of Connally's alleged role in the scam with comments on possible reasons for his "not guilty" verdict when he was tried. Drawn from the next entry.

1261. _____ and Walter McNamara. Milking the Public: Political Scandals of the Dairy Lobby from LBJ to Carter. Chicago: Nelson-Hall, 1980. 300p. Reviews alleged and proven underhanded dealings by the milk producers group during four presidential administrations; the section on price support deals and illegal contributions during the Nixon administration draws on a variety of sources, including the Watergate hearings.

1262. McWhinney, Edward. "Congress and the Presidency and the

Impeachment Power." Indiana Law Review, VIII (1974), 833-851. Examines the Congress' impeachment/trial power, its use in previous cases, and the application of the power to Watergate.

1263. McWilliams, Carey. "Campaign '72." Nation, CCV (September 4, 1972), 132. Suggests Watergate facts will not come out until after the election.

1264. _____. "Campaign '72: The Big Fix." Nation, CCXIV (February 20, 1974), 354-355. Commentary on the ITT case.

1265. _____. "A Contemptible Triumverate." Nation, CCXVII (August 27, 1973), 130-135. Nixon, Haldeman, and Ehrlichman in the light of testimony given before the Ervin panel.

1266. _____. "The Impeachment Saga." Nation, CCXIX (August 17, 1974), 98-101. Reviews and comments upon the work of the House Judiciary Committee.

1267. _____. "The Lawless Administration." Nation, CCXV (October 23, 1972), 354-356. Further commentary on the facts of the Alfred Baldwin confession case as then known.

1268. _____. "Mafia Metaphor." Nation, CCXV (July 10, 1972), 2-3. Equates the Watergate caper with Mafia tactics.

1269. _____. "Nixon vs. the GOP: CREEP." Nation, CCXV (October 30, 1972), 386-388. Examines why the President did not choose to have his re-election run through the Republican National Committee.

1270. _____. "Real Richard: The Tapes As an Airtight Case for Impeachment." Nation, CCXVIII (May 18, 1972), 610-612. Comments on the damning evidence contained in the White House transcripts.

1271. _____. "Too Little, Too Late." Nation, CCXVI (May 14, 1973), 610-611. Critical of White House staff changes, seeing them only as issue dodging.

1272. Magnuson, Edward. "Aftermath of a Burglary." Time, CXIX (June 14, 1982), 33-35. A tenth-anniversary reflection on the changes wrought in American government by the Watergate case.

1273. _____. "Post-Mortem: The Unmaking of a President." Time, CV (May 12, 1975), 72+. Looks at the mistakes made by the White House in the Watergate case.

1274. Magruder, Gail. A Gift of Love. Philadelphia, Pa.: A. J. Holman Co., 1976. 160p. The wife of Jeb Stuart Magruder here presents her recollections of life with her husband during the Watergate crisis; her study of home-life, tension, and marital problems should be compared with the rendering by Maureen Dean, cited above.

1275. Magruder, Jeb Stuart. An American Life: One Man's Road to Watergate. New York: Atheneum, 1974. 338p. Written while awaiting sentencing for his 1973 conviction for lying in connection with the Watergate case, the former presidential aide and deputy CREEP director reviews his life and attempts to suggest some of the reasons he was drawn into the Watergate web and some of the political factors which led to the scandal. One of the earliest Watergate memoirs, this well-written account is chock-full of juicy (at least then) gossip and anecdotes concerning the Nixon White House staffers and how they got along with one another (badly, for the most part). Magruder demonstrates the basic lack of ethics that allowed the case's perpetrators to rationalize their efforts, however illegal, to get Nixon re-elected as being in the national good and, when things went wrong, to attempt to cover them up. Magruder concludes his chronicle with an admission of guilt, declaring "I've helped deal a terrible blow to the political cause I believe in."

1276. _____. From Power to Peace. Waco, Tx.: Word Books, 1978. 224p. After serving seven months, Magruder enrolled in Princeton Theological Seminary where he found peace and a new meaning to life, as here revealed. Contains a few thoughts on Watergate.

1277. _____. "Inside Watergate: Jeb Stuart Magruder's Devastating Testimony." Newsweek, LXXXI (June 25, 1973), 19-24. Recaps Magruder's Ervin Committee testimony in which he revealed details on the planning, approval, financing, and cover-up of the break-in.

1278. _____. "Means." New York Times Magazine (May 19, 1974), 31+. An excerpt from An American Life in which Magruder tells how he first learned about the break-in at the Watergate.

1279. _____. "Reflections on a Course in Ethics: An Interview." Harper's, CCXLVII (October 1973), 59-62+. A discussion between Magruder and William Sloan Coffin regarding their earlier association and, among other things, how Watergate happened.

1280. _____. "Watergate: Magruder Implicates Top Officials." C.Q. Weekly Report, XXXI (June 16, 1973), 1486-1495. A review of his Ervin Committee testimony.

1281. "Main Street Revisited: Changing Views on Watergate." Time, CII (November 12, 1973), 28-29. Looks at public opinion on the case following the summer Ervin panel hearings and finds that many more people believe the President to be involved.

1282. "Making a Federal Case of It: Supreme Court to Rule on the Naming of Nixon As an Unindicted Co-conspirator in the Watergate Cover-up." Newsweek, LXXXIII (June 24, 1974), 29-33. On the high court's decision to review the tapes case (United States v. Nixon) and the legality of a grand jury naming Nixon as unindicted co-conspirator.

1283. "The Making of a Silent Minority." Newsweek, LXXXII (August 27, 1973), 14-17. Another look at public opinion on the case.

1284. Malaney, Gary D. and Terry F. Buss. "A.P. Wire Reports vs. CBS News Coverage of a Presidential Campaign." Journalism Quarterly, LVI (Autumn 1979), 602-610. Examines the reporting of each and the stories released looking for differences, which were found; some comments on Watergate, but not many.

1285. Malone, Dumas and Garry Wills. "Executive Privilege: Jefferson and Burr and Nixon and Ehrlichman." New York Review of Books, XXI (July 18, 1974), 36-40. A distinguished Jefferson scholar and a Nixon watcher compare and contrast the use of executive privilege in the two cases over 100 years apart.

1286. "The Man Everyone Wants to Hear From." Time, CI (April 2, 1973), 12-13. On the anticipated testimony of John Dean.

1287. "Man Overboard." New Republic, CLXVIII (April 21, 1973), 7-8. On Nixon's removal of L. Patrick Gray's name from consideration as FBI Director.

1288. "The Man Who Keeps Asking Why." Time, CII (July 9, 1973), 19-20. A profile of Senator Ervin.

1289. "The Man with the Judicious Gavel." Time, CIV (August 5, 1974), 14-15. A profile of Congressman Rodino.

1290. "The Man Without an Image." Nation, CCXVI (March 12, 1973), 322-324. Comments on Acting FBI Director L. Patrick Gray.

1291. Mangrum, R. C. "Removal of the President: Resignation and the Procedural Law of Impeachment." Duke Law Journal, XXIII (January 1974), 1023-1116. A lengthy consideration of the impeachment process as well as the resignation option.

1292. Manheim, Jarol B. "The Honeymoon's Over: The News Conference and the Development of Presidential Style." Journal of Politics, XLI (February 1979), 55-74. Considers both Nixon's and Ford's positions with the press as the initial period of mutual assessment ends and tough questions begin.

1293. Mankiewicz, Frank. Perfectly Clear: Nixon from Whittier to Watergate. New York: Quadrangle Books, 1973. 239p. Written by McGovern's 1972 national political campaign director, this book examines Nixon's career and his longtime use of "dirty tricks" of the kind that eventually led to Watergate. After an examination of political espionage, the author lists the "White House Horrors," provides biographies of the Watergate 5, and looks at the reason why the Cuban community responded to the Hunt/Liddy call to action. An early assessment of Watergate and the cover-up is provided, plus an appendix containing Nixon's statements on crime, a list of the statutes allegedly broken by the President, and McGovern's comments on corruption. This somewhat loosely organized and uneven series of thoughts includes a fictitious speech written by Mankiewicz for Nixon in which the President would confess to his crimes.

1294. _____. "Politics As Usual: A Veteran Activist in Presidential Campaigns Compares Nixon Politics with the Customary Kind." Progressive, XXXVII (December 1973), 29-32. Adapted from the previous entry.

1295. _____. U.S. vs. Richard M. Nixon: The Final Crisis. New York: Times Books, 1975. 276p. Argues that the important proceedings and related work by the W.S.P.F. amounted to a legal and not a political event; thus, established commentators underrated the chances of Nixon's impeachment and/or resignation. The volume, as the title implies, also provides details on the Supreme Court United States v. Nixon case, but concentrates primarily on the political aspects of the May-August 1974 events. Excerpted in Book Digest, II (May 1975), 79-96.

1296. Manley, John F. "The Presidency, Watergate, and the Public." In: his American Government and Public Policy. New York: Macmillan, 1976. pp. 333-351. An examination of the impact of the crisis on the office of the president and on the confidence of the public in that office.

1297. Mansfield, Harvey C., ed. Congress Against the President. New York: Published for the Academy of Political Science by Praeger, 1975. 200p. A verbatim reprinting of Vol. 32, no. 1 of the Proceedings of the Academy of Political Science consisting of 13 studies by political scientists and government personnel regarding executive-legislative branch relations at the beginning of the 94th

Congress. Includes essays on campaign financing, the growth of White House and Congressional staffs, etc., several of which represent useful reviews of current (1974) and future areas where the Congress and President may face conflict, including the effects of Watergate.

1298. "March 21: Hush-Money Talk." Newsweek, LXXXIII (May 13, 1974), 31-32. An excerpt from the White House transcripts.

1299. "The March 21 Tape: Reprinted from the Wall Street Journal, May 2, 1974." Congressional Record, CXX (May 2, 1974), 12877-12879. The March 21, 1973 Nixon-Dean conversation in which the latter tells the President about a "cancer growing on the presidency."

1300. Marchetti, Victor and John D. Marks. The CIA and the Cult of Intelligence. New York: Alfred A. Knopf, 1974. 398p. The famous CIA-history which sports gaps in the pages due to court-ordered deletions; contains some commentary on the role of the Agency in Watergate.

1301. Margolis, Jack S., comp. The Poetry of Richard Milhous Nixon. Los Angeles, Calif.: Cliff House Books, 1974. Unpaged. Excerpts from the White House transcripts.

1302. Marshall, Eliot. "After the Election." New Republic, CLXVII (November 11, 1972), 11-12. Speculations on the outcome of the Watergate investigations.

1303. _____. "Kleindienst." New Republic, CLXVI (May 13, 1972), 14-16. On the renewed confirmation hearings in which the Attorney General protests his innocence to alleged involvement in the ITT scandal.

1304. Marshall, Jonathan. "A New Watergate Revelation: The White House Death Squad." Inquiry, II (March 5, 1979), 15-21. On Liddy's plans to eliminate columnist Jack Anderson.

1305. Martin, P. L. "Voting on Impeachment: A Dilemma for Candidates." U.S. News and World Report, LXXVII (July 15, 1974), 24-25. On the impact of an impeachment vote by any House Judiciary Committee member facing reelection in the fall.

1306. Marvell, Charles. In Defense of Nixon: A Study in Political Psychology and Political Pathology. Albuquerque, N.M.: American Classical College Press, 1976. 27p. Looks at Nixon's leadership and survival tactics.

1307. "Massacre to Stonewall." Newsweek, LXXXIV (July 29, 1974), 23-26. Recaps part of the House Judiciary Committee report, notably the events surrounding the "Saturday Night Massacre," the tape gap, and the release of the edited White House transcripts.

1308. Mathias, Charles McC., Jr. "Toward a New Beginning: Reprinted from the New York Times, October 26, 1973." Congressional Record, CXIX (October 26, 1973), 35175-35176. Thoughts of the Maryland Republican Senator on the Cox dismissal.

1309. "Maurice H. Stans." In: Eleanora W. Schoenebaum, ed. Political Profiles: The Nixon/Ford Years. New York: Facts on File, Inc., 1979. pp. 615-618. A brief biography of the director of the Finance Committee to Reelect the President.

1310. "Maverick on the Spot: William B. Saxbe." Newsweek, LXXXII (November 12, 1973), 37+. On his nomination to succeed Eliot Richardson as Attorney General.

1311. Max, R. A. "A Judicial Interpretation of the Nixon Presidency." Cumberland Law Review, VI (Spring 1975), 213-242. A review of the courts-Nixon battle on the question of executive privilege.

1312. Maxey, David. "Confidence, with a Little Paranoia: The Committee for the Re-election of the President." Life, LXXIII (September 15, 1972), 23B-33. A contemporary look at CREEP with little hint of wrongdoing.

1313. Mayer, Allan J. "Master of the Power Game." Newsweek, XCVI (December 29, 1980), 13-15. A profile of Alexander Haig.

1314. Mazlish, Bruce. In Search of Nixon: A Psychohistorical Inquiry. Scranton, Pa.: Basic Books, 1972. 187p. Examines the effects of Nixon's family and upbringing on his personality; speculates that Nixon suffered from guilt, insecurity, and personal aggression which carried over into his political life. Reprinted by the Baltimore firm of Penguin Books in 1973.

1315. Meadow, Robert G. "Cross-Media Comparison of Coverage of the 1972 Presidential Campaign." Journalism Quarterly, L (Autumn 1973), 482-488. Examines the reporting by newspapers, TV, and news magazines.

1316. Meany, George. "The Presidency: 'A Dark Shadow of Shame over the Spirit of America.'" American Federationist, LXXX (November 1973), 2-7. A Watergate address by the AFL-CIO boss in October 1973 before the tenth convention of his organization.

1317. Medved, Michael. The Shadow Presidents: The Secret History of the Chief Executives and Their Top Aides. New York: Times Books, 1979. 416p. An anecdotal account, non-scholarly in nature, which treats of the relationship between presidents from Lincoln to Ford and their top assistants. As might be expected, considerable space is given to the relationship between President Nixon and his chief lieutenants, Haldeman, Ehrlichman, and Haig. Unfortunately, the volume devotes little space to the question of problems generated by the growth and expansion of power wielded by top aides.

1318. Mee, Charles I., Jr. "Only Left, Right Have Spoken up on Impeachment--Why the Silence from Middle-of-the-Roaders?: Reprinted from the Los Angeles Times, January 2, 1974." Congressional Record, CXX (January 21, 1974), 184-185. Suggests there is much uncertainty over the nation's fate in the wake of an impeachment and Senate trial.

1319. "Meeting with Republican Congressional Leaders: News Conference of Senator Barry Goldwater, Representative John J. Rhodes, and Senator Hugh Scott Following Their Meeting with the President." Weekly Compilation of Presidential Documents, X (August 12, 1974), 1010-1012. On their August 7 meeting with the president in the Oval Office in which Nixon's Congressional support is examined.

1320. "The Men from CREEP." Newsweek, LXXX (September 25, 1972), 33. Ties the "burglars" to the Nixon reelection organization.

1321. Merrill, John C. "The 'People's Right to Know' Myth." New York State Bar Association Journal, XLV (November 1973), 461-466. Defends the concept of executive privilege and secrecy as necessary to the public good.

1322. Metz, Robert. CBS: Reflections in a Bloodshot Eye. Chicago: Playboy Press, 1975. 428p. A history of the Columbia Broadcasting Corp., with emphasis on CBS TV and the news division in particular. Metz looks at the personalities involved from Murrow to Cronkite and provides some insight into the role of CBS News in covering the Watergate crisis.

1323. Mezvinsky, Edward M. and Doris S. Freedman. "Federal Income Tax Evasion As an Impeachable Offense." Georgetown Law Journal, LXIII (May 1975), 1071-1081. One of the matters investigated by the House Judiciary Committee was Nixon's income taxes and the matter of backdated deeds on gifts of papers to the National Archives.

1324. "Milk Fund, IRS Bugging: Highlights of the Evidence." U.S. News and World Report, LXXVII (July 29, 1974), 19-21.

Evidence developed by the House Judiciary Committee inquiry.

1325. "Milk Group [Committee for Thorough Agricultural Political Education] Gave $462,000 Just Before the Election." C.Q. Weekly Report, XXXI (March 17, 1973), 568-588. An early look at Milk Fund allegations.

1326. "Milk Spills on Connally." Newsweek, LXXXIV (August 12, 1974), 30-31. The Treasury Secretary's alleged role in the scandal.

1327. "Milk Support Price Decision: Information Relating to the Decision." Weekly Compilation of Presidential Documents, X (January 14, 1974), 20-28. White House data showing price supports were not tied to a deal.

1328. "Milking It: Milk Industry Donations." Newsweek, LXXXII (November 26, 1973), 35-36. Data developed by the Ervin Committee hearings.

1329. "Milking the Dairy Co-ops." Time, CIV (July 29, 1974), 20+. On illegal milk industry contributions.

1330. "Milkmen Skimming off More Cream: A.M.P.I. Contributions to the Richard M. Nixon Campaign." Time, CIII (April 8, 1974), 16-17. More on the scandal.

1331. Miller, Arthur S. "The Coming Trial of Richard M. Nixon." Progressive, XXXVIII (June 1974), 15-18. Attempts to apply lessons learned from Johnson's 1868 impeachment.

1332. _____. "Executive Privilege: A Political Theory Masquerading As Law." In: Harold C. Relyea, ed. The Presidency and Information Policy. New York: Center for the Study of the Presidency, 1981. pp. 48-65. A review of the concept with special attention to its use by Nixon.

1333. _____. "Executive Privilege: Its Dubious Constitutionality." Bureaucrat, I (Summer 1972), 136-141. The same data as in the previous citation.

1334. _____. "An Inquiry into the Relevance of the Intentions of the Founding Fathers, with Special Emphasis upon the Doctrine of Separation of Powers: An Address at the University of Arkansas, April 4, 1974." Congressional Record, CXX (November 19, 1974), 36485-36489. Contains much of the information found in the previous two entries.

1335. _____. "Limited Hang Out: The Dialogues of Richard Nixon As a Drama of the Anti-Hero." Harper's, CCXLIX (September 1974), 13-14+. Examines the public attention to the wrong-doings of their President as revealed by the tape transcripts.

1336. _____. "Watergate and Beyond: The Issue Is Secrecy in the Exercise of Government Power." Progressive, XXXVII (December 1973), 15-19. A scathing attack on secrecy, especially executive privilege.

1337. _____. "Watergate Panel Offers Only Band-Aids." Current, CLXV (September 1974), 3-8. Critical of the impeachment articles.

1338. _____. "Who Owns the Nixon Tapes and Papers: Reprinted from the Washington Post, September 21, 1974." Congressional Record, CXX (September 24, 1974), 32501-32502. Argues that they belong to the people.

1339. Miller, Benjamin R. "The Presidency and Separation of Powers: President Nixon Had the Precedents of Many Years and Many Presidents Behind Him When He Refused to Turn over Presidential Papers and Other Materials in Response to the Special Prosecutor's Subpoena." American Bar Association Journal, LX (February 1974), 195-197. Suggests that Nixon was right and Cox wrong in the dispute which led to the latter's dismissal.

1340. Miller, Marvin. The Breaking of a President. 5 vols. City of Industry, Calif.: Therapy Productions, 1974. An impressive collection of materials related to Nixon's fall; an extremely rare bit of "Watergateana."

1341. Miller, Norman C. "Government Agencies Struggle to Keep Going in the Face of Watergate: Reprinted from the Wall Street Journal, January 30, 1974." Congressional Record, CXX (January 31, 1974), 1772. The all-pervasive White House concern with the crisis has left government agencies without direction.

1342. Miller, R. H. The Nixon Haters: How They Did Him In. St. Parsons, W.V.: McClain Printing Co., 1975. 59p. A pro-Nixon book which blames the President's downfall on enemies who sought his head and not on any actions for which he may have been responsible; a diatribe of the first order.

1343. Miller, William Lee. "Some Notes on Watergate and America." Yale Review, LXIII (March 1974), 321-332. On the goodies the crisis has given political cartoonists and moralists alike.

1344. Mishkin, Paul J. "Great Cases and Soft Law: A Comment on United States v. Nixon." UCLA Law Review, XXII (October 1974), 76-91. Finds the verdict does not have lasting impact beyond the immediate crisis.

1345. "Mr. Nixon Comes out Fighting." Newsweek, LXXXII (November 26, 1973), 24-34. A review of the President's speeches and trips, his attacks on Cox and Richardson, and his meeting with congressmen and senators.

1346. "Mr. Nixon Pays the Price." Newsweek, LXXXIII (April 15, 1974), 18-21. The gathering storm over his possible impeachment.

1347. "Mr. Nixon States His Case." Newsweek, LXXXI (June 4, 1973), 16-26. Recaps his statement concerning his staffer's involvement, his sanction of secret operations for national security reasons, and his limiting of the investigation due to a feared CIA link.

1348. "Mr. Nixon's Defense." Newsweek, LXXXIV (July 8, 1974), 26-28+. No hard evidence that he ordered a cover-up.

1349. "Mr. Nixon's Thanksgiving Day Offering: Reprinted from the Washington Post, November 26, 1973." Congressional Record, CXIX (November 26, 1973), 37943-37944. The 18-minute tape gap.

1350. "Mr. Stans, Here Is Your Currency." Time, CIII (March 18, 1974), 18-19. Stans' role in the receipt of illegal campaign contributions.

1351. "Misunderstanding Secrecy." Harper's, CCXLIX (October 1974), 48. A comment on E. Howard Hunt.

1352. Mitchell, John N. "'What Nixon Doesn't Know....'" Time, CII (July 23, 1973), 16-23. Mitchell's Ervin panel testimony shows he withheld information from the President (who didn't inquire deeply), rejected the Liddy plan for massive disruptions, and lists the "White House horrors."

1353. _____. "Watergate: Testimony from Taciturn John Mitchell." C.Q. Weekly Report, XXXI (July 14, 1973), 1865-1876. Same information as in previous entry.

1354. Mitchell, Martha. "How Politics Wrecked My Marriage." Ladies Home Journal, XCI (December 1974), 52+. Claims Mitchell became overly involved after Nixon took him to Washington and especially after he was placed in charge of CREEP.

1355. "The Mitchell Connection." Newsweek, LXXXII (July 16, 1973), 38+. The allegations about his role and his probable Ervin panel testimony.

1356. _____. Newsweek, LXXXIV (November 11, 1974), 38+. Mitchell in court for the Watergate cover-up trial.

1357. "Mitchell-Stans Both Innocent." Newsweek, LXXXIII (May 6, 1974), 23-25. On the Vesco case.

1358. "Mitchell's Secret Fund." Newsweek, LXXX (October 9, 1972), 39. Dispensed for CREEP intelligence.

1359. "Mitchell's White House Horrors." Newsweek, LXXXII (July 23, 1973), 18-23. Mitchell's Ervin Committee testimony reveals Nixon as strangely unconcerned with cover-up details; the former CREEP director's testimony is contrasted with other testimonies before the Senate panel.

1360. Mitgang, H. "John J. Sirica." New York Times Biographical Service, X (August 1979), 1128-1129. A brief biography of the U.S. District Court chief judge.

1361. Mollenhoff, Clark R. "Executive Privilege--A Devious Doctrine: Reprinted from the New York Times, April 13, 1973." Congressional Record, CXIX (April 17, 1973), 12854. Questions the validity of the doctrine in light of Watergate.

1362. _____. "Evils of 'Executive Privilege' Evident in Transcripts: Reprinted from the New York Times, May 14, 1974." Congressional Record, CXX (May 14, 1974), 14644-14645. Condemns the doctrine with examples drawn from the transcripts.

1363. _____. Game Plan for Disaster: An Ombudsman's Report on the Nixon Years. New York: W. W. Norton, 1976. 384p. A former member of the Nixon administration, Mollenhoff resigned in mid-1970 to return to journalism; his account tells of his White House years as well as his peripheral role in uncovering the spreading Watergate scandal. This strident piece of muckraking provides precise accounts of the affairs he uncovered as well as efforts by Haldeman and Ehrlichman to sweep them under the rug. While showing the harried Nixon trapped by the mounting pile of evidence, Mollenhoff uses the President's difficulties to build a damning case against executive privilege, a lawless fiat which the newsman sees as an excuse for the irresponsible exercise of presidential power.

1364. _____. The Man Who Pardoned Nixon. New York: St. Martin's Press, 1976. 312p. A political profile of Gerald R. Ford, the man who succeeded Nixon as U.S. President; contains much information on the controversial pardon granted the Watergate chief executive.

1365. _____. "Questions on Ford's Judgement: Reprinted from the Dallas Morning News, June 1, 1974." Congressional Record, CXX (June 11, 1974), 18827. Reviews the Vice-

President's defense of Nixon and the distance growing between the two men.

1366. "The Momentum Builds." Newsweek, LXXXIII (April 8, 1974), 18-20. The heated desire for Nixon's impeachment.

1367. Monaghan, Frank. Poor Richard's Paradox. New York: Alpha Pub. Co., 1974. 24p. A behavioral analysis of Nixon during the Watergate affair.

1368. Mondale, Walter F. The Accountability of Power: Toward a Responsible Presidency. New York: David McKay, 1975. 248p. Written a year before he became Carter's vice-president, Mondale's book examines the modern presidency and a series of changes he advocates to reduce future presidential transgressions on the liberties of Americans. His chapters examine such topics as presidential campaigns (their running and financing), the growth of White House staff, the decline of Congress as a co-equal branch, the doctrine of executive privilege, the Nixon impeachment process, and presidential relations with the media, in an effort to get behind the myths, practices, and attitudes which led to the current (1975) situation. Although suggestions on character and personality watching are included, the remainder of his reform suggestions lack depth and detail.

1369. "The Money Game: Illegal Corporate Contributions." Newsweek, LXXXII (November 26, 1973), 34. A list of companies making illegal gifts to CREEP.

1370. "The Money Game: Watergate Hush Money." Newsweek, LXXXII (July 2, 1973), 16-17. An early examination of the possibility that Nixon people were offering cash to the Watergate burglars in order to buy their silence.

1371. Monroe, Bill. "Televising Judiciary Hearings Was Milestone for the Press." RTNDA Communicator (September 1974), 2-3. On the importance of the televised impeachment hearings.

1372. Mootry, Russell, Jr. "Frank Wills Must Not Be Forgotten." Ebony, XXXI (June 1976), 100. The Watergate security guard who called police in to make the arrest.

1373. "More Blunt Talk in the Oval Office." Time, CIV (August 19, 1974), 62. Excerpts from the June 23, 1973 transcripts.

1374. "More Bundles for Bebe?: The Watergate Committee's Investigation of Another Secret Campaign Donation." Newsweek, LXXXIII (May 20, 1974), 43-44. On the Hughes donation held three years by Rebozo before being returned.

Watergate   188

1375. "More Network Coverage As Watergate Heats Up." Broad-
       casting, LXXXV (July 30, 1973), 37-38. Intensified cov-
       erage of the Ervin panel hearings.

1376. "More on Deep Throat." Washington Magazine, XI (Decem-
       ber 1975), 22. Suggests the anonymous Woodward and
       Bernstein source was W. Mark Felt.

1377. "More People Believe Network News Than Believe Nixon."
       Broadcasting, LXXXV (November 26, 1973), 21. The
       results of a poll.

1378. "More Questionable Campaign Cash: The Case of Robert L.
       Vesco." Time, CI (March 12, 1973), 19-20. On a do-
       nation from the indicted New Jersey financier.

1379. Morris, Roger. Haig: A General's Progress. Chicago:
       Playboy Press, 1982. A biography of the recently-
       resigned Secretary of State from his early Army days
       through his service with Henry Kissinger and Nixon to
       N.A.T.O. and Reagan. The author digs deeply into the
       general's activities during Watergate and especially probes
       his meetings with Ford prior to Nixon's resignation and
       the granting of the pardon.

1380. Morrow, Lance. "Watergate's Clearest Lesson." Time,
       CXIX (June 14, 1982), 26-28. A ten-year anniversary
       essay around "the point remains, not even a President
       is above the law."

1381. Morse, Wayne L. "Supremacy and Secrecy: The Deeper
       Meaning of Watergate." Nation, CCXVI (June 18, 1973),
       777-779. The secrecy was necessary to Nixon's suprem-
       acy in light of the case.

1382. Mosher, Frederick C., et al. Watergate: Implications for
       Responsible Government. Scranton, Pa.: Basic Books,
       1974. 137p. The commercially-published version of a
       special study commissioned by the Ervin Committee, this
       slim work spells out, in the opinion of a dozen public ad-
       ministration experts, what Watergate revealed as weak-
       nesses in government institutions. Each of the twelve
       make specific suggestions for reforms.

1383. "The Most Critical Nixon Conversations." Time, CIII (May
       13, 1974), 20-39. Excerpts from the White House tran-
       scripts.

1384. Mount, Ferdinand. "The British View of Watergate." Na-
       tional Review, XXVI (January 18, 1974), 77+. A tempest
       in a teapot.

1385. "The Mounting Momentum for Impeachment." Time, CIII

(April 8, 1974), 9-11. Reviews public opinion and Congressional thought on the case.

1386. "Moving in Committee and Court." Time, CIII (April 15, 1974), 18-19. Summarizes the House Judiciary Committee's attempts to gain White House materials and the latest scandal-related indictments.

1387. Moyers, Bill. "Mercy Without Justice." Newsweek, LXXVII (September 23, 1974), 108. Critical of Ford's pardoning of Nixon.

1388. _____. "No Coups, No Tanks, No Mobs." Newsweek, LXXXIV (August 19, 1974), 11. On the peacefulness of Nixon's resignation.

1389. "Much Ado About Haldeman." Time, CXI (February 27, 1978), 16-20+. How his memoirs (q.v.) were roundly condemned as inaccurate.

1390. Mullen, William F. Presidential Power and Politics. New York: St. Martin's Press, 1976. 294p. Concentrates essentially on the powers in the office of a modern president and the dangers inherent in them. With ample Nixon examples, the author nevertheless advances the position that "one does not have to support a weak presidency in order to seek some limitation, some alternative to the present condition of the office."

1391. Murray, J. Edward. "The Free Press and the Watergate Scandal." Grassroots Editor, XIII (July-August 1973), 16-17+. Examines the role of newspapers in getting out word of the affair.

1392. Muson, Howard. "Man for This Season." New York Times Magazine (November 4, 1973), 34-35+. A profile of Judge John J. Sirica.

1393. Myers, Robert J. The Tragedie of King Richard, the Second: The Life and Times of Richard II (1367-1400), King of England (1377-1399) Compared to Those of Richard of America in His Second Administration. Washington, D.C.: Acropolis Books, 1973. 128p. A satirical play which draws parallels between the situations of the two men.

1394. Myerson, Michael. Watergate: Crime in the Suites. New York: International Publications, 1973. 183p. Based on the Watergate hearings and earlier exposés, this book looks into such matters as illegal campaign contributions, the ITT affair, the Milk Fund case, etc. Suffers from a lack of the information unearthed the following year.

1395. "The Mysterious Mr. McCord." Newsweek, LXXXI (April 9, 1973), 24. A profile of the Watergate plumber-burglar.

1396. "The Mystery Deepens on Watergate Tapes." U.S. News and World Report, LXXVI (January 28, 1974), 22-23. Explaining the 18-minute gap.

1397. "The Mystery of the Missing Tapes." Time, CII (November 12, 1973), 22-23. On the disappearance of several tapes Nixon had agreed to hand over.

1398. No entry.

1399. "The Nation Is in a Shambles and Its Survival Is in Question: Reprinted from the Nashville Tennesseean, October 22, 1973." Congressional Record, CXIX (October 30, 1973), 35363. An editorial critical of the Cox firing.

1400. Naughton, James M. "Constitutional Ervin." New York Times Magazine (May 13, 1973), 13+. A look at the career of the Senate Select Committee chairman.

1401. _____. "First Judgement." New York Times Magazine (April 28, 1974), 27-29+. On the verdicts in the first court cases.

1402. _____. "How the Second Best Informed Man in the White House Briefs the Second Worst Informed Group in Washington." New York Times Magazine (May 30, 1971), 9+. An early look at Ron Ziegler and the White House press corps.

1403. _____. "[John M.] Doar Says Pardon Can't Change Facts: Reprinted from the New York Times, September 13, 1974." Congressional Record, CXX (October 3, 1974), 33873. The House Judiciary Committee counsel contends that Nixon was still guilty of the charges made against him.

1404. _____. "Nixon/Congress Battle--The President's Executive Privilege View Brings the Issue Closer to the Crisis Stage: Reprinted from the New York Times, March 14, 1973." Congressional Record, CXIX (March 15, 1973), 8325. On the President's use of the doctrine to block Watergate-related information from reaching Congress.

1405. _____. "Nixon Tape Is Said to Link Milk Prices to Political Gift: Reprinted from the New York Times, June 6, 1974." Congressional Record, CXX (June 6, 1974), 18006. It did not.

1405a. NBC News. "Chronicle of One Television Network's Campaign Coverage During the Last Month of the 1972 Election." In: Thomas E. Patterson and Robert D. McClure, The Unseeing Eye: The Myth of Television Power in National Elections. New York: G. P. Putnam, 1976. pp. 42-46, 208-218. Close coverage which shows the networks made only scattered references to Watergate.

1406. Nelson, Anna K., ed. The Records of Federal Officials: A Selection of Materials from the National Study Commission on Records and Documents of Federal Officials. New York: Garland Publishing Co., 1978. 416p. Contains information on the debate between Nixon and the government over ownership and access to his presidential materials.

1407. Nelson, Bruce. "Seizure Follows Crusty Testimony of Mrs. Beard: Reprinted from the Los Angeles Times." Congressional Record, CXVIII (May 11, 1972), 17108. On the illness of the ITT lobbyist whose memo began an investigation into the possibility of a fix in the corporation's anti-trust suit.

1408. Nelson, Jack. "Anti-Nixon Vote by 21 Dems Seen: Reprinted from the Los Angeles Times, June 28, 1974." Congressional Record, CXX (June 28, 1974), 21744. On the anticipated vote of the Democratic members of the House Judiciary Committee looking into impeachment.

1409. Neustadt, Richard E. "The Constraining of the President: Something Good out of Watergate?" New York Times Magazine (October 14, 1973), 38-39, 100, 110, 112, 114-117. A noted political scientist's views on the possible outcome of the crisis.

1410. _____. Presidential Power: The Politics of Leadership, with Reflections on Johnson and Nixon. New York: John Wiley, 1976. 324p. Includes the author's classic statement with the last few pages devoted to Nixon's difficulties.

1411. _____. Presidential Power: The Politics of Leadership from FDR to Carter. 2nd ed. New York: John Wiley, 1980. 286p. Adds three chapters to the classic account of the uses and abuses of presidential power first published in 1960, which reappraise his analysis of power use by Eisenhower's successors and finds the nation without either an imperial presidency or a dominant Congress. Weakness in the office was the central theme of the 1960 edition and remains the central idea here. Contains a few references to Nixon and Watergate.

1412. Neustadt, Sara Jane. "The (18.5 Minute) Credibility Gap: Analyzing the White House Tapes." Technology Review, LXXVIII (February 1976), 16-18. On the technical analysis ordered by Judge Sirica.

1413. "A New President: An End to a Nation's Agony." U.S. News and World Report, LXXVII (August 19, 1974), 14-16. On Ford's assuming the presidency.

1414. "New Tale of the Tapes: 18 Minutes of Mysterious Buzzing."

Newsweek, LXXXII (December 3, 1973), 26-33. How the 18-minute gap works against Nixon's credibility.

1415. "New Tape Crop." Newsweek, LXXXIII (April 29, 1974), 30-35. Lists possible contents of tapes newly subpoenaed.

1416. New York Times, Staff of. The End of a Presidency. New York: Holt, 1974. 353p. Also published by Bantam Books, this is an instant recounting put together within days of the event. Includes eight essays by staff reporters, including R. W. Apple and James Naughton, a chronology, and documents. Illustrated with 64 pages of photos.

1417. "The Newest Daytime Drama: Hearings of the Senate Select Committee on Presidential Campaign Activities." Time, CI (May 28, 1973), 20-24. On televising the hearings.

1418. "Newsmakers: Egil Krogh." Newsweek, LXXXV (May 26, 1975), 52. A post-Watergate profile.

1419. "Newsmakers: G. Gordon Liddy." Newsweek, LXXXV (January 13 and June 9, 1975), 44, 50-51. Post-Watergate profiles.

1420. "Newsmakers: John D. Ehrlichman." Newsweek, LXXXV (April 21, 1975), 57. A post-Watergate look.

1421. "Newsmakers: John Dean." Newsweek, LXXXV (March 24 and May 5, 1975), 61, 55. Post-Watergate profile.

1422. "Newsmakers: John Mitchell." Newsweek, LXXXV (May 5, 1975), 55. A post-Watergate profile shared with John Dean (see last entry).

1423. "Newsmakers: Sam Ervin." Newsweek, LXXXII (October 22, 1973), 101; LXXXIV (December 30, 1974), 36. Watergate and post-Watergate profiles.

1424. "... the Next Collision." Newsweek, LXXXIII (April 1, 1974), 18-23. After a brief review of Watergate's first year, the article looks at Judge Sirica's turning over of grand jury data to the House Impeachment panel.

1425. "Next Question for Watergate Panel: How to Proceed." C.Q. Weekly Report, XXXI (1973), 2249-2250. On the recessed Ervin panel hearings.

1426. Nikolaieff, George A., ed. The President and the Constitution. Reference Shelf, v. 46, no. 4. New York: H. W. Wilson Co., 1974. 230p. Excerpts from speeches, newspaper accounts, etc. Contents arranged under these headings: "The Demand for Impeachment or Resignation";

"The Watergate Scandal"; "The Growth of Presidential Power"; "War Powers"; "Executive Privilege and Impoundment"; "Impeachment Steps Begin"; and "A President Resigns."

1427. Nix, Mundy. "The 'Meet the Press' Game." In: Gaye Tuchman, ed. The TV Establishment. Englewood Cliffs, N.J.: Prentice-Hall, 1974. pp. 66-71. On the appearance by political figures on the Sunday TV opinion program.

1428. Nixon, Richard M. "Availability of Information from Presidential Tapes: Statement by the President Announcing Procedures." Weekly Compilation of Presidential Documents, IX (October 22, 1973), 1265-1266. The idea of providing selected transcripts.

1429. _____. "Executive Privilege: The President's Statement of March 12, 1973." In: Buel W. Patch, ed. Historic Documents, 1973. Washington, D.C.: Congressional Quarterly, Inc., 1974. pp. 337-342. On why staffers should decline to appear as witnesses; also published in Weekly Compilation of Presidential Documents, IX (March 19, 1973), 253-255.

1430. _____. "From the Official Record--Nixon's History-Making Moves: Text of Statement, October 19, 1973." U.S. News and World Report, LXXV (November 5, 1973), 70-71. Proposal to let Senator John C. Stennis proof any tapes necessary rather than turning them over under subpoena.

1431. _____. "Milk Fund and ITT Statements: Excerpts from Two Presidential Statements [January 8, 1974] Explaining President Nixon's Involvement in 1971 Decisions." In: Robert A. Diamond, ed. Historic Documents, 1974. Washington, D.C.: Congressional Quarterly, Inc., 1975. pp. 3-22. Claims non-involvement in either case and no deals being made.

1432. _____. "News Conference on Watergate, August 22, 1973." In: Buel W. Patch, ed. Historic Documents, 1973. Washington, D.C.: Congressional Quarterly, Inc., 1974. pp. 737-752. Accepts blame for the climate which produced the crisis and restates his position on turning over Oval Office tapes.

1433. _____. "Nixon Interview." National Review, XXVI (January 7, 1974), 632-633. Again expresses no wrongdoing.

1434. _____. "Nixon on Impeachment: Excerpts from Presidential News Conference of February 25, 1974." In: Robert A. Diamond, ed. Historic Documents, 1974.

Washington, D.C.: Congressional Quarterly, Inc., 1975. pp. 145-156. Doesn't expect to be impeached because he sees no grounds.

1435. _____. "Nixon on Impeachment: Excerpts from Three Presidential News Conferences, March 6-19, 1974." In: Robert A. Diamond, ed. Historic Documents, 1974. Washington, D.C.: Congressional Quarterly, Inc., 1975. pp. 189-204. Expresses roughly the same sentiments as in the last entry.

1436. _____. "Nixon on National Security Wiretaps: Excerpts from Sworn Deposition, March 10, 1976." In: Robert A. Diamond, ed. Historic Documents, 1976. Washington, D.C.: Congressional Quarterly, Inc., 1977. pp. 159-168. On the tapes placed on those suspected of leaking information to the press.

1437. _____. "Nixon on White House Transcripts: President Nixon's Address to the Nation [April 29, 1974] Announcing His Plans to Turn Over to the House Judiciary Committee and to Make Public Certain White House-Edited Transcripts of Tape Recorded Presidential Conversations." In: Robert A. Diamond, ed. Historic Documents, 1974. Washington, D.C.: Congressional Quarterly, Inc., 1975. pp. 287-300. The famous White House transcripts.

1438. _____. "Nixon Speaks." Newsweek, LXXXVI (September 1, 1975), 17-18. But says nothing of importance on Watergate.

1439. _____. "Nixon Tells His Side of the Watergate Case: Statement, May 22, 1973." U.S. News and World Report, LXXIV (June 4, 1973), 96-99. Complete text of his May 22 speech.

1440. _____. "Nixon to Managing Editors: Excerpts from a Question-and-Answer Session Between President Nixon and Members of the Associated Press Managing Editors Association at Orlando, Florida, November 17, 1973." In: Buel W. Patch, ed. Historic Documents, 1973. Washington, D.C.: Congressional Quarterly, Inc., 1974. pp. 947-964. All the questions were related to Watergate.

1441. _____. "Nixon's Address to the Nation on the Watergate Case: Radio and Television Address, August 15, 1973." Vital Speeches, XXXIX (September 1, 1973), 674-677. In which the President tells about first learning of the break-in; released as well in U.S. News and World Report, LXXV (August 27, 1973), 77-80.

1442. _____. "Nixon's Address to the Nation on the Watergate Case: Television Address, April 30, 1973." Vital

Speeches, XXXIX (May 15, 1973), 450-452. Nixon's speech on the change in the "palace guard"; also appeared in U.S. News and World Report, LXXIV (May 14, 1973), 70-72.

1443. ———. "Nixon's Attack on News Media: Text of White House News Conference on Middle East Crisis and Watergate, October 26, 1973." In: Buel W. Patch, ed. Historic Documents, 1973. Washington, D.C.: Congressional Quarterly, Inc., 1974. pp. 897-912. In which the chief executive labels the press as "vicious, outrageous, and distorted" in its reporting; also published in C.Q. Weekly Report, XXXI (1973), 2903-2906.

1444. ———. "Nixon's Statements on the Watergate Investigation." C.Q. Weekly Report, XXXII (1974), 2123-2126. Those of March 1974.

1445. ———. "On the Rebound?: Press Conference, August 22, 1973." Newsweek, LXXXII (September 3, 1973), 22-26. The first-learning speech.

1446. ———. "Presidential Tapes and Materials: Address, April 29, 1974." Vital Speeches, XL (June 1, 1974), 482-486. On releasing the White House transcripts.

1447. ———. The Presidential Transcripts in Conjunction with the Staff of the Washington Post. New York: Delacorte Press, 1974. 693p. A reproduction of the edited tapes with an introduction; the paperback, put out by Dell Publishing, was rapidly assembled and on newstands almost instantly.

1448. ———. "The President's Address to the Nation [April 29, 1974], Announcing His Answer to the Subpoena from the House Judiciary Committee." Weekly Compilation of Presidential Documents, X (May 6, 1974), 450-458. On releasing the White House transcripts.

1449. ———. "The President's Letter [May 22, 1974] to Peter W. Rodino, Jr., Chairman of the House Judiciary Committee, in Response to the Committee's Subpoenas." Weekly Compilation of Presidential Documents, X (May 27, 1974), 538. Agreeing to turn over income tax records.

1450. ———. "The President's Own Explanation of Watergate 'Hush Money.'" U.S. News and World Report, LXXVI (March 18, 1974), 20. Excerpts from Nixon's March 6 news conference.

1451. ———. "The President's Resignation Speech." Time, CIV (August 19, 1974), 14. Excerpts.

Watergate

1452. _____. "The President's Statements on the Watergate Investigation." C.Q. Weekly Report, XXXII (August 10, 1974), 2119-2123+. Excerpts from speeches made between August 29, 1972 and April 29, 1974.

1453. _____. Public Papers of the Presidents of the United States: Richard M. Nixon, 1972-1974. 3 vols. Washington, D.C.: Published for the Office of the Federal Register, National Archives and Records Service, by the U.S. Government Printing Office, 1973-1975. Contains all of Nixon's public messages, speeches, and statements, including those on Watergate.

1454. _____. RN: The Memoirs of Richard Nixon. New York: Grosset & Dunlap, 1978. 1,120p. The Watergate segment of Nixon's memoirs are less than candid (according to Senator Ervin who wrote his own memoirs as a rebuttal, q.v.), but constitute mostly a tale of deception, subterfuge, and buck-passing. The 37th president saw his problems in terms of support and loyalty and missed dreams not fulfilled, not in terms of obstructing justice or "dirty tricks."

1455. _____. "Release of Additional Transcripts of Presidential Conversations: Statement by the President, August 5, 1974." Weekly Compilation of Presidential Documents, X (August 12, 1974), 1003-1009. Including those showing his participation in the Watergate cover-up, the so-called "smoking gun."

1456. _____. "Scrambling to Break Clear of Watergate: Television Address of Richard Nixon." Time, CII (August 27, 1973), 11-14. The "first learned about" speech.

1457. _____. Submission of Recorded Presidential Conversations to the Committee on the Judiciary of the House of Representatives by President Richard Nixon. Washington, D.C.: U.S. Government Printing Office, 1974. 1,308p. The official GPO edition of the White House transcripts.

1458. _____. _____. Edited by Gerald Gold. New York: Bantam Books, 1974. 877p. Includes introductory summaries and a background to each segment, a who's who, chronology, the White House summary, a legal argument that accompanied the transcripts, and the text of Nixon's speech to the nation, April 29, 1974. Similar in rapid-production schedule to the version put out by the Washington Post above.

1459. _____. "Tapes That Burst Like a Bombshell: Statement, August 5, 1974." U.S. News and World Report, LXXVII (August 19, 1974), 68. On releasing three tape transcripts covering his June 23, 1972 White House meeting.

1460. _____. "Text of Statement of May 22, 1973 on the Watergate Affair." In: Buel W. Patch, ed. Historic Documents, 1973. Washington, D.C.: Congressional Quarterly, Inc., 1974. pp. 563-576. Also published in C.Q. Weekly Report, IX (May 28, 1973), 693-698.

1461. _____. "The Watergate Investigation: Statement by the President, August 15, 1973." Weekly Compilation of Presidential Documents, IX (August 20, 1973), 991-994. Also printed in U.S. News and World Report, LXXV (August 27, 1973), 81-83.

1462. _____. "The Watergate Investigation: Statement by the President, April 30, 1973." Weekly Compilation of Presidential Documents, IX (May 7, 1973), 433-438.

1463. _____. "Watergate Charges." Vital Speeches, XXXIX (September 1, 1973), 674-677. Text of Nixon's August 15, 1973 address.

1464. _____. "When Nixon Was Asked: 'Would It Not Be Better That You Resign?'" U.S. News and World Report, LXXVI (March 25, 1974), 30. The President's answer at the Chicago Executive Club.

1465. _____ and William B. Saxbe. "Presidential Materials of Richard Nixon: Letter of Agreement Between Former President Nixon and the Administrator of General Services [Arthur F. Sampson], with the Text of a Legal Opinion by the Attorney General, September 8, 1974." Weekly Compilation of Presidential Documents, X (September 16, 1974), 1104-1108. Nixon's agreement with the government on housing his papers and tapes.

1466. "Nixon, Aides' Remarks Re-Open Media Battles." Editor and Publisher (November 3, 1973), 7+. The President's charge that reporting was "outrageous and vicious."

1467. "Nixon and the Media." Newsweek, LXXXI (January 15, 1973), 42-44. On their poor relationship.

1468. "Nixon Counterattack: 'I Have Earned Every Cent.'" C.Q. Weekly Report, XXXI (1973), 3070-3074. The text of the presidential news conference of November 17, 1973 is printed on pp. 3074-3081.

1469. "Nixon Conspiracy Laid Bare." Time, CIV (December 2, 1974), 20+. Testimony in the Watergate cover-up trial.

1470. "The Nixon Crisis: Where Will It Lead?" U.S. News and World Report, LXXVI (May 27, 1974), 17-20. The prospects on impeachment.

1471. "Nixon Deserves Due Process: Reprinted from the Galesburg [Illinois] Register-Mail, May 13, 1974." Congressional Record, CXX (May 20, 1974), 15709. An editorial suggesting the rush to impeachment may be too rapid.

1472. "Nixon Digs in for the Siege." Newsweek, LXXXIII (May 27, 1974), 22-24+. The latest in the White House defense.

1473. "Nixon Digs in to Fight." Time, CIII (February 4, 1974), 13-14. Krogh says Nixon not involved with "plumbers," and Senator Hugh Scott suggests Dean perjured.

1474. "Nixon Encore." Time, CXVIII (October 5, 1981), 25. On possible release of the tapes.

1475. "Nixon-Haldeman Talks: Excerpts from June 23, 1972 Transcripts." Time, CIV (August 19, 1974), 18-19. Planning the cover-up; also printed in U.S. News and World Report, LXXVII (August 19, 1974), 69-70.

1476. "Nixon Has 15 'Sure' Senate Votes, Is Trying for 38: Reprinted from the Boston Globe, May 9, 1974." Congressional Record, CXX (May 9, 1974), 14122-14123. Counting support in the Senate for a possible post-impeachment trial.

1477. "Nixon Has Gone Too Far." Time, CIII (May 20, 1974), 22-23. Public opinion on his refusal to honor subpoenas.

1478. "Nixon Lawyers." Time, CII (July 16, 1973), 16-17. Brief biographies of J. Fred Buzhardt and Leonard Garment.

1479. "Nixon Legacy." C.Q. Weekly Report, XXXII (1974), 2281-2283. On his numerous long-term appointments, e.g., Chief Justice Burger.

1480. "Nixon-Media Feud Keeps Bubbling." Broadcasting, LXXXV (November 12, 1973), 52-53. On the President's remarks, calling them "vicious and outrageous."

1481. "Nixon Mire." Nation, CCXVII (September 3, 1973), 162-163. Comments on his August 15, 1973 address and reasons for not releasing the Oval Office tapes.

1482. "Nixon, Once More, with Feeling." Time, CIX (May 16, 1977), 21-22+. The Nixon-Frost interviews.

1483. "Nixon on TV: Still More Light on Watergate." U.S. News and World Report, LXXXIII (September 12, 1977), 81. Nixon-Frost.

1484. "The Nixon Pardon." In: Robert A. Diamond, ed. Historic Documents, 1974. Washington, D.C.: Congressional Quarterly, Inc., 1975. pp. 811-818. Text and comments.

1485. _____ : Reprinted from the Minneapolis Tribune, September 9, 1974." Congressional Record, CXX (September 11, 1974), 30749. An editorial on the matter.

1486. "The Nixon Poll Wrap-up--Some Astonishing Questions Remain: Reprinted from the Chicago Down Town News, April 1974." Congressional Record, CXX (April 30, 1974), 12473-12474. Those interviewd backed Nixon 5-1.

1487. "The Nixon Presidency." Gallup Opinion Index, XXXIII (June 1974), 1-11. Public opinion concerning.

1488. The Nixon Presidential Press Conferences. New York: E. M. Coleman Enterprises, 1978. 419p. Reprinted; contains an introduction by Helen Thomas, dean of the White House press corps.

1489. "Nixon Presses His Counterattack." Time, CII (November 26, 1973), 15-17. Meetings and speeches during the previous week.

1490. "Nixon Talks." Time, CIX (May 9, 1977), 22-24+. Excerpts from his Frost interviews.

1491. "Nixon Tapes." Newsweek, LXXXII (July 30, 1973), 12-16. After Butterfield revealed their existence, Nixon refused to release them on grounds of executive privilege.

1492. No entry.

1493. "Nixon Tapes--Round Two to Cox." Newsweek, LXXXII (October 22, 1973), 43-44. On the Appellate Court's decision that they should be handed over.

1494. Nixon: The First, Second, Third, Fourth, and Fifth Years of His Presidency. 4 vols. Washington, D.C.: Congressional Quarterly, Inc., 1970-1974. Annual compilations of materials on the Nixon presidency as a whole; the 1972-1974 volumes, especially the last, contain Watergate-related data.

1495. "Nixon--The Odds on Survival Shorten." Time, CIV (August 12, 1974), 9-13. The final pre-resignation days of the Nixon presidency.

1496. "Nixon Turns 61: How Is He Bearing Up?" U.S. News and World Report, LXXVI (January 14, 1974), 22-23. A look at the President's health.

1497. "Nixon vs. Congress: Round Six Will Be the Toughest Yet." U.S. News and World Report, LXXVI (January 7, 1974), 22-23. Democratic efforts to take advantage of Watergate in blocking his programs.

1498. "Nixon vs. the Investigators." U.S. News and World Report, LXXV (August 6, 1973), 11-13. The Cox-Ervin Committee-Nixon struggle over the White House tapes.

1499. "Nixon--What Next?: The Case of the Missing Tapes." Newsweek, LXXXII (November 12, 1973), 24-27+. Revelations that two subpoenaed tapes are missing.

1500. "Nixon's All-Out Drive to Restore Confidence." U.S. News and World Report, LXXV (November 26, 1973), 27-28. "Operation Candor."

1501. "Nixon's Big Push to Head off Impeachment." U.S. News and World Report, LXXVI (April 1, 1974), 23-24. "Operation Candor," continued.

1502. "Nixon's Crisis--And Ford's." Newsweek, LXXXIV (September 23, 1974), 30-34. Facing civil trial, Nixon is rescued by Ford's pardon, which brings the new president much criticism.

1503. "Nixon's Date with the Supreme Court." Time, CIII (June 10, 1974), 19-20+. Anticipated results of United States v. Nixon.

1504. "Nixon's Days in Court Are TV's Too." Broacasting, LXXXVII (August 5, 1974), 18-22. On the historic significance of the televised impeachment hearings.

1505. "Nixon's Defense Strategy." U.S. News and World Report, LXXVII (August 12, 1974), 17-18. Claims of no direct evidence.

1506. "Nixon's Eleventh Hour." Newsweek, LXXXIV (August 12, 1974), 18-21+. On his final days in office.

1507. "Nixon's Emotional Farewell." Time, CIV (August 19, 1968), 68. Comments on.

1508. "Nixon's Farewell: 'I Have Tried To Do What Was Best.'" U.S. News and World Report, LXXVII (August 19, 1974), 71-72.

1509. "Nixon's Future: Should He Be Prosecuted?" C.Q. Weekly Report, XXXII (1974), 2213-2216. Pro and con on the issue.

1510. "Nixon's Last Days." Christian Century, XCI (September 18, 1974), 838-840. Comments on.

1511. "Nixon's Men in the Dock." Newsweek, LXXXIV (October 7, 1974), 43-44. Beginning of the Watergate cover-up trial.

1512. "Nixon's Men: Room for Maneuver?" Newsweek, LXXXIII (April 8, 1974), 20-21. Those on trial for Fielding break-in.

1513. "Nixon's Nightmare: Fighting to Be Believed." Time, CI (May 14, 1973), 17-32. "Palace guard" changes and his latest speech.

1514. "Nixon's Pardon." National Review, XXVI (September 27, 1974), 1085-1086. Comments on.

1515. "Nixon's Popularity." Gallup Opinion Index, XXXII (September 1973), 1-12. Holding firm in some areas, weakening in others.

1516. "Nixon's Role in Watergate." U.S. News and World Report, LXXV (July 9, 1973), 11-13. Recaps John Dean's testimony and cross-examination.

1517. "Nixon's Tapes: How to Settle out of Court." Newsweek, LXXXII (September 24, 1973), 33-35. Describes a plan which would allow Cox to decide which were important and Nixon to retain authority over them.

1518. "Nixon's Thin Defense: The Need for Secrecy." Time, CI (June 4, 1973), 17-23. A statement defending the work of the "plumbers" and the cover-up.

1519. "Nixon's Watergate Tapes: Statement Prepared by Presidential Special Counsel James D. St. Clair." U.S. News and World Report, LXXVI (May 13, 1974), 78-82. Text issued along with the transcripts pointing out Dean's discrepancies.

1520. Nobile, Philip. "Dan Rather Is Going Fishing." Esquire, LXXXI (April 1974), 106-108+. On the CBS News White House correspondent.

1521. _____. "'Extra': How the New York Times Became Second Banana." Esquire, LXXXIII (May 1975), 85-99. Competition with the Washington Post's Woodward and Bernstein.

1522. _____. "What Makes the Apple Machine Run?" More, VI (July-August 1976), 23-28. An interview with New York Times political correspondent R. W. Apple, Jr.

1523. Northey, Rebecca. "Expanding the Mistake of Law Doctrine: United States v. Barker." Boston University Law Review, LVII (November 1977), 882-905. A discussion of Bernard Barker's legal plea regarding his conviction.

1524. "Notes and Comments: The Nixon Interviews." New Yorker,

LIII (May 23, 1977), 27-28. On the former president's encounter with David Frost.

1525. "Notes and Comments: Reactions of Well-Known People in Various Fields to the Edited Transcripts." New Yorker, L (May 20, 1974), 29-31. Most found them disagreeable and unacceptable.

1526. "Notes on Watergate One Year Later." Monthly Review, XXV (May 1974), 1-11. Lessons learned and whereabouts of participants.

1527. "The Notorious Pardon: Some Gaps in Ford's Candor." Nation, CCXIX (November 9, 1974), 455-457. Argues that Ford was not altogether truthful in his pardon statement.

1528. Notson, Robert C. "The Anatomy of Watergate: An Address, January 22, 1974." Congressional Record, CXX (February 5-6, 1974), 2245-2246, 2477-2478. An analysis of why the crisis was occurring.

1529. "Now a White House Inaudibility Gap: The Watergate Tapes." Time, CII (November 19, 1973), 21-22. On the 18-minute gap.

1530. "Now It's a Three-Front Battle over the Tapes." U.S. News and World Report, LXXVI (June 3, 1974), 25-27. Between the courts, special prosecutor, and House Judiciary Committee.

1531. "Now It's the Watergate Two." Newsweek, LXXXI (January 29, 1973), 24-25. Break-in guilty plea of four defendants.

1532. "Now, the Watergate Defense." Newsweek, LXXIV (December 9, 1974), 38+. In the cover-up trial.

1533. Nuechterlein, James A. "Watergate: Toward a Revisionist View." Commentary, LXVIII (August 1979), 38-45. Concerns suggestions that Nixon may not have been all that guilty.

1534. Oberbeck, S. K. "A Plumber's Works." Newsweek, LXXXII (September 10, 1973), 86+. Looks at the publications of E. Howard Hunt.

1535. O'Brien, Francis W. "The Dissenting Opinions of Nixon vs. Sirica: An Argument for Executive Privilege in the White House Tapes Controversy." Southwestern Law Journal, XXVIII (Spring 1974), 373-390. Examines the defense briefs from the White House in the light of national security needs.

1536. O'Brien, Lawrence F. "Watergate and Beyond." In: his

No Final Victories: A Life in Politics from John F. Kennedy to Watergate. Garden City, N.Y.: Doubleday, 1974. pp. 336-362. The author was Democratic chairman at the time of Watergate and it was his records, among others, which were sought by the White House "plumbers" when they broke into the Watergate. O'Brien also describes the party suit against the CREEP organization for damages in the wake of the burglary.

1537. "The Odd Couple at Judiciary." Newsweek, LXXXIII (May 20, 1974), 34-35. Counsels Doar and Jenner.

1538. "Odds on Impeachment Now; In the View of Congressional Leaders Those Transcripts Nixon Made Public Have Hurt the President, Make His Future More Uncertain; How the White House Views Chances of Impeachment." U.S. News and World Report, LXXVI (May 20, 1974), 19-23. The title says it all.

1539. "Of Memory and National Security." Time, CI (June 11, 1973), 19-21. On the denial by Haldeman and Ehrlichman in their Ervin panel testimony of involving the CIA in the coverup.

1540. "Official Version: Watergate Prosecutors Tell Why Nixon Was Not Indicted; A Final Report Answers Some of the Questions in the Minds of Americans About Watergate Decisions, But a Few Mysteries Remain Unsolved." U.S. News and World Report, LXXIX (October 27, 1975), 65-66. Recaps the highlights from the W.S.P.F. final report cited below.

1541. Offutt, Gary S. "Ignorance or Mistake of the Law." Maryland Law Review, XXXVII (Summer 1977), 404-450. On Bernard Barker's legal claim.

1542. O'Leary, Jeremiah. "Ellsberg Judge Met with Nixon: Reprinted from the Washington Star-News, April 30, 1974." In: Book VII, Part IV of U.S. Congress, House, Committee on the Judiciary. Statement of Information: Hearings. 93rd Cong., 2nd sess. Washington, D.C.: U.S. Government Printing Office, 1974. p. 2026. On allegations that Nixon tried to bribe Judge W. Matthew Byrne, Jr.

1543. Oliphant, Tom. "Nixon's New Go-Fer." Ramparts, XII (January 1974), 16-18. A profile of Alexander Haig.

1544. "On the Record." U.S. News and World Report, LXXIV (May 28, 1973), 22+. Claims of White House hush money payments.

1545. "$100,000 Misunderstanding: Bebe Rebozo's Campaign Contribution." Time, CIII (May 6, 1974), 13-14. An illegal contribution and a close Nixon friend.

1546. "One Jump Ahead of the Sheriff." Newsweek, LXXXIX (May 9, 1977), 31. Excerpts from previously unreleased White House transcripts.

1547. "One More Surprise in the Watergate Case: With Senate Hearings Suspended--Maybe Ended--It's in Court That Watergate Fight Is Being Waged." U.S. News and World Report, LXXV (December 10, 1973), 35-36. The mystery over the missing tapes.

1548. "'Operation Chaos': Reprinted from the New York Times, June 11, 1975." Congressional Record, CXXI (June 11, 1975), 18284-18285. Domestic activities of the CIA.

1549. "'Operation Disney World I, II, and III': Reprinted from the Washington Post, November 20-21, 23, 1973." Congressional Record, CXIX (November 26, 1973), 37941-37943. A detailed analysis of the White House strategy designed to restore Nixon's prestige and called "Operation Candor."

1550. "'Operation Friendly Persuasion.'" Newsweek, LXXXIII (March 25, 1974), 22-24+. On the White House effort to persuade influential leaders of Nixon's innocence.

1551. "'Operation Watergate': The Raid on Democratic National Committee Headquarters." Newsweek, LXXX (July 3, 1972), 18-21. Summarizes the initial break-in and gives brief biographies of those caught.

1552. "The Organization Men: Reprinted from the Wall Street Journal, April 4, 1974." Congressional Record, CXX (April 9, 1974), 10313-10314. An editorial asking that there be no more non-party presidential election committees like CREEP.

1553. "The Original Dirty Trickster: Donald R. Segretti." Newsweek, LXXXII (October 15, 1973), 28+. A brief biography.

1554. Orman, John M. Presidential Secrecy and Deception: Beyond the Power to Persuade. Contributions in Political Science, no. 43. Westport, Conn.: Greenwood Press, 1980. 239p. Does not directly relate to Watergate instances in any of the four cases studied (Nixon's concerns Chile), but does attempt to explain the circumstances under which he and others attempted to employ secrecy and deception in policymaking. A useful source for those looking at the manner in which the Nixon White House functioned on foreign policy matters during the life of the Watergate crisis.

1555. Osborne, John. "Appeal to the House." New Republic, CLXIX (October 6, 1973), 11-12. The House Judiciary Committee takes on the task of looking into impeachment possibilities.

1556. _____. "At the Death: Tape Erasure." New Republic, CLXIX (December 8, 1973), 8-10. The 18-minute gap.

1557. _____. "Awaiting Judgement." New Republic, CLXXI (July 27, 1974), 9-11. Preparation of the articles and their report to the floor of the House.

1558. _____. "Back with Dick." New Republic, CLXXVI (May 14, 1977), 8-9. On the Nixon-Frost interviews.

1559. _____. The Fourth Year of the Nixon Watch. New York: Liveright, 1973. 218p. Covers events of 1972-early 1973, including Watergate; based on author's New Republic pieces.

1560. _____. "Guilty Men." New Republic, CLXVII (October 28, 1972), 11-12. The conviction of the Watergate "burglars."

1561. _____. "'I Run the Campaign.'" New Republic, CLXVIII (March 24, 1973), 8-10. Concerns illegal contributions to the Finance Committee to Reelect the President.

1562. _____. "Indictments." New Republic, CLXX (March 16, 1974), 11-13. The grand jury names Nixon an unindicted co-conspirator.

1563. _____. The Last Nixon Watch. Washington, D.C.: New Republic, 1975. 246p. Covers the period 1973-1974; based on the author's New Republic articles.

1564. _____. "Limited Confession." New Republic, CLXVIII (June 2, 1973), 14-15. Thoughts on Nixon's May 22, 1973 statement.

1565. _____. "Nixon Postscript." New Republic, CLXXI (September 7, 1974), 10-13. On the question of who owns the White House tapes.

1566. _____. "Nixon's Devils." New Republic, CLXXV (August 7, 1976), 11-12. Reviews the work of the White House "plumbers."

1567. _____. "One Way Out." New Republic, CLXXI (July 20, 1974), 11-13. On the possibilities of a presidential resignation.

1568. _____. "The Pardon." New Republic, CLXXI (September

28, 1974), 9-11. Reviews Ford's forgiveness of ex-president Nixon.

1569. _____. "President vs. Press." New Republic, CLXVI (April 8, 1972), 11-13. Examines the comments of James Keogh.

1570. _____. "A Shabby Piece of Work." New Republic, CLXXVIII (March 4, 1978), 15-18. A condemnation of Haldeman's memoirs.

1571. _____. "Shades of Meaning." New Republic, CLXXIX (September 15, 1973), 10-12. Clark MacGregor's role in the Watergate investigation.

1572. _____. "Something but the Truth: Television Address About the Watergate Affair." New Republic, CLXVIII (May 12, 1973), 14-16. Suggests Nixon lied in his statement concerning White House staff changes.

1573. _____. "Tactics." New Republic, CLXX (May 11, 1974), 11-12. What was behind the release of the White House transcripts.

1574. _____. "Tapestries." New Republic, CLXX (May 18, 1974), 10-12. J. Fred Buzhardt's story on the Oval Office taping system.

1575. _____. "They Done Him Wrong." New Republic, CLXX (April 27, 1974), 15-17. A look at Nixon's loyal supporters.

1576. _____. "Through the Window." New Republic, CLXVI (April 15, 1972), 15-17. Comments on the ITT scandal.

1577. _____. "To the Brink." New Republic, CLXIX (November 3, 1973), 10-12. Concerns the dismissal of Archibald Cox.

1578. _____. "Was Nixon Sick of Mind?" New York, VIII (April 21, 1975), 37-45. An analysis of the psychological analyses being made on the former president.

1579. _____. "Watergate Miseries." New Republic, CLXIX (July 21, 1973), 16-18. Impact of the unfolding scandal on the White House and President.

1580. Osolin, Charles. "Should Nixon Be Impeached--Mizell Remains Cautious: Reprinted from the Winston-Salem Journal, June 9, 1974." Congressional Record, CXX (June 17, 1974), 19535-19536. Views of North Carolina Congressman Wilmer Mizell.

1581. Ostrow, Ronald J. "Dita Beard Says International Telephone and Telegraph Told Her to Ask Mitchell About Suit: Reprinted from the Los Angeles Times." Congressional Record, CXVIII (May 11, 1972), 17113. The ITT lobbyist's statement on Mitchell and the ITT anti-trust suit.

1582. _____. "FBI Says Same Machine Typed Two Disputed Memos in International Telephone and Telegraph Case: Reprinted from the Los Angeles Times." Congressional Record, CXVIII (May 11, 1972), 17108-17109. On the falseness of the famous Beard memo.

1583. _____. "Former International Telephone and Telegraph Typist Recalls Part of [Beard] Memorandum Referring to Mitchell--Remembers Key Sentence That Ex-Attorney General [Mitchell] Knew of Convention Plans: Reprinted from the Los Angeles Times." Congressional Record, CXVIII (May 11, 1972), 17112-17113. Recollections of secretary Susan Lichtman.

1584. _____. "ITT Reveals Talks with High Officials--Says Its Chief [Harold S. Geneen] Met with Mitchell, Nixon Aides, and Congressmen: Reprinted from the Los Angeles Times." Congressional Record, CXVIII (May 11, 1972), 17104-17105. Admits the meeting more social than underhanded.

1585. _____. "Met ITT Officials, but Didn't Handle Suit, Kleindienst Says: Reprinted from the Los Angeles Times." Congressional Record, CXVIII (May 11, 1972), 17100-17101. Statements made at Kleindienst confirmation hearings.

1586. _____. "Mitchell Denies Discussing ITT Antitrust Cases--Met Corporation Officials Only for Talks on Overall Policy: Reprinted from the Los Angeles Times." Congressional Record, CXVIII (May 11, 1972), 17104. Mitchell disputes Beard memo.

1587. _____. "Mitchell Disputed in ITT Controversy: Reprinted from the Los Angeles Times." Congressional Record, CXVIII (May 11, 1972), 17097-17098. Beard statements.

1588. _____. "Mrs. Beard's Boss Denies He Ordered Her to Write Memo: Reprinted from the Los Angeles Times." Congressional Record, CXVIII (May 11, 1972), 17117. Recollections of William R. Merriam.

1589. _____. "Nixon Ordered Settlement with ITT, Mitchell Quoted As Saying: Reprinted from the Los Angeles Times." Congressional Record, CXVIII (May 11, 1972), 17101-17102. A look at the President's alleged role in the case.

1590. _____. "Panel Will Resume Kleindienst Inquiry: Reprinted from the Los Angeles Times." Congressional Record, CXVIII (May 11, 1972), 17095. The Senate Judiciary Committee re-opening of Kleindienst's confirmation hearings.

1591. _____ and Robert L. Jackson. "Nixon Aides Deeply Upset over 'Tactical Errors' in ITT Affair: Reprinted from the Los Angeles Times." Congressional Record, CXVIII (May 11, 1972), 17102-17103. Concerns not over any illegalities but over handling which brought the matter to the attention of the media.

1592. "The Other Investigator." Time, CII (July 16, 1973), 71+. A profile of Archibald Cox.

1593. "Other Nixon Watergate Men." Time, CIII (March 11, 1974), 20-21. Notes on 18 men who were convicted, indicted, or pleaded guilty.

1594. O'Toole, George. "Enhancing the White House Tapes: Those Missing 18 Minutes." New Republic, LXX (January 19, 1974), 15-18. The work of a Sirica-appointed panel of experts.

1595. _____. "Rose Mary's Machine and the 18-Minute Gap." New Republic, LXX (March 9, 1974), 10-12. Wood's statement on how she caused the erasure.

1596. _____. "Watergate on the Wabash." Penthouse, VIII (September 1976), 53-54, 56, 58, 90, 152-153. Public opinion of the case in predominantly Republican Indiana.

1597. "Outlook in the House." U.S. News and World Report, LXXVII (August 12, 1974), 15-16. Odds on Nixon's impeachment.

1598. "The Oval Office Tapes: Reprinted from the Wall Street Journal, July 10, 1973." Congressional Record, CXIX (July 19, 1973), 24980. An editorial on their potential value in telling who was lying, Dean or the President.

1599. Overland, Doris. "The Great Watergate Conspiracy: A TV Blitzkrieg?" Contemporary Review, CCXXX (July 1978), 29-32. Says network television news largely responsible for forcing Nixon to resign by its massive and continuing coverage of Watergate.

1600. _____. "They Killed a Man." Contemporary Review, CCXXVIII (June 1976), 313-318. The impact of his resignation--perceived by the author as caused by Nixon haters--on the former president.

1601. Paletz, David L. "Television Drama: The Appeals of the

Senate Watergate Hearings." Midwest Quarterly, XXI (Autumn 1979), 63-70. A sense of high drama was maintained as to what people would say and how it would compare with counter-testimony by others.

1602. _____ and Richard J. Vinegar. "Presidents on Television: The Effects of Instant Analysis." Public Opinion Quarterly, XLI (Winter 1977-1978), 488-497. Includes references to the networks' instant analysis of the Watergate speeches and news conferences of Richard M. Nixon.

1603. Paley, William S. As It Happened: A Memoir. Garden City, N.Y.: Doubleday, 1979. 418p. Long-time board chairman of CBS Paley's memoirs cover the history of his network; a few comments are made on his relationship with Richard Nixon before and during the Watergate scandal.

1604. "A Pardon for Nixon and Watergate Is Back." C.Q. Weekly Report, XXXII (September 14, 1974), 2454-2463. A report on the pardon and various reactions to it.

1605. "The Pardon: Questions Persist." Time, CIV (October 28, 1974), 16-18. Questions on whether Nixon had a pre-resignation deal.

1606. "The Pardon That Brought No Peace." Time, CIV (September 16, 1974), 10-12. A review of Ford's action.

1607. Parenti, Michael. "Watergate--The System Worked--For Itself!" In: his Democracy for the Few. 2nd ed. New York: St. Martin's Press, 1977. pp. 164-168. Watergate was put to rest so that big business and other fat cats could get back to their normal routines.

1608. Parris, Judith H. "Congress and the American Presidential System." Current History, LXVI (June 1974), 259-263. On the domination of the former by the latter and the resurgence of Congress as a power during the Watergate crisis.

1609. "Pass the Watergate Soup, Please: Reprinted from the American Bar Association Journal, December 1973." Congressional Record, CXX (January 21, 1974), 186. An editorial comment on the tapes case.

1610. "The Path from Loyalty to Perjury." Newsweek, LXXXI (June 18, 1973), 28-39. Ervin panel testimony of Herbert Porter, Sally Harmony, Robert Reisner, and Hugh Sloan.

1611. Pearl, Arthur. Landslide: The How and Why of Nixon's Victory. Secaucus, N.J.: Citadel Press, 1973. 240p.

The author examines the President's 1972 election victory and finds it loaded with dirty tricks, illegal campaign contributions, etc.

1612. "People: Jeb Stuart Magruder." Time, CV (June 30, 1975), 46. A post-Watergate profile.

1613. "People: John D. Ehrlichman." Time, CV (March 31, 1975), 55; CVII (March 1, 1976), 39. Post-Watergate biography.

1614. "People: John Dean." Time, CIV (November 18, 1974), 52; CV (February 3 and March 17, 1975), 44, 49. Examines Dean's stay in prison.

1615. "People: John Mitchell." Time, CVII (May 31, 1976), 33. A post-Watergate profile.

1616. "People of the United States of America vs. Richard Milhous Nixon." Progressive, XXXVIII (January 1974), 5-7. Another Progressive call for his impeachment.

1617. "People: Sam Ervin." Time, CII (July 9 and November 12, 1973), 29, 77; CIII (February 25, 1974), 53. Brief profiles of the Senate Select Committee chairman.

1618. "People Take It in Stride." Time, CIV (August 19, 1974), 59-60+. Public opinion concerning Nixon's resignation.

1619. "The People's Verdict Is In." Time, CII (September 10, 1973), 18-19. Results of a poll on the credibility of Nixon, Dean, Haldeman, Ehrlichman, and Mitchell as perceived by a sample of American citizens.

1620. Perlez, Jane. "Where Are They Now?" New Times, V (August 22, 1975), 34-40. Post-Watergate profiles of Nixon staffers.

1621. Perry, James M. Us and Them: How the Press Covered the 1972 Election. New York: Clarkson N. Potter, 1973. 279p. After years of attack by the Nixon administration, the press sought out stories about the campaign but often ran into what later became known as "a stonewall" when it came to the Republicans and CREEP.

1622. "Peter W. Rodino." In: Eleanora W. Schoenebaum, ed. Political Profiles: The Nixon/Ford Years. New York: Facts on File, Inc., 1979. pp. 539-542. A brief biography of the House Judiciary Committee chairman.

1623. Peters, Charles. "Blind Ambition in the White House." Washington Monthly, IX (March 1977), 17-21. A look at the "palace guard," with emphasis on John Dean.

1624. Peters, Mike. The Nixon Chronicles. Dayton, Ohio: Lorenz Press, 1976. 168p. A paperback satire, with caricatures and cartoons.

1625. Petersen, Henry E. "'We Were Snookered': Questioning of Henry E. Petersen at Senate Judiciary Committee Hearing." Time, CIV (July 1, 1974), 16. The assistant attorney general's beliefs concerning the involvement of White House staffers in the coverup.

1626. Pett, Saul. "Peter Rodino--In the Eye of the Storm: Reprinted from the Trenton Sunday Times-Advertiser, March 31, 1974." Congressional Record, CXX (April 1, 1974), 8954-8956. A profile of the New Jersey Congressmen who was serving as chairman of the House Judiciary Committee during its impeachment inquiry.

1627. "Phase One of Watergate Ends--Now Its Nixon's Turn." U.S. News and World Report, LXXV (August 20, 1973), 48-50. Reviews Ervin Committee testimony and the upcoming battle between Cox and the White House over possession of the tapes.

1628. Pierpoint, Robert. At the White House: Assignment to Six Presidents. New York: G. P. Putnam, 1981. 240p. The veteran CBS correspondent served at the Nixon White House, and as part of his recollections recalls the friction between his colleague, Dan Rather, and the President.

1629. Pierson, John. "Impeachment Panel Next Week Gets Down to Central Question--At Last It Must Decide What 'High Crimes' Are--Debate May Shift Votes--Birdseed for the Eagle?: Reprinted from the Wall Street Journal, July 23, 1974." Congressional Record, CXX (July 23, 1974), 24826-24827. A preview of the upcoming final chapter in the House Judiciary Committee debate.

1630. Pincus, Ann. "Watergate: Two Who Got Away." Washington Monthly, VIII (November 1976), 43-47. CREEP attorney Paul O'Brien and White House chief of staff Alexander Haig.

1631. Pincus, Walter. "Alexander Haig." New Republic, CLXXI (October 5, 1974), 15-17. Comments on his possible involvement in a deal for Nixon's pardon.

1632. _____. "Babble on the Tapes." New Republic, CLXX (January 5, 1974), 11-13. Examines reasons given for the 18-minute gap.

1633. _____. "Campaign Financing." New Republic, CLXIX (October 27, 1973), 16-19. The need for reform in light of the Watergate illegalities.

1634. _____. "The Case of Peter Flanigan." New Republic, CLXXI (October 19, 1974), 12-13. A look into the matter of selling ambassadorships.

1635. _____. "The Cold War Brought Home." New Republic, CLXVIII (June 23, 1973), 12-15. The use of espionage, illegal entry, bugging, and other tactics by Nixon re-election people.

1636. _____. "The Cover-up Trial: The Trail of Lies." New Republic, CLXXI (November 23, 1974), 9. A comment on the varying testimony of the defendants.

1637. _____. "The Cox Investigation." New Republic, CLXIX (December 8, 1973), 10-13. Its progress before the "Saturday Night Massacre."

1638. _____. "Drippings from the Watergate." New Republic, CLXIX (July 28, 1973), 10-11. White House assistant Richard Moore's statements on the manufacture of White House statements on Watergate and an analysis of the Ervin panel testimony of Herbert Kalmbach.

1639. _____. "The Duping of Richard Helms." New Republic, CLXXII (February 15, 1975), 12-14. On his allowing CIA help to the White House "plumbers."

1640. _____. "Getting to the Bottom of the CIA Cover-up." New Republic, CLXXI (September 28, 1974), 11-13. The break-in at the office of Daniel Ellsberg's psychiatrist, L. Fielding.

1641. _____. "GOP Money Scandal." New Republic, CLXVIII (April 21, 1973), 17-21. On the financing of the Watergate affair.

1642. _____. "How the FBI and CIA Played the Game." New Republic, CLXVIII (June 16, 1973), 19-23. On their role in the initial Watergate investigation.

1643. _____. "Hushabye Boodle." New Republic, CLXX (June 8, 1974), 8-9. Concerns the use of campaign funds for Watergate hush money.

1644. _____. "The Latest Cover-up." New Republic, CLXVIII (June 30, 1973), 14-17. Looks at three stages of the cover-up, how they fell apart, and White House reactions to each.

1645. _____. "Loose Ends: Questions the Ervin Committee Should Ask." New Republic, CLXIX (September 8, 1973), 19-21. How did the various White House figures hear of the break-in and what was the substance of the Nixon-Haldeman-Ehrlichman meeting on June 20, 1972.

1646. ———. "Misusing the FBI." New Republic, CLXVIII (February 24, 1973), 17-18. The role of L. Patrick Gray.

1647. ———. "More Watergate Lies." New Republic, CLXVIII (April 7, 1973), 19-23. As reported in the confirmation hearings on L. Patrick Gray.

1648. ———. "New Pieces in the Watergate Puzzle." New Republic, LXX (April 13, 1974), 13-14. A consideration of the report given by Earl J. Silbert.

1649. ———. "Nixon's Knowledge." New Republic, CLXX (April 6, 1974), 16-19. Reviews the President's statements concerning his reactions to the earlier Watergate investigations.

1650. ———. "Obstructing Justice." New Republic, CLXIX (September 1, 1973), 21-23. On the delay in the FBI's investigation of campaign contributions.

1651. ———. "Politics and the FBI." New Republic, CLXVII (November 11, 1972), 14-17. The role of the FBI in fostering dirty tricks.

1652. ———. "Prosecutor Jaworski's 'Operation Townhouse.'" New Republic, CLXIX (December 22, 1973), 10. Investigation of a secret White House fund-raising operation.

1653. ———. "Puzzling Prosecution: More Unanswered Watergate Questions." New Republic, CLXVIII (June 2, 1973), 15-19.

1654. ———. "Raising Money to Run." New Republic, CLXIX (October 13, 1973), 16-18. Considers the work of Herbert Kalmbach.

1655. ———. "Rose Mary Woods Mystery: Who Dunnit?" New Republic, CLXX (February 2, 1974), 14-17. On the 18-minute tape gap.

1656. ———. "Running for Cover." New Republic, CLXIX (July 7, 1973), 14-16. Why John Dean chose to testify.

1657. ———. "The Silbert-Petersen Puzzle." New Republic, CLXXI (July 6, 1974), 15-16. More on their Watergate investigations.

1658. ———. "Was It Only John Dean?: Somebody's Lying." New Republic, CLXIX (June 22, 1974), 11-13. Reaction to the testimony by members of the "palace guard."

1659. ———. "Watergate: Act III." New Republic, CLXXII

(January 18, 1975), 17-18. On the outcome of the Watergate cover-up trial.

1660. _____. "Watergate Lies." New Republic, CLXVIII (February 17, 1973), 11-14. How CREEP sought to disassociate itself from the Watergate burglars through evasions and lies.

1661. _____. "Watergate Teasers: Listeners to the White House Tapes." New Republic, CLXIX (November 24, 1973), 14-15. Thoughts on the opinions expressed by those who had listened.

1662. _____. "The Watergate Trial." New Republic, CLXXI (November 9, 1974), 10-12. On using the tapes as evidence.

1663. _____. "Watergate Whodunnit: The Transcripts Don't Tell the Whole Truth." New Republic, CLXX (May 25, 1974), 15-17. On the inadequacy of the edited White House transcripts.

1664. Pious, Richard M. The American Presidency. Scranton, Pa.: Basic Books, 1979. 491p. Drawing on the examples of various presidents, including Richard Nixon, the author examines the factors associated with success or failure when chief executives assert their constitutional prerogatives. Pious asserts that the changes wrought in the office come from constitutional issues and not from "less significant electoral and partisan factors." A useful background study for students of Watergate.

1665. "Plea Bargaining--What It Is, Why It's Under Fire in Watergate." U.S. News and World Report, LXXVII (July 8, 1974), 18+. On the practice of allowing defendants to plead to lesser crimes in exchange for their cooperation or testimony.

1666. "The Plumbers Go on Trial." Newsweek, LXXXIV (July 8, 1974), 31-33. The Fielding break-in trial.

1667. Poliock, Andrew. "Nixon's Man on the Watergate Panel." Today's Speech, XXIII (Fall 1975), 7-12. The statements and work of Florida's Senator Edward Gurney.

1668. "Political Dynamite." Newsweek, LXXXIV (July 29, 1974), 36-37. The White House transcripts.

1669. Polk, James R. "The Covert Collector--GOP's [Herbert] Kalmbach: Reprinted from the Washington Evening-Star, February 2, 1972." In: U.S. Congress, Senate, Committee on the Judiciary. Richard G. Kleindienst--Resumed: Hearings. 92nd Cong., 2nd sess. Washington,

D.C.: U.S. Government Printing Office, 1972. pp. 440-442. Kalmbach's work in raising 1972 campaign funds from large contributors.

1670. _____. "Is Dean Too Deeply Involved?: Reprinted from the Washington Star-News, March 31, 1974." Congressional Record, CXX (April 11, 1974), 10789. On Dean's effectiveness as a government witness.

1671. _____. "Letter Reveals Milk Lobby Offer: Reprinted from the Washington Star-News, October 24, 1973." Congressional Record, CXIX (October 24, 1973), 34955-34956. Compare with Dita Beard's memo on ITT.

1672. _____. "Piracy and Politics: That $200,000 Contribution." New Republic, CLXVIII (March 17, 1973), 18-21. Given by financier Robert Vesco.

1673. Polsby, Nelson W. "Watergate: Alienation and Accountability in the Nixon Administration." In: his Political Promises: Essays and Commentary on American Politics. New York and London: Oxford University Press, 1974. pp. 3-14. An essay on the workings and non-workings of the "palace guard."

1674. Popkin, Richard H. and Barry Glassner. "Candidate for 'Deep Throat.'" Focus/Midwest, no. 66 (1975), 8-13. Conjecture on the possible role of Robert F. Bennett as the anonymous source of Woodward and Bernstein.

1675. Porter, Laurenda W. "The White House Transcripts: Group Fantasy Events Concerning the Mass Media." Central States Speech Journal, XXVII (Spring 1976), 272-279. Reviews the manner in which the media employed the edited transcripts, including the reading of certain sections and reenactment of others.

1676. Porter, Paul A. "Impeachment and TV--Impeding the Process of Justice: Reprinted from the Washingtin Post, May 4, 1974." Congressional Record, CXX (May 9, 1974), 13874-13875. Against televising the proceedings.

1677. Porter, William E. Assault on the Media: The Nixon Years. Ann Arbor, Mich.: University of Michigan Press, 1976. 320p. A chronological account, 1969-1974, of the orchestrated efforts of the White House to harass representatives of the media, e.g., the litigation against journalists who sought to protect confidentiality, anti-trust actions against television networks, etc. Certain relevant documents are appended. Much on Watergate.

1678. Powers, Thomas. The Man Who Kept the Secrets: Richard Helms and the CIA. New York: Alfred A. Knopf, 1979.

416p. The only book-length biography of the former CIA Director; includes a useful look at his involvement in the Watergate case.

1679. _____. "Nixon Finale." Commonweal, CIII (May 7, 1976), 307-309. Comments on a deposition by the former president.

1680. _____. "The Rise and Fall of Richard Helms: Survival and Sudden Death in the CIA." Rolling Stone (December 16, 1976), 46+. Taken from an early draft of the book cited above.

1681. "Preliminary Nixon Poll Result--65 Per Cent Disapprove of Nixon: Reprinted from the Novato [California] Advance, February 6, 1974." Congressional Record, CXX (March 27, 1974), 8577-8578. The results of a local poll.

1682. "The Presidency at Stake: Reprinted from the Peoria Journal-Star, March 3, 1974." Congressional Record, CXX (March 11, 1974), 6229. An editorial on the stakes in the House Judiciary Committee impeachment inquiry.

1683. "The President and the Law: Reprinted from the Washington Star-News, October 22, 1973." Congressional Record, CXIX (October 23, 1973), 34792-34793. An editorial on the dismissal of Archibald Cox.

1684. "The President and the Special Prosecutor: Reprinted from the Washington Post, November 29, 1973." Congressional Record, CXIX (November 29, 1973), 38595-38596. An editorial on Nixon's relationship to Jaworski.

1685. "The President Fights Back: Where Watergate Stands Now." U.S. News and World Report, LXXIV (June 4, 1973), 15-18. Nixon's May 22, 1973 Watergate address.

1686. "The President Gambles on Going Public." Time, CIII (May 13, 1974), 10-14+. On the release of the edited White House transcripts.

1687. "President Nixon and the Presidency: Reprinted from the Philadelphia Evening Bulletin, March 20, 1974." Congressional Record, CXX (March 21, 1974), 7830-7831. Editorializes that Nixon is the issue in Watergate, not the presidency as an institution.

1688. "President Nixon's Resignation." In: Robert A. Diamond, ed. Historic Documents, 1974. Washington, D.C.: Congressional Quarterly, Inc., 1975. pp. 683-695. Includes Nixon's letter of resignation and his address to the nation.

1689. "The President Prepares His Answer." Time, CIII (May 6, 1974), 11-12. Why Nixon chose to send the House Judiciary Committee edited transcripts instead of the actual tapes.

1690. "The President Shores up His Command." Time, CI (June 18, 1973), 11-14. On the appointment of new White House staffers and assistants.

1691. "The President vs. Congress--The Score Since Watergate: A Special Report." National Journal, VIII (1976), 730-748. Suggests that Congress is no longer the weaker branch.

1692. "Presidential Support: Nixon Score Hits Record Low." C.Q. Weekly Report, XXXI (1973), 2344-2351. Standing in the public opinion polls.

1693. "Presidential Tapes and Documents: Analysis, Index, and Particularized Claims of Executive Privilege for Subpoenaed Materials, Filed by Special Counsel to the President, November 26, 1973, U.S. District Court for the District of Columbia, Miscl. no. 47-73." Weekly Compilation of Presidential Documents, IX (December 9, 1973), 1370-1377.

1694. "Presidential Tapes and Documents: The President's Letter to Senator Sam J. Ervin, Jr., Chairman, Senate Select Committee on Presidential Campaign Activities, in Response to the Committee's Subpoenas, January 4, 1974." Weekly Compilation of Presidential Documents, X (January 7, 1974), 11-12. Full text.

1695. "Presidential Year Dominated by Watergate." In: 1974 Congressional Quarterly Almanac. Washington, D.C.: Congressional Quarterly, Inc., 1975. pp. 903-906. A chronology based on data from the firm's C.Q. Weekly Report.

1696. "The President's Lawyer and GOP Fund Raiser: Herbert Kalmbach." Time, XCIX (March 27, 1972), 33-34. A capsule biography.

1697. "The President's Privilege: Reprinted from the Washington Post, March 19, 1973." Congressional Record, CXIX (March 19, 1973), 8354. An editorial on executive privilege.

1698. "The President's Strategy for Survival." Time, CIII (March 25, 1974), 11-14+. Delay.

1699. "The President's Tape Transcripts: Summary Memorandum."

Congressional Record, CXX (May 2, 1974), 12921-12924. Shows contradictions in Dean's Ervin panel testimony.

1700. "The Press and the Watergate Hearings: Phase One." Columbia Journalism Review, XII (November-December 1973), 26-57. An analysis of press coverage of the Ervin Committee hearings.

1701. "Pressing Hard for the Evidence." Time, CIII (April 1, 1974), 9-12. Judge Sirica gives grand jury data to the House Judiciary Committee.

1702. Price, Raymond. With Nixon. New York: Viking Press, 1977. 398p. The former president's chief speechwriter offers what amounts to a friend's apology for the administration. Admiring Nixon's philosophy, the author believes Watergate to have been of less consequence than the President's foreign policy achievements. Nixon, he charges, was the victim of a double standard exacerbated by an unfair media that examined his alleged sins more closely than those of his predecessors. Should be compared with the memoirs of William Safire (below) and the volume by Lasky (above), which is more of a polemic than this, but which also finds Nixon's behavior to be no worse than that of earlier chief executives.

1703. "The Price of Loyalty." New Republic, CLXX (April 27, 1974), 9-10. The case of Herbert L. Porter.

1704. "The Price of Plea-Bargaining." Newsweek, LXXXIII (June 17, 1974), 27+. The Fielding break-in trial.

1705. "Probing the Telltale Tape." Newsweek, LXXXIII (January 28, 1974), 14-16+. Looks at the mystery of the 18-minute tape gap.

1706. "Profile, Leon Jaworski--The New Special Prosecutor." C.Q. Weekly Report, XXXI (November 3, 1973), 2901. A brief biography.

1707. Progressive, Editors of. "A Call to Action: Reprinted from the Progressive, December 1973." Congressional Record, CXIX (November 14, 1973), 36998-36999. An editorial seeking the President's impeachment.

1708. "The Prosecutor Departs." Time, CIV (October 21, 1974), 38. On Jaworski's return to private law practice.

1709. "The Prosecution Wraps up Its Case with Fresh Evidence." U.S. News and World Report, LXXVII (December 2, 1974), 27-28. The Watergate cover-up trial.

1710. "The Prosecution Zeroes in on John Mitchell." U.S. News and World Report, LXXVII (November 11, 1974), 26. Watergate cover-up trial.

1711. "Protecting the Special Prosecutor: Reprinted from the Washington Post, November 16, 1973." Congressional Record, CXIX (November 16, 1973), 37548-37549. Suggests that the next one not be allowed to be fired.

1712. Prouty, L. Fletcher. "An Inside Look." Ramparts, XII (October 1973), 21-23. On Watergate and the role of the CIA therein.

1713. "Psychological Fallout: How Other Professionals See It." Today's Health (August 1973), 19+. Effect of Watergate on the U.S.'s mental health.

1714. "Psywar on the Potomac." Newsweek, LXXXIII (February 18, 1974), 25-27. Nixon's refusal to submit further tapes to Leon Jaworski and Haig's assertions that Dean's testimony is and was false.

1715. "Public: Disillusioned." Time, CIII (May 20, 1974), 18+. Public opinion.

1716. "The Public's Right to Know." Nation, CCXV (September 18, 1972), 195-196. Seeks the appointment of a special prosecutor independent of Kleindienst.

1717. "Pushing Ahead the Impeachment Inquiry." Time, CIII (March 18, 1974), 9-12. Work of the House Judiciary Committee.

1718. Pynn, R. E., ed. Watergate and the American Political Process. New York: Praeger, 1975. 246p. Essays by scholars and journalists, most of which are excerpted from other sources. A good "Watergate reader."

1719. "Question Now: Will Nixon Try to Curb TV Journalism?" Broadcasting, LXXXV (November 5, 1973), 22-25. A review of the administration's response to TV Watergate coverage.

1720. "Questions About Gray." Time, CI (March 5, 1973), 14-15. Raised during his FBI confirmation hearings.

1721. "The Quiet-Stall Survival Strategy." Time, CIII (February 25, 1974), 12-13. Adopted by the White House in light of the House impeachment drive.

1722. Ramis, Timothy V. "Executive Privilege: What Are the Limits?" Oregon Law Review, LIV (Spring 1975), 81-103. Suggests the practice has value if kept within certain limits.

1723. Randolph, Robert C. and Daniel C. Smith. "Executive Privilege and the Congressional Right of Inquiry." Harvard Journal of Legislation, X (June 1973), 621-671. Points out Nixon administration development of the control of information and suggests Congressional remedies.

1724. Rangell, Leo. "Lessons from Watergate: A Derivative for Psychoanalysis." Psychoanalytic Quarterly, XXXV (1976), 37-61. Unavailable for review.

1725. Rangell, Leo. The Mind of Watergate: An Exploration of the Compromise of Integrity. New York: W. W. Norton, 1980. 318p. A "psychochronicle" of the public response to the growing evidence against Nixon, a duplicity which many found reflected their own tensions between aggressive ambition and proper moral values all are supposed to live by. The public, the author argues, knew of the President's dishonesty and elected to live with it until it could no longer deny or tolerate his guilt. Looks at Nixon's early career and political fortunes, to assess his character. Should be compared with the work by James D. Barber cited above.

1726. Rasberry, Robert W. The "Technique" of Political Lying. Washington, D.C.: University Press of America, 1981. 289p. Examines how politicians, Nixon included, could use a variety of deceptive techniques to lie and bend the truth to their own advantage.

1727. Raspberry, William. "Corruption Without Precedent: Reprinted from the Washington Post, October 29, 1973." Congressional Record, CXIX (October 29, 1973), 35253. Compares Watergate with previous political scandals.

1728. _____. "Why Ask If He's Guilty?: Reprinted from the Washington Post, November 20, 1973." Congressional Record, CXIX (November 26, 1973), 37944. Comments on the administration's "Operation Candor."

1729. Rather, Dan. "The Unmaking of a President [and] Where Watergate Led." In: his The Camera Never Blinks: Adventures of a TV Journalist. New York: Ballantine Books, 1977. pp. 238-275. Published simultaneously by the New York firm of William Morrow, Rather's memoirs highlight his Watergate experience as CBS News White House correspondent and include a vivid picture of his sharp questioning of and responses from an embattled President Nixon.

1730. _____ and Gary Paul Gates. The Palace Guard. New York: Harper & Row, 1974. 326p. The two CBS employees look both at the Nixon entourage (Haldeman, Ehrlichman, Kissinger, Mitchell, etc.) and the changes in style and concept in the office of the presidency in the post-LBJ administration. The interactions of personnel are presented in anecdotal style and, naturally, the book is loaded with references to Watergate and how the most competent aides were pushed aside by Haldeman and Ehrlichman.

1731. Ratner, Leonard G. "Executive Privilege, Self-Incrimination, and the Separation of Powers Illusion." UCLA Law Review, XXII (October 1974), 92-115. Was executive privilege being used to hide one's guilt?

1732. Raven, Bertram H. "The Nixon Group." Journal of Social Issues, XXX (Fall 1974), 297-320. Nixon's advisors were not a close-knit team but were held together by mutual dependence on the President.

1733. Rebozo, Charles G. ("Bebe"). "Excerpts from an Interview by Walter Cronkite, December 19, 1973." In: Buel W. Patch, ed. Historic Documents, 1973. Washington, D.C.: Congressional Quarterly, Inc., 1974. pp. 975-981. A three-part interview carried on CBS December 19-21, 1973 in which a range of Watergate-related questions are asked, especially about Rebozo's role with Howard Hughes.

1734. "Recycling General Haig: Reprinted from the New York Times, September 18, 1974." Congressional Record, CXX (September 19, 1974), 31825-31826. Post-Watergate fate of the White House chief of staff.

1735. No entry.

1736. Reedy, George. "Impeachment on TV--No Barriers Between the Public and the Facts: Reprinted from the Washington Post, April 29, 1974." Congressional Record, CXX (May 9, 1974), 13874. Supports the idea of televising the proceedings.

1737. _____. "On the Isolation of Presidents." In: Rex G. Tugwell and Thomas E. Cronin, eds. The Presidency Reappraised. New York: Praeger, 1974. pp. 119-132. President Johnson's press secretary comments on the isolation of modern presidents, especially Nixon, and the rise of greater power in the White House staff.

1738. _____. "The President and the Press: Struggle for Dominance." Annals of the American Academy of Political and Social Science, no. 427 (September 1976), 65-72. Examines the manner whereby the president attempts to control the flow of unfavorable information and the press is forced to dig for it.

1739. _____. The Presidency in Flux. New York: Columbia

University Press, 1973. 133p. Suggests the White House staff creates presidential isolation leading presidents into developing grandiose and unrealistic views of themselves and their objectives.

1740. Reeves, Richard. "What Ehrlichman Really Thought of Nixon." New York, IX (May 10, 1976), 40-42. As revealed in his Watergate cover-up trial testimony and his political novels.

1741. "Reflections on the Resignation: A Symposium." National Review, XXVI (August 30, 1974), 954-962+. Asks questions like: Was it necessary?, What would have happened had Nixon not resigned?, etc.

1741a. Reford, Emmette S. "Watergate: A Test of Constitutional Democracy." In: John H. Hallowell, ed. Prospects for Constitutional Democracy: Essays in Honor of R. Taylor Cole. Durham, N.C.: Duke University Press, 1976. pp. 183-197. Briefly reviews the application of the Constitution in the crisis.

1742. Reichley, A. James. Conservatives in an Age of Change: The Nixon and Ford Administrations. Washington, D.C.: Brookings Institution, 1981. 482p. The author studies the role of conservative ideology, a distinguishable tradition in U.S. political history, in the deliberations of those two administrations and how that ideology led to positions on various issues. With regard to Nixon's approach, Reichley shows the evolution of the policy for dealing with Congress and the conservative ideology impact on various topics from welfare to Watergate. Interestingly enough, the Brookings Institution was singled out as a "plumbers" target, but the idea was scrapped before implementation.

1743. _____. "Getting at the Roots of Watergate." Fortune, LXXXVIII (July 1973), 90-93+. Roots are identified as being in political corruption, questionable Washington moral standards, the technology of espionage (bugging, etc.), money, and the imperial presidency. Reprinted in Current, CLIV (September 1973), 3-11 as "What Reforms Are Needed?"

1744. _____. "Let's Reform Campaign Financing, but Let's Do It Right." Fortune, LXXXVIII (December 1973), 94-97+. Suggests that the reforms should not discriminate against individual giving, only the excesses and illegalities witnessed in earlier campaigns.

1745. "The Reluctant Inquisitor: Henry Petersen." Newsweek, LXXXIV (July 1, 1974), 26. A brief profile.

1746. Relyea, Harold C. "Executive Privilege: A Brief Overview." In: U.S. Congress, House, Committee on Government Operations. The Availability of Information to Congress: Hearings. 93rd Cong., 1st sess. Washington, D.C.: U.S. Government Printing Office, 1973. pp. 264-274. A history of the doctrine with emphasis on its expansion by Nixon. Dusted off and updated for inclusion in the author's edited The Presidency and Information Policy (New York: Center for the Study of the Presidency, 1981), pp. 1-33 under the title "The Presidency and the People's Right to Know."

1747. Rembar, Charles. "The Grand Inquest." Esquire, LXXX (November 1973), 123-126+. A look at the Watergate investigation with emphasis on the Ervin Committee hearings.

1748. _____. "How Much Due Process Is Due a President?: Reprinted from the New York Times Magazine, July 21, 1974." Congressional Record, CXX (July 23, 1974), 24716-24717. The same as to any average citizen.

1749. "Removal of the President: Resignation and the Procedural Law of Impeachment." Duke Law Journal, XXIII (1974), 1023+. Questions whether an impeachment process should continue once its object had resigned.

1750. "Re-opening ITT." Time, CII (November 12, 1973), 51-52. New evidence in the case.

1751. "Reply Brief Regarding Court Order Requiring Production of Recordings and Documents: Reply Brief Filed by Attorneys for the President in the United States Court of Appeals for the District of Columbia Circuit, September 19, 1973." Weekly Compilation of Presidential Documents, IX (September 24, 1973), 1154-1163. Full text.

1752. "Representative Rarick Says He Would Not Vote for Impeachment Now: Reprinted from the Baton Rouge Sunday Advocate, July 28, 1974." Congressional Record, CXX (July 30, 1974), 25892. The opinion of Louisiana Congressman John R. Rarick.

1753. "Republican Revolt over Watergate." Time, CI (April 9, 1973), 16-17. Calls by Republican leaders for the scandal to be cleaned-up.

1754. "Republicans Running Hard in Watergate Shadow." C.Q. Weekly Report, XXXII (1974), 351-356. The effect of the scandal on the campaign of Republicans in the fall 1974 elections.

1755. "The Reselling of the President." Time, CII (July 9, 1973),

20-21. Efforts to show that Nixon was not involved with Watergate.

1756. "Resignation: An Act of Statesmanship." Time, CIII (April 1, 1974), 10-11. Opinions on how Nixon's quitting would be received.

1757. "Resignation vs. Impeachment." New Republic, CLXX (May 25, 1974), 5-6. On the options facing the President.

1758. "Resignations Impede White House Work and Initiatives." C.Q. Weekly Report, XXXI (May 5, 1973), 1069-1070. The texts of the President's April 30 statement on the resignations of Kleindienst, Haldeman, and Ehrlichman. Their respective letters of resignation are printed on pp. 1075-1076.

1759. "Response to Special Prosecutor's Petition for Supreme Court Review: Brief Filed by Attorneys for the President in Opposition to the Special Prosecutor's Petition, May 30, 1974." Weekly Compilation of Presidential Documents, X (June 3, 1974), 562-564. Full text.

1760. "Response to Subpoena of Recordings and Documents: Brief in Opposition Filed by Attorneys for the President in the United States District Court for the District of Columbia, August 7, 1973--In the United States District Court for the District of Columbia, in re: Grand Jury Subpoena Duces Tecum Issued to Richard M. Nixon, or Any Subordinate Officer, Official, or Employee with Custody or Control of Certain Documents or Objects." Weekly Compilation of Presidential Documents, IX (August 13, 1973), 961-971. Full text.

1761. "Responsibility in the Oval Office--'The Presidency Is a Public Trust': Reprinted from the Washington Post, August 8, 1974." Congressional Record, CXX (August 8, 1974), 27332-27333. An editorial on impeachment hearing rhetoric.

1762. Reston, James. "The President's Papers: Reprinted from the New York Times, August 18, 1974." Congressional Record, CXX (September 19, 1974), 31821. On the post-resignation fate of Nixon's documents and tapes.

1763. _____. "The Tapes Buy Time: Reprinted from the New York Times, October 24, 1973." Congressional Record, CXIX (October 30, 1974), 35498. Concerns the Cox dismissal.

1764. Reston, James, Jr. "The Breaking of Richard Nixon." Playboy, XXV (April 1978), 93+. Pressures from within and without the White House in the summer of 1974 which brought about the President's resignation.

1765. Reynolds, William A. "'That Little Jap': Reprinted from the Pryor [Oklahoma] Daily Times, August 22, 1973." Congressional Record, CXIX (September 10, 1973), 29081. On the insult to Ervin panel member Senator Daniel Inouye by attorney John Wilson.

1766. Rezneck, Daniel A. "Is Judicial Review of Impeachment Coming?" American Bar Association Journal, LX (July 1974), 681-685. Suggests that the Supreme Court's granting of judicial review when Adam Clayton Powell was ousted from the House entitles Nixon to the same review should he be impeached.

1767. Rhodes, Irwin S. "What Really Happened to the Jefferson Subpoenas?" American Bar Association Journal, LX (January 1974), 52-54. Suggests that the arguments in the Watergate tapes case are similar to those in the Aaron Burr case a century and a half earlier.

1768. "Richard G. Kleindienst." In: Current Biography Yearbook 1973. New York: H. W. Wilson Co., 1974. pp. 132-133. A brief profile.

1769. _____. In: Eleanora W. Schoenebaum, ed. Political Profiles: The Nixon/Ford Years. New York: Facts on File, Inc., 1979. pp. 360-361. A capsule biography.

1770. "Richard M. Nixon." In: Eleanora W. Schoenebaum, ed. Political Profiles: The Nixon/Ford Years. New York: Facts on File, Inc., 1979. pp. 466-479. The largest biography in the Schoenebaum compilation.

1771. "Richard M. Nixon: End of a Remarkable Career." C.Q. Weekly Report, XXXII (1974), 2083-2091. A review of the President's political career.

1772. "The Richard Nixon Story--A Tumultuous Career." U.S. News and World Report, LXXVII (August 19, 1974), 33-36. A post-resignation summary.

1773. "Richard Nixon Stumbles to the Brink." Time, CII (October 29, 1973), 12-14+. The dismissal of Archibald Cox.

1774. "Richard Nixon's Collapsing Presidency." Time, CIII (May 20, 1974), 15-17. Examines reaction to the White House transcripts.

1775. Richardson, Elliot L. "The Battle over the Tapes: Elliot Richardson Tells His Side of the Story." U.S. News and World Report, LXXV (November 5, 1973), 64-65. Excerpts from Richardson's October 23 press conference in which he discusses the dismissal of Archibald Cox.

1776. _____. "The First Job Is to Restore Confidence: An Interview." U.S. News and World Report, LXXV (September 3, 1973), 22-27. On the appointment of Special Prosecutor Cox.

1777. _____. "The Saturday Night Massacre." Atlantic, CCXXXVII (March 1976), 40-44, 69-71. On his resignation and the dismissal of Archibald Cox.

1778. _____. "Sense of Strain: The Testimony of Elliot L. Richardson Before the Senate Judiciary Committee." Time, CII (November 19, 1973), 27-28. Richardson on the reasons for the Cox dismissal.

1779. _____. "Statement by Richardson: Reprinted from the New York Times, May 8, 1973." In: Book IX, Part I of U.S. Congress, House, Committee on the Judiciary. Statement of Information: Hearings. 93rd Cong., 2nd sess. Washington, D.C.: U.S. Government Printing Office, 1974. p. 140. On the search for a Watergate special prosecutor.

1780. "Richardson, Cox Win Judiciary Committee Approval." C.Q. Weekly Report, XXXI (1973), 1313-1315. On the former's confirmation as Attorney General and the latter's as Special Prosecutor.

1781. Richman, A. "Burglary Brings Fame to [James] McCord." Biographical News, I (December 1974), 1426. A quick profile.

1782. Riemer, Neal. "Watergate and Prophetic Politics." Review of Politics, XXXVI (April 1974), 284-297. Unavailable for review.

1783. Rieselbach, Leroy N. "In the Wake of Watergate." Review of Politics, XXXVI (July 1974), 371-393. The need for Congressional reforms, especially in campaign financing.

1784. Ringle, William. "Claims of Nixon 'Not Knowing' Won't Wash: Reprinted from the San Bernadino [California] Sun, July 14, 1973." Congressional Record, CXIX (July 25, 1973), 25870. Doubts on Nixon's statements.

1785. The Ripon Society and Clifford W. Brown, Jr. "The Campaign of 1972: Watergate." In: their Jaws of Victory: The Game-Plan Politics of 1972, The Crisis of the Republican Party, and the Future of the Constitution. Boston: Little, Brown, 1974. pp. 89-114. Assesses the impact of Watergate on all three parts of the subtitle. Watergate is seen as a scandal not made by Republicans but by the President and his aides--one perceived as having an effect on the party if not on the Constitution.

1786. "Ripping Open an Incredible Scandal." Time, CI (April 30, 1973), 11-17. The beginning flood of statements, a chronology, law suits pending, Kleindienst's withdrawal from the investigation, and John Dean about to testify.

1787. "The Rise-and-Fall of Mr. Law-and-Order." Newsweek, LXXXI (April 30, 1973), 18. Going from Attorney General to Watergate suspect was the fate of John Mitchell.

1788. "Robert Mardian." In: Eleanora W. Schoenebaum, ed. Political Profiles: The Nixon/Ford Years. New York: Facts on File, 1979. pp. 423-424. A brief biography.

1789. "Robert U. ("Bob") Woodward." In: Eleanora W. Schoenebaum, ed. Political Profiles: The Nixon/Ford Years. New York: Facts on File, Inc., 1979. pp. 677-678. Another brief biography of the Washington Post reporter.

1790. Roberts, Chalmers M. "Foreign Policy Under a Paralyzed Presidency." Foreign Affairs, LII (July 1974), 675-689. Adrift and largely the product of Henry Kissinger, whose memoirs (q.v.) this article should be compared to.

1791. Robinson, Michael J. "The Impact of the Televised Watergate Hearings." Journal of Communications, XXIV (Spring 1974), 17-30. An analysis of the impact of the hearings on the public and on lawmakers alike.

1792. _____. "Television and American Politics, 1956-1976." Public Interest, no. 48 (Summer 1977), 3-39. A twenty-year review with some comment on Watergate.

1793. Roche, John P. "From Kennedy to Ford: TV and the Presidency." TV Guide, XXIII (May 24, 1975), A5-A6. The high point was Kennedy and the low, Nixon.

1794. _____. "Has CBS News Failed in Its Duty to America?" TV Guide, XXIV (October 19, 1974), A5-A6. In its coverage of Watergate.

1795. _____. "A Word Edgewise--Impeachment Battle Shapes up As a Public Opinion Contest: Reprinted from the AFL-CIO News, May 18, 1974." Congressional Record, CXX (May 23, 1974), 16341-16342. A conservative view of the value of the impeachment quest.

1796. Roddy, Joseph. "Notes on the Biggest Bankroll Theory." More, V (May 1975), 18-21. Haldeman and Watergate hush money.

1797. Rodgers, W. H. "Geneen and Nixon: Mirror Images of Power." Nation, CCXVII (October 1, 1973), 302-305. Compares the President to the board chairman of ITT, Harold Geneen.

1798. Rodino, Peter W., Jr. "Congressional Review of Executive Action." Seton Hall Law Review, V (Spring 1974), 489-525. A duty as detailed by the chairman of the House Judiciary Committee.

1799. Roemer, John. "Gordon Liddy: He Bungled into the White House." Rolling Stone (July 19, 1973), 24-28. How Liddy came to be a "plumber"; looks at his FBI and prosecuting attorney careers.

1800. Rogovin, Mitchell. "Revenuers vs. Republicans: If CREEP Filed a Tax Return." New Republic, CLXIX (July 7, 1973), 16-18. On the hiding of secret funds.

1801. "The Role of the Presidency." Current, VI (July 1973), 3-26. A symposium featuring the opinions of John Gardner, Robert Bowie, Irving Kristol, Arthur Schlesinger, Jr., Robert Brustein, Theodore Hesburgh, and Henry Steele Commanger.

1802. "Ronald L. Ziegler." In: Eleanora W. Schoenebaum, ed. Political Profiles: The Nixon/Ford Years. New York: Facts on File, Inc., 1979. pp. 688-690. A capsule biography of Nixon's Press Secretary.

1803. "Rose Mary Woods." In: Eleanora W. Schoenebaum, ed. Political Profiles: The Nixon/Ford Years. New York: Facts on File, Inc., 1979. pp. 676-677. A profile of the President's long-time personal secretary.

1804. "Rose Mary's Boo-Boo." Newsweek, LXXXII (December 10, 1973), 26-29+. The 18-minute tape gap.

1805. "Rose Woods: The Fifth Nixon." Time, CII (November 19, 1973), 22. A quick look at their relationship.

1806. Rosen, G. R. "President Nixon Should Resign." Dunn's, CIII (February 1974), 63-65. Written on behalf of the business community.

1807. Rosenbaum, David E. "Watergate Unit Suspends Investigator over a Leak: Reprinted from the New York Times, November 20, 1973." Congressional Record, CXIX (November 21, 1973), 37842-37843. The firing of C. Scott Armstrong.

1808. Rosenbaum, Robert. "Ah, Watergate!" New Republic, CLXXXVI (June 23, 1982), 15-16+. A tenth anniversary reflection.

1809. Rosenfield, L. W. "August 9, 1974: The Victimage of Richard Nixon." Communications Quarterly, XXIV (Fall 1976), 19-23. The President's resignation and his addresses to nation and staff are analyzed.

1810. Rositzke, Harry. "The CIA and Watergate." In: his The CIA's Secret Operations. New York: Reader's Digest Press, 1977. pp. 219-226. A brief review of the Agency's involvement with the "plumbers" and the attempt to have it block the FBI's early investigation.

1811. Rothenberg, A. B. "Why Nixon Taped Himself." Psychoanalytic Review, LXII (1975), 201-233. Character defects and a desire not to be contradicted by history and historians.

1812. "Round Two in Nixon's Counterattack." Time, CII (December 3, 1973), 14-17. White House attempts to discredit Elliot Richardson and the bombshell of the 18-minute tape gap.

1813. Rourke, Francis E. "Presidential Power: The Convenience of Secrecy." Nation, CCXV (July 1972), 39-42. The uses by the Nixon administration of executive privilege.

1814. _____. "Watergate and the Presidency--Watergate, Its Implications for Responsible Government: A Report Prepared by a Panel of the National Academy of Public Administration at the Request of the Senate Select Committee on Presidential Campaign Activities--Executive Fallibility and Presidential Management Styles." Administration and Society, VI (August 1974), 155-177. Undertaken before the expiration of the Ervin panel, this report considers the bad affects of the scandal and suggests possible measures to restore what the title calls "responsible government."

1815. Rovere, Richard H. "Letter from Washington." New Yorker, CLXVIII (June 9, 1973), 103-109. Wonders why foreign governments have not taken advantage of President Nixon's Watergate troubles to create mischief.

1816. _____. _____. New Yorker, CLXIX (July 16, 1973), 66-70. Argues that Nixon simply did not appreciate what John Dean was trying to tell him about White House staff culpability in the scandal.

1817. _____. _____. New Yorker, L (September 16, 1974), 134-135. Commentary on the Nixon pardon.

1818. Rowan, Carl T. "Little Public Outcry over the 'Watergate Caper': Reprinted from the Philadelphia Evening Bulletin,

September 4, 1972." Congressional Record, CXVIII (September 5, 1972), 29432. An analysis of public reaction to early reports of the affair.

1819. Rowan, Hobart. "A Crisis of Leadership: Reprinted from the Washington Post, November 29, 1973." Congressional Record, CXIX (November 29, 1973), 38784. Comments on Nixon's dilemma as a weakened leader.

1820. Royster, Vermont. "A Bitter Spirit That Won't Die: Reprinted from the Wall Street Journal, September 23, 1974." Congressional Record, CXX (September 24, 1974), 32304-32305. The continuing bad taste left in the mouths of people by the pardon.

1821. _____. "The Public Morality: Afterthoughts on Watergate." American Scholar, XLIII (Spring 1974), 249-259. Comments on the need for a different morality in government from that which existed when Watergate became an issue.

1822. _____. "Thinking Things over--The Impeachment Imperative: Reprinted from the Wall Street Journal, May 29, 1974." Congressional Record, CXX (May 29, 1974), 16853-16854. Comments on the rush to judgement.

1823. Rubin, Richard L. "The Presidency in the Age of Television." American Political Science Proceedings, XXXIV (Summer 1981), 138-152. Looks at the impact of TV on presidential activities; contains a few comments on the troubles of Richard Nixon.

1824. "The Rush Toward Judgement in the Watergate Case." U.S. News and World Report, LXXV (September 17, 1973), 33-34. Latest grand jury and court verdicts and indictments.

1825. "Rushing Ahead the Impeachment Inquiry." Time, CIII (March 18, 1974), 9-12. The work of the House Judiciary Committee staff.

1826. Russell, Dick. "Argosy Interview: Charles Colson." Argosy, CCCLXXXIII (March 1976), 29+. Includes the former counsel's views on Nixon's involvement in the cover-up.

1827. Ryan, R. A. "Impeachment Prober Is Used to Tough Spots." Biographical News, I (January 1974), 21. A capsule biography of John Doar.

1828. Saffell, David C., ed. American Government: Reform in the Post-Watergate Era. Cambridge, Mass.: Winthrop, 1976. 267p. A collection of essays on political reform, including contributions by Henry Steele Commanger, Eugene J.

McCarthy, Nelson Polsby, David Broder, Elizabeth Drew, James Reston, Gaylord Nelson, etc.

1829. _____. Watergate: Its Effects on the American Political System. Cambridge, Mass.: Winthrop, 1974. 371p. Featuring a few general pieces on the presidency as an institution, this volume is a "Watergate reader," including contributions from a number of important press and government figures, as well as political scientists.

1830. Safire, William. Before the Fall: An Inside View of the Pre-Watergate White House. Garden City, N.Y.: Doubleday, 1975. 704p. A Nixon speech writer who resigned before the scandal broke tells a sympathetic yet objective story about the more human side of the Nixon White House; should be compared with Raymond Price's memoirs cited above. Abridged in Saturday Evening Post, CCXLVII (April 1975), 42-43+.

1831. _____. "Deck Being Stacked by the Judiciary Committee: Reprinted from the Richmond [Virginia] Times-Dispatch, January 17, 1974." Congressional Record, CXX (January 23, 1974), 657-658. Critical of the House inquiry.

1832. _____. "Into an Era of Investigation: Reprinted from the Washington Evening-Star, July 12, 1973." Congressional Record, CXIX (July 13, 1973), 23854-23855. Comments on the large number of Watergate-related investigations.

1833. _____. "Jail for the Chief?: Reprinted from the New York Times, May 13, 1974." Congressional Record, CXX (May 14, 1974), 14683-14684. Speculates that the "crimes of Watergate" might lead to Nixon's imprisonment should he be found guilty.

1834. _____. "Last Days in the Bunker." New York Times Magazine (August 18, 1974), 6+. On the ambience of the Nixon White House in the final days before the President's resignation.

1835. _____. "The Press Is the Enemy." New York, VIII (January 27, 1975), 41-44, 47-50. Reviews the Nixon administration's battle with the press, especially during the dark days of Watergate.

1836. _____. "Who's What Around the White House: Let Henry and Al and George and Mel Do It." New York Times Magazine (November 11, 1973), 38-39+. Looks at the work and pecking-order of White House staffers.

1837. St. Clair, James D. "News Conference of Special Counsel, July 22, 1974." Weekly Compilation of Presidential Documents, X (July 29, 1974), 822-828. Regarding his defense of Nixon before the House Judiciary Committee.

1838. _____. "St. Clair Speaks." Newsweek, LXXXVIII (October 25, 1976), 40. Nixon lied to him about being involved in the cover-up.

1839. Salant, Richard S. "Nixon and Watergate Are Gone: Now Do the People Love Us?" Quill, LXII (November 1974), 23-26. On how the public remains skeptical about the media's motives.

1840. _____. "Salant Says Media Shouldn't Wallow in Watergate." Broadcasting, LXXXVII (September 30, 1974), 35-36. Comments on continuing analysis of the crisis and the pardon.

1841. Salman, S. "The Wages of Sincerity." Newsweek, LXXXV (February 17, 1975), 19-20. The prison term of John Dean.

1842. "Sam Ervin's Last Harrumph." Newsweek, LXXXIV (July 22, 1974), 47-48. The Senate Select Committee completes its work.

1843. Sampson, Anthony. The Sovereign State of ITT. New York: Stein and Day, 1973. 323p. Sampson examines the history and political involvements of International Telephone and Telegraph concentrating on both domestic and foreign operations. An expanded edition published in a 335-page edition by the Greenwich, Conn., firm of Fawcett in 1974 brings the story up to the Watergate era, complete with the story of Dita Beard's memo and the Kleindienst hearings.

1844. "Samuel Dash." In: Eleanora W. Schoenebaum, ed. Political Profiles: The Nixon/Ford Years. New York: Facts on File, Inc., 1979. pp. 160-162. A capsule biography.

1845. "Samuel J. Ervin." In: Current Biography Yearbook 1973. New York: H. W. Wilson Co., 1974. pp. 120-122. A brief profile.

1846. _____. In: Eleanora W. Schoenebaum, ed. Political Profiles: The Nixon/Ford Years. New York: Facts on File, Inc., 1979. pp. 192-195. A more complete biography than that in the last entry.

1847. San Francisco Bay Area Kapitalistate Group. "Watergate on the Eighteenth Brumaire of Richard Nixon." Kapitalistate: Working Papers of the Capitalist State, III (Spring 1975), 3-24. Unavailable for review.

1848. Saxbe, William B. "If Nixon Is Impeached--What Then?: An Interview." U.S. News and World Report, LXXVI (February 4, 1974), 22-26+. Richardson's successor as Attorney General explains the trial process as well as the rules of succession to the Oval Office.

1849. "Saxbe: Nixon's Second Selection from Congress." C.Q. Weekly Report, XXXI (1973), 2896-2900. On the Ohio senator's nomination to be Attorney General; includes a nice profile.

1850. "Scandals As an Issue." New Republic, LXVII (September 23, 1972), 8-9. Seems to be having no impact on 1972 electorate other than increased cynicism.

1851. Schell, Jonathan. "Reflections: The Time of Illusion." New Yorker, LI (June 2-July 7, 1975), 42-48+, 70-71+, 55-56+, 60-88+, 39-44+, 38-48+. Forms the basis for the next entry whose annotation applies to this citation.

1852. _____. The Time of Illusion. New York: Alfred A. Knopf, 1976. 392p. Based on the New Yorker articles cited in the entry above. Schell argues that the 1969-1974 Nixon administration developed "a new form of rule, in which images were given precedence over substance in every phase of government," an "illusion" created in order to keep up U.S. credibility as a great power with the rest of the world. The author goes on to contend that when Nixon employed spies, burglars, and extortionists and employed the IRS, CIA, and FBI to destroy his opposition, the President actually believed that he was saving not only his own country but the world. Provides an interesting and complex picture of the web of conspiracy the Nixon White House wove and which fell apart with the Watergate scandal.

1853. Schlesinger, Arthur M. "Can Psychiatry Save the Nation?" Saturday Review (September 7, 1974), 10-16. On the then-vogue idea of subjecting presidents to character analysis.

1854. _____. "Executive Privilege--A Murky History: Reprinted from the Wall Street Journal, March 30, 1973." Congressional Record, CXIX (April 2, 1973), 10615-10616. A brief history of the process, highlighting its expansion by the Nixon administration.

1855. _____. The Imperial Presidency. Boston: Houghton, Mifflin, 1973. 541p. Users should also see the same year's Popular Library reprint which includes an epilogue, "The Vice Presidency: A Modest Proposal," not found in the hardback edition. A well-known critique of the growth of anonymous presidential power since 1789, mostly via war powers. In his discussion of Nixon, the author sees him as usurping Congressional authority and engaged in intimidation, secrecy, executive privilege and presidential prerogatives in a concentrated effort to change the constitutional balance of power. At the end of the study, Schlesinger urges Nixon's impeachment.

1856. _____. "Is the Presidency Too Powerful?" Reader's Digest, CVII (December 1975), 87-93. Sees the abuses of the Nixon administration over and the need for an activist presidency arising once more.

1857. _____. "Nixon Since the Broadcast." New Statesman and Nation, LXXXV (May 18, 1973), 715-717. His position since announcing the resignations of his top aides.

1858. _____. "The Runaway Presidency." Atlantic, CCXXXII (November 1973), 43-55. Based on the Nixon section of his book, The Imperial Presidency.

1859. _____. "Watergate and the Corruption of Language." Today's Education, LXIII (September 1974), 25-27. Comments on those "Watergate words and phrases" which came into Americans' language as a result of their exposure to the crisis.

1860. _____. "What If We Don't Impeach Him?" Harper's, CCXLVIII (May 1974), 12-18. Argues that many Americans will lose their freedom and rights if Nixon's imperial presidency continues, and that Congress will go into an even steeper decline.

1861. _____. "Who Owns a President's Papers?" Manuscripts, XXVII (Summer 1975), 178-182. Comments on the Nixon claim to ownership reprinted from the February 26, 1975 issue of the Wall Street Journal.

1862. Schnapper, Morris B., ed. Presidential Impeachment: A Documentary Overview. Washington, D.C.: Public Affairs Press, 1974. 144p. Prints many of the documents submitted to the House Judiciary Committee, including pro-impeachment briefs by such groups as the A.C.L.U. and the President's defense delivered by his attorneys. Unfortunately, it has no index.

1863. Schorr, Daniel. Clearing the Air. Boston: Houghton Mifflin, 1977. 333p. This CBS newsman was deeply involved in the coverage of Watergate, for which he won three Emmy awards. His account tells of his being wiretapped by the FBI and of the difficulty of investigative reporting in the tension-filled atmosphere surrounding the case.

1864. _____. "The FBI and Me." Columbia Journalism Review, XIII (November 1974), 8-14. How the FBI kept track of this reporter's activities.

1865. Schwartz, Bernard. "Bad Presidents Make Hard Law: Richard M. Nixon in the Supreme Court." Rutgers Law Review, XXXI (May 1978), 22-38. A further look at the issues in United States v. Nixon.

1866. Schwartz, Herman. "Six Years of Tapping and Bugging." Civil Liberties Review, I (Summer 1974), 26-37. Details the covert data gathering practices of the Nixon administration.

1867. Scott, Austin. "Laser 'Bug' in Nixon Office Reported: Reprinted from the Washington Post, April 21, 1975." In: U.S. Congress, Senate, Committee on the Judiciary, Subcommittee on Constitutional Rights. Surveillance Technology, 1976: Report. 94th Cong., 2nd sess. Washington, D.C.: U.S. Government Printing Office, 1976. pp. 1001-1003. Details on the kinds of bugs maintained in Nixon's Oval Office before Watergate.

1868. Scott, Peter D. "From Dallas to Watergate: The Longest Cover-up." Ramparts, XII (November 1973), 12-20+. Draws a line from the cover-up of the Kennedy assassination to Watergate showing that many of the same people and techniques were involved in both.

1869. Seamans, Andrew. "Developing the Internal Security Mission." In: Richard O. Wright, ed. Whose FBI? LaSalle, Ill.: Open Court Publishing, 1974. pp. 139-172. A general account with some references to Watergate.

1870. "A Secret Agent Named Tony." Newsweek, LXXXI (May 28, 1973), 38. Profiles Tony Ulasewicz.

1871. "The Secretary and the Tape Tangle." Time, CII (December 10, 1973), 15-18+. Rose Mary Woods and her explanation for the 18-minute tape gap.

1872. Seelye, John. Dirty Tricks; Or, Nick Novin's Natural Nobility. New York: Liveright, 1974. 152p. A satire on the Watergate case.

1873. ———. "The Measure of His Company: Richard M. Nixon in Amber." Virginia Quarterly Review, LIII (Autumn 1977), 241-257. Unavailable for review.

1874. Segretti, Donald H. "Dirty, but Surely Beyond Tricks: Donald Segretti's Testimony." Time, CII (October 15, 1973), 20-21. Segretti's testimony on "dirty tricks" to the Ervin panel.

1875. ———. "Watergate--A Big Bag of Anti-Muskie Campaign Tricks." C.Q. Weekly Report, XXXI (October 6, 1973), 2630+. Excerpts from Segretti's opening statement to the Ervin Committee.

1876. Self, Edwin F. "Thanks Sam, I Needed That: An Interview with Sam Ervin." San Diego Magazine, XXVII (April 1975), 24-38. A wide-ranging interview with much on Watergate.

1877. "Self-Incriminating Nixon Tapes: Excerpts." In: Robert A. Diamond, ed. Historic Documents, 1974. Washington, D.C.: Congressional Quarterly, Inc., 1975. pp. 673-682. Excerpts from the June 23, 1972 tape.

1878. "Selling the People Short." Progressive, XXXVIII (March 1974), 5-6. Suggests citizens are wise to Nixon's defense strategies.

1879. Semple, Robert B., Jr. "Richard M. Nixon: A Tentative Evaluation." In: Philip C. Dolce and George H. Skau, eds. Power and the Presidency. New York: Scribners, 1976. pp. 164-174. Attempts to show how Nixon misused his power.

1880. "The Senate Prepares to Judge." Time, CIV (August 12, 1974), 12. In the likely event Nixon is impeached by the full House.

1881. "Senate-White House Clash: The FBI's Man in a Squeeze." U.S. News and World Report, LXXIV (March 26, 1973), 33. The confirmation problems of L. Patrick Gray.

1882. "Sentencing the Plumbers: Excerpts from the Court Proceedings." In: Robert A. Diamond, ed. Historic Documents, 1974. Washington, D.C.: Congressional Quarterly, Inc., 1975. pp. 661-672. The sentencing was actually accomplished in early 1975.

1883. "Sense of Climax." Newsweek, LXXXIV (July 22, 1974), 14-18. Examines the problems facing the President.

1884. "Separation of Powers and Executive Privilege: The Watergate Briefs." Political Science Quarterly, LXXXVIII (December 1973), 582-654. Examines both sides of the question; provides texts.

1885. "Seven Charged, a Report, and a Briefcase." Time, CIII (March 11, 1974), 11-14+. The Watergate grand jury findings and the move by Judge Sirica to provide grand jury data to the House Judiciary Committee.

1886. "Seven Days in August." Newsweek, LXXXIV (August 19, 1974), 10-20. Events leading up to and including the Nixon resignation.

1887. "Seven Tumultous Days." Time, CII (November 5, 1973), 13-14. Events in the week following the "Saturday Night Massacre."

1888. Seymour-Ure, Colin. "Presidential Power, Press Secretaries, and Communications." Political Studies, VIII (June 1980), 253-270. A president's power, the author argues, depends to a large extent on his ability to communicate, and his press secretaries are important to that end; gives examples, including Nixon and Ziegler.

1889. Shanahan, Eileen. "Nixon Asked Data on [George] Wallace Tax, Panel Was Told: Reprinted from the New York Times, July 17, 1974." Congressional Record, CXX (August 1, 1974), 26439-26440. The House Judiciary Committee hears how the IRS was employed for political purposes.

1890. Shapiro, William. "The Ziegler Memorandum: A Five Point Plan to Prevent Impeachment." Washington Magazine, V (January 1974), 41-45. "Operation Candor."

1891. Shapley, Deborah. "Watergate: 1972 Campaigners Tried to Use R & D Agencies." Science, CLXXXV (July 12, 1974), 124-127. Government funding to such groups was allocated according to their "responsiveness" to the Nixon campaign.

1892. Shartar, Martin. "John Dean Talks About Jimmy Carter, the Nixon White House, Watergate, and the Things He'll Never Tell: An Interview." Atlanta, XVI (January 1977), 46-48. A brief but wide-ranging talk.

1893. "Shattered Justice Department." Newsweek, LXXXII (November 5, 1973), 36-37. Impact on employees of the "Saturday Night Massacre."

1894. Shawcross, William. "Can Nixon Last?" New Statesman and Nation, LXXXVI (November 9, 1973), 671-672. A British journalist and Watergate-watcher evaluates the impact of the "Saturday Night Massacre."

1895. _____. "Counts in the Nixon Indictment." New Statesman and Nation, LXXXVI (August 3, 1973), 139-140. Summation of the Ervin panel testimonies.

1896. _____. "The Fortunes of Richard Nixon." New Statesman and Nation, LXXXVI (October 19, 1973), 544-545. A look at his uncompromising position in the tapes case.

1897. _____. "The March of Truth." New Statesman and Nation, LXXXV (June 29, 1973), 948-949. A review of early Ervin Committee testimony.

1898. _____. "Nixon, the Tapes, and Mr. Cox." New Statesman and Nation, LXXXVI (October 26, 1973), 583-584. Issues in the "Saturday Night Massacre."

1899. _____. "Options Now for Nixon." New Statesman and Nation, LXXXVI (December 7, 1973), 843-845. Raises the question of resignation or impeachment.

1900. _____. "Saga of the Tapes." New Statesman and Nation, LXXXVI (November 30, 1973), 797-798. Looks at the mysterious 18-minute gap.

1901. _____. Sideshow: Kissinger, Nixon, and the Destruction of Cambodia. New York: Simon and Schuster, 1979. 467p. The question of the secret bombing was hotly debated during the House Judiciary Committee, but details on those operations, herein well covered, lie outside the purview of this guide. Those seeking details may wish to consult my Air War Southeast Asia, 1961-1973 (Metuchen, N.J.: The Scarecrow Press, 1979).

1902. _____. "Truth, Wealth, and the Watergate." New Statesman and Nation, LXXXV (April 6, 1973), 483-484. CREEP and illegal campaign contributions.

1903. _____. "Will Checkers Ride Again?" New Statesman and Nation, LXXXV (April 27, 1973), 603-604. Examines the President's televised Watergate statements.

1904. Shear, Marie. "Stoolies, Ciphers, and Alibis: Women in the White House Transcripts." ETC, XXXIII (March 1976), 88-92. Examines references to women in the White House edited transcripts.

1905. Sherrill, Robert. "Zealots for Nixon: Gaudy Night at the Watergate." Nation, CCXV (September 25, 1972), 230-234. An early assessment of the connection between the Watergate burglars and the Nixon staff.

1906. "Showdown Before the Justices." Time, CIV (July 15, 1974), 13-14. United States v. Nixon, the great tapes case.

1907. "Showdown: Richard Nixon's Refusal to Surrender Watergate Tapes." Newsweek, LXXXII (August 6, 1973), 12-17. Provides the President's reasons and reviews the legal steps being taken to obtain them.

1908. Sickels, Robert J. Presidential Transactions. Englewood Cliffs, N.J.: Prentice-Hall, 1974. 184p. Attempts to apply "exchange theory"--a personal calculation of self-interest on a rational basis prior to action--to the presidential arena; the assessment of Nixon's battle with the Supreme Court does not, however, rest on that theory but rather on traditional political analysis.

1909. Sidey, Hugh. "Guilty Until Proven Innocent." Time, CI (May 14, 1973), 19. Blames the scandal on the secrecy and isolation within the administration.

1910. _____. "Memories of a Prosecutor." Time, CIV (November 4, 1974), 22. Jaworski reflects on Watergate and Nixon's guilt.

1911. _____. Portrait of a President. New York: Harper & Row, 1975. 189p. A picture book on President Ford, with sections on Nixon's departure and the pardon.

1912. _____. "Sadness in Mid-America." Time, CI (April 30, 1973), 18. Considers the opinions of people in Greenfield, Iowa.

1913. _____. "Second Sight on the Pardon." Time, CIV (October 7, 1974), 23. Reviews the impact of the pardon.

1914. _____. "Violation of the Public Trust." Time, CIII (May 13, 1974), 14. Reactions to the White House edited tape transcripts by former presidential aides.

1915. _____. "Watergate and the Classroom." Today's Education, LXI (January-February 1974), 23-25. Looks at courses set up nationwide to study the case; suggests steps necessary to rid America of the so-called Watergate mentality.

1916. _____. "We Cannot Run Away." Time, CIII (June 24, 1974), 33. Views of Iowa Congressman Edward Mezvinsky of the House Judiciary Committee.

1917. Sigel, Roberta S. "Affect for Government and Its Relation to Policy Output Among Adolescents." American Journal of Political Science, XXI (February 1977), 111-134. The impact of Watergate on the political inclination of youth.

1918. "Silbert's Promotion: Reprinted from the Washington Star-News, January 7, 1974." In: U.S. Congress, Senate, Committee on the Judiciary. Nomination of Earl J. Silbert to Be United States Attorney: Hearings. 93rd Cong., 2nd sess. Washington, D.C.: U.S. Government Printing Office, 1974. p. 107. An editorial on his fitness to become D.C.'s U.S. Attorney.

1919. Silbey, Franklin. "General Haig--A Lethal Precedent: Reprinted from the Nation, September 24, 1973." Congressional Record, CXIX (September 20, 1973), 30770-30773. On his appointment and work as White House chief of staff.

1920. No entry.

1921. Simons, Howard. "Watergate As a Catalyst." Montana Journalism Review, no. 18 (1975), 12-15. The rebirth of muckraking journalism.

1922. Sirica, John J. "Highlights of Judge Sirica's Decision."

Time, CII (September 10, 1973), 17. Enforcing subpoena for nine presidential taped conversations.

1923. ———. "The Judge Commands the President." Time, CII (September 10, 1973), 14-16. The main points in Sirica's ruling against Nixon in the tapes case.

1924. ———. "Sirica Decision on Grand Jury Report on Nixon: Excerpts from U.S. District Court John J. Sirica's Decision to Turn over a Sealed Grand Jury Report and Briefcase of Evidence to the House Judiciary Committee for Use in Its Impeachment Probe." In: Robert A. Diamond, ed. Historic Documents, 1974. Washington, D.C.: Congressional Quarterly, Inc., 1975. pp. 225-234. Texts.

1925. ———. "Text of Statement, March 23, 1973, on Sentencing the Five Defendants Who Pleaded Guilty." In: Buel W. Patch, ed. Historic Documents, 1973. Washington, D.C.: Congressional Quarterly, Inc., 1974. pp. 419-423. On sentencing the Watergate burglars; text.

1926. ———. "Text of Statement on Sentencing G. Gordon Liddy, March 23, 1973." In: Buel W. Patch, ed. Historic Documents, 1973. Washington, D.C.: Congressional Quarterly, Inc., 1974. pp. 418-419. Includes comments on Liddy's refusal to co-operate with the prosecution.

1927. ———. "Sirica Decision: The Watergate Tapes." New Republic, CLXIX (September 8, 1973), 7-9. Looks at the tapes decision and points out where it falls short.

1928. ———. To Set the Record Straight: The Break-in, the Tapes, the Conspirators, the Pardon. New York: W. W. Norton, 1979. 394p. Writing in his foreword, Sirica says:

> From beginning to end, the Watergate case took five years to work its way through the United States District Court in Washington. From the fall of 1972, when indictments were first returned against the original suspects, until late in the fall of 1977, I was involved in nearly every phase of that proceeding.... I have tried to tell the story of the Watergate case as I saw it from the bench. And I have tried to tell something of my own life's story so that people may know a bit about the kind of person I am.

Written with the assistance of a Time magazine reporter, John F. Stacks, Sirica's memoirs confirm most of what has been reported elsewhere and is an excellent rebuttal of those critics who thought he should not have been such an activist in the case. The book sets forth the judge's views on the main points of its subtitle and adds in one convenient place reprints of his opinions and the opinions on his opinions rendered by various appellate courts.

1928a. Sititich, Mary F. "The Butterfly Blues." Air Progress, XXXVI (May 1975), 4+. A look at Alexander Butterfield's post-Watergate job as FAA Administrator.

1929. "Skeleton in the GOP Closet." Newsweek, LXXX (September 4, 1972), 38. A GAO report charges the Republicans with questionable bookkeeping and wonders where some of its funds came from.

1930. Skelton, William. "This Is Marrrvin Zindler." TV Guide, XXIV (February 8, 1975), 14-16. Comments on former White House press secretary Ronald Ziegler.

1931. "Slugging It Out over the ITT Affair." Time, XCIX (March 20, 1972), 12-15. Examines the charges and investigations surrounding the Beard memo.

1932. "A Small Nixon Defense Team Has Recruiting Problems." C.Q. Weekly Report, XXXII (March 23, 1974), 741-744. On the President's problems in finding defense counsel.

1933. Smith, Cecil. "Ratings Soar for Watergate on PBS: Reprinted from the Los Angeles Times, June 20, 1973." Congressional Record, CXIX (August 1, 1973), 27381-27382. The public's response to the uninterrupted hearings.

1934. Smith, Chesterfield H. "The Constitutional Crisis: Reprinted from the New York Times, October 23, 1973." Congressional Record, CXIX (October 23, 1973), 34858-34859. Thoughts on the Cox dismissal by the president of the American Bar Association.

1935. _____. "Reactions to Watergate--Threats to Justice: An Address." Congressional Record, CXX (January 23, 1974), 662-664. The rush toward impeachment.

1936. Smith, Franklin B. The Assassination of President Nixon. Rutland, Vt.: Academy Books, 1976. 93p. Pro-Nixon columns reprinted from the New York Times and Burlington Free Press between March 1973 and August 1974.

1937. "Snooping on the 'Enemies.'" Newsweek, LXXXIV (July 29, 1974), 26-29. Reviews the atmosphere leading to the creation of the "plumbers," and recaps their activities.

1938. Sobel, Lester A., ed. Money and Politics: Contributions, Campaign Abuses, and the Law. New York: Facts on File, Inc., 1974. 204p. Contents: Political Spending Soars.--1972 Campaign.--Watergate Revelations.--Controversial Contributions.--Agnew's Downfall.--Other Developments. Taken from the weekly service, Facts on File, this is an excellent source for dry details on the ITT, Milk, and other scandals.

1939. _____. Presidential Succession: Ford, Rockefeller, and the 28th Amendment. New York: Facts on File, Inc., 1975. 225p. Another useful tool drawn from the pages of Facts on File, this volume is based on newspaper accounts, Senate hearings, official and unofficial texts; covers the appropriate Watergate events.

1940. Sobel, Robert, ed. Biographical Directory of the United States Executive Branch, 1774-1977. 2nd rev. ed. Westport, Conn.: Greenwood Press, 1977. 503p. Includes personnel of the Nixon administration who were involved in Watergate and related matters.

1941. "Social Scientists Speak on Watergate." Society, X (September-October 1973), 15-27. Various aspects of the affair are covered by Murray Weidenbaum, Herbert Marcuse, Robert Nisbet, Ithiel de Sola Pool, Stuart Umpleby, and Edward Schneier.

1942. Sofaer, A. D. "Executive Privilege: An Historical Note." Columbia Law Review, LXXV (November 1975), 1318-1321. Traces the history of the concept, with some comments on Nixon's use.

1943. "Some Familiar Notes Sung by John Dean." Broadcasting, LXXXV (July 3, 1973), 30+. A report on his Ervin panel testimony before live TV cameras.

1944. Sommer, Michael. "Televising Impeachment: Eight Viewpoints." RTNDA Communicator (August 1974), 4-5. Includes the views of Fred Friendly, James Reston, George Reedy, the ACLU, and others.

1945. Sorensen, Theodore C. Watchmen in the Night: Presidential Accountability After Watergate. Cambridge, Mass.: M.I.T. Press, 1975. 178p. Based on a series of lectures delivered at MIT in the fall of 1974, this slim volume contends that "emotions may still run too high to permit a careful and objective evaluation of long-standing institutional arrangements." Nevertheless, he dismisses most of the post-Watergate proposals to decrease presidential power in favor of Congress, which he sees as being too inflexible to perform in an executive setting. To prevent future Watergates, the former Kennedy aide suggests that presidents be made more accountable to the courts, Congress, and the press.

1946. _____. "Watergate and American Foreign Policy." World

Today, XXX (December 1974), 497-503. Contends that U.S. policy suffered through Nixon's full-time preoccupation with the scandal.

1947. Soule, John W. "Cognitive Dissonance and Public Reactions to Watergate." Experimental Study of Politics, V (February 1976), 1-19. Unavailable for review.

1948. "Speaking of Money and Politics." Time, CII (July 30, 1973), 21-22. Covers the Ervin Committee testimony of Herbert Kalmbach, Tony Ulasewicz, Frederick LaRue, Robert Mardian, and Gordon Strachan.

1949. "Special Prosecution Force Issues Final Report." C.Q. Weekly Report, XXXIII (1975), 2214. Contains a few excerpts; the report is cited below.

1950. "The Specter in the Dock." Newsweek, LXXXIV (October 28, 1974), 26-27+. Nixon and the Watergate cover-up trial.

1951. Spencer, Patricia L. "Separation of Powers--Bills of Attainder--Presidential Papers--Chief Executive's Right to Privacy." Akron Law Review, XI (Fall 1977), 373-386. Offers thoughts and comments on each sub-topic.

1952. Spencer, Stewart. "Pardon Was Surely Respectable--Venomous Criticism of Ford Has Some Disturbing Implications: Reprinted from the Charlotte [North Carolina] News, September 24, 1974." Congressional Record, CXX (September 24, 1974), 32511-32512. Supports the Ford action.

1953. Sperling, Godfrey, Jr. "Survey--Republicans Agitated by Transcripts: Reprinted from the Christian Science Monitor, May 14, 1974." Congressional Record, CXX (May 15, 1974), 14943. Looks at GOP reaction to the edited White House transcripts.

1954. "The Spies Who Came in for the Heat." Newsweek, LXXX (September 18, 1972), 40-45. An early assessment of the White House "plumbers" and their operations; includes eleven biographies of major figures.

1955. "Spotlight on the Tape Vault." Newsweek, LXXXIV (August 5, 1974), 24-25. Notes then current handling of the subpoenaed White House tapes.

1956. Spragens, William C. From Spokesman to Press Secretary: White House Media Operations. Washington, D.C.: University Press of America, 1980. 243p. A review of the role of presidential press secretaries from the early days through the Carter Administration's early days, examining the manner in which they changed from simple readers of statements to active media influences. Contains a section on the role of Ronald Ziegler during Watergate.

1957. Sprague, R. E. "June 1972 Raid on Democratic Party Headquarters." Computers and Automation, XXI (August, October, December 1972), 33-36, 18-26+, 24-30. An early assessment of the Watergate case, planning, tactics, and outcomes.

1958. _____. "The Lessons of Watergate." Computers and Automation, XXII (August 1973), 36-43. Drawn in light of the Ervin Committee hearings.

1959. _____. "Nixon, Ford, and the Political Assassinations in the United States." Computers and People, XXIV (January 1975), 27-31. Attempts to draw a line between those two presidents and illegal intelligence operations within the borders of the United States.

1960. _____. "The Watergate Crime and Cover-up Strategy." Computers and Automation, XXII (March 1973), 26-30. Assembles a pattern based on the knowledge then available.

1961. "The Spreading Stain." Newsweek, LXXXII (June 4, 1973), 25. The Watergate roles of the FBI, CIA, SEC, and State Department.

1962. "The Spy and the All-American Boy." Time, CIV (November 11, 1974), 21+. The fate of "plumber" E. Howard Hunt.

1963. "Spy in the Cold." Time, CI (January 29, 1973), 17-20. Promising them money, Hunt persuades four Watergate burglars to plead guilty.

1964. "Spy in the White House: The Question of Alexander Butterfield's Contact with the CIA." Time, CVI (July 21, 1975), 14. Examines the possibility that Butterfield was an Agency plant.

1965. "The Spy Who Took the Fall." Newsweek, LXXXII (October 8, 1973), 38. Hunt.

1966. "Spying at White House Orders." U.S. News and World Report, LXXIV (June 11, 1973), 19-21. Reports on the internal intelligence activities of the Nixon White House and how they led to the activities of the "plumbers."

1967. "Spying Gone Haywire." Time, CIV (July 29, 1974), 18-20+. The "plumbers'" operations.

1968. "The Staff Cox Left Behind." Time, CII (December 3, 1973), 18-21. Looks at the Watergate task force and the background of its leaders.

1969. "Stand-up Texan for a Tough Case." Time, CII (November 12, 1973), 45-46. Profiles Leon Jaworski.

1970. Stans, Maurice. "Stans' Statement." C.Q. Weekly Report, XXXI (June 16, 1973), 1495-1497. Testimony before the Ervin Committee.

1971. _____. The Terrors of Justice: The Untold Side of Watergate. New York: Everest House, 1978. 478p. Finance Director of CREEP, the former Commerce Secretary was acquitted in the Vesco case but later pleaded guilty to minor infractions of the campaign finance law. Regarded as the "Watergate paymaster," he argues in this memoir that he was a victim of double standards in an unfair, witch-hunting atmosphere created by politicians and, especially, the press. Stans rebuts every charge, intimation, accusation, and insinuation leveled at him during the three-year investigation in the longest (and in the view of some critics, the dullest) apology of any major figure in the case.

1972. "Stanton, Rather Say White House Made Open Threats." Broadcasting, LXXXVI (May 6, 1974), 32-33. Against CBS for its reporting of the affair.

1973. Steiger, Paul. "Aide to Nixon Called ITT 'Mastermind': Reprinted from the Los Angeles Times." Congressional Record, CXVIII (May 11, 1972), 17103-17104. The role of Peter M. Flanigan.

1974. Stein, Howard F. "Silent Complicity at Watergate." American Scholar, XLIII (Winter 1973), 21-37. A deep analysis of the social and psychological climate that led to the scandal.

1975. "A Step Ahead of the Curve." Newsweek, LXXXIII (May 13, 1974), 38-39. Looks at the PR value of the edited White House transcripts.

1976. Stephenson, D. Grier, Jr. "Mild Magistracy of the Law: United States v. Richard M. Nixon." Intellect, CIII (February 1975), 288-292. Reasons why the Supreme Court case was not earth-shaking.

1977. "Stepping Up the Pressure." Newsweek, LXXXIII (January 21, 1974), 19-21. The end of "Operation Candor."

1978. Stern, Sol. "Watergate Footnote: The Selling of Frank Wills." New York Times Magazine (November 10, 1974), 32-33+. The unsuccessful efforts of the Watergate security guard to cash in on the fame of his accidental role.

1979. Stevenson, Robert L. "The Audience for the Impeachment

Hearings." Journal of Broadcasting, XX (Spring 1976), 159-168. Examines who watched and why.

1980. "The Stiff Price of Watergate." Newsweek, LXXXV (March 3, 1975), 14-15. Profiles those participants jailed.

1981. "Stiff Sentences." Time, CIV (August 12, 1974), 21-22. The sentencing of John Dean and John Ehrlichman.

1982. Stokes, George. "The Story of P.: Computer Analysis of the Watergate Tapes." Harper's, CCXLIX (October 1974), 6-9+. The 18-minute gap and assorted background noises.

1983. Stone, I. F. "The Fix: Reprinted from the New York Review of Books." Congressional Record, CXX (September 25, 1974), 32667-32668. On ownership of the presidential tapes.

1984. _____. "Impeachment." New York Review of Books (June 28, 1973), 12-19. Considers the early possibilities in light of history.

1985. "Stonewall Nixon at War." Newsweek, LXXXIII (June 3, 1974), 22-25. Examines Nixon's refusals to answer tape subpoenas.

1986. "The Story of a GOP Trickster." Newsweek, LXXX (October 30, 1972), 30-36. Profiles Donald Segretti.

1987. "Story of the Big Cover-up." Newsweek, LXXXIII (March 11, 1974), 23-29. Grand jury indictments of Haldeman, Ehrlichman, Colson, Mitchell, Strachan, Mardian, and Parkinson on cover-up charges.

1988. Strachan, Kristine. "Self-Incrimination, Immunity, and Watergate." Texas Law Review, LVI (May 1978), 791-834. Examines the plea-bargaining arrangements of the scandal.

1989. Strackbein, O. R. "Crime As the Sole Basis of Impeachment." Congressional Record, CXX (April 3, 1974), 9694-9695. Supports that argument.

1990. _____. "Impeachment--A Primitive Political Weapon." Congressional Record, CXX (June 24, 1974), 20825-20826. Finds it to be a weapon of revenge.

1991. _____. "Impeachment As a Political Weapon." Congressional Record, CXX (April 24, 1974), 11795-11796. Can be employed to force presidents to do the will of Congress.

1992. _____. "Impeachment Perspective--Looking in the Mirror of History." Congressional Record, CXX (May 23, 1974), 16285. Examines earlier impeachment efforts in U.S. history in the light of Watergate.

1993. _____. "Why Impeachment?" Congressional Record, CXX (July 17, 1974), 28888-28889. Because the public demands it.

1994. No entry.

1995. "Stress Test--Who's Lying?" Newsweek, LXXXII (July 23, 1973), 19. Psychological Stress Evaluator evaluations of the stress on Colson, Mitchell, Haldeman, and Dean.

1996. Stroud, K. "Mo Fiddled While Dean Burned." Ms, IV (November 1975), 46+. John Dean's wife's activities during the Watergate crisis.

1997. "The Struggle for Nixon's Tapes." Time, CII (September 3, 1973), 29-33. Reviews the pro and con arguments presented in briefs before Judge Sirica.

1998. "Subpoena for Nixon." Time, CIII (February 11, 1974), 14. During John Ehrlichman's trial for the Fielding break-in.

1999. "Subpoena of Materials Relating to the Ellsberg Case." Weekly Compilation of Presidential Documents, X (June 3, 1974), 565-568. Letter to Judge Gesell from St. Clair regarding materials subpoenaed by Colson and Ehrlichman in the Fielding break-in.

2000. "Subpoena of Presidential Tapes and Materials: Documents Filed by Attorneys for the President, Moving to Quash the Subpoena Issued by the U.S. District Court for the District of Columbia, May 1, 1974." Weekly Compilation of Presidential Documents, X (May 6, 1974), 473-484. Full text.

2001. "Subpoena of Presidential Tapes and Materials: Document Submitted [April 30, 1974] to the House Judiciary Committee in Answer to the Committee's Subpoena." Weekly Compilation of Presidential Documents, X (May 6, 1974), 459-469. Full text.

2002. "Subpoena of Presidential Tapes by the Senate Select Committee on Presidential Campaign Activities: Memorandum Filed by Attorneys for the President [May 10, 1974] in Response to the Committee's Memorandum." Weekly Compilation of Presidential Documents, X (May 13, 1974), 505-509.

2003. "Subpoenas (Con't)." Time, CI (March 12, 1973), 62. Notes of reporters subpoenaed for Democratic and Republican lawsuits.

2004. _____. Time, CI (April 2, 1973), 65. Reports that the subpoenas were quashed as a violation of the First Amendment.

2005. Sundquist, James L. "Needed--A Workable Check on the Presidency: Reprinted from the Brookings Bulletin, Fall 1973." Congressional Record, CXX (January 30, 1974), 1499-1501. Looks for curbs on presidential power and excesses.

2006. _____. "Reflections on Watergate: Lessons for Public Administration." Public Administration Review, XXXIV (September-October 1974), 453-461. Looks at ways to curb presidential excesses and the growth of administrative staffs in light of the crisis.

2007. "Supreme Court Case: Brief Filed by Attorneys for the President, June 21, 1974, in the Supreme Court of the United States, October Term, 1973, nos. 73-1766 and 73-1834: United States of America, Petitioner v. Richard M. Nixon, President of the United States, Cross Petitioner v. United States of America, Respondent; On Writs of Certiorari Before Judgement to the United States Court of Appeals for the District of Columbia Circuit." Weekly Compilation of Presidential Documents, X (July 1, 1974), 657-709. Questions of court jurisdiction, executive privilege, and separation of powers among the branches of government.

2008. "Supreme Court Case: Reply Brief Filed by Attorneys for the President, July 1, 1974, in the Supreme Court of the United States, October 1973 Term, nos. 73-1766 and 73-1834: United States of America, Petitioner v. Richard M. Nixon, President of the United States, Cross Petitioner v. United States of America, Respondent; On Writs of Certiorari Before Judgement to the United States Court of Appeals for the District of Columbia Circuit." Weekly Compilation of Presidential Documents, X (July 8, 1974), 772-787. Addresses the same questions as the previous entry.

2009. "Suppressing Evidence." New Republic, CLXIX (August 11, 1973), 5-7. Comments on the President's refusal to release his tapes.

2010. "Surprises and Contradictions in the Mitchell-Stans Case." U.S. News and World Report, LXXVI (March 25, 1974), 29-30. Concerns their trial.

2011. "Surviving in the Bull's Eye." Time, CIII (May 27, 1974), 19-20. The artful dodging of Alexander Haig.

2012. Sussman, Barry. The Great Cover-up: Nixon and the Scandal of Watergate. New York: T. Y. Crowell, 1974. 151p. With opinion and appraisal of the whole Watergate affair, this detailed and absorbing account was written by a Washington Post official who was first City Editor and then head of the Post's special Watergate task force. Sussman both helped to supervise and direct the work of Woodward and Bernstein, and here offers frank insights into the story of how his newspaper covered the crisis.

2013. Swayduck, Edward. "Sabotage: Since 1946, Nixon's Political Stock-in-Trade." Lithopinion, VIII (Summer 1973), 2-7. Traces the use of "dirty tricks" in all Nixon-related campaigns.

2014. Sweeney, Louise. "Bar President Would Vote Impeachment: Reprinted from the Christian Science Monitor, June 14, 1974." Congressional Record, CXX (July 2, 1974), 22088. Reports on the conversion of Nixon-supporter Chesterfield Smith.

2015. "Symposium: The Meaning of Watergate." Current, CLV (October 1973), 3-29. Contains excerpts from articles by Hans Morgenthau, Ramsey Clark, Stanley Cloud, Arthur Kinoy, and Barbara Tuchman.

2016. "Symposium: United States v. Nixon." UCLA Law Review, XXII (October 1974), 1-140. Contents: "The Incarnation of Executive Privilege," by Raoul Berger.--"Mr. Nixon Loses but the Presidency Largely Prevails," by Louis Henkin.--"Presidential Prerogative and Judicial Review," by Kenneth L. Karst.--"A Political and Constitutional Review of United States v. Nixon," by William Van Alstyne.

2017. "Symposium: United States v. Nixon--An Historical Perspective." Loyola of Los Angeles Law Review, IX (December 1975), 11-66. Similar in thrust to the previous entry.

2018. Szulc, Tad. "The CIA and the Plumbers." New Republic, CLXIX (December 29, 1973), 19-21. Reviews the assistance given the latter by the former.

2019. _____. Compulsive Spy: The Strange Career of E. Howard Hunt. New York: Viking Press, 1974. 180p. Using newspaper accounts and Washington contacts, the author focuses on Hunt's career in intelligence from his OSS days in Burma to his activities on behalf of the White House "plumbers"; Szulc, a veteran reporter on spy matters, argues that Hunt's CIA conditioning and personal flaws led to his involvement in the Watergate affair.

2020. _____. "How Nixon Used the CIA." New York, VIII (January 20, 1975), 28-33. Examines not only the Watergate incident, but other domestic intelligence operations in which the Agency was involved.

2021. _____. "Spy Compulsion." New York Times Magazine (June 3, 1973), 11+. A review of Hunt's career.

2022. _____. "Super Contributors." New Republic, CLXIX (August 11, 1973), 15-17. Looks at the large companies and "fat-cats" involved in providing illegal or questionable support to CREEP.

2023. "Tackling Toward the Impeachment Line." Time, CIV (July 8, 1974), 14-15. On the renewed push for a final vote by the House Judiciary Committee.

2024. "Tales from the Men Who Took Orders." Time, CI (June 4, 1973), 26-30. Examines the Ervin Committee testimony of McCord, Caulfield, Barker, Ulasewicz, Baldwin, and Gerald Alch.

2025. "Tales of 'Hush Money.'" U.S. News and World Report, LXXV (July 30, 1973), 19. Herbert Kalmbach's Ervin panel testimony.

2026. Talmey, Allene. "Who Broke the Watergate Story, and How?" Vogue, CLXII (August 1973), 96-97+. Credits Woodward and Bernstein.

2027. "Tangled Trail of a Campaign Contribution: Investigation of Contributions of Armand Hammer and Tim M. Babcock to the Nixon Campaign." Business Week (September 21, 1974), 84+. Follows the WSPF inquiry.

2028. "The Tangled Web They Wove." Newsweek, LXXXIV (December 2, 1974), 32+. Covering the Watergate cover-up trial.

2029. "The Tapes: A Nine-Month Battle for Disclosure." C.Q. Weekly Report, XXXII (May 4, 1974), 1077. A chronology, July 17, 1973-April 29, 1974.

2030. "Tapes Mystery--Roadblocks Facing the New Prosecutor: Nixon's Latest Troubles over Watergate--Missing Tapes and a Congressional Fight for an Investigator Who Can't Be Fired or Curbed by the President." U.S. News and World Report, LXXV (November 12, 1973), 21-23. Covers the events listed in the subtitle.

2031. "Tapes Ruin Image Nixon Sought: Reprinted from the Flint [Mich.] Journal, May 5, 1974." Congressional Record, CXX (May 8, 1974), 13848. An editorial on the edited White House transcripts.

2032. "The Tapes That Sealed His Doom." Newsweek, LXXXIV (August 19, 1974), 33-34. Repeats the contents of the "smoking gun" tapes which proved the President was involved in the Watergate cover-up.

2033. Tapia, Raul R., John P. Jones, and Michael O. Levine.

"Congress vs. the Executive: The Role of the Courts." Harvard Journal of Legislation (February 1974), 352-403. Discusses the reasons for increases in such cases.

2034. "Tattletale Gray." Time, CI (January 15, 1973), 20. L. Patrick Gray.

2035. Taylor, Lawrence. "Wilson, ITT Accounts in Apparent Conflict: Reprinted from the St. Louis Post-Dispatch, April 10, 1972." In: U.S. Congress, Senate, Committee on the Judiciary. Richard G. Kleindienst--Resumed: Hearings. 92nd Cong., 2nd sess. Washington, D.C.: U.S. Government Printing Office, 1972. pp. 905-907. Congressman Bob Wilson and the ITT stories differed on an alleged $400,000 GOP convention guarantee.

2036. Taylor, Walter. "Impeachment Panel Evidence--IRS Chiefs Balked at Pressure." Congressional Record, CXX (July 18, 1974), 24182. A report on attempted misuse of the tax service.

2037. _____. "White House Got IRS Data on Reporter: Reprinted from the Washington Star-News, May 29, 1974." Congressional Record, CXX (July 22, 1974), 24498-24499. The reporter in question was James R. Polk.

2038. "Teamsters, Watergate Connection." Time, CX (August 8, 1977), 28. On an illegal contribution by the former.

2039. "Televising Impeachment: Reprinted from the Chicago Tribune, July 24, 1974." Congressional Record, CXX (July 29, 1974), 25618. An opposing editorial.

2040. "Telling the Tape Tale." Newsweek, LXXXIV (May 13, 1974), 136. How publishers printed the White House transcripts quickly.

2041. "Telltale Tape Deepens Nixon's Dilemma." Time, CIII (January 28, 1974), 13-18. The experts' report on the 18-minute tape gap.

2042. "Tense Games of the Tapes." Newsweek, LXXXII (August 13, 1973), 16-23. Bob Haldeman's testimony and his version of the clandestine tapes.

2043. ter Horst, Jerald F. Gerald Ford and the Future of the Presidency. New York: Third Press, 1974. 247p. In addition to providing a biography of his friend, ter Horst, Ford's first press secretary who resigned over the Nixon pardon, uses this account to analyze the traumatic effect of Watergate on the presidency.

2044. Terkel, Studs. "View from the Second Story." Rolling Stone

(November 7, 1974), 32-36. Two professional burglars give their opinions on the technique of the Watergate break-in.

2045. "Test for Jaworski." Time, CII (November 19, 1973), 27. Suggests potential pitfalls the new prosecutor may encounter.

2046. "A Texan Who Goes His Own Way." Time, CIII (March 11, 1974), 12-13. Another Jaworski profile.

2047. Thatcher, C. Marshall. "United States v. Nixon: What Price Unanimity?" Ohio Northern Law Review, II (Summer 1974), 303-317. Wonders if any of the Supreme Court justices compromised themselves.

2048. Theoharis, Athan G. "Bureaucrats Above the Law: Double-Entry Intelligence Files." Nation, CCXXV (October 22, 1977), 393-397. FBI domestic surveillance.

2049. _____. "From the Cold War to Watergate." Intellect, CIII (October 1974), 20-26. Discusses the conflict between national security and civil liberties.

2050. _____. Spying on Americans: Political Surveillance from Hoover to the Houston Plan. Philadelphia, Pa.: Temple University Press, 1978. 360p. Examines the history of domestic intelligence from the '30's to 1970 with some comment on political "dirty tricks" under Nixon.

2051. "There Can't Be a Quick Fix." New Republic, CLXVIII (May 5, 1973), 7-9. Reviewing campaign '72 "dirty tricks."

2052. "They Had a Little List." Newsweek, LXXXII (July 9, 1973), 14-15. The White House "enemies list."

2053. "The Thickening ITT Imbroglio." Time, XCIX (March 27, 1972), 28+. The Kleindienst hearings on his involvement.

2054. Thimmesch, Nick. "The Abuse of Richard Nixon." The Alternative (April 1976), 5-8. Compares Nixon's administration with that of his predecessors in light of the Church panel's intelligence findings.

2055. _____. "The Clamor to Drive Nixon Out." Reprinted from the Chicago Tribune, February 7, 1974." Congressional Record, CXX (February 19, 1974), 3494-3495. Suggests the President's critics are ganging up on him.

2056. _____. "The Final Days of John Mitchell." New York, X (June 27, 1977), 11-12. The fate of the CREEP director.

2057. _____. "Richard Nixon Speaks His Mind." Saturday Evening Post, CCLI (March 1979), 64-66+. An interview with the former president.

2058. "The 'Third-Rate Burglary' That Toppled a President: Watergate and the White House." U.S. News and World Report, LXXVII (August 19, 1974), 24-26+. A summary of the main events from 1972-1974.

2059. "Thirty Days for Lying." Time, CIII (April 22, 1974), 17. The trial of Herbert Porter.

2060. "Thirty One Persons, Nine Firms Already Linked to Watergate: Reprinted from the Washington Star-News, March 1, 1974." Congressional Record, CXX (March 1, 1974), 4946-4947. A rundown on those caught up in the scandal.

2061. "'This Is Hard Work.'" Newsweek, LXXXIV (July 29, 1974), 24-25. An excerpt from the June 4, 1973 White House tape transcript.

2062. "This Is Your President--Warts and All." Newsweek, LXXXIII (May 13, 1974), 18-19. Revelations about Nixon revealed by the transcripts.

2063. Thomas, Helen. "The Day the President Left Without the Press." Editor and Publisher, CVII (January 5, 1974), 9+. A visit to Camp David during the Watergate period.

2064. _____. "Watergate." In: her Dateline: White House. New York: Macmillan, 1975. pp. 125-226. In these anecdotal memoirs of a veteran UPI correspondent, the problems of the press in covering Nixon during the Watergate crisis are fully explored. Compare with Rather's The Camera Never Blinks cited above.

2065. Thomas, Norman C. "Watergate and the Presidency: A Preliminary Assessment." In: his The Presidency in Contemporary Context. New York: Dodd, Mead, 1975. pp. 318-330. A preliminary examination of the impact of the crisis on the institution of the presidency, e.g., relations with Congress, press, etc.

2066. Thompson, Fred D. At That Point in Time: The Inside Story of the Senate Watergate Committee. New York: Times Books, 1975. 275p. The three Republican senators on the Ervin panel chose Thompson as their counsel during the conduct of the inquiry, and his reputation became somewhat that of an obstructionist. The author provides information on various procedures employed by the committee, "leaks," press relations, the writing of the final report, and interesting commentary on the CIA and members of the Democratic Committee in relation to the break-in. Thompson's recollections should be read in conjunction with those of Senator Ervin (q.v.) and majority counsel Samuel Dash (q.v.).

2067. _____. "Fred Thompson Speaks--A Little Late." National Review, XXVII (October 10, 1975), 1099-1100. Excerpts and comments based on the previous entry.

2068. _____. "One Lawyer's Perspective on Watergate." Oklahoma Law Review, XXVII (1974), 226+. An early version of the sentiments expressed in the minority counsel's memoirs cited above.

2069. Thompson, Hunter S. Fear and Loathing: On the Campaign Trail '72. New York: Popular Library, 1974. 512p. A "new journalist" who followed the campaign for Rolling Stone, Thompson has absolutely nothing good to say about Richard Nixon and not just because of the Watergate affair, which is only briefly mentioned. This is a good example of the kind of polemic which existed in the investigation-ridden atmosphere of Washington in 1973-1974.

2070. "Those Two-Track Tapes." Newsweek, LXXXIV (July 22, 1974), 19-20. Examines some of the differences between White House and House Judiciary Committee versions of the edited tape transcripts.

2071. "The Tide Turns Back Toward Impeachment." Time, CIV (July 22, 1974), 8-9. On the release of the Ervin Committee report and as noted in the last entry, the revelation of differences in Nixon-House tape versions.

2072. Tillinghast, Diana S. "Information Seeking on Watergate and President Nixon's Resignation and Attitudes Toward Nixon and the Mass Media." Unpublished PhD Dissertation, Michigan State University, 1976. An interesting attempt to differentiate between the kinds of people who sought information on the crisis and their attitudes towards the President and the press.

2073. "To the Circus with the Organ Grinder." Time, CII (July 30, 1973), 8-9. A look at Senator Ervin and his hearings.

2074. Todd, J. T. "Watergate As a Management Problem: What Hindsight Can Teach Us." Management Review, LXII (December 1973), 18-23. Examines the control of the burglars and the cover-up and the bungling involved in the affair.

2075. Todd, William B. "The White House Transcripts." Bibliographic Society of America Papers, LXVIII (July 1974), 267-296. Reviews the edited version of the tapes and the comments made upon them.

2076. "Top Republicans Size Up Impact of Watergate on Their Party." U.S. News and World Report, LXXV (July 30, 1973), 20-21. Thoughts of eleven GOP senators and representatives.

2077. "The Tortoise on the Hill." Newsweek, LXXXIII (June 10, 1974), 23-25. Comments on the slowness of the impeachment process.

2078. Totenberg, Nina. "Obiter Dicta from the Watergate Press Table." New York, VIII (January 20, 1975), 38-43. A review of press coverage of the Watergate cover-up trial.

2079. "Tough Guy." Time, CII (September 24, 1973), 24-25. Lists grounds for a possible Colson indictment in the Fielding case.

2080. "The Transition: Nixon Resigns, Ford Takes Over." C.Q. Weekly Report, XXXII (August 10, 1974), 2971-2076+. A review of the events.

2081. "Translating Watergate." Newsweek, LXXXI (August 6, 1973), 47. The problems of foreign press people covering the crisis.

2082. Trejise, James, et al. Watergate--A Crisis for the World: A Survey of British and French Press Reaction Toward an American Political Crisis. New York: Pergamon Press, 1980. 260p. A review of the affair as reported and analyzed for European readers by the leading newspapers of the Anglo-French community.

2083. Tretik, Stanley. They Could Not Trust the King: Nixon, Watergate, and the American People. New York: Collier-Macmillan, 1974. 197p. A non-chronological photographic essay with explanatory notes and extraordinarily interesting illustrations. See especially the hard look of John Ehrlichman at the Ervin Committee hearings. Barbara Tuchman contributes a useful introduction.

2084. Trewhitt, H. L. "Haig's Last Stand?" Newsweek, LXXXIII (May 27, 1974), 32. His role as White House chief of staff.

2085. "Trial." New Yorker, L (April 15, 1974), 32-33. The Fielding break-in trial.

2086. "Trial and Error." Newsweek, LXXXIII (March 11, 1974), 30-31. Indictments by the Watergate grand jury.

2087. "The Trial Begins, Minus Its Star." Time, CIV (October 14, 1974), 15-16. The Watergate cover-up trial.

2088. "Trial Scenario." Newsweek, LXXXIII (March 25, 1974), 30-31. Examines what a Senate trial of the president might be like as well as those proceedings covering his associates.

2089. Trillin, Calvin. "U.S. Journal: The Midwest." New Yorker, CLXVIII (June 9, 1973), 84-87. Examines the reactions of Midwesterners, especially Kansans, to Watergate.

2090. "Triple Threat to Illegal Givers." Business Week (October 20, 1973), 33-34. The investigations of the Ervin panel and Special Prosecutor into those firms making illegal gifts.

2091. Trotter, R. J. "Watergate: A Psychological Perspective." Science News, CVI (December 14, 1974), 378. A brief review of the principals' mind set.

2092. "Trying to Get the T-R-U-T-H." Time, CIV (November 4, 1974), 21-22+. The Watergate cover-up trial.

2093. "Trying to Govern As the Fire Grows Hotter." Time, CI (May 21, 1973), 13-14. Profiles new White House staffers and notes administration efforts to shore up its image with the public.

2094. Tugwell, Rex G. and Thomas E. Cronin, eds. The Presidency Reappraised. New York: Praeger, 1974. 312p. A series of revisionist essays, some indexed elsewhere in this bibliography, which examine the institution of the presidency in the light of Watergate.

2095. Turner, William W. "Patrick Gray, Nixon's Man at the FBI." New Republic, CCXV (November 27, 1972), 524-527. A brief assessment of the man and his work.

2096. "Two Versions of Key Watergate Tapes: A Sampling." U.S. News and World Report, LXXVII (July 22, 1974), 16. Differences in the edited White House version and the edition given to the House Judiciary Committee.

2097. Tyler, John E. Access to Presidential Materials. FOI Center Report, no. 346. Columbia, Mo.: School of Journalism, University of Missouri, 1975. 7p. A brief assessment with emphasis on the Nixon papers and tapes.

2098. "Ultimatum to the President." Time, CII (November 12,

1973), 38-40. A note on GOP conditions for supporting Nixon after the Cox dismissal.

2099. "Unanimous No to Nixon." Time, CIV (August 5, 1974), 20+. The outcome of United States v. Nixon.

2100. "Unexpurgated Liddy." Time, CIV (October 7, 1974), 86. On G. Gordon Liddy's refusal to comment.

2101. Ungar, Sanford J. "Counterintelligence and Internal Security." In: his FBI: An Uncensored Look Behind the Walls. Boston: Little, Brown, 1976. pp. 111-146. A review of the development of those functions with some little attention paid to the Watergate gambit.

2102. _____. "Kleindienst Approved 11-4, As Panel Ends ITT Probe: Reprinted from the Washington Post, April 28, 1972." In: Book V, Part II of U.S. Congress, House, Committee on the Judiciary. Statement of Information: Hearings. 93rd Cong., 2nd sess. Washington, D.C.: U.S. Government Printing Office, 1974. pp. 860-861. Comments on the Kleindienst-ITT affair as resolved by the Senate Judiciary Committee.

2103. _____. "Kleindienst Faces Further Questions: Reprinted from the Washington Post, April 27, 1972." In: Book V, Part II of U.S. Congress, House, Committee on the Judiciary. Statement of Information: Hearings. 93rd Cong., 2nd sess. Washington, D.C.: U.S. Government Printing Office, 1974. p. 859. Senate Judiciary Committee questions to the Attorney General on the ITT case.

2104. _____. "No Nixon Role in ITT Case, Mitchell Says: Reprinted from the Washington Post, March 10, 1972." In: Book V, Part II of U.S. Congress, House, Committee on the Judiciary. Statement of Information: Hearings. 93rd Cong., 2nd sess. Washington, D.C.: U.S. Government Printing Office, 1974. pp. 857-858. Kleindienst's predecessor clears the President of involvement.

2105. _____. "Undoing of the Justice Department: After the 'Saturday Night Massacre.'" Atlantic, CCXXXIII (January 1974), 29-34. After examining the history of the Justice Department 1969-1973, the Post reporter shows how the politics of the administration invaded the department's functions and culminated in the Cox dismissal.

2106. "The Unholy Impeachment Process." National Review, XXVI (April 26, 1974), 499. Comments upon the unwholesomeness of the process.

2107. "(Unintelligible) or (Inaudible)." Newsweek, LXXXIII (May 13, 1974), 22. Wonders what caused the unintelligible

Watergate 258

or inaudible sections in the edited White House tape transcripts.

2108. "The Unmaking of the President." Time, CIV (August 19, 1974), 15A+. A lengthy review of the crisis and the steps which led to the President's resignation.

2109. United States. Appellate and Other Court Actions. The following court cases were heard in 1973-1974 and are entered here as drawn from pp. 166-170 of the 1975 final report of the Watergate Special Prosecution Force:

Watergate Break-in

1. United States v. James W. McCord, Jr. (U.S.C.A. D.C. Cir. 73-2252)
2. United States v. G. Gordon Liddy (U.S.C.A. D.C. Cir. 73-1565)
3. United States v. E. Howard Hunt, Jr. (U.S.C.A. D.C. Cir. 73-2199)
4. United States v. Bernard L. Barker (U.S.C.A. D.C. Cir. 73-2185)
5. United States v. Eugenio R. Martinez (U.S.C.A. D.C. Cir. 73-2186)
6. United States v. Frank A. Sturgis (U.S.C.A. D.C. Cir. 73-2187)
7. United States v. Virgilio Gonzalez (U.S.C.A. D.C. Cir. 73-2188)

Convictions of original Watergate defendants upheld by U.S. Court of Appeals. See United States v. Liddy, 509 F. 2d 482 (1974); United States v. McCord, 509 F. 2d 334 (1974); United States v. Barker, 514 F. 2d 208 (1975); United States v. Hunt, 514 F. 2d 270 (1975). McCord and Liddy appealed convictions after trial by jury. Others appealed denial of motions to withdraw pleas of guilty.

Petitions for writs of certiorari filed in the Supreme Court by Liddy (Sup. Ct. 74-5678), McCord (Sup. Ct. 74-988), and Barker (Sup. Ct. 74-6308) were denied on January 27, 1975, April 21, 1975, and June 9, 1975, respectively.

* * *

8. United States v. George Gordon Liddy (U.S.C.A. D.C. Cir. No. 73-1564)
9. In Re Grand Jury Proceedings, George Gordon Liddy (U.S.C.A. D.C. Cir. No. 73-1562)

Liddy, who had been sentenced for his conviction in the break-in of the Democratic National Committee, was adjudged in civil contempt for refusing to testify before a grand jury after being granted immunity. He was ordered confined, and execution of sentence in the criminal case was suspended during his confinement for civil contempt.

On October 10 and December 12, 1974, the Court of Appeals affirmed the action of the District Court. See United States v. Liddy, 506 F. 2d 1293 (1974) and 510 F. 2d 669 (1974). Liddy's petition for writ of certiorari filed in the Supreme Court (Sup. Ct. 74-5828) was denied on March 17, 1975.

* * *

10. United States v. George Gordon Liddy (U.S.C.A. D.C. Cir. No. 73-1753)
    Appeal from district judge's denial of motion to reduce sentence pending.

Watergate Cover-up

1. In Re Application of United States Senate Select Committee on Presidential Campaign Activities (U.S.D.C. D.C. Misc. No. 70-73)
   Senate Select Committee applied for use immunity for Jeb Stuart Magruder and John W. Dean III pursuant to 18 U.S.C. §§ 6001, 6005 on May 19, 1973. Special Prosecutor sought an order requiring the immunized witness to testify before the Committee in executive session in order to prevent pre-trial publicity. Court granted the immunity orders without condition on June 12, 1973.
2. Haldeman v. Sirica (U.S.C.A. D.C. Cir. No. 74-1364), 501 F. 2d 714 (1974).
3. Strachan v. Sirica (U.S.C.A. D.C. Cir. No. 74-1368)
   Petition for a writ of mandamus to prohibit transfer of Grand Jury report to the House Judiciary Committee investigation into possible impeachment of President Nixon denied on March 21, 1974.
4. Mitchell, et al. v. Sirica (U.S.C.A. D.C. Cir. No. 74-1492), 502 F. 2d 373 (1974).
   Petition for a writ of mandamus to recuse Judge Sirica denied on June 7, 1974.
5. Mitchell, et al. v. Sirica (Sup. Ct. No. 73-2001)
   Petition for a writ of certiorari to review above ruling concerning recusal of Judge Sirica denied on July 25, 1974.
6. Haldeman v. Sirica (U.S.C.A. D.C. Cir. No. 74-1727)
   Petition for a writ of mandamus challenging validity of grand jury extension act and seeking dismissal of the indictment denied on August 14, 1974.
7. Haldeman v. Sirica (Sup. Ct. No. 74-236)
   Petition for a writ of certiorari to review denial of mandamus relating to grand jury extension denied on November 11, 1974.
8. Ehrlichman v. Sirica (U.S.C.A. D.C. Cir. No. 74-1826)
   Haldeman v. Sirica (U.S.C.A. D.C. Cir. No. 74-1826)
   Petition for a writ of mandamus or prohibition seeking a continuance of the case. The Court suggested a 3-4 week continuance as appropriate for further trial preparation on August 22, 1974.

9. Ehrlichman v. Sirica (Sup. Ct. No. A-93), 419 U.S. 1310 (1974).
Application for a stay of trial pending consideration of petition for a writ of mandamus or prohibition denied on September 2, 1974.
10. Strachan v. Sirica (U.S.C.A. D.C. Cir. No. 74-1868)
Petition for a writ of mandamus filed under seal seeking dismissal of indictment on grounds of immunity denied on September 20, 1974.
11. Mitchell v. Sirica (U.S.C.A. D.C. Cir. No. 74-1878)
12. Ehrlichman v. Sirica (U.S.C.A. D.C. Cir. No. 74-1876)
Petitions for writs of mandamus seeking an indefinite postponement of the trial denied on September 20, 1974.
13. Mitchell & Haldeman v. Sirica (Sup. Ct. No. A-217)
Application for a stay of the trial pending petition for a writ of certiorari from denial of petition for writ of mandamus or prohibition denied on September 27, 1974.
14. Mitchell, Haldeman, Ehrlichman, Mardian & Parkinson v. Sirica (U.S.C.A. D.C. Cir. No. 74-1949)
Petition for a writ of prohibition seeking to alter trial judge's procedures for exercising peremptory challenges of prospective jurors denied on October 11, 1974.
15. United States v. Haldeman (U.S.C.A. D.C. Cir. No. 75-1381)
United States v. Ehrlichman (U.S.C.A. D.C. Cir. No. 75-1382)
United States v. Mardian (U.S.C.A. D.C. Cir. No. 75-1383)
United States v. Mitchell (U.S.C.A. D.C. Cir. No. 75-1384)
Appeals from convictions in United States v. Mitchell pending.

Fielding Break-in

1. United States v. De Diego (U.S.C.A. D.C. Cir. No. 74-1769), 511 F. 2d 818 (1975).
Dismissal of charges against Felipe De Diego reversed; case remanded for hearing.
2. United States v. John D. Ehrlichman (U.S.C.A. D.C. Cir. No. 74-1882)
3. United States v. Bernard L. Barker (U.S.C.A. D.C. Cir. No. 74-1883)
4. United States v. Eugenio Martinez (U.S.C.A. D.C. Cir. No. 74-1884)
5. United States v. G. Gordon Liddy (U.S.C.A. D.C. Cir. No. 74-1885)
Defendants' appeals of convictions pending.
6. United States v. John D. Ehrlichman (U.S.C.A. D.C. Cir. No. 74-1921)
Government's appeal of trial judge's setting aside of the jury's verdict on one count of the indictment (18 U.S.C. § 1001) voluntarily dismissed by the government.

Subpoenas for Presidential Tape Recordings

1. In Re Grand Jury Subpoena Duces Tecum Issued to Richard M. Nixon or any Subordinate Officer, Official or Employee with Custody or Control of Certain Documents or Objects. Richard M. Nixon, Appellant (U.S.D.C. D.C. Misc. No. 47-73), 360 F. Supp. 1 (1973)
   On August 29, 1973, Chief Judge John Sirica enforced a grand jury subpoena to Richard M. Nixon for nine presidential recordings. After the ruling was upheld, hearings were conducted concerning two missing conversations and an $18\frac{1}{2}$-minute gap on a third tape.
2. Nixon v. Sirica (U.S.C.A. D.C. Cir. No. 73-1962), 487 F. 2d 700 (1973).
3. United States v. Sirica (U.S.C.A. D.C. Cir. No. 73-1967) Cross-petitions for writs of mandamus to review order enforcing grand jury subpoena. Order of district court, with modifications upheld on October 12, 1973.
4. Nixon v. Sirica (U.S.C.A. D.C. Cir. Nos. 74-1618, 74-1753)
   Appeal and petition for mandamus to review Judge Sirica's order of June 12, 1974, reconsidering earlier ruling that the final portion of the September 15, 1972, Nixon-Haldeman-Dean conversation, subpoenaed by the grand jury, was subject to a valid claim of privilege. On August 6, 1974, the appellant moved for voluntary dismissal which was granted on August 7.
5. United States v. Nixon (Sup. Ct. No. 73-1766), 418 U.S. 683 (1974)
   Nixon v. United States (Sup. Ct. No. 73-1834)
   Petition and cross petition for writ of certiorari before judgment to review Judge Sirica's May 20, 1974, order enforcing Special Prosecutor's trial subpoena for 64 presidential tape recordings issued April 16, 1974. Writs were granted on May 31, 1974; arguments were heard July 8, 1974; and a unanimous Court upheld the lower court order on July 24, 1974. (See United States v. Mitchell, 377 F. Supp. 1326 (1974).)

Nixon Tapes and Documents

1. Nixon v. Sampson (U.S.D.C. D.C. Civil No. 74-1518)
2. Reporters Committee for Freedom of the Press v. Sampson (U.S.D.C. D.C. Civil No. 74-1533)
3. Lillian Hellman v. Sampson (U.S.D.C. D.C. Civil No. 74-1551)
   Consolidated suits seeking enforcement of and challenging agreement relating to custody of tapes and documents compiled during the Nixon Administration.
4. Nixon v. Richey (U.S.C.A. D.C. Cir. No. 75-1063), 513 F. 2d 427 (1975), 513 F. 2d 430 (1975)

Petition for writ of mandamus granted staying effectiveness of district judge's decision in Nixon v. Sampson.

5. Richard M. Nixon v. Administrator, General Services Administration (U.S.D.C. D.C. Civil No. 74-1852)
Suit challenging the constitutionality of the Presidential Recordings and Materials Preservation Act concerning the custody and disposition of tapes and documents compiled during the Nixon Administration.

Miscellaneous Appellate Proceedings

1. Howard Edwin Reinecke v. Parker (U.S.C.A. D.C. Cir. No. 74-1533)
Petition for a writ of mandamus seeking transfer of plaintiff's case to U.S. District Court for the Northern District of California denied on June, 1974.
2. United States v. Dwight L. Chapin (U.S.D.C. D.C. Cir. No. 74-1648), 515 F. 2d 1274 (1975)
Conviction affirmed. Petition for a writ of certiorari in the Supreme Court pending.
3. United States v. Howard Edwin Reinecke (U.S.C.A. D.C. Cir. No. 74-2068)
Appeal of criminal conviction pending.
4. United States v. Hon. Robert Hill, U.S. District Judge (U.S.C.A. Fifth Cir. No. 74-3738)
United States v. Ray Cowan and Jake Jacobsen, Defendants, and Wayne O. Woodruff, et al., Special Prosecutors, Appellees (U.S.C.A. Fifth Cir. No. 74-3941)
Appeals from the appointment of a special prosecutor by district judge after the government agreed to dispose of pending federal charges against Jacobsen upon his agreement to plead guilty to a charge in U.S. District Court for the District of Columbia. Petition for mandamus filed November 22, 1974. Both actions pending.
5. United States v. Gasch (U.S.C.A. D.C. Cir. No. 75-1452)
Petition for writ of mandamus to set aside order of district judge transferring trials of Frank DeMarco and Ralph Newman to the Central District of California and the Northern District of Illinois, respectively, denied.
6. United States v. Tim M. Babcock (U.S.C.A. D.C. Cir. No. 74-1285)
Appeal challenging judge's authority to impose prison sentence under 2 U.S.C. § 441 for misdemeanor violation.

2110. ____. Commission on CIA Activities Within the United States. "Watergate Activities." In: Its Report. Washington, D.C.: U.S. Government Printing Office, 1975. pp. 172-207. Comments on the Agency's assistance to the White House "plumbers."

2111. ____. Congress. House. Committee on Armed Services. Special Subcommittee on Intelligence. Inquiry into the

Alleged Involvement of the Central Intelligence Agency in the Watergate and Ellsberg Matters: Report. 93rd Cong., 1st sess. Washington, D.C.: U.S. Government Printing Office, 1973. 23p. Another look at the help provided to the "plumbers."

2112. _____. _____. _____. Committee on Government Operations. Presidential Records Act of 1978: Hearings. 95th Cong., 2nd sess. Washington, D.C.: U.S. Government Printing Office, 1978. 896p. Testimony on housing and access to presidential papers; much comment on the Nixon documents.

2113. _____. _____. _____. _____. Presidential Records Act of 1978: Report. 95th Cong., 2nd sess. Washington, D.C.: U.S. Government Printing Office, 1978. 24p. The committee's recommendations based on the testimony in the previous citation.

2114. _____. _____. _____. _____. Subcommittee on Foreign Operations and Government Information. Availability of Information to Congress: Hearings. 93rd Cong., 1st sess. Washington, D.C.: U.S. Government Printing Office, 1973. 361p. An examination of the executive branch's information policies, especially executive privilege.

2115. _____. _____. _____. _____. _____. Telephone Monitoring Practices by Federal Agencies: Hearings. 93rd Cong., 2nd sess. Washington, D.C.: U.S. Government Printing Office, 1974. 293p. Much testimony on FBI taps in relation to the Watergate affair.

2116. _____. _____. _____. Committee on House Administration. Disapproving Certain Regulations Proposed by the General Services Administration Implementing the Presidential Recordings and Materials Preservation Act: Report. 94th Cong., 1st sess. Washington, D.C.: U.S. Government Printing Office, 1975. 69p. Critical of the GSA-Nixon deal on non-access to the White House tapes.

2117. _____. _____. _____. _____. 94th Cong., 2nd sess. Washington, D.C.: U.S. Government Printing Office, 1976. 27p. Another dissention.

2118. _____. _____. _____. _____. Presidential Recordings and Materials Preservation Act: Report. 93rd Cong., 2nd sess. Washington, D.C.: U.S. Government Printing Office, 1974. 25p. Expresses the committee's concern on the Nixon-GSA arrangement.

2119. _____. _____. _____. _____. Subcommittee on Printing. The Public Documents Act: Hearings. 93rd Cong., 2nd sess. Washington, D.C.: U.S. Government Printing Office,

1974. 234p. Includes comments on the handling of the Nixon documents.

2120. ___. ___. ___. ___. Implementation of Title I of the Presidential Recordings and Materials Act: Hearings. 94th Cong., 1st sess. Washington, D.C.: U.S. Government Printing Office, 1975. 567p. The largest section of testimony on the proposed limitation of access to the Nixon materials, with comments on how best to preserve and protect them.

2121. ___. ___. ___. Committee on Internal Security. Domestic Intelligence Operations for Internal Security Purposes: Hearings. 93rd Cong., 2nd sess. Washington, D.C.: U.S. Government Printing Office, 1974. 590p. Includes some references to the covert actions of the White House "plumbers."

2122. ___. ___. ___. Committee on the Judiciary. "Breakdown of the Staff and Biographies of Counsel." In: Book III of its Impeachment Inquiry: Hearings. 93rd Cong., 2nd sess. Washington, D.C.: U.S. Government Printing Office, 1974. pp. 2141-2156. Includes brief résumés on John M. Doar, Albert E. Jenner, Jr., and 37 other individuals.

2123. ___. ___. ___. ___. Brief on Behalf of the President of the United States: Hearings. 93rd Cong., 2nd sess. Washington, D.C.: U.S. Government Printing Office, 1974. 123p. Presentation by James D. St. Clair; also includes the White House lawyer's "An Analysis of the Scope of an Article of Impeachment," pp. 103-123.

2124. ___. ___. ___. ___. Comparison of White House and Judiciary Committee Transcripts of Eight Recorded Presidential Conversations: Hearings. 93rd Cong., 2nd sess. Washington, D.C.: U.S. Government Printing Office, 1974. 63p. Comparison of passages appearing in the two publications Submission of Recorded Presidential Conversations.... and Transcripts of Eight Recorded Presidential Conversations, both cited below.

2125. ___. ___. ___. ___. "Comparison of White House, House Judiciary Transcripts." In: Robert A. Diamond, ed. Historic Documents, 1974. Washington, D.C.: Congressional Quarterly, Inc., 1975. pp. 301-390. Contains the bulk of the previous citation, both of which show significant variations between the transcripts submitted and released.

2126. ___. ___. ___. ___. Constitutional Grounds for Presidential Impeachment: Report. 93rd Cong., 2nd sess. Washington, D.C.: U.S. Government Printing Office, 1974.

60p. A guide prepared to assist the House Judiciary Committee in its impeachment inquiry; concludes that an impeachable offense need not be a criminal act. Also published as Appendix II of Book III of the Committee's Impeachment Inquiry: Hearings, pp. 2157-2218.

2127. _____. _____. _____. _____. Debate on Articles of Impeachment: Hearings. 93rd Cong., 2nd sess. Washington, D.C.: U.S. Government Printing Office, 1974. 562p. These July 24-30 discussions were televised to the American people.

2128. _____. _____. _____. _____. "Donohue Resolution and Articles of Impeachment." Appendix VII of Book III of Impeachment Inquiry: Hearings. 93rd Cong., 2nd sess. Washington, D.C.: U.S. Government Printing Office, 1974. pp. 2253-2258. The resolution of Massachusetts Democratic Congressman Harold D. Donohue is presented.

2129. _____. _____. _____. _____. Errata: Hearings. 93rd Cong., 2nd sess. Washington, D.C.: U.S. Government Printing Office, 1974. 23p. Examines the questions of mistakes in the inquiry.

2130. _____. _____. _____. _____. "Impeachment Articles: Texts of the Three Articles of Impeachment, Adopted July 27-30, 1974." In: Robert A. Diamond, ed. Historic Documents, 1974. Washington, D.C.: Congressional Quarterly, Inc., 1975. pp. 655-660. These articles are reprinted in a variety of sources cited elsewhere in this bibliography.

2131. _____. _____. _____. _____. "Impeachment Debate: The Arguments for and Against." U.S. News and World Report, LXXVII (August 5, 1974), 57-60. Summaries of the arguments presented in the fourth citation back.

2132. _____. _____. _____. _____. Impeachment Inquiry, Books I-III, January 31-July 28, 1974: Hearings. 3 pts. 93rd Cong., 2nd sess. Washington, D.C.: U.S. Government Printing Office, 1974. Contains full details on the inquiry from its earliest days to its conclusion.

2133. _____. _____. _____. _____. Impeachment Inquiry Procedures. 93rd Cong., 2nd sess. Washington, D.C.: U.S. Government Printing Office, 1974. 2p. The rules by which the inquiry would be conducted; also printed as Appendix VI of Book III of its Impeachment Inquiry: Hearings, pp. 2249-2252.

2134. _____. _____. _____. _____. "The Impeachment Investigation of Richard M. Nixon." In: its History of the Committee on the Judiciary of the House of Representatives: Committee Print. 97th Cong., 2nd sess. Washington, D.C.: U.S. Government Printing Office, 1982. pp. 28-36. A brief history of the investigation.

2135. ____. ____. ____. ____. Impeachment of Richard M. Nixon, President of the United States: [Final] Report, Together with Supplemental, Additional, Separate, Dissenting, Minority, Individual, and Concurring Views. 93rd Cong., 2nd sess. Washington, D.C.: U.S. Government Printing Office, 1974. 528p. Together with the Ervin Committee final report (q.v.), this is one of the two best sources for basic data on the Watergate affair. Excerpts are printed in a variety of sources including C.Q. Weekly Report, XXXII (August 31, 1974), 2352-2358, Robert A. Diamond, ed. Historic Documents, 1974 (Washington, D.C.: Congressional Quarterly, Inc., 1975), pp. 713-764, and Congressional Record, CXX (August 20, 1974), 29219-29361.

2136. ____. ____. ____. ____. Introduction by R. W. Apple, Jr. New York: Viking Press, 1975. 755p. The commercially-published version of the GPO report with the assistance and commentary of staff members of the New York Times.

2137. ____. ____. ____. ____. Impeachment: Selected Materials on the Procedure. 93rd Cong., 2nd sess. Washington, D.C.: U.S. Government Printing Office, 1974. 900p. A revised edition of a 1971 work containing historical and parliamentary information on how the process works in the United States, both in the 20th century and before. A variety of scholarly articles are reprinted within.

2138. ____. ____. ____. ____. Minority Memorandum on Facts and Law: Hearings. 93rd Cong., 2nd sess. Washington, D.C.: U.S. Government Printing Office, 1974. 164p. A Republican document stressing the need for law and fact in arriving at grounds for impeachment.

2139. ____. ____. ____. ____. "More from the House Committee: Milk Fund and IRS." U.S. News and World Report, LXXVII (July 29, 1974), 19-21. Recaps evidence on Nixon's mishandling of those two articles.

2140. ____. ____. ____. ____. "Procedures for Handling Impeachment Inquiry Material." Appendix III of Book III of Impeachment Inquiry: Hearings. 93rd Cong., 2nd sess. Washington, D.C.: U.S. Government Printing Office, 1974. pp. 2219-2222. The manner in which materials would be housed, handled, and released to the media.

2141. ____. ____. ____. ____. "Special Inquiry Staff and Biographies of Counsel." In: Book III of Impeachment Inquiry:

Hearings. 93rd Cong., 2nd sess. Washington, D. C.: U.S. Government Printing Office, 1974. pp. 2234-2236. Includes brief resumes on counsels Terry R. Kirkpatrick, Lawrence Lucchino, Theodore R. Tetzlaff, and Ben A. Wallis, Jr.

2142. _____. _____. _____. Statement of Information, Appendices I-IV: Hearings. 93rd Cong., 2nd sess. 4 pts. Washington, D. C.: U. S. Government Printing Office, 1974. Contents: Appendix I--Presidential Statements on the Watergate Break-in and Its Investigation; Appendix II--Papers in Criminal Cases Initiated by the Watergate Special Prosecution Force, June 27, 1973-August 2, 1974; Appendix III--Supplemental Documents; Appendix IV--Political Matters Memoranda, August 13, 1971-September 18, 1972.

2143. _____. _____. _____. Statement of Information, Background Memorandum: Hearings. 93rd Cong., 2nd sess. Washington, D. C.: U. S. Government Printing Office, 1974. 6p. Contents: "White House Staff" and "President Nixon's Campaign Organizations."

2144. _____. _____. _____. Statement of Information, Books I-XII: Hearings. 93rd Cong., 2nd sess. 21 pts. Washington, D. C.: U. S. Government Printing Office, 1974. Contents: Book I, Events Prior to the Watergate Break-in, December 2, 1971-June 17, 1972; Book II, Events Following the Watergate Break-in, June 17, 1972-February 9, 1973; Book III, Part I, Events Following the Watergate Break-in, June 20, 1972-March 22, 1973; Book III, Part II, Events Following the Watergate Break-in, June 20, 1972-March 22, 1973; Book IV, Part I, Events Following the Watergate Break-in, March 22, 1973-April 30, 1973; Book IV, Part II, Events Following the Watergate Break-in, March 22, 1973-April 30, 1973; Book IV, Part III, Events Following the Watergate Break-in, March 22, 1973-April 30, 1973; Book V, Part I, Department of Justice/ITT Litigation--Richard Kleindienst Nomination Hearings; Book V, Part I, Department of Justice/ITT Litigation--Richard Kleindienst Nomination; Book VI, Part I, Political Contributions by Milk Producers' Cooperatives--The 1971 Milk Price Support Decision; Book VI, Part II, Political Contributions by Milk Producers' Cooperatives/The 1971 Milk Price Support Decision; Book VII, Part I, White House Surveillance Activities and Campaign Activities; Book VII, Part II, White House Surveillance Activities and Campaign Activities; Book VII, Part III, White House Surveillance Activities and Campaign Activities; Book VIII, Internal Revenue Service; Book IX, Part I, Watergate Special Prosecutor's/Judiciary Committee's Impeachment Inquiry; Book IX, Part II, Watergate Special Prosecutor's/Judiciary Committee's Impeachment Inquiry; Book X, Tax

Deductions for Gift of Papers; Book XI, Bombing of Cambodia; Book XII, Impoundment of Funds/Government Expenditures on President Nixon's Private Properties at San Clemente and Key Biscayne. This material constitutes, together with the Ervin Committee hearings (q.v.), the richest trove of information on the Watergate case.

2145. _____. _____. _____. Statement of Information Submitted on Behalf of President Nixon, Books I-IV: Hearings. 93rd Cong., 2nd sess. 4 pts. Washington, D.C.: U.S. Government Printing Office, 1974. Contents: Book I, Events Following the Watergate Break-in, June 19, 1972-March 1, 1974; Book II, Department of Justice/ITT Litigation; Book III, Political Contributions by Milk Producers' Cooperatives/The 1971 Milk Price Support Decision; Book IV, White House Surveillance Activities. Prepared by White House lawyers in response to the inquiry of the House Judiciary Committee.

2146. _____. _____. _____. "Status Report As of April 24, 1974." Appendix V of Book III of Impeachment Inquiry: Hearings. 93rd Cong., 2nd sess. Washington, D.C.: U.S. Government Printing Office, 1974. pp. 2237-2248. Reports the work of the Impeachment Inquiry Staff.

2147. _____. _____. _____. Summary of Activities of the Committee on the Judiciary, House of Representatives. 93rd Cong., 1st sess. Washington, D.C.: U.S. Government Printing Office, 1974. 38p. Examines a few of the initial calls for impeachment.

2148. _____. _____. _____. _____, 93rd Congress. 93rd Cong., 2nd sess. Washington, D.C.: U.S. Government Printing Office, 1975. 72p. A review of the work of the committee as a whole, including the impeachment events.

2149. _____. _____. _____. Summary of Information: Hearings. 93rd Cong., 2nd sess. Washington, D.C.: U.S. Government Printing Office, 1974. 177p. A recap of the data contained in the 21 parts of the Statement of Information.

2150. _____. _____. _____. Testimony of Witnesses, Books I-III: Hearings. 93rd Cong., 2nd sess. 3 pts. Washington, D.C.: U.S. Government Printing Office, 1974. Contents: Book I, Alexander Butterfield, Paul O'Brien, and Fred C. LaRue; Book II, William O. Bittman, John N. Mitchell, and John W. Dean, 3rd; Book III, Henry E. Petersen, Charles W. Colson, and Herbert W. Kalmbach.

2151. _____. _____. _____. Transcripts of Eight Recorded Presidential Conversations: Hearings. 93rd Cong., 2nd sess. Washington, D.C.: U.S. Government Printing Office, 1974. 218p. Reproduces additional White House tape transcripts.

2152. _____. _____. "Work of the Impeachment Inquiry Staff As of February 5, 1974." Appendix I of Book III of Impeachment Inquiry: Hearings. 93rd Cong., 2nd sess. Washington, D.C.: U.S. Government Printing Office, 1974. pp. 2135-2156. A review of the work conducted from its beginning on January 31 to this date.

2153. _____. _____. "Work of the Impeachment Inquiry Staff As of March 1, 1974." Appendix IV of Book III of Impeachment Inquiry: Hearings. 93rd Cong., 2nd sess. Washington, D.C.: U.S. Government Printing Office, 1974. pp. 2223-2236. A review of the work conducted in February 1974.

2154. _____. _____. Subcommittee on Civil and Constitutional Rights. FBI Oversight: Hearings. 95th Cong., 1st and 2nd sess. Washington, D.C.: U.S. Government Printing Office, 1978. 391p. Hearings on the effort to curb excesses in the FBI.

2155. _____. _____. _____. FBI Counterintelligence Programs: Hearings. 93rd Cong., 2nd sess. Washington, D.C.: U.S. Government Printing Office, 1975. 47p. A brief look with passing references to events of the Watergate era.

2156. _____. _____. Subcommittee on Courts, Civil Liberties, and the Administration of Justice. Political Intelligence in the Internal Revenue Service--The Special Service Staff: A Documentary Analysis. 93rd Cong., 2nd sess. Washington, D.C.: U.S. Government Printing Office, 1974. 344p. Examines the White House use of the IRS against its political enemies.

2157. _____. _____. Subcommittee on Criminal Justice. Authority to Issue Final Report by Special Prosecutor: Hearings. 94th Cong., 1st sess. Washington, D.C.: U.S. Government Printing Office, 1975. 30p. Examines the need for a WSPF final report, which was eventually published and which is cited below.

2158. _____. _____. _____. Pardon of Richard M. Nixon and Related Matters: Hearings. 93rd Cong., 2nd sess. Washington, D.C.: U.S. Government Printing Office, 1975. 271p. An investigation to see if a deal was struck between Nixon officials and Gerald Ford; includes the latter's testimony.

2159. _____. _____. Select Committee on Intelligence. U.S. Intelligence Agencies and Activities, Domestic Intelligence Programs: Hearings. 94th Cong., 1st sess. Washington, D.C.: U.S. Government Printing Office, 1975. 175p. Includes many references to illegal or questionable FBI/CIA/IRS activities during the Watergate era.

2160. ____. ____. Joint Committee on Congressional Operations. Special Report Identifying Court Proceedings and Actions of Vital Interest to the Congress. 94th Cong., 2nd sess. Washington, D.C.: U.S. Government Printing Office, 1974. 566p. A reprinting of the proceedings in United States v. John Mitchell, et al. and United States v. Richard M. Nixon, et al. plus Richard M. Nixon v. United States.

2161. ____. ____. Joint Committee on Internal Revenue Taxation. Investigation of the Special Service Staff of the Internal Revenue Service: Hearings. 94th Cong., 1st sess. Washington, D.C.: U.S. Government Printing Office, 1975. 114p. Another look at Nixon's questionable use of the IRS.

2162. ____. ____. Joint Committee on Printing. Official Congressional Directory. 3 vols. Washington, D.C.: U.S. Government Printing Office, 1972-1974. Useful for learning more about the Senators and Representatives involved in the Watergate probes.

2163. ____. ____. Senate. Committee on Foreign Relations. Dr. [Henry] Kissinger's Role in Wiretapping: Hearings. 93rd Cong., 2nd sess. Washington, D.C.: U.S. Government Printing Office, 1974. 409p. Looks at the alleged role of Nixon's National Security Advisor on placing and ordering FBI bugs on NSC staff members.

2164. ____. ____. ____. ____. Report on the Inquiry Concerning Dr. Kissinger's Role in Wiretapping, 1969-1971: Review and Findings. 93rd Cong., 2nd sess. Washington, D.C.: U.S. Government Printing Office, 1974. 6p. Based on the previous citation.

2165. ____. ____. ____. ____. Nomination of Alexander M. Haig, Jr. to Be Secretary of State: Hearings. 97th Cong., 1st sess. 2 pts. Washington, D.C.: U.S. Government Printing Office, 1981. Includes a variety of questions asked concerning his role as Nixon's White House chief of staff.

2166. ____. ____. ____. ____. Nomination of Richard Helms to Be Ambassador to Iran and CIA International and Domestic Activities: Hearings. 93rd Cong., 2nd sess. Washington, D.C.: U.S. Government Printing Office, 1974. 109p. Features a number of questions on CIA assistance to the "plumbers."

2167. ____. ____. ____. ____. Subcommittee on Surveillance. Warrantless Wiretapping and Electronic Surveillance: Report. 94th Cong., 1st sess. Washington, D.C.: U.S. Government Printing Office, 1975. 11p. A brief recap of known information on illegal practices.

2168. ____. ____. ____. Committee on Government Operations. Disapproving Certain Regulations Proposed by the Administrator of General Services Under Section 104 of the Presidential Recordings and Materials Preservation Act: Report. 94th Cong., 1st sess. Washington, D.C.: U.S. Government Printing Office, 1975. 49p. A similar report of 24 pages was also issued in 1976; both disapprove of National Archives' handling of the Nixon tapes and documents.

2169. ____. ____. ____. ____. GSA Regulations Implementing Presidential Records and Materials Preservation Act: Hearings. 94th Cong., 1st sess. Washington, D.C.: U.S. Government Printing Office, 1975. 457p. Hearings on the manner in which the National Archives proposed to handle the Nixon tapes and documents.

2170. ____. ____. ____. ____. Preservation, Protection, and Public Access with Respect to Certain Tape Recordings and Other Materials: Report. 93rd Cong., 2nd sess. Washington, D.C.: U.S. Government Printing Office, 1974. 10p. A recap of the arrangements for handling Nixon's materials.

2171. ____. ____. ____. ____. The Presidential Records Act of 1978: Hearings. 95th Cong., 2nd sess. Washington, D.C.: U.S. Government Printing Office, 1978. 45p. Examines many of the concerns raised in the previous three citations.

2172. ____. ____. ____. ____. Watergate Reorganization and Reform Act of 1975: Hearings. 94th Cong., 1st sess. Washington, D.C.: U.S. Government Printing Office, 1976. 745p. Hearings on reforms suggested in the executive branch as the result of the Watergate scandal. An accompanying 117-page Report was also issued.

2173. ____. ____. ____. ____. Subcommittee on Intergovernmental Relations. Executive Privilege--Secrecy in Government: Hearings. 94th Cong., 2nd sess. Washington, D.C.: U.S. Government Printing Office, 1976. 647p. Examines the state of the doctrine two years after Watergate; includes many references to the manner in which it was employed by Richard Nixon.

2174. ____. ____. ____. ____. Subcommittee on Intergovernmental Relations and Committee on the Judiciary, Subcommittees on Separation of Powers and Administrative Practice and Procedure. Executive Privilege, Secrecy in Government, Freedom of Information: Hearings. 93rd Cong., 1st sess. 3 pts. Washington, D.C.: U.S. Government Printing Office, 1973. Hearings held during 1973 which, in the case of executive privilege, directly bear on Nixon's relations with Congress during the crisis.

2175. ____. ____. ____. Committee on the Judiciary. "From the Record--Both Sides of the Kleindienst Case: Excerpts from Reports of the Senate Judiciary Committee." U.S. News and World Report, LXXII (May 22, 1972), 74-78+. Much on the ITT case and the Attorney General's alleged involvement.

2176. ____. ____. ____. ____. "ITT Affair--Politics and Justice: Hearings Before the Senate Judiciary Committee." Newsweek, LXXIX (March 20, 1972), 24-26+. Includes much of the data from the previous citation.

2177. ____. ____. ____. ____. Nomination of Clarence M. Kelly to Be Director of the Federal Bureau of Investigation: Hearings. 93rd Cong., 1st sess. Washington, D.C.: U.S. Government Printing Office, 1973. 192p. Much on Kelly's anticipated role in handling the Watergate investigation.

2178. ____. ____. ____. ____. Nomination of Earl J. Silbert to Be United States Attorney: Hearings. 94th Cong., 1st sess. Washington, D.C.: U.S. Government Printing Office, 1975. 278p. Includes much information on Silbert's handling of the Watergate probe.

2179. ____. ____. ____. ____. Nomination of Elliot L. Richardson to Be Attorney General: Hearings. 93rd Cong., 1st sess. Washington, D.C.: U.S. Government Printing Office, 1973. 287p. The majority of these hearings are devoted to Watergate.

2180. ____. ____. ____. ____. Nominations of Joseph T. Sneed to Be Deputy Attorney General and Robert H. Bork to Be Solicitor General: Hearings. 93rd Cong., 1st sess. Washington, D.C.: U.S. Government Printing Office, 1973. 26p. Bork would eventually find himself the officer dismissing Archibald Cox.

2181. ____. ____. ____. ____. Nomination of Laurence H. Silberman to Be Deputy Attorney General: Hearings. 93rd Cong., 2nd sess. Washington, D.C.: U.S. Government Printing Office, 1974. 40p. As with the previous two citations, this also contains biographical data.

2182. ____. ____. ____. ____. Nomination of Louis Patrick Gray, 3rd, to Be Director, Federal Bureau of Investigation: Hearings. 93rd Cong., 1st sess. Washington, D.C.: U.S. Government Printing Office, 1973. 714p. Gray's nomination was eventually withdrawn by the Nixon administration after he was unable to weather a storm of Watergate-related criticism.

2183. ____. ____. ____. ____. Nomination of Richard G. Kleindienst: Supplemental Report, Together with Individual Views. 92nd Cong., 2nd sess. Washington, D.C.: U.S. Government Printing Office, 1972. 26p. The Committee's views on his ITT involvement are here noted.

2184. _____. ____. ____. ____. Nomination of Richard G. Kleindienst to Be Attorney General and Louis Patrick Gray, 3rd, to Be Deputy Attorney General: Hearings. 92nd Cong., 2nd sess. Washington, D.C.: U.S. Government Printing Office, 1972. 93p. These original nominations encountered little opposition as neither ITT nor Watergate had yet become scandals.

2185. _____. ____. ____. ____. Richard G. Kleindienst--Resumed: Hearings. 92nd Cong., 2nd sess. 2 pts. Washington, D.C.: U.S. Government Printing Office, 1972. After ITT broke, Kleindienst asked that his nomination hearings be reopened in an effort to clear his name.

2186. _____. ____. ____. ____. Nomination of William B. Saxbe to Be Attorney General: Hearings. 93rd Cong., 1st sess. Washington, D.C.: U.S. Government Printing Office, 1973. 97p. The maverick Republican senator from Ohio was confirmed and served out Nixon's administration.

2187. _____. ____. ____. ____. Nomination of William D. Ruckelshaus to Be Deputy Attorney General: Hearings. 93rd Cong., 1st sess. Washington, D.C.: U.S. Government Printing Office, 1973. 116p. Ruckelshaus would also retire rather than dismiss Archibald Cox.

2188. _____. ____. ____. ____. Refusals by the Executive Branch to Provide Information to the Congress, 1964-1973: Report. 93rd Cong., 2nd sess. Washington, D.C.: U.S. Government Printing Office, 1974. 571p. Includes much information on the controversial practice of executive privilege.

2189. _____. ____. ____. ____. Special Prosecutor: Hearings. 93rd Cong., 1st sess. 2 pts. Washington, D.C.: U.S. Government Printing Office, 1973. This set represents the Senate's investigation of the "Saturday Night Massacre" and its consideration of the role of a special prosecutor; testimony is provided by Archibald Cox, Elliot Richardson, Robert Bork, Leon Jaworski, etc.

2190. _____. ____. ____. ____. Subcommittee on Administrative Practice and Procedure. FBI Statutory Charter: Hearings. 95th Cong., 2nd sess. 2 pts. Washington, D.C.: U.S. Government Printing Office, 1978. An effort to find ways to guard against FBI political involvement à la Watergate.

2191. ____. ____. ____. ____. Warrantless Wiretapping: Hearings. 92nd Cong., 2nd sess. Washington, D.C.: U.S. Government Printing Office, 1973. 221p.

2192. ____. ____. ____. ____. Warrantless Wiretapping, 1974: Hearings. 93rd Cong., 2nd sess. Washington, D.C.: U.S. Government Printing Office, 1974. 519p. Both of these references contain information on illegal practices of the Watergate era, some of which were part of the case under review here.

2193. ____. ____. ____. Subcommittee on Constitutional Rights. Political Intelligence in the IRS--The Special Service Staff: A Documentary Analysis. 93rd Cong., 2nd sess. Washington, D.C.: U.S. Government Printing Office, 1974. 344p. Another study of the politicization of the IRS by the Nixon White House.

2194. ____. ____. ____. ____. Subcommittee on Separation of Powers. Removing Politics from the Administration of Justice: Hearings. 93rd Cong., 2nd sess. Washington, D.C.: U.S. Government Printing Office, 1974. 529p. Examines the various ways in which the Nixon White House employed the FBI, IRS, and CIA in illegal activities.

2195. ____. ____. ____. Committee on Ways and Means. Subcommittee on Oversight. Internal Revenue Service Intelligence Operations: Hearings. 94th Cong., 1st sess. Washington, D.C.: U.S. Government Printing Office, 1975. 100p. The illegal use of the IRS by the Nixon administration against its enemies.

2196. ____. ____. ____. Select Committee on Presidential Campaign Activities. Presidential Campaign Activities of 1972: Appendix to the Hearings, Legal Documents Relating to the Select Committee Hearings. 93rd Cong., 1st and 2nd sess. 2 pts. Washington, D.C.: U.S. Government Printing Office, 1974. Includes motions and transcripts of the various Watergate-related court actions in the Federal court system.

2197. ____. ____. ____. ____. Presidential Campaign Activities of 1972, Books I-XXVI: Hearings. 93rd Cong., 1st and 2nd sess. 26 pts. Washington, D.C.: U.S. Government Printing Office, 1973-1974. Contents: Books I-IX, Watergate Investigation; Books X-XII, Campaign Practices; Book XIII, Campaign Financing; Books XIV-XVII, Milk Fund Investigation; Books XVIII-XX, Watergate and Related Activities, Responsiveness Program; Books XXI-XXIV, The Hughes-Rebozo Investigation and Related Matters; Book XXV, Supplemental Material on Campaign Practices and Finances; Book XXVI, Exhibits Relating to Chapter 8 of the Final Report (q.v.). The whole was indexed in 1981 by Hedda Garza, whose contribution is cited above in our Reference Section. Together with the House Judiciary Committee inquiry noted above, this is one of the richest troves of Watergate-related material extant. The so-called Senate Watergate Committee was formed in early 1973 and was chaired by North Carolina Democratic senator Sam J. Ervin, Jr., a noted authority on the Constitution. The first nine volumes contain the explosive testimony of Dean, Haldeman, Ehrlichman, etc.

2198. ____. ____. ____. ____. Draft of Final Report. 93rd Cong., 2nd sess. 3 pts. Washington, D.C.: U.S. Government Printing Office, 1974. This draft should be compared with the Final Report cited below.

2199. ____. ____. ____. ____. The Final Report. 93rd Cong., 2nd sess. Washington, D.C.: U.S. Government Printing Office, 1974. 1,250p. In addition to chapters on the investigative procedures of the committee and the views of individual members, this report sets forth findings in an arrangement equivalent to the "books" of hearings cited in the citation before last. Should be used in conjunction with the final report of the House Judiciary Committee impeachment inquiry cited above. Excerpts from the final report were published in a variety of sources, e.g. "Impeachment Crisis--'Tragic Happenings': Final Report of the Senate Watergate Committee, U.S. News and World Report, LXXVII (July 22, 1974), 68-70, and "Senate Watergate Report: Excerpts, July 12, 1974," in Robert A. Diamond, ed., Historic Documents, 1974 (Washington, D.C.: Congressional Quarterly, Inc., 1975), pp. 599-620.

2200. ____. ____. ____. ____. Watergate Hearings: Break-in and Cover-up. New York: Viking Press, 1973. 886p. Edited by the staff of the New York Times and with an introduction by R. W. Apple, this was a quickly-assembled and published (also by Bantam Books) compilation of excerpts from the May-August 1973 testimony. Also includes a chronology, brief biographies, and selected Nixon statements on Watergate. A similar 2-volume work, The Senate Watergate Report, was published by the New York firm of Dell in 1976.

2201. ____. ____. ____. Select Committee to Study Government Operations with Respect to Intelligence Activities. The Federal Bureau of Investigation: Hearings. 94th Cong., 1st sess. Washington, D.C.: U.S. Government Printing Office, 1976. 1,000p. Investigations by the group chaired by Senator Frank Church into the illegal activities of the FBI; contains statements on Watergate.

Watergate   276

2202. ____. ____. ____. ____. The Huston Plan: Hearings. 94th
       Cong., 1st sess. Washington, D.C.: U.S. Government
       Printing Office, 1976. 403p. Looks into the massive
       Nixon administration plan for illegal political espionage.

2203. ____. Department of Justice. "Amended Guidelines for the
       Special Prosecutor: Reprinted from the Federal Register,
       November 7, 1973." In: U.S. Congress, Senate, Com-
       mittee on the Judiciary. Nomination of William B. Saxbe
       to Be Attorney General: Hearings. 93rd Cong., 1st
       sess. Washington, D.C.: U.S. Government Printing
       Office, 1973. pp. 17-21. Designed to insure political
       independence from the White House.

2204. ____. ____. "Duties and Responsibilities of the Special Pros-
       ecutor." C.Q. Weekly Report, XXXI (May 26, 1973),
       1314. As originally set out for Archibald Cox; also pub-
       lished in the Congressional Record, CXIX (October 23,
       1973), 34778.

2205. ____. ____. The Law of Impeachment. 2 pts. Washington,
       D.C., 1974. Working papers prepared by the Office of
       Legal Counsel; includes a discussion of what constitutes
       an impeachable offense, a history of constitutional pro-
       visions relating to the process, and statements from his-
       tory on impeachment, judicial review, and executive priv-
       ilege.

2206. ____. ____. Legal Aspects of Impeachment. 3 pts. Wash-
       ington, D.C., 1974. More working papers from the Of-
       fice of Legal Counsel which further discuss the points
       noted in the annotation to the previous citation.

2207. ____. ____. Watergate Special Prosecution Force (WSPF).
       WSPF First Anniversary Report. Washington, D.C.,
       1974. Unpaged. A brief review of the work undertaken.

2208. ____. ____. ____. Report. Washington, D.C.: U.S. Gov-
       ernment Printing Office, 1975. 277p. Reports on the
       activities of the WSPF, including the current status of
       cases handled by the Office of the Special Prosecutor and
       a description of the Special Prosecutor's relations with
       other units of government. Appendices include a list of
       staff, chronology, and bibliography. Should be used in
       conjunction with the final reports of the House Judiciary
       Committee and Senate Watergate Committee, both of which
       are cited above. Excerpts from the final report appeared
       in a variety of sources, including: "Final Report: Ex-
       cerpts, October 16, 1975," in Robert A. Diamond, ed.
       Historic Documents, 1975 (Washington, D.C.: Congres-
       sional Quarterly, Inc., 1976), 633-690 and "Official Ver-
       sion," U.S. News and World Report, LXXIX (October 27,
       1975), 65-66.

2209. ____. District Court for the District of Columbia. The EOB Tape of June 20, 1972: Report on a Technical Investigation Conducted for the U.S. District Court for the District of Columbia, by an Advisory Panel on White House Tapes. Washington, D.C., 1974. 65p. The experts' analysis of the 18-minute tape gap.

2210. ____. ____. Review of a Report Submitted to the U.S. District Court for the District of Columbia Entitled "The Tape of June 20, 1972." Stanford, Calif.: Stanford Research Institute, 1974. Another look at the 18-minute tape gap.

2211. ____. Library of Congress, Congressional Research Service. "Impeachment Defense Counsel for the President: Report." Congressional Record, CXX (July 31, 1974), 26019-26024. Examines possible presidential defenses against the articles.

2212. ____. ____. Resolved That the Powers of the Presidency Should Be Curtailed: A Collection of Excerpts and a Bibliography Relating to the Intercollegiate Debate Topic, 1974-1975. Washington, D.C.: U.S. Government Printing Office, 1974. 328p. Useful background information on a variety of Watergate-related subjects such as executive privilege.

2213. ____. ____, Government and General Research Division. "The Present Limits of Executive Privilege." Congressional Record, CXIX (March 28, 1973), H2243-H2246. A review of the history of the concept; note that this reference comes from the daily, not the bound, edition.

2214. ____. National Study Commission on Records and Documents of Federal Officials. Final Report. Washington, D.C.: U.S. Government Printing Office, 1977. 137p. Examines housing and access to such papers, including those of former president Richard M. Nixon.

2215. ____. ____. Memorandum of Law. Washington, D.C.: U.S. Government Printing Office, 1977. 347p. An examination of the various laws relating to, among other things, presidential papers and documents.

2216. ____. ____. Memorandum of Findings on Existing Custom or Law, Fact and Opinion. Washington, D.C.: U.S. Government Printing Office, 1977. 373p. A review of existing statutes.

2217. ____. Supreme Court. "Supreme Court on Nixon Tapes: Full Text of the Supreme Court's Decision Ordering President Nixon to Surrender Subpoenaed White House Tape Recordings." In: Robert A. Diamond, ed. Historic

Documents, 1974. Washington, D.C.: Congressional Quarterly, Inc., 1975. pp. 621-638. The text of opinion in United States v. Nixon.

2218. _____. _____. "Supreme Court on Wiretapping: Excerpts from Ruling on Abuses of the Federal Wiretapping Statute by Former Attorney General John N. Mitchell and His Justice Department Subordinates, May 13, 1974." In: Robert A. Diamond, ed. *Historic Documents, 1974.* Washington, D.C.: Congressional Quarterly, Inc., 1975. pp. 391-406. Excerpts from United States v. Mitchell.

2219. "United States vs. Richard M. Nixon, President, et al." *Time,* CIV (July 22, 1974), 10-17. Describes the case in detail and speculates on the President's next moves. Includes biographical data on the Supreme Court justices.

2220. "Unpardonable." *Progressive,* XXXVIII (October 1974), 5-6. An editorial opposing the Ford pardon of Richard Nixon.

2221. "Unpardonable Offenses." *New Republic,* CLXXI (September 21, 1974), 5-6. Additional reaction to the Nixon pardon.

2222. "The Unsinkable John Dean." *Newsweek,* LXXXIV (November 4, 1974), 32+. His testimony in the Watergate cover-up trial.

2223. Van Alstyne, William. "No Doubtful Authority Ought to Be Exercised: The Impeachment of Richard Nixon." *Congressional Record,* CXX (May 9, 1974), 13958-13959. Warns the House Judiciary Committee against legal mistakes in its articles of impeachment.

2224. _____. "A Political and Constitutional Review of United States v. Nixon." *UCLA Law Review,* XXII (October 1974), 116-140. Examines the Constitutional aspects of the case in light of the politics of the situation.

2225. _____. "President Nixon: Toughing It Out with the Law." *American Bar Association Journal,* LIX (December 1973), 1398-1402. Compares Nixon's use of executive privilege in several instances and notes that such claims have diverted attention from his conduct to the question of presidential power under the Constitution.

2226. _____. "The Third Impeachment Article: Congressional Bootstrapping." *American Bar Association Journal,* LX (October 1974), 1199-1202. Questions the legality and validity of the third article.

2227. Van der Linden, Frank. "President Is Hurt by 'Palace Guard': Reprinted from the *Washington Star,* April 22, 1973." *Congressional Record,* CXIX (April 30, 1973),

13693. The effects of the resignations of Haldeman and Ehrlichman.

2228. ———. "Raps Impeachment Vote Push: Reprinted from the Homewood-Flossmoor [Illinois] Star, May 12, 1974." Congressional Record, CXX (May 14, 1974), 14682. The opinions of Attorney General William Saxbe.

2229. Van Valkenberg, W. E. "Impeachment: God Save the King from Overzealous Subordinates." Utah Law Review, XXIII (Spring 1974), 71-91. Examines the role of the impeachment inquiry staff in pushing for articles.

2230. Varnado, S. L. "Watergate As Drama." National Review, XXV (August 31, 1973), 945+. Comments on the televising of the Ervin panel hearings.

2231. Vartabedian, Robert A. "A Case Study in Contemporary Apologia: The Self-Defense Rhetoric of Richard Nixon." Unpublished PhD Dissertation, University of Oklahoma, 1981. A brand new look at the strategy employed by the former president in his Watergate statements and speeches.

2232. "Verdict on a Trickster." Newsweek, LXXXIII (April 15, 1974), 30+. Dwight L. Chapin.

2233. "Verdict on Chapin." U.S. News and World Report, LXXVI (April 15, 1974), 16. Guilty of "dirty tricks."

2234. "Verdict on Watergate." Newsweek, LXXXV (January 13, 1975), 16-18. The outcome of the cover-up trial.

2235. "A Very Definitive Decision: Supreme Court's Ruling on the Case of Subpoenaed White House Tapes." Newsweek, LXXXIV (August 5, 1974), 23-26. The outcome of United States v. Nixon.

2236. "Vesco: Too Hot to Handle." Newsweek, LXXXI (March 12, 1973), 20-21. On his effort to provide illegal contributions.

2237. Vestal, Bud. "This Is the Week That Was for Gerry Ford: Reprinted from the Jackson [Michigan] Citizen Patriot, August 14, 1974." Congressional Record, CXX (August 22, 1974), 30139-30140. A chronicle of the week when Nixon resigned and Ford became president.

2238. Vidich, A. J. "Political Legitimacy in Bureaucratic Society: An Analysis of Watergate." Social Research, XLII (Winter 1975), 778-811. Unavailable for review.

2239. "Villain Vindicated." Time, CI (May 14, 1973), 100. Nixon's role in the attempt at press conciliation.

2240. "Violation of His Constitutional Oath." Time, CIV (August 12, 1974), 14-15. The House Judiciary Committee's articles of impeachment.

2241. Volz, Joseph. "None of the President's Men." Washington Magazine, X (July 1975), 46-51. The tapes and White House aides are discussed.

2242. Von Hoffman, Nicholas. "The Breaking of a President." Penthouse, VIII (March 1977), 47-48, 50, 52, 150, 152-153. Traces the pressures on Nixon to resign in the final days of Watergate.

2243. _____. "The First All-Out Felony Cabinet: Reprinted from the Washington Post, September 18, 1972." Congressional Record, CXIX (September 19, 1972), 31364-31365. Looks at the record of past and sitting cabinet members of the Nixon administration.

2244. _____. "First They Convict Nixon, Then They Try Him: Reprinted from the Chicago Tribune, April 24, 1974." Congressional Record, CXX (April 29, 1974), 12263-12264. Critical of the rush to impeachment.

2245. _____. "How Nixon Got Strung Up." New Republic, CLXXXVI (June 23, 1982), 24-27. A tenth-anniversary analysis of the push to oust the former president.

2246. _____. Make-Believe Presidents: Illusions of Power from McKinley to Carter. New York: Pantheon Books, 1978. 260p. Presidential power, the author contends, works really well or corruptly only when other powers in the Federal system assent to its use or when corporate elites or ruling classes favor it. Contains some comments on the downfall of Nixon which are touched on in his other articles cited here.

2247. _____ and Garry Trudeau. The Fireside Watergate. New York: Sheed and Ward, 1973. 150p. A book of humorous readings; co-author Trudeau is the creator of the Doonesbury comic strip.

2248. Vose, Clement E. "Nixon's Archival Legacy." Political Science, X (Fall 1977), 432-438. Against the former president's control of access to the papers.

2249. _____. "Presidential Papers As a Political Science Concern." Political Science, VIII (Winter 1975), 8-18. Another look at the possible problems of limited access.

2250. "Vote of No Confidence." Newsweek, LXXXIII (March 4, 1974), 16-19. The House Judiciary Committee decision for an impeachment inquiry.

2251. "Voters: Nixon Should Go." Time, CIV (May 13, 1974), 19. Public opinion on the edited White House transcripts.

2252. Wade, Nicholas. "20 June Tape Critics Fault Logic of Experts' Final Report." Science, CLXXXIV (June 21, 1974), 1261-1262+. Many disagreed with the findings of Judge Sirica's special panel.

2253. _____. "Watergate Tapes: Critics Question Main Conclusion of Expert Panel." Science, CLXXXIII (February 22, 1974), 732-734. Similar to previous citation; reprinted in Congressional Record, CXX (April 11, 1974), 10910-10911.

2254. _____. "Watergate: Verification of Tapes May Be an Electronic Standoff." Science, CLXXXII (December 14, 1973), 1108-1110. Comments on Judge Sirica's panel's investigation of the 18-minute tape gap.

2255. Wagner, Randolph G. "Public Response to Watergate." Unpublished PhD Dissertation, Yale University, 1981. A study of public opinion on the crisis, 1972-1974.

2256. Waldie, Jerome R. "Playing Politics with Justice: Reprinted from Nation, September 28, 1974." Congressional Record, CXX (September 24, 1974), 32493-32495. The California Democratic Congressman and member of the House Judiciary Committee was critical of Ford's pardon of Nixon.

2257. _____. "Unconscionable Pardon." Nation, CCXIX (September 28, 1974), 263-266. Identical to the previous citation.

2258. Waldrop, Frank C. "The Connecticut Eel." Washington Magazine, XII (August 1977), 7. A brief profile of L. Patrick Gray, 3rd.

2259. Wallen, H. "Pat Buchanan Gets It Right." Washington Post Potomac (December 9, 1973), 12-13+. A study of one of Nixon's most controversial speech writers.

2260. Walsh, Denny. "Corruption Among the Nixon Entourage." Focus/Midwest, no. 57 (1972), 8-12. A study of the activities of Attorney General Richard Kleindienst.

2261. Walter C. McCrone Associates. "Microanalytical Analysis of Beard Memorandum." In: U.S. Congress, Senate, Committee on the Judiciary. Richard G. Kleindienst--Resumed: Hearings. 92nd Cong., 2nd sess. Washington, D.C.: U.S. Government Printing Office, 1973. pp. 860-864. Contends that the Dita Beard ITT memo was a hoax.

2262. Walters, R. "What Did Ziegler Say, and When Did He Say It?" Columbia Journalism Review, XIII (September-October 1974), 30-35. Examines the statements of White House press secretary Ron Ziegler.

2263. Walters, Vernon K. Silent Missions. Garden City, N. Y.: Doubleday, 1978. 654p. The Deputy Director of CIA during Watergate, this retired Lt. General has much to say about his Agency's role in the scandal.

2264. Walthall, Timothy. "Impeachment--Stealing Fire from the Gods: Reprinted from the New England Law Review." Congressional Record, CXX (May 7, 1974), 13584-13587. Argues that impeachment is a last-resort political weapon which should be employed carefully.

2265. Waltner, Tim. "The Crisis of the Presidency: Reprinted from the Freeman [South Dakota] Courier, October 25, 1973." Congressional Record, CXIX (October 30, 1973), 35362. Reaction to the dismissal of Archibald Cox.

2266. Wanniski, Jude. "When Did the President Know?: Reprinted from the Wall Street Journal, May 3, 1974." Congressional Record, CXX (May 15, 1974), 14757-14758. Suggests he knew much earlier than previously indicated.

2267. "The War for Nixon Tapes: Court Order to Surrender Tapes." Newsweek, LXXXII (September 10, 1973), 19-22. Examines the basis for Judge Sirica's decision and reactions to it.

2268. Warren, Earl. "Government Secrecy: Corruption's Ally." American Bar Association Journal, LX (May 1974), 550-552. The former Supreme Court Chief Justice argues that a free press is necessary to stimulate the opening of government affairs at all levels.

2269. "Was Justice Done?" Newsweek, LXXXIV (September 16, 1974), 19-21+. Comment on the Nixon pardon.

2270. "Was Justice Finally Done?" Newsweek, LXXXV (January 13, 1975), 19-20+. The outcome of the Watergate cover-up trial.

2271. Wasby, ----. "The Presidency Before the Courts." Capital University Law Review, VI (1976), 35+. Unavailable for review.

2272. "Washing Dirty Dollars." New Republic, CLXVIII (May 19, 1973), 5-7. The matter of undisclosed contributions to the GOP campaign of '72.

2273. Washington Post, Staff of. The Fall of a President. New

York: Delacorte, 1974. 232p. Also issued by Dell in paperback, this quickie volume is similar to the New York Times' The End of a Presidency cited above. Includes thirteen essays by Post staffers, including Woodward/Bernstein, a chronology, and important documents such as the articles of impeachment.

2274. _____, eds. Year of Scandal: How the Washington Post Covered Watergate and the Agnew Crisis. Washington, D.C.: Washington Post Writers Group, 1973. A review of the scandals and the process of the paper's coverage.

2275. "Watching Nixon: A Symposium." Newsweek, LXXXIX (May 16, 1977), 28-29+. Reactions to the former president's comments in his Frost interviews.

2276. "Watergate." New Republic, CLXXI (November 30, 1974), 9-10. Comments on the cover-up trial.

2277. Watergate: A Dramatic Public Disclosure by Nixon." C.Q. Weekly Report, XXXII (1974), 1067-1104. The text of the April 30, 1974 White House summary of taped presidential conversations which were provided to the House Judiciary Committee is printed at pp. 1078-1086, the text of Nixon's televised April 29, 1974 address in which he revealed that he would make public edited versions of his tapes is printed at pp. 1101-1104, and the text of the controversial March 21, 1973 transcript of the President's Oval Office meeting with Dean and Haldeman is printed at pp. 1087-1101.

2278. "Watergate: A Dramatic Switch by the White House." C.Q. Weekly Report, XXXI (1973), 895-898. The President's attempt to be more open in light of the Cox firing criticism.

2279. "Watergate: A Hard Look at Presidential Impeachment." C.Q. Weekly Report, XXXI (1973), 2831-2853. Examines the idea as initially raised; texts of letters, documents, and memos relating to the Cox dismissal are printed at pp. 2848-2853.

2280. "Watergate: A Historic Constitutional Confrontation." C.Q. Weekly Report, XXXI (July 28, 1973), 2031-2051. The battle for the White House tapes.

2281. "Watergate: A Historic Subpoena to the President." C.Q. Weekly Report, XXXII (1974), 923-926. Text of Judge Sirica's effort to obtain the White House tapes.

2282. "Watergate: A Presidential Court Appeal on Tapes." C.Q. Weekly Report, XXXI (September 8, 1973), 2391-2393. Nixon's lawyers appealed subpoenas for the tapes.

2283. "Watergate: A Presidential Denial of Involvement." C.Q. Weekly Report, XXXI (May 26, 1973), 1255-1270. Reprints the President's statement and the testimony of others.

2284. "Watergate: A Renewed Climate of Confrontation." C.Q. Weekly Report, XXXII (1974), 1327-1330. The end of what had been a brief breathing period in winter 1974.

2285. "Watergate: A 'Sinister Force' in Blank on Tape." C.Q. Weekly Report, XXXI (1973), 3201-3209. Reviews the $18\frac{1}{2}$-minute tape gap.

2286. "Watergate: A Threat to Arrest White House Officials." C.Q. Weekly Report, XXXI (1973), 654-655. For their lack of cooperation.

2287. "Watergate: A Week of Action Related to the Tapes." C.Q. Weekly Report, XXXII (July 13, 1974), 1795-1809. Leading up to the Supreme Court contest.

2288. "Watergate Accusers Pile Up Evidence." U.S. News and World Report, LXXVII (November 25, 1974), 77. Data gathered in support of the Watergate cover-up trial.

2289. The Watergate Affair. Crisis Paper, no. 30. London: Atlantic Educational Publications, 1973. 20p. A summary of events for British school teachers.

2290. "Watergate: Aiming for End of Hearings by November 1." C.Q. Weekly Report, XXXI (1973), 2461-2467. The end of the Ervin panel hearings with notes on what had thus far been revealed.

2291. "Watergate: An Inconclusive Report on Gap in Tape." C.Q. Weekly Report, XXXI (December 15, 1973), 3270-3271+. Presented by Judge Sirica's special panel.

2292. "Watergate and a Dangerous World: Reprinted from the Washington Star-News, October 28, 1973." Congressional Record, CXIX (October 30, 1973), 35498-35499. Editorializes on the need for presidential leadership in a time of troubles.

2293. "Watergate and Impeachment in Perspective." C.Q. Weekly Report, XXXII (1974), 3444-3449. Attempts to separate facts from assumptions.

2294. "Watergate and the CIA." U.S. News and World Report, LXXIV (June 4, 1973), 19. Agency aid to the "plumbers."

2295. "Watergate and the Election." National Review, XXV (August 17, 1973), 879-880. Examines the crisis in the light of the 1972 election results.

2296. "Watergate Anniversary." Newsweek, LXXXIX (June 20, 1977), 10+. The fifth anniversary of the break-in.

2297. "Watergate Anniversary and Watergate Prosecution Status: Reprinted from the Nashville Tennesseean, June 17, 1974." Congressional Record, CXX (June 20, 1974), 20388-20389. Recaps indictments and trials held to date.

2298. "Watergate: Appointments, Hearings, Missing Tapes." C.Q. Weekly Report, XXXI (November 3, 1973), 2879-2895. Reviews events during the preceding week.

2299. "Watergate: Approval of Subpoena Power for Judiciary." C.Q. Weekly Report, XXXII (1974), 291-295. House panel receives power to compel testimony and documents delivery.

2300. "Watergate: As Nixon Picks Up the Pieces, Big Changes Are Taking Place." U.S. News and World Report, LXXIV (May 14, 1973), 17-19. Staff and other changes in light of the resignation of key members of the "palace guard."

2301. "Watergate Bargains: Were They Necessary?" Time, CIII (June 24, 1974), 64. Critical of plea bargaining in various witness cases.

2302. "Watergate: Battle over the Meaning of Words." C.Q. Weekly Report, XXXII (1974), 1735-1741. As the House Judiciary Committee drew up its articles of impeachment.

2303. "Watergate Blockbuster." National Review, XXVI (May 24, 1974), 569-570. The release of the edited White House tape transcripts.

2304. "Watergate Blotter." Nation, CCXVI (May 14, 1973), 614-616. Shows how White House statements changed as new proof emerged.

2305. "Watergate: Both Sides Agree Nixon Also Is on Trial." U.S. News and World Report, LXXVII (October 28, 1974), 72-74. The cover-up trial of former key aides.

2306. "The 'Watergate Caper': A Chronology of Events." C.Q. Weekly Report, XXXII (1974), 2292-2293. A brief chronology from June 1974-August 9, 1974.

2307. _____. C.Q. Weekly Report, XXX (September 9, 1972), 2293-2294. Covers events from April 4-September 6, 1972.

2308. "Watergate: Capital's Unwholesome Preoccupation." C.Q. Weekly Report, XXXI (April 28, 1973), 1007-1010. A chronology covering the period April 20-26, 1973.

2309. "The Watergate Case: What's It All About?" U.S. News and World Report, LXXIV (April 16, 1973), 27-29. An early assessment of the scandal's significance.

2310. "Watergate Cast of Characters." C.Q. Weekly Report, XXXI (May 5, 1973), 1065-1068. Suggests many have similar backgrounds.

2311. "Watergate Casualties: The List Grows Longer." U.S. News and World Report, LXXVII (August 12, 1974), 23. The fates of Dean, Connally, Ehrlichman, and Ed Reinecke.

2312. "Watergate: Chapin Indictment, Krogh Guilty Plea." C.Q. Weekly Report, XXXI (December 1, 1973), 1735-1741. A review of those events.

2313. Watergate Classics [a Play Presented at] the Yale Repertory Theater, November 16, 1973-January 26, 1974. New Haven, Conn.: Yale School of Drama, 1974. 126p. An original play which had 27 performances.

2314. "Watergate Chronology, July 25-31, 1974." C.Q. Weekly Report, XXXII (August 3, 1974), 2924-2926. Details events in the period of the Supreme Court hearing on the tape case.

2315. The Watergate Coloring Book. Vancouver, B.C.: Watergate Publishing Co., 1973. 24p. Presents caricatures and cartoons on events and personnel.

2316. "Watergate Committee Hearings of 'Utmost Gravity.'" C.Q. Weekly Report, XXXI (May 19, 1973), 1191-1200. The opening of the Ervin Committee hearings.

2317. "Watergate Committee Hears 33rd Witness [and] Recesses." C.Q. Weekly Report, XXXI (August 11, 1973), 2188-2191+. Excerpts from Gray's testimony and the text of a March 30, 1973 memo from Colson to Haldeman.

2318. "Watergate Cont'd." Time, XCVIII (August 14, 1972), 21-22. A summary of events to that date.

2319. _____. Newsweek, LXXXI (February 19, 1973), 23-24. The investigation of Donald Segretti.

2320. "Watergate: Continued Hearings by a Tired Committee." C.Q. Weekly Report, XXXI (August 4, 1973), 2110-2134. A chronology and excerpts from the prepared statement of H.R. Haldeman.

2321. "Watergate: Continued Hearings on Tapes, Prosecutor." C.Q. Weekly Report, XXXI (1973), 2045-2959. Recaps the Senate Judiciary Committee hearings on the independence of the Special Prosecutor after the Cox dismissal.

2322. "Watergate Coverup Indictments." In: Robert A. Diamond, ed. Historic Documents, 1974. Washington, D.C.: Congressional Quarterly, Inc., 1975. pp. 157-184. Text of indictment returned against seven former White House and Nixon re-election campaign officials and aides on March 1, 1974.

2323. "Watergate Cover-up Trial Opens After Two Years." C.Q. Weekly Report, XXXII (1974), 2676-2677. A recap of opening events.

2324. "Watergate Defenders." Newsweek, LXXXIV (October 14, 1974), 68. Lawyers for the seven defendants in the cover-up trial.

2325. "Watergate Defense Strategy: Put the Blame on Nixon." U.S. News and World Report, LXXVII (December 9, 1974), 62. The cover-up strategy of the seven defendants.

2326. "Watergate: Defining the Law on Deadline." Time, CIII (March 18, 1974), 50-52. The role of lawyer-reporters like Fred Graham and Carl Stern.

2327. "Watergate: Denials of Extortion of Milk Producers." C.Q. Weekly Report, XXXI (December 29, 1973), 3457. The solicitation of illegal contributions in return for favors.

2328. "Watergate: Disagreements Between Senate [and] Prosecutor." C.Q. Weekly Report, XXXI (1973), 1349-1358. Attempts by Mr. Cox to get the Ervin Committee to forego its hearings.

2329. "Watergate: Disintegrating Support for the President." C.Q. Weekly Report, XXXII (1974), 1151-1204. Public opinion and Congressional support crumbling in light of the tape transcripts.

2330. "Watergate Drags Pat Gray Under." Newsweek, LXXXI (April 16, 1973), 21-23. On Nixon's withdrawal of Gray's name for consideration as FBI Director.

2331. "Watergate: Drip, Drip, Drip." Newsweek, LXXXII (December 24, 1973), 17-18. Nixon tax revelations and the work of Sirica's panel of tape experts.

2332. "Watergate: Ehrlichman Says Nixon Fooled Him." C.Q. Weekly Report, XXXII (1974), 3337-3338. His testimony at the cover-up trial.

2333. "Watergate Evidence." Newsweek, LXXXIV (July 22, 1974), 26-46. Recaps almost entirely the House Judiciary Committee's description of the evidence on events from December 2, 1971-April 30, 1973 and reprints lawyer St. Clair's reply brief.

2334. "The Watergate Experience: Lessons for Empirical Theory." American Politics Quarterly, III (October 1975), 355-476. Partial Contents: "Young Voters' Reactions to Early Watergate Issues," by Steven H. Chaffee and Lee B. Becker; "Student Attitudes Toward Mr. Nixon: The Consequences of Negative Attitudes Toward a President for Political System Support," by Harrell R. Rodgers, Jr. and Edward B. Lewis; "Stability of Support for the Political System: The Initial Impact of Watergate," by Paul M. Sniderman, et al.; and "Watergate and the Media: A Case Study of Agenda-Setting," by David H. Weaver, et al.

2335. "Watergate Fallout: Government in Disarray." U.S. News and World Report, LXXXIII (August 6, 1973), 15-17. Officials in and out of government give their views on the effect of the scandal.

2336. "Watergate: Fewer Resignation Calls, More Subpoenas." C.Q. Weekly Report, XXXII (1974), 1263-1265. The push to settle the question of the President's involvement.

2337. "Watergate: Fight Against Time--Who's to Blame for Delay?" U.S. News and World Report, LXXVI (June 10, 1974), 29. The continuing battle over the tapes.

2338. "Watergate Flooding." National Review, XXIIV (April 13, 1973), 406-407. Suggests Nixon's misreading of the scandal and how to handle it led to the political crisis.

2339. "Watergate: Grand Jury Names Nixon Co-Conspirator." C.Q. Weekly Report, XXXII (June 8, 1974), 1467-1472. Events surrounding the President's naming as an unindicted co-conspirator.

2340. "Watergate Hearings--Perhaps Longer Than Expected." C.Q. Weekly Report, XXXI (July 7, 1973), 1800-1804. Looks at the work ahead of the Ervin panel.

2341. "Watergate: Hints of Compromise on Subpoenaed Tapes." C.Q. Weekly Report, XXXII (1974), 52-57. The hopes evaporated almost as quickly as they surfaced.

2342. "Watergate: House Committee Moves to Center Stage." C.Q. Weekly Report, XXXII (1974), 487-492. The start of the Judiciary Committee's impeachment inquiry.

2343. "Watergate: House [Judiciary] Committee Efforts to Get Sealed Report." C.Q. Weekly Report, XXXII (March 9,

1974), 591-598. The Grand Jury report was eventually turned over by Judge Sirica.

2344. "Watergate: How the Lid Blew Off." U.S. News and World Report, LXXIV (May 14, 1973), 20+. Reviews events following the trial of the Watergate burglars.

2345. "Watergate: Hunt, Magruder Join Witness List." C.Q. Weekly Report, XXXII (1974), 3052-3054. In the cover-up trial.

2346. "Watergate: Hunt Memo Asking Money Revealed." C.Q. Weekly Report, XXXII (1974), 3099-3100. By the former Watergate burglar in the days before the first trial.

2347. "Watergate Idiocy." National Review, XXII (November 10, 1972), 1231-1232. Suggests the events were beyond the realm of normal "dirty tricks."

2348. "Watergate: Implication of Four Presidential Aides." C.Q. Weekly Report, XXXI (March 31, 1973), 700-701. Those mentioned include Dean, Haldeman, and Ehrlichman.

2349. "Watergate: Increasing Criticism by Republicans." C.Q. Weekly Report, XXXI (1973), 760-761. Demands that the scandal be cleaned up.

2350. "Watergate: Indications of Deliberate Tape Erasures." C.Q. Weekly Report, XXXII (January 19, 1974), 82-89. Report of Sirica's panel of tape experts.

2351. "Watergate: Indictment of Plumbers Chief Krogh." C.Q. Weekly Report, XXXI (October 13, 1973), 2700-2706. Includes a summary of his work with the White House "plumbers."

2352. "Watergate: Indictments, High Level Reorganization." C.Q. Weekly Report, XXXI (May 12, 1973), 1119-1122+. The resignations of Haldeman and Ehrlichman and the dismissal of Dean.

2353. "Watergate Investigators' Office Work." Office, LXXVIII (October 1973), 45+. A look at the office set-up for the staff of the Special Prosecutor.

2354. "Watergate Issues." Time, XCVIII (August 28, 1972), 20. The role of CREEP.

2355. _____: Part I, Is Publicity Dangerous?" Time, XCIX (June 18, 1973), 61-62. Suggests publicity will hamper future prosecutions.

2356. _____: Part II, Must a President Testify?" Time, XCIX

(June 18, 1973), 62. Looks at precedents and opinions on subpoenaing a president.

2357. "Watergate: Magruder Implicates Top Officials." C.Q. Weekly Report, XXXI (1973), 1486-1497. His Ervin Committee testimony.

2358. "Watergate: Mixed Response to Pledge of Cooperation." C.Q. Weekly Report, XXXII (1974), 230-234. Not all believed the President's pledge.

2359. "Watergate: Most Damaging Charges Yet by Dean." C.Q. Weekly Report, XXXI (1973), 1710-1727. His Ervin panel testimony that Nixon knew and approved the cover-up.

2360. "Watergate Moves into a Crucial Stage." U.S. News and World Report, LXXV (July 2, 1973), 25-26. Anticipates Dean's testimony and recaps that given earlier to the Ervin Committee.

2361. "Watergate: Near Showdown on White House Records." C.Q. Weekly Report, XXXI (July 21, 1973), 1931-1946. The battle for the tapes.

2362. "Watergate: Nixon, Cox Failure to Agree on Tapes." C.Q. Weekly Report, XXXI (1973), 2503-2506. This failure led to the "Saturday Night Massacre."

2363. "Watergate: Nixon Goes Public, Pledges Disclosure." C.Q. Weekly Report, XXXI (November 19, 1973), 3010-3018. "Operation Candor."

2364. "Watergate: Nixon Role Becomes Trial Defense." C.Q. Weekly Report, XXXII (1974), 2953-2955. Strategy of the defendants in the cover-up trial.

2365. "Watergate: Nixon's Angels Stand Firm." Business Week (June 2, 1973), 21-22. The President's backers remain committed but desire tougher contribution rules.

2366. "Watergate: Nixon's Conservative Support Wanes." C.Q. Weekly Report, XXXII (1974), 719-725. In light of the tape transcripts.

2367. "Watergate: Nixon's Mood at a Time of Trouble." U.S. News and World Report, LXXIV (May 21, 1973), 24-25. Unnamed sources close to the President convey his concern.

2368. "Watergate Notes." Time, CIII (June 10, 1974), 22+. The activities of John Dean are discussed.

2369. "Watergate: Now It's a Federal Case." Newsweek, LXXX (September 25, 1972), 31-32. Looks at Federal indictments in DC and Florida and the upcoming testimony of Alfred Baldwin.

2370. "Watergate: Now the Courts Move In." U.S. News and World Report, LXXV (September 10, 1973), 15-17. Provides details on trials and court battles related to the scandal.

2371. "Watergate: Now the Stage Is Set for the Full Story." U.S. News and World Report, LXXIV (May 21, 1973), 17-19. The opening of the Ervin Committee hearings.

2372. "Watergate on TV: Time Essay." Time, CI (June 25, 1973), 14-15. Coverage of the Ervin panel hearings.

2373. "Watergate I: The Evidence to Date." Time, CII (August 20, 1973), 16-18. Evidence as revealed by the Ervin panel hearings.

2374. "Watergate: Ongoing Battles for White House Evidence." C.Q. Weekly Report, XXXII (June 1, 1974), 1407-1412. The pursuit of the tapes.

2375. "Watergate Opens." Newsweek, LXXXI (January 15, 1973), 16-17. The trial of the Watergate burglars.

2376. "Watergate: Pardon Repercussions Continue." C.Q. Weekly Report, XXXII (1974), 2557-2558. Opposition to the Ford action.

2377. "Watergate: Phase IV." Nation, CCXVI (May 7, 1973), 578-579. Asks what did Nixon know.

2378. "Watergate: Playing the Tapes Brings Case Alive." C.Q. Weekly Report, XXXII (1974), 3004-3005. Reaction after the tapes are finally handed over and played.

2379. "Watergate: Plenty to Probe." Newsweek, LXXXI (February 12, 1973), 25-26. Questions remaining after the trial of the Watergate burglars.

2380. "Watergate: Prosecution Finishes Its Case." C.Q. Weekly Report, XXXII (1974), 3207-3208. In the cover-up trial.

2381. "Watergate: Prosecution Nears End of Its Case." C.Q. Weekly Report, XXXII (1974), 3156-3158. In the cover-up trial.

2382. "Watergate: Putting All the Evidence in Focus." C.Q. Weekly Report, XXXII (1974), 1847-1860. The House Judiciary Committee's final report.

2383. "Watergate Questions: Nixon Leaves Many Unanswered."
C.Q. Weekly Report, XXXI (1973), 2244-2248. The text
of his August 15, 1973 statement is printed at pp. 2287-
2291.

2384. "Watergate: Religious Issues and Answers." Christian Century (September 26, 1973), 937-942. To the question of what is the central religious issue posed by the scandal, 22 religious leaders provide their answers.

2385. "Watergate Revisited." National Review, XXXIV (June 25, 1982), 740-741. A tenth-anniversary assessment.

2386. _____. Progressive, XLVI (July 1982), 11. A tenth-anniversary note.

2387. "Watergate Role." Time, CXVI (December 29, 1980), 12. Of Alexander Haig.

2388. "Watergate Rolls On." Time, C (September 11, 1972), 18-19. Charges and counter-charges on financial misdeeds by CREEP and the Nixon campaign.

2389. "Watergate: St. Clair Begins Nixon Defense." C.Q. Weekly Report, XXXII (June 29, 1974), 1671-1679. His statements to the House Judiciary Committee.

2390. "The Watergate Scandal." In: 1973 Congressional Quarterly Almanac. Washington, D.C.: Congressional Quarterly, Inc., 1974. pp. 1007-1053. A succinct review of the information revealed in 1973.

2391. "Watergate Scandal: A Senate Search for the Truth." C.Q. Weekly Report, XXXI (1973), 834-847. A review of the work of the Ervin panel.

2392. "Watergate Sentencing." In: Robert A. Diamond, ed. Historic Documents, 1975. Washington, D.C.: Congressional Quarterly, Inc., 1976. pp. 141-154. Excerpts from the court transcript of February 21, 1975.

2393. "Watergate: Seven Indictments May Assist House Inquiry." C.Q. Weekly Report, XXXII (1974), 531-539. Cover-up indictments by the Watergate grand jury.

2394. "Watergate: Shifting Perspectives." National Review, XXV (May 25, 1973), 565-566. U.S. and European public opinion is mild with only the media and politicians concerned at this point.

2395. "The Watergate Six: Stage Is Set for the Big Trial." U.S. News and World Report, LXXVII (October 7, 1974), 40. Opening of the cover-up trial.

2396. "Watergate: Six Months in Prison for Plumber Krogh." C.Q. Weekly Report, XXXII (January 26, 1974), 131-136. Reviews his activities before sentencing.

2397. "Watergate Tales--Analysis of the Stages of the Watergate Case Covered by the Transcripts." Newsweek, LXXXIII (May 13, 1974), 24+. Looks for the answer to the question: how much did Nixon know?

2398. "Watergate Taps." Time, C (September 18, 1972), 18-19. Democratic chairman O'Brien's charge that his phones were tapped prior to the burglary.

2399. "Watergate: Tapes Document Cover-up Story." C.Q. Weekly Report, XXXII (1974), 3142-3144. Finally providing support for the story by John Dean.

2400. "Watergate Tapes--The Puzzle Persists." U.S. News and World Report, LXXV (December 17, 1973), 37. Testimony on the $18\frac{1}{2}$-minute gap.

2400a. "Watergate: Testimony." C.Q. Weekly Report, XXXI (1973), 1865-1876. Reviews his Ervin Committee statements, with many excerpts.

2401. "Watergate: The Birds Are Singing." Newsweek, LXXXI (April 9, 1973), 16-17+. The statements of Dean and others like McCord and Magruder.

2402. "Watergate: The Cast Shrinks." Newsweek, LXXXI (January 22, 1973), 23-24. E. Howard Hunt pleads guilty.

2403. "Watergate: The Dam Bursts." Newsweek, LXXXI (April 20, 1973), 16-17+. On the increased flow of statements from McCord, Dean, etc.

2404. "Watergate: The Eye of the Storm." Newsweek, LXXXI (June 11, 1973), 19-24. Dean's testimony is countered by that from Haldeman and Ehrlichman.

2405. "Watergate: The Last Act." Newsweek, LXXXV (January 6, 1975), 13-15. The outcome of the cover-up trial.

2406. "Watergate: The President's Men Speak Out in His Defense." U.S. News and World Report, LXXV (August 13, 1973), 21-23. Excerpts from the Ervin panel testimony of Ehrlichman and Haldeman.

2407. No entry.

2408. Watergate: The View from the Left. Introductions by Linda Jenness and Andrew Pulley. New York: Pathfinder Press, 1973. 95p. Includes a series of essays and addresses on the topic of Watergate, such as C. Jaquith's "Labor and Black Leaders Led the 'Enemies List,'" Fred Halstead's "How We Foiled Nixon's Dirty Tricks," and D. Morrison's "Watergate and the Black Movement." Much polemic and little based on data revealed after the middle of the Ervin Committee hearings.

2409. "Watergate: Three More Shocks for the President." U.S. News and World Report, LXXVI (June 17, 1974), 24-27. Colson's guilty plea, the unindicted co-conspirator judgement, and a possible contempt of court citation allegedly planned by Judge Gesell.

2410. "Watergate Trial." Newsweek, LXXX (August 14, 1972), 20-21. Bernard Barker, G. Gordon Liddy, and financial entanglements.

2411. "Watergate Trial: Guilty Pleas by Four More Defendants." C.Q. Weekly Report, XXXI (1973), 104-105. Now all of the Watergate burglars have pleaded.

2412. "Watergate: Trial's Final Arguments Are Made." C.Q. Weekly Report, XXII (1974), 3450-3451. The cover-up trial's final phase.

2413. "Watergate Upheaval: Is Government at a Standstill?" U.S. News and World Report, LXXIV (May 28, 1973), 17-19. Shifts and vacancies in executive branch posts since the crisis started and what effect they might have on government operations.

2414. "Watergate: Very Offensive Security." Newsweek, LXXX (October 23, 1972), 35-36. Explores the reasons for White House dirty tricks against the campaign of George McGovern.

2415. "Watergate: Vital Work Ahead for Senate Committee." C.Q. Weekly Report, XXXI (1973), 3063-3069. Scenario for the upcoming Ervin Committee hearings.

2416. "Watergate: Was the President Deceived?" U.S. News and World Report, LXXIV (April 30, 1973), 16-19. Recaps Nixon's April 17, 1973 address to the nation.

2417. Watergate Wasn't All My Fault. Chicago: Playboy Press, 1975. 190p. Nine short, humorous tales concerning the crisis.

2418. "Watergate--Where Will It All Lead?: Day After Day More Revelations About Watergate." U.S. News and World Report, LXXIV (June 18, 1973), 17-21. Evidence emerging from the Ervin panel hearings.

2419. "Watergate: White House Criticism of House Inquiry." C.Q. Weekly Report, XXXII (March 16, 1974), 651-658. Questions the methods employed and leaks of information.

2420. "Watergate: White House Shake-up." In: Buel W. Patch, ed. Historic Documents, 1973. Washington, D.C.: Congressional Quarterly, Inc., 1973. pp. 499-514. Includes the text of the President's April 30, 1973 TV address and the texts of the letters of resignations of Kleindienst, Haldeman, and Ehrlichman, the announcement of the withdrawal of Gray's nomination, and the text of Gray's April 27, 1973 resignation letter.

2421. "Watergate--Who's Telling the Truth?" U.S. News and World Report, LXXV (July 23, 1973), 19-21. Contrasts Dean's statements with others made at the Ervin hearings.

2422. "Watergate: Will Nixon Be the Big Loser?" U.S. News and World Report, LXXIV (May 7, 1973), 19-20. Opinions of Congressmen and anonymous White House aides.

2423. "Watergate Windup: The Long, Slow Process Begins." U.S. News and World Report, LXXVII (October 14, 1974), 26. The opening of the cover-up trial.

2424. Watergate Without Words: Cartoons and Art of America's Greatest Political Scandal. San Francisco, Calif.: Straight Arrow Publishers, 1975. 93p. Caricatures and cartoons from several sources concerning the crisis and its personalities.

2425. "Watergate Wit." Time, CI (June 25, 1973), 94. TV-radio shows, comedy acts, record albums, and bumper stickers are surveyed.

2426. "Watergate: Witnesses Finish, Trial Nears End." C.Q. Weekly Report, XXXII (1974), 3393-3394. The cover-up trial.

2427. "Watergate's Curious Cast of Characters." Newsweek, LXXXI (April 30, 1973), 22. Brief portraits of some of the personnel involved.

2428. "Watergate's Forgotten Man." Progressive, XXXVIII (January 1974), 12. Frank Wills.

2429. "Watergate's Impact on the Future As Political Scientists See It." U.S. News and World Report, LXXV (December 3, 1973), 78-82. A poll shows expectations in future elections, changes in the political system, and impact on public opinion.

2430. "Watergate's Issue Now: Do You Believe John Dean?" U.S.

News and World Report, LXXVII (November 4, 1974), 19-20. The attempt by defense attorneys in the cover-up trial to destroy the effectiveness of the testimony of the government's key witness.

2431. "Watergate's Key Witness." Senior Scholastic, CLXXXIII (October 25, 1973), 12-18. A special report on and profile of John Dean.

2432. "Watergate's Legacy for '74." Newsweek, LXXXII (December 31, 1973), 10-11. Possible scenarios for the scandal's uncovering in the new year.

2433. "Watergate's New Chapter--Is Mitchell the Key?" U.S. News and World Report, LXXV (July 16, 1973), 21-22. Anticipates his Ervin Committee testimony.

2434. "Watergate's Widening Waves of Scandal." Time, CI (April 2, 1973), 11-12. Reports on McCord's letter to Judge Sirica.

2435. "Waterlogged Justice?: Reprinted from the Washington Star-News, June 21, 1974." Congressional Record, CXX (June 25, 1974), 21114-21115. An editorial on House Judiciary Committee leaks.

2436. Waters, Charles. "The Agony of Egil Krogh." Washingtonian, IX (May 1974), 60-67. The fate of the White House "plumber" who pleaded guilty.

2437. Watkins, H. D. "American's Gift Sparks Scrutiny." Aviation Week and Space Technology, XCIX (July 16, 1973), 24-25. An illegal campaign contribution which led investigators to others.

2438. Ways, Max. "Watergate As a Case Study in Management: Farcical and Self-Destructive Blunders Emerged from a Tragic Flaw in the Nixon White House--Self-Pity." Fortune, LXXXVIII (November 1973), 108-111+. A classic tragedy with poor communication, poor targeting, and terrible cost effectiveness.

2439. "We Also Accepted Cash." Newsweek, LXXXIII (April 29, 1974), 35. John Mitchell and CREEP.

2440. "Weakened White House: New Questions for Business." Business Week (May 5, 1973), 18-19. The White House shake-ups leave businessmen wondering whom in government to deal with.

2441. Weaver, David H., Maxwell E. McCombs, and Charles Spellman. "Watergate and the Media: A Case Study in Agenda-Setting." American Politics Quarterly, III (1975),

458-472. Examines the role of the media in covering and promoting the investigation of the scandal.

2442. Weaver, Paul. "The New Journalism and the Old: Thoughts After Watergate." Public Interest (Spring 1974), 67-88. Comments on the rise of investigative journalism à la Woodward/Bernstein.

2443. Webb, Julian. "Impeachment Is a Procedure, Not a Crisis: Reprinted from the Donalsonville [Georgia] News, May 1, 1974." Congressional Record, CXX (May 21, 1974), 15925-15926. Looks at the process in light of legality and not that of crisis.

2444. Wechsler, William A. "The Doctrine of the Separation of Powers and Judicial Review of Impeachment: Prize Essay, Loomis School, Hartford, Connecticut." Congressional Record, CXX (May 20, 1974), 15377-15381. Reviews the doctrines and precedents in light of the rush to impeachment.

2445. Weckel, Ted. "Watergate--Requiem for a President: Reprinted from the Chicago News, June 18, 1974." Congressional Record, CXX (June 25, 1974), 21108-21109. Suggests that Nixon would soon be out of office.

2446. Wehrwein, Austin C. "Measuring the Limits of a Pardon's Force: Reprinted from the Minneapolis Star, September 18, 1974." Congressional Record, CXX (October 3, 1974), 33798-33799. A study of the precedent in presidential pardons undertaken in light of Ford's action.

2447. Weicker, Lowell, Jr. Chilling Effect. Garden City, N.Y.: Doubleday, 1974. The Connecticut Republican senator recalls his service on the Ervin Committee and provides his perspective on the Nixon presidency in light of the evidence revealed in the summer 1973 hearings.

2448. _____. "The Politics of Reform: An Interview." Center Magazine, VIII (January 1975), 36-39. Suggests that Watergate will lead to certain reforms which should prove beneficial.

2449. Weissman, Stephen, ed. Big Brother and the Holding Company: The World Behind Watergate. New York: Ramparts Press, 1974. 350p. A collection of essays by radical writers taken mostly from Ramparts and The New York Review of Books which suggest that a Nixon resignation would not really be a vindication of the system but another cover-up, as the scandal is merely a symptom of a larger society filled with various injustices.

2450. West, S.G., et al. "Ubiquitous Watergate: An Attributional

Analysis." Journal of Personnel and Social Psychology, XXXII (July 1975), 55-68. Unavailable for review.

2451. Westerbeck, Colin L., Jr. "The Last Syllable of Recorded Time." Commonweal, CIV (May 27, 1977), 339-340. Thoughts on Nixon's interviews with David Frost.

2452. "What and Who Is Impeachable?" Newsweek, LXXXIII (February 18, 1974), 27-28. The quest for grounds for an impeachment.

2453. "What Cover-up?" New Republic, CLXVII (September 9, 1972), 7-8. The investigation of donations to CREEP.

2454. "What Does It All Mean?" Newsweek, LXXXIV (August 19, 1974), 52-59. Reactions to Nixon's resignation.

2455. "What Mitchell and Dean Said About Their Talks with the President." U.S. News and World Report, LXXV (November 12, 1973), 104-105. Excerpts from their testimony before the Ervin Committee.

2456. "What Should the President Do Now?" Newsweek, LXXXI (May 14, 1973), 39-40. A series of interviews with people in and out of government.

2457. "What the CIA Knew." Newsweek, LXXXIV (July 15, 1974), 29. Concerning planning for the break-in and the following cover-up.

2458. "What the People Say." U.S. News and World Report, LXXVII (August 12, 1974), 19-22. Public opinion on impeachment.

2459. "What the President Knew." Newsweek, LXXXIII (May 13, 1974), 24-30. Transcripts show him aware of the cover-up earlier than his statements indicated.

2460. "What the Secret Police Did." Newsweek, LXXXI (June 11, 1973), 20-21. Looks at the "plumbers'" activities and plans then under investigation.

2461. "What the Tapes Might Show: The Tapes Being Sought by the House Judiciary Committee." Newsweek, LXXXIII (April 1, 1974), 20-21. That President Nixon was involved in the cover-up.

2462. "Whatever Happened to Mitchell's Re-election Committee?" U.S. News and World Report, LXXV (July 16, 1973), 22. Remained in business after the election to settle accounts.

2463. Wheeler, Harvey and Robert M. Hutchins. "The Constitution Under Strain." Center Magazine, VII (March-April 1974),

43-52. An examination of the Constitutional aspects of the Watergate case.

2464. Wheeler, Michael. Lies, Damn Lies, and Statistics: The Manipulation of Public Opinion in America. New York: Liveright, 1976. 298p. A discussion of political polls with useful coverage of efforts to show that Richard Nixon's popularity was holding fast during the early phases of Watergate.

2465. "Where Did All That Money Go?" Newsweek, LXXXI (May 7, 1973), 24-25. A look at financial shenanigans in the GOP presidential campaign of '72.

2466. "Where Impeachment Stands Now." U.S. News and World Report, LXXVII (July 15, 1974), 18-20. Apparently very certain to come.

2467. "Where the Cox Probe Left Off." Time, CII (November 5, 1973), 23-26. Scenarios as to where Cox's pre-dismissal probe was heading.

2468. "Whispers About Colson." Newsweek, LXXXI (March 5, 1973), 21. "Plumbers'" work by the White House special counsel.

2469. White, Theodore H. America in Search of Itself: The Making of the President, 1956-1980. New York: Harper & Row, 1982. White's tale is more than just that of the election of 1980 or of those since 1956 prior to it, but of the flow and stresses in American society since the time of President Eisenhower; Watergate and the legacy it left receives the full measure of this veteran journalist's attention.

2470. _____. Breach of Faith: The Fall of Richard Nixon. New York: Atheneum, 1975. 373p. Excerpted in Reader's Digest, CVI (May 1975), 204-206+; with background on Nixon's career, this is a blow-by-blow description of the end of Nixon's presidency that should be compared with Woodward and Bernstein's The Final Days cited below.

2471. _____. Making of the President 1972. New York: Atheneum, 1973. 391p. Provides a general description of Nixon and a close-up look at the election campaign, although first-hand reporting on Watergate-related events is limited.

2472. _____. "Teddy White on Watergate." Newsweek, LXXXII (July 30, 1973), 20. Discusses the impact of Watergate and dirty tricks on the 1972 election as noted in his Making of the President 1972 last cited.

2473. _____. "Watergate in Perspective." Reader's Digest, CIII (November 1973), 102-109. An effort to find a pattern in events then taking place.

2474. White, Thomas S. "Reliance on Apparent Authority As Defense to Criminal Prosecution." Columbia Law Review, LXXVII (June 1977), 775-809. Dissects the contention of the former White House staffers that they were just carrying out Nixon's orders and wishes in the cover-up.

2475. White, William S. "The Perils of Presidential Resignation: Reprinted from the Washington Post, May 10, 1974." Congressional Record, CXX (May 23, 1974), 16341. Suggests much confusion might surround it.

2476. _____. "Presidents and the Press--An Adversary Relationship?: Excerpts from an Address." Intellect, CV (November 1976), 128-129. Contains a few comments on Nixon's relations with the press.

2477. "White House Deathwatch." Newsweek, LXXXIV (August 19, 1974), 77-78. Events immediately preceding Nixon's resignation.

2478. "White House Intrigue." Time, CII (July 2, 1973), 14. Alleged intrigue between Colson and Dean.

2479. "White House Study of Nixon Support in the 93rd Congress." C.Q. Weekly Report, XXXII (1974), 80-81. Found 100 pro-impeachment votes in January 1974.

2480. "White House Tape Erasures." In: Robert A. Diamond, ed. Historic Documents, 1974. Washington, D.C.: Congressional Quarterly, Inc., 1975. pp. 23-28. Text of the Report by the Sirica-appointed panel of tape experts on the causes of the $18\frac{1}{2}$-minute gap in a subpoenaed presidential tape recording.

2481. "White House View: Why the Tapes Worry Nixon." U.S. News and World Report, LXXVI (May 6, 1974), 26-27. The explanation of an anonymous White House aide.

2482. Whitehead, Robert, Jr. "Poll Watching: Do We Really Know How the Public Feels About Impeachment?" Columbia Journalism Review, XII (March-April 1974), 3-6. Suggests that the polls of public opinion are not accurate; compare with Michael Wheeler's book cited above.

2483. Whiteside, Thomas. "Annals of Television: The Nixon Administration and Television." New Yorker, LI (May 17, 1975), 41-48+. A review of relations, which were bad for the most part.

2484. Whitney, David C. The American Presidents. Garden City, N.Y.: Doubleday, 1978. 532p. Profiles from Washington to Carter; the chapter on Nixon is the longest in the book.

2485. "Who Owns the Tapes?" Time, CIV (September 30, 1974), 97+. A review of the controversy.

2486. "Who Was 'Deep Throat'?" Washington Magazine, X (May 1975), 30. Speculates that it was W. Mark Felt.

2487. "Who's in Charge at the White House?" U.S. News and World Report, LXXVI (March 4, 1974), 27-29. The work of Alexander Haig.

2488. "Who's in Charge There?" Time, CIII (January 21, 1974), 12-14. Another look at Haig's activities.

2489. "Who's Sorry Now?" Newsweek, LXXXIV (November 25, 1974), 39-40. The cover-up trial.

2490. "Why Ervin Heads Senate Inquiry." U.S. News and World Report, LXXIV (May 28, 1973), 29. Because of his knowledge of the Constitution.

2491. "Why It Was Better to Give...." Time, CII (November 26, 1973), 18+. A look at contributions by corporations to Nixon's 1972 campaign.

2492. "Why Nixon Went on the Witness Stand." U.S. News and World Report, LXXXII (May 16, 1977), 27-29. Reasons for being interviewed by David Frost.

2493. "Why the Tapes Are Needed." New Republic, CLXX (February 23, 1974), 7-9. To prove or disprove the many allegations surrounding the case.

2494. "Why They Did What They Did." Nation, CCXVI (June 11, 1973), 738-740. Enumerates political motivations for the "plumbers" and the cover-up.

2495. "Why Those Tapes Were Made." Time, CIII (April 22, 1974), 14-15. To guard Nixon's future reputation.

2496. Wicker, Tom. "Mr. Nixon Takes a Whitewash: Reprinted from the New York Times, October 23, 1973." Congressional Record, CXX (October 24, 1973), 34965-34966. Comments on the Cox dismissal.

2497. _____. "Reflections of Ruckelshaus--Inside Report on the FBI: Reprinted from New York Times Magazine, August 19, 1973." In: U.S. Congress, Senate, Committee on the Judiciary. <u>Nomination of William D. Ruckelshaus to Be Deputy Attorney General: Hearings</u>. 93rd Cong., 1st sess. Washington, D.C.: U.S. Government Printing Office, 1973. pp. 51-61. Reflections by Ruckelshaus on his brief duty as Interim FBI Director between the death of J. Edgar Hoover and the nomination of L. Patrick Gray, 3rd.

2498. _____. "A Step Short of Impeachment: Reprinted from the <u>New York Times</u>, March 5, 1974." <u>Congressional Record</u>, CXX (March 27, 1974), 8567-8568. Reports on the idea of having a special presidential election.

2499. Wiedrich, Bob. "Nixon's Retreat Behind the Walls: Reprinted from the <u>Chicago Tribune</u>, August 8, 1974." <u>Congressional Record</u>, CXX (August 8, 1974), 27656-27657. The President's isolation in the face of certain impeachment.

2500. Wieghart, James. "FBI Chief to Tell of Burning Hunt File--Learns Folders Held Fake Government Cables: Reprinted from the <u>New York Daily News</u>, April 27, 1973." In: Book IV, Part III of U.S. Congress, House, Committee on the Judiciary. <u>Statement of Information: Hearings</u>. 93rd Cong., 2nd sess. Washington, D.C.: U.S. Government Printing Office, 1974. p. 1617. The actions of L. Patrick Gray.

2501. Wiener, Jon. "Tocqueville, Marx, Weber, Nixon: Watergate in Theory." <u>Dissent</u>, XXIII (Spring 1976), 171-180. How the scandal would appear in the theories of the first three men named.

2502. Wigdor, David and Alexandra. "The Future of Presidential Papers." In: Harold C. Relyea, ed. <u>The Presidency and Information Policy</u>. New York: Center for the Study of the Presidency, 1981. pp. 92-101. Includes some history of the Nixon-GSA deal of late 1974.

2503. Will, George F. "Capitol Issues: Newspaper Coverage of Watergate." <u>National Review</u>, XXVI (February 15, 1974), 190. Critical of the massive interest of the press in the scandal.

2504. _____. "For Congress--A 'Make or Break' Test: Reprinted from the <u>Washington Post</u>, May 28, 1974." <u>Congressional Record</u>, CXX (June 3, 1974), 17317. Reasons for the impeachment rush.

2505. _____. "Goal Line Stand: Nixon's Battle to Hold Public Opinion." <u>National Review</u>, XXV (December 21, 1973), 1400. "Operation Candor."

2506. _____. "Richard Nixon's Seventh Crisis." New York Times Magazine (July 8, 1973), 7+. Watergate compared to the crises in the President's book, Six Crises.

2507. _____. "Sauerkraut Ice Cream." National Review, XXV (July 6, 1973), 726. Contends various statements on Watergate are as indigestible as sauerkraut ice cream.

2508. _____. "Stay Tuned." National Review, XXV (November 9, 1973), 1228. Comments on the dismissal of Archibald Cox.

2509. _____. "Unraveling." National Review, XXV (May 11, 1973), 514. Praises Washington Post for uncovering the scandal.

2510. "Will They Pick the Carcass?" Newsweek, LXXXIV (September 9, 1974), 19-21. The continuing work of the Watergate Special Prosecution Force.

2511. Williams, D. A. "Hunt's Tales of Watergate." Newsweek, LXXXIX (March 7, 1977), 22. Comments on the recollections of the Watergate burglar.

2512. Wills, Garry. "Nixon Deserves Watergate: Reprinted from the Washington Post, September 18, 1972." Congressional Record, CXVIII (September 19, 1972), 31364. Thoughts on the allegations in light of the election.

2513. Wilson, Gerald L. "The Strategy of Explanation: Richard M. Nixon's August 8, 1974 Resignation Speech." Communication Quarterly, XXIV (Summer 1976), 14-20. An analysis of the President's speech in which he claimed the loss of political support rather than wrongdoing was the reason for his quitting.

2514. Wilson, Richard. "Archibald Cox and Impeachment: Reprinted from the Houston Post, January 31, 1974." Congressional Record, CXX (February 5, 1974), 2241-2242. Views of the former Special Prosecutor.

2515. _____. "House Is Far Cry from Grand Jury: Reprinted from the Washington Star-News, April 1, 1974." Congressional Record, CXX (April 3, 1974), 9682. Reports that the House Judiciary Committee is not the same as the Watergate Grand Jury.

2516. _____. "Impeachment Efforts Are on Shaky Ground: Reprinted from the San Diego Union, February 18, 1974." Congressional Record, CXX (March 27, 1974), 8566. The complicated start of the House Judiciary Committee inquiry.

2517. _____. "No Case Yet for Impeachment: Reprinted from the Washington Evening Star, October 29, 1973." Congressional Record, CXIX (November 1, 1973), 35683. Despite the Cox dismissal.

2518. _____. "Why Professor Cox Had to Go: Reprinted from the Washington Evening Star, October 27, 1973." Congressional Record, CXIX (November 1, 1973), 35683. Because he was perceived to be unreasonable in his tape demands.

2519. Winter, Robert K., Jr. Watergate and the Law. Washington, D.C.: American Enterprise Institute for Public Policy Research, 1974. 85p. The subtitle explains the content: "Political Campaigns and Presidential Power."

2520. Winter, Ruth. "Scientists Analyze the Voices of Nixon, Haldeman, Ehrlichman, and Dean." Science Digest, LXXXIX (June 1976), 62-68. A study of the Watergate tapes to learn who was telling the truth.

2521. Wise, David. The American Police State: The Government Against the People. New York: Random House, 1976. 437p. Veteran student of intelligence matters Wise examines the various wrongdoings by U.S. intelligence and federal police agencies during the Nixon administrations, paying special attention to the work of the FBI and the "plumbers"; the CIA connection is explored on pp. 226-256.

2522. _____. "Colby of CIA, CIA of Colby." New York Times Magazine (July 1, 1973), 8-9+. The Deputy Director of CIA who testified before the Ervin panel.

2523. _____. "The Defending of the President." New York Times Magazine (May 26, 1974), 10-11+. The work of the President's special counsels, e.g. James D. St. Clair.

2524. _____. "The Kissinger Wiretaps." New Times, VII (October 29, 1976), 25-28, 30-34, 70-72. Finds the Secretary of State did order them placed on his NSC officials.

2525. _____. The Politics of Lying: Government Deception, Secrecy, and Power. New York: Random House, 1973. 415p. An attack on government deception and secrecy condoned by the Nixon administration; stresses that they were caused by changes in the American character since World War II as reflected in Nixon and his "palace guard."

2526. _____. "The President and the Press." Atlantic, CCXXXI (April 1973), 55-64. A look at the long-standing feud between the Nixon White House and the news media, especially since the beginning of Watergate.

2527. Wise, Helen D. What Do We Tell the Children?: Watergate and the Future of Our Country. New York: Braziller, 1974. 116p. The then-president of the National Education Association gives parents and teachers a synopsis of the scandal and discusses lessons which might be drawn from it in a most unreadable fashion. Many characters are not identified and the work lacks documentation of any kind for statements quoted. Still, it may at one time have been useful for parents who had to explain the Watergate mess to their kids, many of whom are now in college and mostly unconcerned with the affair.

2528. Witcover, Jules. "How Well Does the White House Press Perform?" Columbia Journalism Review, XII (November-December 1973), 39-43. Witcover's analysis was written at the peak period of public interest in the case and offers sobering reflections on the press's role in promoting that interest.

2529. "With Thanks to Frank Wills." Ebony, XXIII (June 1973), 94-95. Calls attention to the security guard who found the tape over the door in the Watergate and called in police.

2530. "Witness Richard Nixon Is Excused." Time, CIV (December 16, 1974), 27-28. Evidence in the Watergate cover-up trial.

2531. "Witness to Watergate: TV Brings It All Home." Broadcasting, LXXXIV (May 21, 1973), 20-21. Televising the Ervin Committee hearings.

2532. "Witnesses to a Spreading Stain." Time, CII (August 20, 1973), 14-15. Final Ervin panel testimony by Gray, Kleindienst, and Petersen, all of whom mention White House interference in the investigation and prosecution of the case.

2533. Wolfe, Burton H. The Devil and Dr. Noxin. San Francisco, Calif.: Wild West Press, 1973. 218p. An original satirical play modeled on Marlowe's Faust.

2534. Woll, Peter. "Executive Immunity from the Judicial Process." In: his Constitutional Law: Cases and Comments. Englewood Cliffs, N.J.: Prentice-Hall, 1981. pp. 152-162. The most recent interpretation, which contains some references to President Nixon's relations with the courts during the Watergate crisis.

2535. Woodcock, George. "Weimar and Watergate." Canadian Forum, LIV (May-June 1974), 6-10. A comparison of Germany before Hitler with the U.S. under Nixon during and before Watergate.

2536. "Woodstein Meets 'Deep Throat': The Work of Reporters Carl Bernstein and Bob Woodward." Time, CIII (April 22, 1974), 55+. A review of the investigative reporting on Watergate by the two noted Washington Post correspondents.

2537. Woodstone, Art. The Head of Richard Nixon. New York: Popular Library, 1976. 286p. A British author links facts, quotes, and his own speculations together to portray Nixon as a "neurologically compulsive psychological reactionary whose hostilities menace himself and the world." This extreme polemic and poor example of pseudopsychology was first published in 1972 as a 248-page hardback by St. Martin's Press, New York.

2537a. Woodward, Comer Van. Responses of Presidents to Charges of Misconduct. New York: Dell Publishing Co., 1974. 401p. A paperback reprint of a study undertaken for the House Judiciary Committee's impeachment inquiry staff with an added introduction by Woodward; primarily an historical review.

2538. Woodward, Robert U. ("Bob"). "O'Brien Sues GOP Campaign--Lays Blame for Bugging on White House: Reprinted from the Washington Post, June 21, 1972." In: Book II of U.S. Congress, House, Committee on the Judiciary. Statement of Information: Hearings. 93rd Cong., 2nd sess. Washington, D.C.: U.S. Government Printing Office, 1974. pp. 302-304. Reports the reactions of the chairman of the Democratic National Committee, whose office was broken into.

2539. _____. "Watergate on the Record--Sort Of: An Interview." Time, CVII (May 3, 1976), 17. Woodward suggests that many questions are yet to be fully answered.

2540. _____ and Carl Bernstein. "Ervin Insists Aides Testify Under Oath: Reprinted from the Washington Post, April 3, 1973." In: Book IV, Part I of U.S. Congress, House, Committee on the Judiciary. Statement of Information: Hearings. 93rd Cong., 2nd sess. Washington, D.C.: U.S. Government Printing Office, 1974. pp. 498-500. The chairman of the Senate Select Committee on Presidential Campaign Activities sets the ground rules for testimony at the so-called 1973 "Watergate hearings."

2541. _____. The Final Days. New York: Simon and Schuster, 1976. 476p. Excerpted in Newsweek, LXXXVII (April 5-12, 1976), 39-46+, 53-60+, and reprinted the same year in a 529-page paperback edition by the New York firm of Avon Books. The two famed Washington Post reporters here give us their sequel to the earlier All the President's Men (cited above under Bernstein and

Woodward). The massive tome is divided into two parts: first, a look at people and events of Watergate from Dean's firing on April 30, 1973 to late July 1974; the second, an extremely detailed examination of the last two weeks--the final days--of the Nixon presidency. This book was a blockbuster best-seller and perhaps the most controversial of the so-called "instant histories" to emerge from Watergate. The embattled President is shown to have been drinking heavily, in a suicidal mood, and on the brink of mental disintegration. His wife was seen as imbibing the drink while his aides and defense attorneys, especially Haig and St. Clair, were seen maneuvering in a variety of last-ditch efforts to save the Oval Office, their boss, and their hides. Lies are exposed and gossip is repeated. Perhaps the most controversial passage, later addressed by both Nixon and Kissinger in their memoirs (cited above) has to do with the two men kneeling together in silent prayer on the eve of the President's resignation. The Woodward/Bernstein account needs to be employed in conjunction with all the post-1976 memoirs and biographies noted above, but will remain one of the most intimate accounts of the scandal for years to come.

2542. _____. "Ford Disputed on Events Preceding Nixon Pardon: Reprinted from the Washington Post, December 18, 1975." Congressional Record, CXXII (September 30, 1976), 34287-34288. Exposes some of the lingering doubt existing even after the President testified before a Congressional committee that no deal had been made for a pardon.

2543. _____. "History on the Run: An Interview." Library Journal, CI (May 1, 1976), 1089-1095. An interview granted on publication of their The Final Days, which explains their observations and reporting methods.

2544. _____. "Interview." Mademoiselle, LXXIX (August 1974), 300-301. Another set of comments on their Watergate experiences.

2545. _____. "McCord Takes Fifth 20 Times--Effort to Gain Immunity Seen: Reprinted from the Washington Post, March 30, 1973." In: Book IV, Part I of U.S. Congress, House, Committee on the Judiciary. Statement of Information: Hearings. 93rd Cong., 2nd sess. Washington, D.C.: U.S. Government Printing Office, 1974. pp. 488-489. On Watergate burglar James McCord's refusal to cooperate with investigators.

2546. _____. "Mitchell Is Linked to Bugging Plans: Reprinted from the Washington Post, March 29, 1973." In: Book IV, Part I of U.S. Congress, House, Committee on the

Judiciary. Statement of Information: Hearings. 93rd Cong., 2nd sess. Washington, D.C.: U.S. Government Printing Office, 1974. pp. 432-433. CREEP Director John N. Mitchell's involvement in plans for the Watergate break-in.

2547. _____. "Report Critical of Stans--Secret Fund Shift Known, Probe Likely: Reprinted from the Washington Post, September 13, 1972." Congressional Record, CXX (August 7, 1974), 22271-22272. Maurice Stans, director of the Finance Committee to Reelect the President, and the laundering of campaign contributions.

2548. _____. "Stans Denies GOP Money Funded Watergate Break-in: Reprinted from the Washington Post, August 9, 1972." Congressional Record, CXIX (August 11, 1972), 27890.27891. On the use of laundered funds to pay for the "plumbers'" equipment and personnel.

2549. _____ and E. J. Bachinski. "White House Consultant Tied to Bugging Figure: Reprinted from the Washington Post, June 20, 1972." In: Book II of U.S. Congress, House, Committee on the Judiciary. Statement of Information: Hearings. 93rd Cong., 2nd sess. Washington, D.C.: U.S. Government Printing Office, 1974. pp. 232-233. The relationship between Charles Colson and Howard Hunt.

2550. _____ and Scott Armstrong. The Brethren: Inside the Supreme Court. New York: Simon and Schuster, 1979. 467p. A lengthy history of the modern Supreme Court; the court's hearing of United States v. Nixon is covered on pp. 287-347.

2551. _____. "The Nixon Tapes Conspiracy." Newsweek, XCIV (December 10, 1979), 86-87. An excerpt from the last citation.

2552. No entry.

2553. "The World on Watergate." Newsweek, LXXXIV (August 12, 1974), 40. A sampling of foreign editorial opinion.

2554. "Would You Believe Judiciary's Leaks?: Reprinted from the New York Times, June 20, 1974." Congressional Record, CXX (June 20, 1974), 20349. An editorial concerning unauthorized leaks.

2555. Wright, Frank. "Stans' Tactics Shocked GOP Fund Raisers: Reprinted from the Minneapolis Tribune, November 28, 1973." Congressional Record, CXIX (November 28, 1973), 38303-38304. Concerns the collection of illegal contributions and methods for securing contributions from big business.

2556. Wright, Gerald C., Jr. "Constituency Response to Congressional Behavior: The Impact of the House Judiciary Committee Impeachment Votes." Western Political Quarterly, XXX (September 1977), 401-410. Analyzes the impact of Congressmen's votes on their home districts and the opinions of people in those districts on the decisions of their representatives.

2557. Yap, Diosdado M., ed. Know Your Congress, 1973 and 1974. 2 vols. Washington, D.C.: Capital Publications, 1973-1974. Lists members, staffs, and committees; useful for information on who in Congress was involved in dealing with the various aspects of the Watergate case.

2558. Yoder, Edwin M., Jr. "Shell-Shock--Over-Reacting to the Pardon: Reprinted from the Greensboro [North Carolina] Daily News, September 24, 1974." Congressional Record, CXX (September 24, 1974), 32512. A look at the public's reaction to the Nixon pardon.

2559. Zeisel, Hans. "The Jury Selection in the Mitchell-Stans Conspiracy Trial." American Bar Foundation Research Journal, no. 1976 (Spring 1976), 151-174. A review of the process whereby jurors were chosen.

2560. "Zero Defect: The White House." New Republic, CLXIX (September 1, 1973), 7-9. Another look at the role of Chuck Colson.

2561. Ziegler, Ronald L. "Hypocrisy in Action: Ron Ziegler's Misleading Statements on Watergate." Commonweal, XCVIII (September 21, 1973), 490. An analysis of the White House press secretary's various statements and comments on the events of the crisis to date.

2562. _____. "Watergate Special Prosecution Force and Department of Justice: Remarks of Press Secretary." Weekly Compilation of Presidential Documents, IX (October 29, 1973), 1271-1272. Ziegler's comments on the Cox dismissal.

2563. Zimmer, Troy A. "The Impact of Watergate on the Public's Trust in People and Confidence in the Mass Media." Social Science Quarterly, LIX (March 1979), 743-751. The crisis brought questions on both as to motives and performance.

2564. Zimmerman, Fred L. "Taking a Look at 'Operation Candor': Reprinted from the Wall Street Journal, December 7, 1973." Congressional Record, CXIX (December 7, 1973), 40323-40324. An examination of the Nixon Administration's so-called effort to be more open and forthright on Watergate.

2565. Zinner, Paul E. "How the Kremlin Covered-up Watergate: A Study in Self Protection." New Leader, LVII (October 28, 1974), 12-13. Moscow papers and radio said little about the crisis in order to keep the Russian people from wondering about Soviet leaders and their possible misdeeds.

THE SOUNDS OF WATERGATE: RECORDS, VIDEO- AND AUDIO-TAPE RECORDINGS

Introduction: Although millions of words poured out over the public air waves during the Watergate crisis, they have long since been quieted by history. Fortunately, some effort was made at the time, or in the years just after, to provide a sound record of the affair, in discussions, readings of the transcripts, actual speeches, and some humor. One college even undertook to video-tape significant sections of the crisis while it was unfolding. To provide access to some of these materials, those we have uncovered are all entered here in this section, "the sounds of Watergate."

Burns, Jack, Avery Schreiber, and Ann Elder. The Watergate Comedy Hour. Little David, 1976. (LD 1010). 33 1/3 rpm, stereo disc, 34 min. An edited version of the sound recording issued in 1973 as Hidden Records ST11202, this is a series of satirical skits performed by the authors, et al., including Fannie Flagg. Contents: Watergate Comedy Hour.--The Plan--The Break-in--Special Investigator--The Investigation--Youth Wants to Know--The Meeting--Ron Ziegler Meets the Press--The Reverend and the President--The President's Prayer.

Burns, James MacGregor and Jack W. Peltason. Resurrection of the Party System Through Control of Campaign Financing. Center for the Study of Democratic Institutions, 1976. (Tape 674; Constitutional Principles: Their Validity and Vitality Today, no. 12). 1 reel, 3 3/4 lps, 1/2-track, mono, 5-inch tape recording, 31 min., 48 sec. Also issued as a 7 1/2 lps full-track tape and as a cassette. James M. Burns and Jack W. Peltason discuss the rejuvenation of the party system and the role of campaign financing, reformed from the Watergate evils, in that process. Edited from a post-conference meeting held by the Center for the Study of Democratic Institutions, December 9-14, 1973.

Cleveland, Harlan, et al. The National Security Obsession. Center for the Study of Democratic Institutions, 1976. (Tape 669; Constitutional Principles: Their Validity and Vitality Today, no. 7). 1 reel, 3 3/4 lps, 1/2-track, mono, 5-in. tape recording, 1 hr., 14 min., 31 sec. Also issued as a 7 1/2 lps full-track tape and as a cassette. Cleveland and others discuss national security in relation to some of the problems involved in Watergate, and consider the concept of security and its effective limits. Edited from the proceedings of a conference held for the Center for the Study of Democratic Institutions, December 9-14, 1973.

Ex-President Nixon Addresses the Nation Series. Antioch Video, 1980. 1/2-inch videotape, color, sound, 30-40 min. Available from the Communications Study Center of Antioch College, Yellow Springs, Ohio. Titles of interest here include: First Watergate Speech, June 1973; Press Conference, October 26, 1973; Press Conference, March 19, 1974--In Houston; The Resignation Process: The Events and News Building Toward Resignation (covers events from August 6 through Ford's swearing-in); Second Watergate Speech, August 15, 1973.

Hurst, James W. and Robert M. Hutchins. Separation of Powers: A Post-Watergate Perspective. Center for the Study of Democratic Institutions, 1976. (Tape 671; Constitutional Principles: Their Validity and Vitality Today, no. 9). 1 reel, 3 3/4 lps, 1/2-track, mono, 5-in. tape recording, 59 min., 35 sec. Also issued as a 7 1/2 lps full-track tape and as a cassette. Hurst and Hutchins discuss the separation of powers and the allocations of powers among the principal lawmaking agencies of the government; some mention of Watergate. Edited from the proceedings of a conference held for the Center for the Study of Democratic Institutions, December 9-14, 1973.

Lasch, Christopher, et al. Constitutional Implications of Watergate: A Summing Up. Center for the Study of Democratic Institutions, 1976. (Tape 673; Constitutional Principles: Their Validity and Vitality Today, no. 11). 1 reel, 3 3/4 lps, 1/2-track, mono, 5-in. tape recording, 48 min., 46 sec. Also issued as a 7 1/2 lps full track tape and as a cassette. A group discussion in which the participants summarize, in a final session, specific constitutional remedies presented at the December 9-14, 1973 conference from which this recording was edited.

_____. The Modern Presidency: How You Play the Game. Center for the Study of Democratic Institutions, 1976. (Tape 665; Constitutional Principles: Their Validity and Vitality Today, no. 3). 1 reel, 3 3/4 lps, 1/2-track, mono, 5-in. tape recording, 49 min., 25 sec. Also issued as a 7 1/2 lps full track tape and as a cassette. Lasch, et al., discuss the presidency in relation to some of the constitutional issues and problems involved in Watergate, and examine the conditions and values that led to abuses and excesses of executive power. Edited from the proceedings of a conference held for the Center for the Study of Democratic Institutions, December 9-14, 1973.

Molner, Don, comp. Watergate. Folkways, 1973. (FD 5551-5553). 33 1/3 disc, various times. Three records taken principally from the Ervin Committee hearings; descriptive notes inserted into each slipcase. Contents: No. 1, The Break-in; No. 2, The Testimony of Jeb Stuart Magruder: A Question of Ethics; No. 3, "I Hope the President Is Forgiven": John W. Dean, III, Testifies.

Mondale, Walter F., et al. American Democracy in the 1970's.

Center for the Study of Democratic Institutions, 1975. (Tapes 628-629). 2 reels, 3 3/4 lps, 1/2-track, mono, 5-inch tape recordings, 54 min., 9 sec. and 45 min., 54 sec. Also issued in two cassettes. Senator Mondale, et al., discuss Watergate at a 1974 symposium and examine the extent to which the Nixon presidency imperiled the balance of power between government branches.

Nixon, Richard M. The Checkers Speech, The Resignation Speech. Lava Mt., 1974. (RMN 235). 33 1/3, stereo, disc. Presents these two speeches exactly as heard when given originally. Includes a song, "The Day Man Flew," performed by Juanteen Folks and Alix Pascal.

———. Resignation of a President--August 8, 1974. Capitol Records, 1974. (SJ 11350). 33 1/3 disc, 15 min., 16 sec. and 17 min., 48 sec. Nixon's resignation and White House farewell speeches; descriptive notes are provided on the slipcase.

The Nixon Years. Pioneer Audio Lab, 1976. 1 reel, 7 1/2 lps. mono, 7-in. tape recording, 60 min. Presents recorded instances from Nixon's career from Checkers in 1952 through his 1974 resignation as president; includes comments and testimony by various people.

The Tapes: Submission of Recorded Presidential Conversations to the Committee of the Judiciary of the House of Representatives. Historical Record Presentations Co. of Tulsa, 1974. (HRS 3025). 2, 33 1/3 stereo discs. or 2 cassettes. A dramatization of excerpts from the tapes as recorded between September 15, 1972 and April 30, 1973; various readers.

The Watergate Primer. Waterfall Records, 1973. (WFL 66). 2, 33 1/3 stereo discs. Recording of a radio show originally produced on Boston's WBCN and broadcast on May 13, 1973; consists of narration, excerpts from statements of Watergate participants, sound effects, and satirical songs.

The Watergate Tapes--A Re-Creation. Voice Over Books, 1974. (Cassette 00974). 1 stereo cassette, 69 min. Highlights of Nixon's key transcripts, narrated by Bernard Elsmann and read by Will Jordan and Jerry Orbach.

Wheeler, John H., Herbert Alexander, and Harry S. Ashmore. The Impact of Watergate on the Electoral Process. Center for the Study of Democratic Institutions, 1976. (Tape 672; Constitutional Principles: Their Validity and Vitality Today, no. 10). 1 reel, 3 3/4 lps, 1/2-track, mono, 5-inch. tape recording, 58 min., 42 sec. Also issued as a 7 1/2 lps full track tape and as a cassette. Focuses on the impact of Watergate on the electoral process with discussions of deficiencies in the Constitution which led to the excesses. Edited from the proceedings of a conference held for the Center for the Study of Democratic Institutions, December 9-14, 1973.

Winter, Ralph K., Jr., et al. Watergate, the Courts, and Impeachment. American Enterprise Institute for Public Policy Research, 1974. 1 cassette, 60 min. A discussion on the topic recorded on March 14, 1974.

APPENDIX

Magazines and Journals Containing at Least One Article Relative to This Bibliography

Across the Board
Administration and Society
Air Progress
Akron Law Review
Alternative
America
American Archivist
American Bar Association Journal
American Bar Foundation Research Journal
American Federationist
American Journal of Political Science
American Lawyer
American Opinion
American Political Science Proceedings
American Political Science Review
American Politics Quarterly
American Psychologist
American Scholar
American Spectator
Annals of the American Academy of Political and Social Science
Argosy
Armed Forces and Society
Armed Forces Journal International
ASNE Bulletin
Atlanta
Atlantic
Atlas
Aviation Week and Space Technology

Bibliographic Society of America Papers
Biographical News
Black Scholar
Book Digest
Boston
Boston University Law Review
Broadcasting
Bureaucrat
Business Economics
Business Week

C.Q. Weekly Report
California Bar Journal
Canadian Forum
Capital University Law Review
Case and Comment
Case Western Reserve Law Review
Catholic University Law Review
Center Magazine
Center Report
Central States Speech Journal
Chicago Tribune Magazine
Christian Century
Christianity and Crisis
Christianity Today
Chronicle of Higher Education
Civil Liberties Review
Coast
Columbia Journalism Review
Columbia Law Review
Commentary
Commonweal
Communication Research
Communications Quarterly

Computers and Automation
Congressional Record
Connecticut Law Review
Contemporary Politics
Contemporary Review
Criminal Law Bulletin
Cumberland Law Review
Current
Current History

DePaul Law Review
Detroit
Duke Law Journal
Dunn's

Ebony
Editor and Publisher
Emory Law Journal
Encounter
Esquire
ETC
Experimental Study of Politics

Federal Communications Bar Journal
Focus/Midwest
Forbes
Fordham Law Review
Foreign Affairs
Fortune
Freedomways

Gallup Opinion Index
Georgetown Law Journal
Gold Coast Pictorial
Good Housekeeping
Grassroots Editor

Harper's
Harvard Journal of Legislation
Harvard Law Review
History of Childhood Quarterly

Illinois Bar Journal
Indiana Law Review
Inquiry
Intellect

International Socialist Review

Journal of Broadcasting
Journal of Communications
Journal of Personnel and Social Psychology
Journal of Politics
Journal of Psychohistory
Journal of Social Issues
Journal of Social Psychology
Journalism Quarterly

Kapitalistate

Ladies Home Journal
Law Library Journal
Library Journal
Life
Lithopinion
Los Angeles
Loyola Law Review
Loyola of Los Angeles Law Review

McCalls
Macleans
Mademoiselle
Manuscripts
Maryland Law Review
Midwest Quarterly
Mississippi Law Journal
Modern Age
Montana Journalism Review
Monthly Review
More
Ms.

Nation
National Civic Review
National Journal
National Review
New Leader
New Republic
New Statesman and Nation
New Times
New York Magazine
New York Review of Books
New York State Bar Association

Journal
New York Times Biographical
 Service
New York Times Magazine
New Yorker
New West
Newsweek
Nieman Reports
North Carolina Central Law
 Journal
North Carolina Law Review

Office
Ohio State Law Journal
Oklahoma Bar Association
 Journal
Oklahoma Law Review
Oregon Law Review

Pacific Sociological Review
Parade Magazine
Penthouse
People
Pepperdine Law Review
Playboy
Political Psychology
Political Science
Political Science Quarterly
Political Studies
Present Tense
Presidential Studies Quarterly
Progressive
Publisher's Weekly
Psychoanalytic Quarterly
Psychoanalytic Review
Psychology Today
Public Finance Quarterly
Public Interest
Public Opinion Quarterly

Quill

Ramparts
Reader's Digest
Record of the Association of
 the Bar of the City of New
 York
Redbook
Review of Politics

Ripon Quarterly
Rolling Stone
RTNDA Communicator
Rutgers Law Review

St. John's Law Review
San Diego Magazine
Saturday Review
Saturday Review of Literature
Saturday Review World
Science
Science Digest
Science News
Senior Scholastic
Seton Hall Law Review
Simulations and Games
Social Research
Social Science Quarterly
Society
Sociometry
South Atlantic Quarterly
Southern California Law Review
Southern Speech Communication
 Journal
Southwestern Law Journal
Speech Monographs
Stanford Law Journal
Studies in Contemporary Com-
 munism

Technology Review
Temple Law Quarterly
Texas Monthly
Theology Today
Time
Today's Education
Today's Health
Today's Speech
Trial
TV Guide

UCLA Law Review
U.S. News and World Report
University of Colorado Law Re-
 view
University of Missouri-Kansas
 City Law Review
University of Pennsylvania Law
 Review
University of Toledo Law Review

University of Toronto Law
  Journal
Utah Law Review

Virginia Quarterly Review
Vital Speeches
Vogue

Washington Journalism Review
Washington Magazine
Washington Monthly

Washington Post Potomac Magazine
Washingtonian
Weekly Compilation of Presidential Documents
Western Political Quarterly
World Studies
World Today

Yale Law Journal
Youth and Society

SUBJECT INDEX

ABC News 72
Abstracts and Indexes 27-61
Agnew, Spiro T. 87-89, 413, 758, 842, 3227
Aiken, George T. 90
Alch, Gerald 2024
American Airlines 2437
Anderson, Jack 126-135, 407, 854, 950-952, 1080, 1208-1210, 1304; see also Beard, Dita; ITT; Liddy, G. Gordon
Andrews, John K., Jr. 137
Anniversaries see Watergate Anniversaries
Annuals and Dictionaries 62-71
Apple, R. W., Jr. 1522; see also New York Times
Armstrong, C. Scott 1807
Associated Milk Producers, Inc. see Milk Fund Scandal
Associated Press 1072, 1284; see also Press coverage of Watergate events

Babcock, Tim M. 2027; see also Campaign contributions and financing
Baker, Howard H., Jr. 173-174, 532, 667, 670; see also U.S. Congress, Senate, Select Committee on Presidential Campaign Activities
Baldwin, Alfred C., 3rd 178, 1267, 2024, 2197-2200, 2369; statements and testimony 178, 883
Barker, Bernard 169-170, 230, 232, 418, 1143, 1225, 1523, 1541, 1551, 1882, 2197-2200, 2410; statements and testimony 191, 883, 2024; see also "Plumbers"; Watergate Break-in
Beard, Dita 126, 129-132, 135, 204, 291, 703, 951-952, 1036, 1407, 1581-1583, 1586-1588, 1671, 1843, 1931, 2261; see

also Anderson, Jack; ITT Scandal
Bennett, Robert F. 1674
Ben-Veniste, Richard 218
Bernstein, Carl 99, 212, 234, 299, 373, 560, 618, 717, 835, 854, 888, 1176, 1192, 1239, 1376, 1674, 2012, 2026, 2442, 2536; see also Press coverage of Watergate events; Washington Post; Woodward, Robert U. ("Bob")
Bibliographies 1-26
Bork, Robert H. 281, 653, 1893, 2180; see also Cox, Archibald, dismissal of
Brinkley, David 304
Brinkley, Jack 1067
Brown, Edmund G., Jr. 286
Buchanan, Patrick 321-322, 392, 842, 2259
Buckley, James L. 324, 819
"Bugs" see Kissinger, Henry; Watergate Break-in; Wiretapping
Butterfield, Alexander P. 98, 261, 557, 1213, 1491, 1928a, 1964, 2150; see also Tapes, Revelation of
Buzhardt, J. Fred 550, 605, 1478, 1574; see also Nixon, Richard M., Defense of
Byrne, W. Matthew, Jr. 138, 1542

Campaign contributions and financing 85, 112, 140, 153, 168, 172, 191a, 205, 213, 229, 235, 245, 248, 278, 286-290, 364, 381-382, 418, 504, 507, 533, 562, 576, 588, 613-614, 648, 672, 713, 731-732, 797, 912, 925, 948-949, 951-952, 1010, 1016-1030, 1032-1034, 1036-1038, 1109, 1131, 1161, 1226-1227, 1251, 1275-1280, 1298, 1350, 1352-1360, 1368-1370, 1374, 1378, 1394, 1544-1545, 1561, 1581-1591, 1634, 1641, 1643, 1650, 1652, 1654, 1669, 1671-1672, 1742-

319

Index   320

1744, 1783, 1796, 1800, 1891, 1902, 1929, 1931, 1938, 1970-1971, 2009, 2022, 2027, 2035, 2038, 2090, 2144-2145, 2197-2200, 2272, 2410, 2437, 2439, 2452, 2465, 2491, 2519, 2547-2548, 2555; see also Committee to Re-elect the President; Hughes, Howard; ITT Scandal; Kalmbach, Herbert; Milk Fund Scandal; Mitchell, John N.; Rebozo, Charles ("Bebe"); Smith, C. Arnold; Stans, Maurice

Campaign disruptions 111, 149, 191a, 207, 233, 235-236, 354, 512, 584, 598, 660, 828, 920, 1042, 1208-1210, 1227, 1247, 1275-1280, 1293-1294, 1352-1360, 1368, 1611, 1621, 1635, 1651, 1874-1875, 2013, 2050-2051, 2069, 2197-2200, 2295, 2414, 2471-2472, 2519; see also Committee to Re-elect the President; Liddy, G. Gordon; Segretti, Donald

Caulfield, Jack 2024

CBS News 159, 321, 792, 854-856, 906, 1006, 1284, 1322, 1794; see also Rather, Dan; Schorr, Daniel; Television coverage of Watergate events

Central Intelligence Agency 113, 145, 174, 252, 259, 414, 429-430, 458, 497, 562, 593, 629, 767, 858, 892, 904, 934, 953-957, 1213, 1241, 1300, 1347, 1539, 1548, 1639, 1642, 1678, 1680, 1712, 1810, 1851-1852, 1961, 1964, 2018-2021, 2110-2111, 2159, 2194, 2197-2200, 2263, 2294, 2457, 2521-2525; see also Colby, William; Helms, Richard; Hunt, E. Howard; "Plumbers"; Watergate Break-in; Watergate Break-in, cover-up; Watergate investigation

Chapin, Dwight 616, 782, 2232-2233, 2312

Chronologies 118, 398, 447, 583, 994, 1126, 1695, 2029, 2058, 2083, 2108, 2237, 2306-2308, 2314

CIA see Central Intelligence Agency

Clawson, Kenneth 655, 1219

Colby, William E. 414-415, 2522; statements and testimony 415; see also Central Intelligence Agency

Colson, Charles W. ("Chuck") 264, 326, 339, 391, 419-430, 519, 755, 858, 955, 1001, 1082, 1254, 1826, 1987, 1995, 1999, 2079, 2197-2200, 2409, 2468, 2478, 2549, 2560; statements and testimony 421-422, 424, 1214, 2150, 2197, 2199; see also "Plumbers"; Watergate Break-in, cover-up

Committee to Re-elect the President 111, 235-236, 239, 245, 263, 278, 358, 418, 505, 648, 920, 945, 1109, 1166, 1171, 1208-1210, 1247, 1251, 1269, 1275-1280, 1312, 1320, 1352-1360, 1369-1370, 1536, 1552, 1561, 1621, 1660, 1800, 1970-1971, 2022, 2143-2144, 2197-2200, 2354, 2388, 2439, 2452, 2462; see also Campaign contributions and financing; Campaign disruptions; Liddy, G. Gordon; Magruder, Jeb Stuart; Mitchell, John N.; Stans, Maurice

Congressional opinion on Watergate see Public opinion on Watergate; Republican Party

Connally, John see Milk Fund Scandal

Constitutional aspects of Watergate see Executive privilege; Impeachment grounds and process; United States v. Richard M. Nixon

Contributions see Campaign contributions and financing

Conyers, John, Jr. 452-453

Cox, Archibald 147, 180, 214, 218, 438, 532, 605, 666, 722, 1101, 1133, 1154, 1167, 1345, 1493, 1498, 1592, 1637, 1776, 1780, 2328, 2362, 2467, 2514; dismissal as Special Prosecutor 86, 195, 228, 243, 281, 320, 375, 442, 487, 498-502, 605-608, 644, 653, 664, 685, 723-724, 827, 852-853, 973, 1011, 1014, 1167, 1193, 1197-1198, 1201, 1236, 1307-1308, 1339, 1399, 1517, 1577, 1683, 1763, 1773, 1775, 1777-1779, 1887, 1893-1894, 1898, 1934, 2098, 2105, 2189, 2265, 2278, 2321, 2362, 2496, 2508, 2518, 2562; statements 486-496; see also Tapes, Subpoena of

CREEP see Committee to Re-elect the President

Cushman, Robert E. 893

Dash, Samuel 532, 674, 899-900, 1844; see also U.S. Congress, Senate, Select Committee on Presidential Campaign Activities
Dean, John W., 3rd 136, 141, 237-238, 352, 468, 535-537, 539, 541, 544, 548-549, 569, 609, 611, 628, 636, 681, 687, 785, 806, 858, 899-900, 902, 909, 932, 935, 1005, 1041, 1062, 1066, 1100, 1111, 1238, 1286, 1299, 1421, 1473, 1516, 1519, 1614, 1619, 1623, 1656, 1658, 1670, 1786, 1816, 1841, 1892, 1981, 1995-1996, 2052, 2311, 2348, 2360, 2368, 2431, 2478, 2520; dismissal as White House Counsel 277, 328, 367, 537, 1572, 2352; statements and testimony 123, 367, 483, 537-538, 540, 542-543, 545-547, 550-551, 555-556, 667, 679, 772, 843, 909, 1248, 1516, 1699, 1943, 2150, 2197-2200, 2222, 2359, 2401, 2403, 2421, 2430, 2455; see also Ehrlichman, John; Haldeman, H. R.; U.S. Congress, Senate, Select Committee on Presidential Campaign Activities
Dean, Maureen ("Mo") 535-536, 552-553, 624, 876, 1996
"Deep Throat" see Bernstein, Carl; Woodward, Robert U. ("Bob")
Dictionaries and Annuals 62-71
"Dirty tricks" see Campaign disruptions; Committee to Re-elect the President; Segretti, Donald
Doar, John 305, 590, 720, 899-900, 1403, 1537, 1827, 2122; see also U.S. Congress, House, Committee on the Judiciary--Impeachment hearings and inquiry
DuMas, George N. 465

Ehrlichman, John D. 154, 457, 537, 636-638, 646, 753-754, 806, 858, 1061, 1082, 1238, 1265, 1317, 1363, 1420, 1613, 1619, 1623, 1730, 1981, 1987, 1998-1999, 2083, 2311, 2348, 2520; resignation as Domestic advisor 165, 267, 277, 328, 367, 537, 636, 858, 1572, 1758, 2227, 2352, 2420; statements and testimony 121-122, 503, 628-639, 651, 836, 1539, 1740, 2197-2200, 2332, 2404, 2406; see also Dean, John W., 3rd; Haldeman, H. R.; Nixon, Richard M., defense of; U.S. Congress, Senate, Select Committee on Presidential Campaign Activities; Watergate Break-in, cover-up
Eisenhower, David 101, 641-642
Eisenhower, Julie Nixon 101, 624, 715, 1081
Ellsberg Break-in see Fielding Break-in
Ellsberg Break-in Trial see Fielding Break-in Trial
Ervin, Sam J., Jr. 401, 520, 600, 612, 663, 667, 669, 777, 891, 1181, 1238, 1288, 1400, 1423, 1617, 1842, 1845-1846, 1876, 2073, 2490; statements 666-670, 2197-2199; see also U.S. Congress, Senate, Select Committee on Presidential Campaign Activities
Ervin Committee see U.S. Congress, Senate, Select Committee on Presidential Campaign Activities
Executive privilege 76, 162, 180, 219, 220-222, 225, 250, 285, 303, 345, 349, 402, 408, 470-479, 491, 599, 661-662, 676, 683, 690-693, 763, 770-771, 844, 862, 878, 885, 960, 1091, 1104, 1148, 1152, 1154, 1170, 1185, 1213, 1256, 1285, 1311, 1321, 1332-1334, 1336, 1361-1363, 1368, 1404, 1429, 1434, 1478, 1491, 1535, 1693-1694, 1697, 1722-1723, 1731, 1746, 1813, 1854-1855, 1884, 1693-1694, 1697, 1722-1723, 1731, 1746, 1813, 1854-1855, 1884, 1896, 1907, 1942, 1951, 2114, 2173-2174, 2188, 2213, 2225; see also Cox, Archibald; Jaworski, Leon; Nixon, Richard M., defense of; Tapes, Subpoena of; United States v. Richard M. Nixon

FBI see Federal Bureau of Investigation

Index 322

Federal Bureau of Investigation 113, 145, 252, 429, 497, 574, 629, 717, 822, 834, 904, 934, 1096, 1241, 1642, 1646-1647, 1650-1651, 1810, 1851-1852, 1863-1864, 1869, 1961, 2048-2050, 2101, 2154-2155, 2159, 2190, 2194, 2197-2201, 2497, 2521, 2524-2525; see also Central Intelligence Agency; Gray, L. Patrick; Watergate Break-in, cover-up
Felt, W. Mark 717, 1317, 2486
Fielding, Fred F. 1111; see also Dean, John W.
Fielding Break-in 170, 638, 659, 782, 1208-1210, 2144; see also "Plumbers"
Fielding Break-in Trial 100, 123, 134, 292, 326, 380, 389, 421-422, 424, 637, 646, 729, 755, 794, 1000, 1214, 1401, 1512, 1666, 1704, 1998-1999, 2079, 2085, 2109, 2197-2200
Finance Committee to Re-elect the President see Campaign contributions and financing; Committee to Re-elect the President; Stans, Maurice
Flanigan, Peter 1634, 1973; see also ITT Scandal
Ford, Gerald R. 272, 274, 276, 735-748, 928, 1292, 1364-1365, 1413, 1416, 1911, 1939, 1959, 2043, 2541-2542; see also Nixon, Richard M., pardon of; Nixon, Richard M., resignation of
Frampton, George, Jr. 218

Garment, Leonard 1478; see also Nixon, Richard M., defense of
"Gemstone" see Harmony, Sally; Magruder, Jeb Stuart
Geneen, Harold S. 588, 1123, 1584, 1797; see also ITT Scandal
Gesell, Gerhard 729, 794, 1999, 2409
Goldwater, Barry 331, 809-810, 819, 1319; see also Republican Party
Goodwin, Richard N. 392
Graham, Fred 1221, 2326
Gray, L. Patrick 712, 934, 1156, 1287, 1290, 1646, 2034, 2095, 2197-2200, 2258, 2420; confirmation hearings of 237-238,

511, 561, 823-825, 1647, 1720, 1881, 2182, 2330, 2420; statements and testimony 123, 468, 2197-2200, 2500, 2532; see also Federal Bureau of Investigation; Watergate Break-in, cover-up
Gregory, Thomas 920
Gurney, Edward 1667

Haig, Alexander M., Jr. 97, 605, 848, 1004, 1134, 1229, 1313, 1317, 1379, 1543, 1630-1631, 1734, 1919, 2011, 2083, 2387, 2487-2488, 2541; statements and testimony 140, 267, 280, 851-853, 2165; see also Nixon, Richard M., resignation of
Haldeman, H. R. ("Bob") 142, 457, 630, 687, 753-754, 804, 806, 845, 849, 858, 1082, 1238, 1265, 1317, 1363, 1389, 1570, 1619, 1623, 1730, 1796, 1987, 1995, 2348, 2520; resignation as White House chief of staff 165, 267, 277, 328, 367, 858, 1572, 1758, 2227, 2352, 2420; statements and testimony 121, 269, 468, 651, 858-859, 1539, 2042, 2197-2200, 2320, 2404, 2406; see also Dean, John W., 3rd; Ehrlichman, John D.; Watergate Break-in, cover-up
Hammer, Armand 2027
Harlow, Bryce N. 267
Harmony, Sally 127, 610
Harwood, Richard 392
Helms, Richard 259, 1639, 1678, 1680; statements and testimony 468, 861, 2166; see also Central Intelligence Agency
Hersh, Seymour 212, 854; see also New York Times
Higby, Lawrence 140
Hoover, J. Edgar 569; see also Federal Bureau of Investigation
Hughes, Howard 140, 205, 570, 614, 731, 948-949, 1226, 1374, 1733, 2197-2199; see also Campaign contributions and financing; Rebozo, Charles ("Bebe")
Hunt, E. Howard 169, 339, 619-620, 681, 893, 953-957, 999, 1005, 1208-1210, 1225, 1241-1242, 1293, 1351, 1534, 1551, 1882, 1962-1963, 1965-1966, 2018-2021, 2109, 2345-2346, 2375, 2379, 2500, 2511, 2549;

statements and testimony 124, 953-957, 2197-2200, 2402; see also Central Intelligence Agency; Fielding Break-in; "Plumbers"; Watergate Break-in
Huston, Tom C. 354, 2202
Huston Plan see Huston, Tom C.

Immunity for Witnesses see Watergate Special Prosecution Force, immunity and plea bargaining
Impeachment grounds and process 106, 114, 163, 199, 223-224, 250, 285, 302, 310-312, 402, 432, 445, 462, 494, 508, 530, 581, 725-727, 752, 802, 833, 837, 930, 942, 965, 969-994, 1013, 1093, 1148, 1150, 1157, 1262, 1291, 1323, 1331, 1337, 1749, 1767, 1848, 1860, 1862, 1880, 1984, 1989-1993, 2088, 2106, 2123, 2126-2129, 2131-2138, 2140, 2205-2206, 2223, 2264, 2293, 2443-2444, 2452, 2514-2517; see also U. S. Congress, House, Committee on the Judiciary--Impeachment inquiry and hearings
Impeachment sentiment see Public opinion on Watergate
Indexes and Abstracts 27-61
Indictments of Watergate figures see Watergate Grand Jury
Inouye, Daniel 1002, 1765
Internal Revenue Service 113, 252, 355, 679, 1040, 1155, 1168, 1234, 1852, 1889, 2036-2037, 2139, 2156, 2159, 2161, 2193-2195
IRS see Internal Revenue Service
ITT Scandal 85, 91, 126-129, 131-132, 135, 204, 229, 253, 286-291, 330, 356, 397, 461, 507, 570, 588, 689, 703, 706, 875, 890, 951-952, 1001, 1017-1030, 1036-1038, 1119-1123, 1128, 1227, 1250, 1264, 1303, 1394, 1407, 1431, 1576, 1581-1591, 1750, 1843, 1938, 1973, 2035, 2053, 2102-2104, 2144-2145, 2175-2176, 2183, 2185, 2197-2200; see also Anderson Jack; Beard, Dita; Campaign contributions and financing; Geneen, Harold S.; Kleindienst, Richard; Mitchell, John N.;

Wilson, Bob

Jaworski, Leon 92, 103, 128, 143, 180, 218, 313, 485, 605, 645, 694, 817, 890, 959, 969, 975, 985, 998, 1040, 1045-1054, 1103, 1186-1187, 1652, 1684, 1706, 1708, 1714, 1910, 1969, 2045-2046, 2197-2200; appointment as Special Prosecutor 203, 1048, 1050; see also Tapes, Subpoena of; Watergate Special Prosecution Force
Jenner, Albert 1537, 2122; see also U. S. Congress, House, Committee on the Judiciary--Impeachment inquiry and hearings
Jordan, Barbara 1074

Kalmbach, Herbert 1032, 1654, 1669, 1696; statements and testimony 121, 1084, 1638, 1948, 2025, 2150, 2197-2200; see also Campaign contributions and financing; Watergate Break-in, cover-up
Kelly, Clarence M. 2177
Kissinger, Henry 894, 904, 1112, 1379, 1730, 2163-2164, 2524, 2541; see also Nixon, Richard M., resignation of; Watergate and foreign relations; wiretapping
Klein, Herbert G. 1114-1116
Kleindienst, Richard G. 411, 644, 899-900, 1119-1123, 1224, 1303, 1768-1769, 1786, 2184; implication in ITT Scandal 126, 129, 135, 291, 330, 1036-1037, 1119-1122, 1250, 1303, 1585, 1590, 1843, 2053, 2102-2103, 2144-2145, 2175-2176, 2183, 2185, 2260; resignation as Attorney General 165, 1758, 2424; statements and testimony 1119-1112, 2197-2200, 2532; see also Anderson, Jack; Beard, Dita
Krogh, Egil 627, 659, 782, 1144-1145, 1418, 1473, 2312, 2351, 2396, 2436; see also "Plumbers"

LaRue, Fred 239, 1948, 2150
Leeper, Paul 258
Lessons of Watergate see Watergate, lessons and effects
Liddy, G. Gordon 110, 306, 358,

Index 324

407, 573, 733, 783-784, 1191, 1208-1210, 1242, 1304, 1352, 1419, 1799, 1926, 2100, 2109, 2410; see also Committee to Re-elect the President; "Plumbers"
Los Angeles Times 854

McCord, James 178, 339, 358, 696, 883, 926, 1043, 1238, 1240, 1243, 1293, 1551, 1781, 1882, 1928, 2109; statements and testimony 696, 883, 926, 1395, 2024, 2197-2200, 2401, 2403, 2434, 2545; see also "Plumbers"; Sirica, John J.; Watergate Break-in
MacGregor, Clark 1571; see also Committee to Re-elect the President
Magruder, Gail 624, 1274
Magruder, Jeb Stuart 127, 216, 284, 573, 675, 902-903, 1055-1058, 1171, 1238, 1274-1280, 1612, 2345; statements and testimony 902, 1275, 1277, 1280, 2197-2199, 2357, 2401; see also Watergate Break-in, cover-up
Mardian, Robert 239, 753-754, 1082, 1788, 1948, 1987; statements and testimony 907, 2197-2199; see also Committee to Re-elect the President
Martinez, Eugenio R. 191, 403, 750, 1225, 1293, 1551, 1882, 2109; see also Fielding Break-in; "Plumbers"; Watergate Break-in
Merriam, William R. 1588
Mezvinsky, Edward 1916
Milk Fund Scandal 161, 247, 364, 448-449, 570, 689, 732, 1032-1034, 1161, 1166, 1227, 1235, 1260-1261, 1324-1330, 1394, 1405, 1431, 1938, 2139, 2144-2145, 2197-2199, 2327; see also Campaign contributions and financing
Mitchell, John N. 123, 239, 358, 366, 555, 753-754, 912, 1065, 1257, 1352-1360, 1422, 1615, 1710, 1730, 1787, 1987, 1995, 2010, 2056, 2439, 2462, 2546, 2559; implication in ITT Scandal 126, 130-132, 135, 1123, 1128, 1250, 1581, 1583-1584, 1586-1587, 1589, 2104; statements and testimony 651, 907, 1064, 1128, 1352-1353, 1359, 2150, 2197-2200, 2433, 2455; see also Beard, Dita; Committee to Re-elect the President; Watergate Break-in, cover-up
Mitchell, Martha 624, 1257, 1354
Mizell, Wilmer 1580
Mollenhoff, Clark 212
Moore, Richard 1638

Neal, James F. 485, 899-900; see also Watergate Special Prosecution Force
Nedzi, Lucien 767
Nelson, Jack 212
New York Times 854, 1521-1522
Nixon, Patricia 101, 534, 624, 716, 2541
Nixon, Richard M. 1009, 1088, 1454, 1770-1772, 1879, 2520; defense of 83, 169, 242, 262, 275, 319, 341, 385, 465, 472-479, 513, 550, 567, 602, 686, 697, 798, 929, 939, 969-994, 1050, 1073, 1102, 1184, 1233, 1348, 1472, 1478, 1505, 1837-1838, 1878, 1890, 1907, 1932, 1985, 2000-2004, 2123, 2145, 2211, 2333, 2389, 2404, 2406, 2523, 2541; family of 101, 1182, 2541; interviews with David Frost 105, 698, 773-775, 795, 805, 923, 1045, 1482-1483, 1490, 1524, 1558, 2275, 2451, 2492; pardon of 152, 211, 283, 293, 295, 323, 376, 443, 454, 526, 625, 645, 652, 682, 700, 705, 735-745, 880, 918, 962, 1044, 1134, 1148, 1153, 1200, 1229, 1246, 1252, 1254, 1364, 1387, 1403, 1484-1485, 1502, 1514, 1527, 1568, 1604-1606, 1817, 1820, 1911, 1913, 1952, 2043, 2220-2221, 2256-2257, 2269-2270, 2376, 2446, 2542, 2558; psychological and character studies of 75, 171, 185-190, 197, 298, 301, 313, 320, 370, 384, 393-394, 406, 464, 507a, 577, 647, 747, 757, 872, 1009, 1180, 1215, 1217, 1293, 1306, 1314, 1367, 1578, 1724-1725, 1811, 1851-1853, 1974, 2091, 2367, 2499, 2537, 2541; resignation of 322, 324, 332, 334, 360, 432, 459, 480, 508, 559, 641-642, 695, 699, 704,

746, 807, 809-810, 894, 927, 962, 1072, 1112, 1253, 1295, 1340, 1342, 1388, 1416, 1451-1452, 1507-1508, 1567, 1618, 1688, 1741, 1749, 1756-1757, 1764, 1809, 1833-1834, 1886, 1899, 1911, 1939, 2080, 2237, 2242, 2273, 2454, 2469, 2475, 2477, 2513, 2541; statements of 115, 217, 328, 367, 446, 871, 963-964, 1092, 1184, 1213, 1335, 1345, 1347, 1428-1465, 1468, 1507-1508, 1685, 1688, 1809, 1903, 2057, 2231, 2277, 2283, 2383, 2416, 2424, 2507, 2513, 2541

O'Brien, Lawrence 1168, 1234, 1536, 2398, 2538
O'Brien, Paul 1630, 2150
O'Neill, Thomas ("Tip") 305
Operation Candor see Public opinion on Watergate
Operation Chaos see Central Intelligence Agency

Palace Guard see Colson, Charles; Dean, John W., 3rd; Ehrlichman, John D.; Haldeman, H. R.; White House staff
Parkinson, Kenneth 1082, 1987
Petersen, Henry E. 886, 899-900, 1625, 1653, 1657, 1745, 2150, 2532; see also Watergate Break-in, investigation of
Plea bargaining see Watergate Special Prosecution Force--Immunity and plea bargaining
"Plumbers" 111, 115, 145, 170, 174, 191, 230, 235, 292, 326, 380, 407, 423, 574, 627, 637, 656, 659, 750, 794, 892, 953-957, 1208-1210, 1238, 1242, 1320, 1560, 1566, 1639, 1810, 1851-1852, 1882, 1937, 1954, 1963, 1966-1967, 2018-2021, 2197-2199, 2294, 2351, 2460, 2468, 2521; see also Barker, Bernard; Colson, Charles; Committee to Re-elect the President; Fielding Break-in; Hunt, E. Howard; Liddy, G. Gordon; McCord, James; Martinez, Eugenio; Watergate Break-in
Polk, James R. 212, 925, 2037
Porter, Herbert 1610, 1703, 2059

Presidency, office of the 171, 179, 186-189, 227, 320, 362, 435, 509, 516, 811-812, 870, 1088, 1130, 1173-1174, 1390, 1409-1411, 1426, 1608, 1664, 1687, 1739, 1855-1856, 1858, 1908, 1945, 2094, 2246, 2469, 2471, 2484, 2552
Press coverage of Watergate events 206, 212, 234, 265-266, 315-316, 363, 372, 383, 388, 392, 395-396, 400, 416, 480-481, 531, 563, 573, 585, 604, 617-618, 622, 654, 658, 684, 816, 838-840, 847, 867, 875, 888-889, 941, 1075, 1085-1087, 1114-1117, 1125, 1160, 1172, 1206, 1219-1220, 1258, 1284, 1292, 1315, 1391, 1466-1467, 1480, 1488, 1675-1677, 1835, 1921, 2078, 2239, 2268, 2441-2442, 2476, 2503, 2526, 2528, 2541, 2563; see also names of reporters; television coverage of Watergate events
Public opinion on Watergate 107, 155-156, 217, 249, 254, 260, 262, 267, 315, 335, 353, 365, 368, 374, 377, 404, 527-528, 579, 608, 680, 721, 777, 788, 821, 837, 841, 847, 895, 914, 936-937, 967-969, 979-980, 984, 1044, 1069, 1105-1107, 1113-1116, 1124, 1127, 1141, 1158, 1164, 1175, 1205, 1245, 1281, 1283, 1296, 1318, 1377, 1385, 1477, 1486-1487, 1500-1501, 1515, 1549-1550, 1596, 1618-1619, 1681, 1687, 1692, 1715, 1728, 1753-1754, 1774, 1795, 1818, 1820, 1878, 1890, 1912, 1917, 1947, 1975, 1977, 2089, 2251, 2255, 2329, 2363, 2366, 2422, 2454, 2456, 2458, 2464, 2479, 2484, 2505, 2563-2564

Rather, Dan 82, 151, 175, 215, 417, 523-525, 529, 854, 1177, 1522, 1628, 1729, 1972; see also television coverage of Watergate events
Reasoner, Harry 304
Rebozo, Charles G. ("Bebe") 168, 205, 532, 570, 672, 731, 948, 1227, 1374, 1545, 1733, 2197-2199; see also Campaign contributions and financing; Hughes,

Howard
Reisner, Robert 1610
Republican Party 314, 463, 809-810, 1753-1754, 1785, 1929, 2076; see also Goldwater, Barry
Rhodes, John J. 331, 1319
Richardson, Elliot 411, 605-606, 644, 724, 868, 1236, 1345, 1775-1780, 1812, 1893, 2179, 2197-2200; see also Cox, Archibald, dismissal of
Rodino, Peter W. 176, 305, 387, 612, 985, 1249, 1289, 1622, 1626, 1798; see also U.S. Congress, House, Committee on the Judiciary--Impeachment inquiry and hearings
Ruckelshaus, William D. 2187, 2197-2199, 2497; see also Cox, Archibald, dismissal of
Ruth, Henry 899-900; see also Watergate Special Prosecution Force

St. Clair, James D. 169, 262, 275, 590, 686, 929, 969, 1073, 1102, 1233, 1519, 1837-1838, 2123, 2333, 2389, 2523; see also Nixon, Richard M., defense of; Tapes, Subpoena of; United States v. Richard Nixon
"Saturday Night Massacre" see Bork, Robert; Cox, Archibald, dismissal of; Richardson, Elliot; Ruckelshaus, William D.
Saxbe, William 868, 965, 1310, 1848-1849, 2186, 2228
Schorr, Daniel 529, 854, 1863-1864; see also television coverage of Watergate events
Scott, Hugh 331, 1319, 1473
Segretti, Donald H. 149, 592, 1553, 1874-1875, 1986, 2197-2200, 2319; see also Campaign disruptions
Senate Watergate Committee see U.S. Congress, Senate, Select Committee on Presidential Campaign Activities
Separation of Powers see Executive privilege
Sevareid, Eric 304
Sheraton Corp. see ITT Scandal
Sidey, Hugh 854
Silberman, Laurence H. 2181
Silbert, Earl J. 114, 537, 898-900, 1039, 1648, 1653, 1657, 1918, 2178; see also Watergate Break-in, investigation of
Sirica, John J. 74, 138, 180, 438, 472, 676, 696, 734, 891, 926, 938, 1008, 1047, 1063, 1077-1078, 1149, 1169, 1195-1196, 1240, 1360, 1392, 1424, 1701, 1885, 1922-1928, 2196, 2281, 2434, 2541; see also McCord, James; Tapes, Subpoena of; Watergate Break-in, cover-up trial
Sloan, Hugh 358, 945, 1610
Smith, C. Arnholt 153, 172, 229; see also Campaign contributions and financing
Smith, Howard K. 304
Special Prosecutor see Cox, Archibald; Jaworski, Leon; Watergate Special Prosecution Force
Stans, Maurice 123, 248, 912, 919, 1309, 1350, 1357, 1971, 2010, 2547-2548, 2555, 2559; statements and testimony 651, 902, 1970, 2197-2199; see also Campaign contributions and financing; Committee to Re-elect the President
Stennis, John 827, 1430
Stern, Carl 2326
Strachan, Gordon 1082, 1948, 1987; statements and testimony 121, 2197-2199
Sturgis, Frank A. 759, 2109; see also "Plumbers"

Tapes of presidential conversations, edited White House transcripts 78, 95, 180, 182, 270, 335, 347, 372, 440, 469, 522, 554, 575, 579, 603, 608, 611, 623, 688, 766, 780-781, 916, 923-927, 966, 1009, 1050, 1108, 1190, 1215, 1218, 1270, 1298-1299, 1301, 1307, 1335, 1362, 1373, 1383, 1428, 1437, 1446-1448, 1453, 1455, 1457-1459, 1470, 1519, 1525, 1538, 1546, 1661-1663, 1668, 1675, 1686, 1689, 1699, 1774, 1904, 1914, 1953, 1975, 2031-2032, 2040, 2061-2062, 2070-2071, 2075, 2096, 2124-2125, 2251, 2277, 2303, 2329, 2366, 2397, 2399, 2459, 2461, 2481; $18\frac{1}{2}$-minute gap 108, 140, 157, 180, 371, 917, 938, 1050, 1089, 1307, 1349, 1396, 1412, 1414, 1529, 1556, 1594-1595,

1632, 1655, 1705, 1804, 1812, 1871, 1900, 1982, 2041, 2107, 2209-2210, 2252-2254, 2285, 2291, 2331, 2350, 2400, 2480; Missing subpoenaed 74, 180, 1397, 1499, 1547, 2030, 2298; Ownership of 79, 93, 323, 451, 455-456, 587, 749, 864, 921, 943, 1204, 1207, 1244, 1338, 1406, 1465, 1474, 1565, 1762, 1861, 1983, 2097, 2109, 2112-2113, 2116-2120, 2168-2171, 2214-2216, 2248-2249, 2485, 2502; Revelation of 98, 180, 261, 333, 338, 557, 1491, 1574, 1865, 2042; Subpoena of 74, 92, 124, 143, 169, 180, 200-202, 220, 226-227, 298, 345, 347, 437-439, 444, 467, 470-479, 490, 493-495, 498, 565, 661-662, 664, 667, 676, 692-693, 827, 831, 844, 852-853, 890, 943, 1050-1054, 1076-1077, 1133, 1154, 1169, 1196, 1311, 1386, 1415, 1448, 1477-1478, 1493, 1498, 1517, 1530, 1609, 1627, 1693-1694, 1714, 1751, 1759-1760, 1896, 1907, 1922-1928, 1955, 1985, 1998-2004, 2009, 2109, 2267, 2280-2282, 2287, 2336-2337, 2341, 2361, 2374, 2461, 2493; Supreme Court case see United States v. Richard M. Nixon

Television coverage of Watergate events 159, 193-194, 206, 240, 265-266, 304, 307, 315, 388, 392, 395, 400, 480-481, 526, 532, 563-564, 568, 578, 580, 582, 622, 626, 654, 684, 720, 727, 768-769, 789-792, 838-840, 842, 854-856, 892, 897, 906, 909, 914, 1003, 1006, 1085-1087, 1090, 1114-1117, 1125, 1138, 1160, 1163, 1165, 1172, 1189, 1202, 1221, 1284, 1315, 1321, 1368, 1371, 1375, 1377, 1405a, 1417, 1427, 1443, 1466-1467, 1488, 1503, 1599, 1601-1603, 1675-1677, 1719, 1729, 1736, 1791-1794, 1823, 1835, 1839-1840, 1863-1864, 1933, 1943-1944, 1972, 1979, 2039, 2072, 2230, 2372, 2390-2391, 2441, 2483, 2531, 2541, 2563; see also Press coverage of Watergate events; Rather, Dan; Schorr, Daniel

Thompson, Fred D. 557, 2066-2068
Time, Inc. 854
Transcripts see Tapes of presidential conversations--edited White House transcripts

Ulasewicz, Tony 883, 1870, 1948, 2024, 2197-2199
U.S., Congress, House, Committee on the Judiciary--Articles of Impeachment 148, 271, 351, 390, 433, 452, 710-711, 720, 751, 776, 992, 997, 1337, 1557, 2130, 2223, 2226, 2240, 2302
_____._____.--Impeachment inquiry and hearings 77, 106, 120, 246, 255, 271, 273, 282, 305, 307, 341-346, 350, 359, 387, 409-410, 432-433, 439-441, 444, 452-454, 508, 517, 566, 580-581, 603, 608, 610, 612, 640, 649, 689, 697, 720, 727, 734-734a, 768, 776, 779, 787, 798, 801, 820, 829-831, 833, 846, 858, 865-866, 881, 897, 899-900, 910, 915, 927-930, 946, 950, 971-973, 1050, 1070, 1073-1074, 1079-1080, 1093, 1157, 1172, 1184, 1202-1203, 1205, 1233, 1235, 1249, 1266, 1297, 1305, 1307, 1346, 1371, 1386, 1408, 1424, 1471, 1503, 1555, 1597, 1629, 1676, 1701, 1717, 1736, 1761, 1798, 1822, 1825, 1831-1832, 1880, 1883, 1885, 1901, 1916, 1940, 1944, 1979, 2001, 2023, 2039, 2070-2071, 2077, 2122-2158, 2223, 2250, 2299, 2302, 2333, 2342-2343, 2382, 2419, 2435, 2461, 2466, 2469-2470, 2515-2517, 2541, 2554, 2556; see also Impeachment, grounds and process; Rodino, Peter
_____._____.--members of 120, 176, 350, 720, 826
_____._____.--staff 106, 409, 720, 983, 1297, 1825, 2122, 2141, 2152-2153, 2229, 2557
_____. Senate, Select Committee on Presidential Campaign Activities 85, 87, 89, 121, 124, 160, 173, 240, 255, 260, 294, 325, 327, 357, 368, 396, 401, 415, 437-439, 463, 468, 474, 475, 479, 483, 503, 505, 520-521, 532, 537-547, 555-557, 572,

578, 580, 611-612, 628-629, 631, 638-639, 662, 664, 666-674, 707-708, 769, 772, 788, 857-858, 866, 882-883, 891, 899-900, 902, 907, 909, 919, 931, 975, 999, 1002-1003, 1006a, 1015, 1034, 1050, 1064, 1084, 1099-1100, 1138, 1151, 1163-1165, 1172, 1188, 1228-1229, 1238, 1248, 1265, 1275-1280, 1355, 1375, 1382, 1417, 1425, 1498, 1539, 1601, 1610, 1627, 1638, 1667, 1699-1700, 1747, 1791, 1832, 1842, 1874-1876, 1895, 1897, 1933, 1948, 1958, 1970-1971, 2002, 2066-2068, 2073, 2090, 2230, 2290, 2316-2317, 2328, 2340, 2360, 2371-2373, 2406, 2415, 2418, 2421, 2433, 2469-2470, 2522, 2531-2532, 2540-2541
———. District Court for the District of Columbia see Gesell, Gerhard; Sirica, John J.
United States v. Barker 1143, 1523, 1541, 2109
United States v. Mitchell 218, 2109, 2196, 2218
United States v. Nixon 158, 180, 196, 210, 219, 349, 408, 470-471, 478, 697, 763-765, 793, 846, 850, 879, 885, 911, 976-977, 1047, 1050, 1146, 1194, 1199, 1211, 1213, 1282, 1295, 1344, 1503, 1865, 1906, 1908, 1976, 2007-2008, 2016-2017, 2047, 2099, 2109, 2160, 2196, 2217, 2219, 2224, 2235, 2541, 2550-2551; see also Executive privilege; Tapes, Subpoena of

Vesco, Robert 123, 248, 570, 1016, 1357, 1378, 1672, 2010, 2236, 2559; see also Campaign contributions and financing; Mitchell, John N.; Stans, Maurice
Volner, Jill 778

Wallace, George 1889
Walters, Vernon 562, 1178, 2263; see also Central Intelligence Agency
Washington Post 99, 167, 234-235, 321, 618, 816, 835, 854, 888, 1035, 1109, 1176, 1239, 2012, 2273-2274; see also Bernstein, Carl; Woodward, Robert U. ("Bob")
Watergate and Foreign relations/reactions 340, 450, 521, 608, 704, 848, 869, 894, 922, 940, 961-962, 1112, 1384, 1554, 1790, 1815, 1894-1900, 1902-1903, 1945, 2081-2082, 2289, 2292, 2394, 2553, 2465; see also Kissinger, Henry
Watergate anniversaries 104, 159, 177, 427, 558, 589, 1005, 1526, 2296-2297, 2385-2386
Watergate Break-in 178, 191, 230, 235, 258, 339, 357, 396, 403, 423, 453, 594, 657, 953-957, 1144-1145, 1208-1210, 1225-1228, 1230, 1240-1243, 1293, 1531, 1551, 1905, 1957, 1960, 2044, 2144, 2197-2199, 2438, 2521, 2546; see also Barker, Bernard; Hunt, E. Howard; McCord, James; Martinez, Eugenio; "Plumbers"
Watergate Break-in Cover-up 94, 109, 154, 184, 235, 239, 344, 352, 379, 396, 419-430, 457, 483-485, 537-551, 569, 636, 667, 681, 687, 696, 755, 815, 858, 953-957, 1082, 1227-1230, 1238, 1242-1243, 1247, 1273, 1275-1280, 1293, 1298-1299, 1352-1360, 1363, 1475, 1516, 1518, 1536, 1539, 1544, 1623, 1625, 1643-1644, 1658, 1796, 1816, 1826, 1905, 1960, 2074, 2144-2145, 2197-2200, 2344, 2379, 2438, 2459, 2475, 2478, 2494, 2500, 2525, 2532; see also Dean John W., 3rd; Colson, Charles; Ehrlichman, John D.; Haldeman, H. R.; Mitchell, John N.; Watergate Break-in Cover-up Trial
Watergate Break-in Cover-up Trial 100, 150, 181, 485, 513, 632, 636, 650, 651, 709, 734, 753-754, 786, 808, 1078, 1083, 1356, 1469, 1511, 1532, 1636, 1659, 1662, 1709-1710, 1928, 3078, 3087, 2092, 2109, 2234, 2276, 2288, 2305, 2323-2325, 2332, 2364, 2380-2381, 2392, 2395, 2399, 2405, 2412, 2423, 2426, 2430, 2489, 2430; see also Ehrlichman, John D.; Haldeman, H. R.; Mardian, Robert; Mitchell, John N.; Sirica, John J.
Watergate Grand Jury 127-128, 143,

379, 389, 595, 642, 729, 964, 1050, 1082, 1195, 1282, 1424, 1562, 1701, 1824, 1885, 1924, 1928, 1987, 2086, 2322, 2339, 2342, 2393, 2409
Watergate, investigation of 96, 114, 414-415, 576, 629, 636, 650, 886, 899-900, 934, 1039, 1263, 1302, 1347, 1452, 1461-1462, 1571, 1625, 1637, 1642, 1646, 1648, 1650, 1652-1653, 1657, 1786, 1810, 1918, 2144-2145, 2467, 2532; see also Central Intelligence Agency; Federal Bureau of Investigation; Silbert, Earl J.
Watergate, lessons and effects of 104, 116, 155-156, 173, 179, 206, 209, 251, 269, 309, 314, 317, 361-362, 365, 369, 386, 399, 404, 426-427, 434, 436, 463, 506, 596, 615, 790, 799-800, 813, 887, 895, 993, 1041, 1107, 1129, 1132, 1259, 1305, 1341, 1380-1382, 1409-1411, 1497, 1526, 1724, 1783, 1785, 1814, 1821, 1828-1829, 1850, 1941, 1946, 1958, 2005-2006, 2015-2016, 2076, 2309, 2334-2335, 2413, 2429, 2478, 2519, 2527, 2556
Watergate, religious and moral aspects 244, 298, 301, 369, 377, 420, 426, 507a, 701, 708, 728, 879, 944, 958, 1237, 1343, 1725, 2384
Watergate, satire and humor on 257, 296, 337, 714, 718, 1089, 1097, 1232, 1343, 1393, 1872, 2313, 2315, 2417, 2424-2425, 2533
Watergate Special Prosecution Force 144, 218, 318, 605, 778, 899-900, 1011, 1050, 1052, 1094, 1103, 1295, 1540, 1711, 1807, 1949, 1968, 2157, 2207-2208, 2288, 2353, 2510; immunity and plea bargaining 327, 537, 874, 1118-1123, 1665, 1704, 1988, 2196, 2301, 2534
Weicker, Lowell P., Jr. 160, 2197-2200, 2447-2448
White House "enemies" see Dean, John W., 3rd
White House Special Investigations Unit see "Plumbers"
White House Staff 73, 94, 208, 235, 275-277, 280, 308, 509, 514, 730, 761, 851, 896, 1004, 1012, 1071, 1092, 1271, 1317, 1368, 1730, 1732, 1737, 1739, 1830-1836, 1909, 1940, 2093, 2143, 2286, 2298, 2300, 2474
Wiggins, Charles E. 341
Wills, Frank 1372, 1978, 2428, 2529; see also Watergate Break-in
Wilson, Bob 588, 2035; see also ITT Scandal
Wilson, John 1765
Wiretapping 354, 476, 497, 574, 594, 894, 904, 947, 1098, 1112, 1227, 1436, 1851-1852, 1866, 1869, 1937, 1959, 2115, 2163-2164, 2167, 2191-2192, 2521; see also Federal Bureau of Investigation; Kissinger, Henry; "Plumbers"; Watergate Break-in
Woods, Rose Mary 140, 157, 371, 624, 1595, 1655, 1803, 1805, 1871; see also Tapes, $18\frac{1}{2}$-minute gap
Woodward, Robert U. ("Bob") 99, 234, 299, 560, 618, 717, 835, 854, 888, 1176, 1179, 1192, 1239, 1376, 1674, 1789, 2012, 2026, 2442, 2536; see also Bernstein, Carl; Washington Post

Ziegler, Ronald 164, 266, 279, 889, 1075, 1101, 1114-1117, 1139, 1317, 1402, 1802, 1888, 1890, 1930, 1956; statements and testimony of 141, 144, 265, 1103, 2262, 2561-2562; see also Press coverage of Watergate events; television coverage of Watergate events

REF E 860 .S64 1983